What Is African Art?

What Is African Art?

A SHORT HISTORY

Peter Probst

The University of Chicago Press   Chicago and London

The University of Chicago Press, Chicago 60637
The University of Chicago Press, Ltd., London
© 2022 by The University of Chicago
All rights reserved. No part of this book may be used or reproduced in any manner
whatsoever without written permission, except in the case of brief quotations in critical
articles and reviews. For more information, contact the University of Chicago Press,
1427 E. 60th St., Chicago, IL 60637.
Published 2022
Printed in the United States of America

31 30 29 28 27 26 25 24 23 22   1 2 3 4 5

ISBN-13: 978-0-226-79301-6 (cloth)
ISBN-13: 978-0-226-79315-3 (paper)
ISBN-13: 978-0-226-79329-0 (e-book)
DOI: https://doi.org/10.7208/chicago/9780226793290.001.0001

Library of Congress Cataloging-in-Publication Data

Names: Probst, Peter, author.
Title: What is African art? : a short history / Peter Probst.
Description: Chicago : University of Chicago Press, 2022. |
    Includes bibliographical references and index.
Identifiers: LCCN 2022006679 | ISBN 9780226793016 (cloth) |
    ISBN 9780226793153 (paperback) | ISBN 9780226793290 (ebook)
Subjects: LCSH: Art, African—Study and teaching—History. |
    Art, African—Historiography.
Classification: LCC N7380 .P76 2022 | DDC 709.6—dc23/eng/20220317
LC record available at https://lccn.loc.gov/2022006679

∞ This paper meets the requirements of ANSI/NISO Z39.48-1992 (Permanence of Paper).

CONTENTS

Introduction

What is African art? What do we have in mind, or rather, what do we talk about when we talk about African art? This book is about the shifting answers to this question. The discursive and institutional space I focus on is the field of African art studies or, if you will, the Africanist art world. My aim is to give the reader an understanding of how members of this world have continuously filled the notion of African art with new meanings and why these shifts manifest wider societal transformations.

Since this book is very much about context, let me begin by providing the personal context out of which it emerges. The idea for the book results from a seminar I have been teaching off and on since 2005. Professionally and personally, the year was a turning point for me. At that time, I had not only recently relocated from Germany to the US but had moved from an anthropology to an art history department.

In the 1980s, when I studied in Berlin and at Cambridge University, my understanding of African art was informed by studies about power objects, popular urban painting, spirit possession, and masked performances. As I saw it the field belonged firmly to anthropology. Art history departments in Germany did not offer courses on African art but focused solely on European traditions. At times curators of the nearby Berlin Ethnological Museum offered courses on African, Mesoamerican, or Oceanic art. While we were all aware of the colonial history of the museum's collections, debates in the department focused more on the then prominent critique of ethnographic authority and practices of ethnographic representation.

Lectures and seminar discussions did not draw sharp distinctions between anthropological and art-historical approaches to African art. Yes, one could discern different ways of seeing, but to me they were complementary. I did not conceive "art" and "society" as opposites. The field was small and easily encompassed both disciplines. The common denominator was an interest in *traditional art*, a term that by then had replaced colonial and market designations like *primitive* and *tribal art*. At times there were special exhibitions where one could see "modern" African art—the category "contemporary" was hardly used yet. But these were fleeting opportunities. The only permanent place to see modern African art was the Center for African Art and Culture (Iwalewa Haus) at the University of Bayreuth in the south of Germany. In German Africanist circles at that time, the center was famous for allowing visitors to meet and converse with African artists, writers, and musicians in a relaxed, club-like atmosphere. Back then, however, African art was just one of many things I was interested in. It was only much later—in the late 1990s, after having done fieldwork in Malawi and Cameroon and having worked at the Berlin Ethnological Museum and the Free University of Berlin—that I moved to Bayreuth to start a new position at the center. It was only then that I began to conceive of the field of African art as my professional home.

Students studying African art today find themselves in a very different environment. The landscape has changed drastically. First, anthropology is no longer a major voice in the field. Art history has taken over. Nowadays, books on African art are mostly written by scholars trained in art history rather than anthropology. Second, while indigenous or traditional art still has its audience, it has lost its privileged position to modern and contemporary art. The latter has not only won the favor of students, it has also become an investment. Big auction houses such as Christie's, Sotheby's, and Bonham's have their own departments selling modern and contemporary art from Africa and its diasporas, or "Global Africa," as the field is now conceived. Art journals regularly inform readers about emerging artists "to look out for," and art fairs, like 1:54, provide annual international platforms for finding and buying the work of upcoming artists. In addition, the continent now has its own landscape of art shows, the biennales in Dakar, Bamako, and Cairo being only the most prominent venues (fig. I.1).

For critics and curators, the critical success of contemporary art has brought its own questions. For instance, should a large metal assemblage by El Anatsui, arguably one of the most well-known and successful contemporary artists from the continent, be exhibited in the gallery of contemporary art or in the "African Gallery" (fig. I.2)? Should a wall label actually name the nationality of an artist whose work is on display? Why is this information necessary? To answer these questions by simply referencing the effects of "globalism" misses at least two key developments and debates. One such development is the debate about contemporaneity. In the 1980s anthropology underwent a self-critical

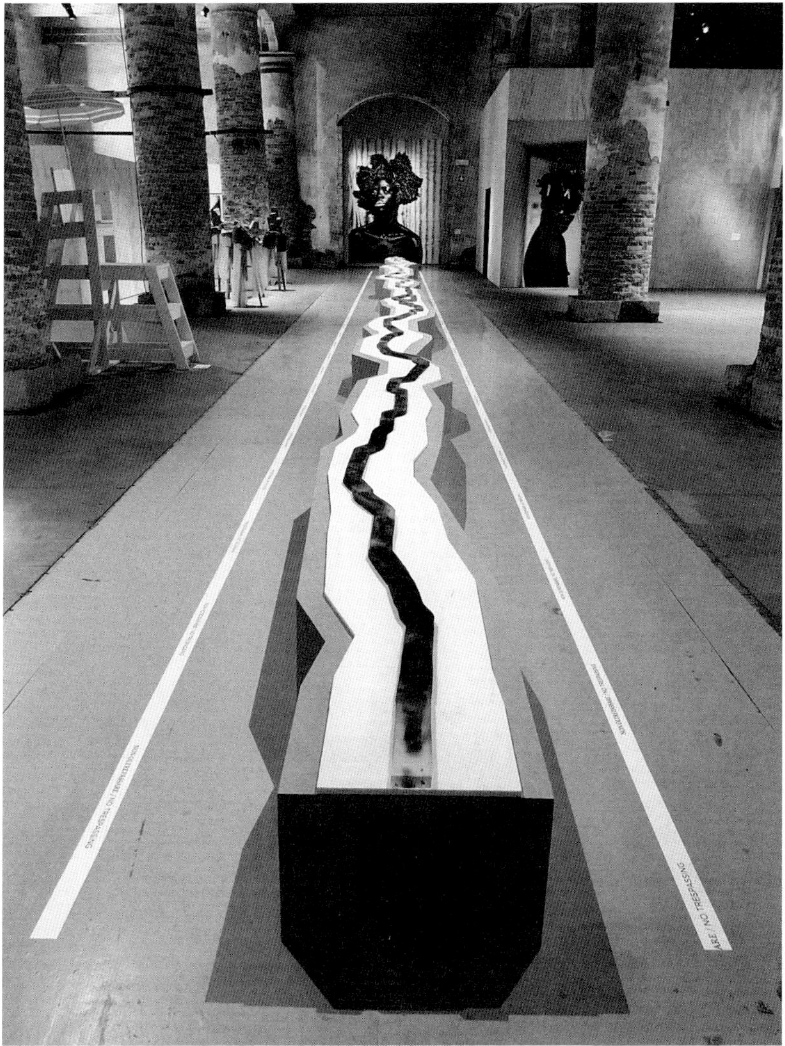

I.1 African artists are now a permanent fixture at international biennales: Otobong Nkanga, *Veins Aligned*, from 2018, with photographs by Zanele Muholi in the back. Installation view, Venice Biennale, August 2019. Photo: the author.

analysis by examining how the discipline's historical usage of concepts like "primitive" or "tribal" deployed the category of time as a means of holding its subjects at a temporal and ethical distance.[1] The critique focused especially on modes of anthropological writing and representation. While ethnographic fieldwork means sharing time with subjects and accepting rules of reciprocity, the subsequent scholarly discussion of the fieldwork's findings reintroduced a distance by labeling the beliefs

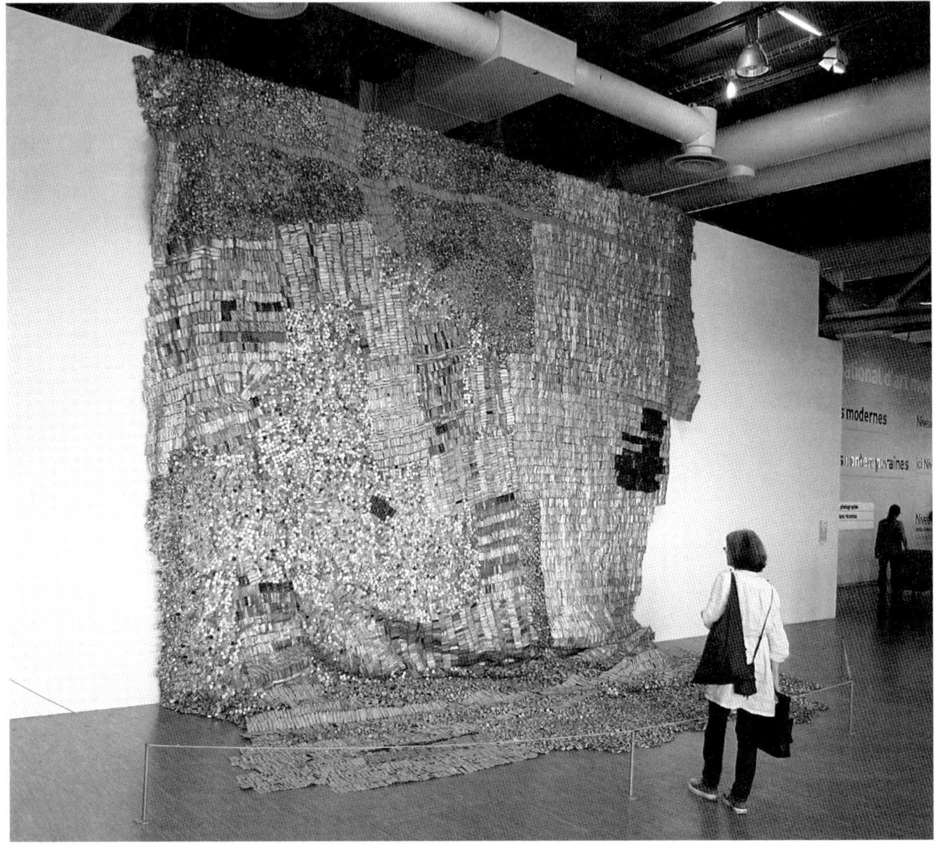

I.2 El Anatsui, *Sasa*, 2004. Bottle tops and copper wire, 8.4 × 6.4 m. Installation view, Musée National d'Art Moderne, Centre Pompidou, Paris, 2011. Photo: Susan Mullin Vogel. © El Anatsui.

and practices of the people with whom one lived together as "tribal," "traditional," or "premodern." Anthropology's acknowledgment of this "denial of coevalness" (Fabian) was therefore a breakthrough that powerfully aligned with studies exploring Africa as an "invention" and "idea" rooted in imperial and colonial discourses of power.[2] Today these works have become standard references that inform not only public reasoning about racism and inequality but also the visit to an art museum. Artists, critics, and curators often question and challenge the popular practice of framing an artist and/or artwork by using geographical specifications.[3] As a result, audiences have learned to be sensitive to the images the signifier "Africa" conjures. While colonialism has officially come to an end, its images, stereotypes, and structural dynamics have not.

Though related, the second development is not so much an effect of theory but of media technology and migration. Today we can go online and see and hear artists from different parts of the globe presenting their work. The internet has become a virtual space that we share with other users, allowing us to encounter the "other" in new ways. The new media environment has affected the public's view of anthropological and/or ethnological museums as predigital spaces of encounters with cultural otherness. In the past, anthropology museums aimed to provide the objects on display with cultural meaning and context. While the aesthetic quality of objects was acknowledged, objects were not primarily presented as art but as vehicles or gateways into the understanding of other cultures. Nowadays, such representations are seen as flawed and outdated, uneasy remnants and reminders of the colonial past.

The critique is especially virulent in Europe, where colonialism provided the origin of anthropological museums. After all, it was during the late nineteenth and early twentieth centuries, the height of colonialism, that African artifacts poured into Euro-American museums and were classified as "primitive art." To distance themselves from this origin, many anthropology museums have renamed themselves "Museums of World Art" or "World Cultures," but with limited effects, however, since such rebrandings have not resolved questions of restitution and ownership. Nor do relabelings such as "World Art" and/or "World Cultures" somehow exempt the art world from reckoning with the past. On the contrary, with tens of thousands of African refugees trying to make their way across the Mediterranean into Europe, the so-called migrant crisis, has brought the colonial past back to consciousness with full force.

Tellingly, the influx of migrant subjects has prompted the reflux of ethnographic objects. On November 27, 2017, during a visit to Burkina Faso, French president Emmanuel Macron acknowledged that "African heritage can't just be in European private collections and museums" and pledged to commission a report that would look into the modalities of restitution. A year later, on November 23, 2018, the Senegalese novelist and economist Felwine Sarr and the French art historian Bénédicte Savoy released a detailed report that expounded why, what, and when African cultural property housed in French museums should be restituted.[4] As they argued,

> On a continent where 60% of the population is under the age of 20 years-old, what is first and foremost of great importance is for young people to have access to their own culture, creativity, and spirituality from other eras that certainly have evolved since, but whose knowl-

edge and recognition can no longer merely be reserved for those re-siding in Western countries or for those who count themselves among the African diaspora living in Europe.[5]

As it happened, the release of the report coincided with two widely noted museum events. The first happened on December 6, 2018, only a week later, when Senegalese president Macky Sall ceremoniously inaugurated the new Musée des civilisations noires in Dakar. In his opening remarks, Sall thanked the Chinese government for its generous financial and tech-nical assistance in building the museum and stressed the duty of African peoples to remain "vigilant sentinels of the heritage of the ancients," a re-minder that was quickly linked to the debate over the restitution of some ten thousand pieces of Senegalese art from France.[6] Two days later, on December 8, the AfricaMuseum in Tervuren, on the outskirts of Brus-sels, reopened its doors after a decade of revamping the neoclassical building and overhauling its racist presentation of Belgium's former col-ony (fig. I.3).[7] With more than one hundred thousand artifacts, Tervuren still houses the world's largest collection of Congolese art. Like Sall in Senegal, Congo's president Joseph Kabila requested the restitution of large numbers of objects from Tervuren's collection. This time, however, the demand came with a moratorium. As president Kabila explained, the restitution of objects should wait till the completion of the country's new national museum, designed and built by South Korea. Meanwhile, the Belgian government has officially agreed to transfer legal ownership to the Democratic Republic of the Congo. The process of repair and restitu-tion has started. In November 2021, France returned twenty-six works looted in the late nineteenth century from the Kingdom of Dahomey to the Republic of Benin. Likewise, German government officials and museum directors have officially committed to return a "substantial amount" of "Benin Bronzes" to Nigeria. The first returns are expected to take place in 2023/2024 and will likely be housed in the planned Edo Museum of West African Art in Benin City, a new structure designed by the renowned architect David Adjaye.[8]

Objects and Fields

Things have changed. Some sixty years after the end of colonialism, re-lations between the Global South and the Global North are being re-defined, and history is being reconsidered. These shifts also inform the project at hand.

As noted, the decision to embark on a historiography of African art studies has its origins in a history of theories and methods seminar on

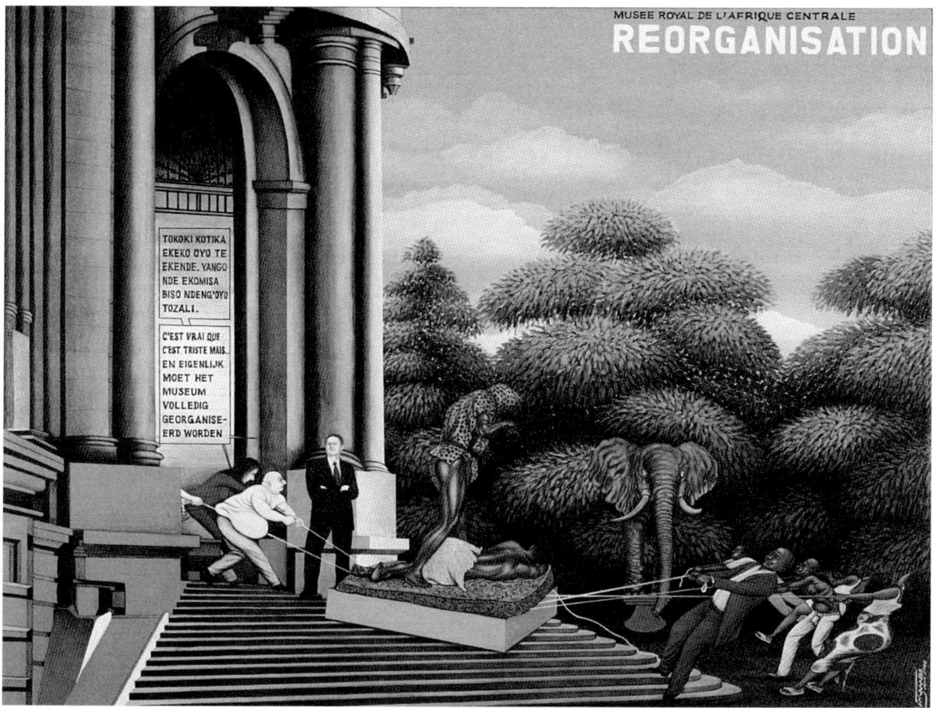

I.3 Chéri Samba, *Réorganisation*, 2002. Oil on canvas, 104 cm × 134 cm. Collection RMCA Tervuren. Samba's painting depicts the struggle for control over the representation of Congolese culture between members of Belgium's African diaspora museum staff and members of Belgium's Congolese diaspora and staff members of what was then still the Royal Museum for Central Africa. The Lingala reads, "We cannot accept this work being removed. It has made us who we are." The French reads, "It's true that it's sad but . . ." And the Dutch reads, "The museum really must be completely reorganized." Meanwhile, Samba's painting has been turned into a large reproduction that is installed on a wall immediately before the entrance to the introductory gallery of the renovated and rebranded AfricaMuseum. It is thus the first artwork visitors encounter when they enter the museum. © Magnin-A Gallery, Paris.

African art I have been teaching at irregular intervals since 2005. By then, the debate on *Provincializing Europe* was in full swing, and the contours of a new inclusive Global Art History were taking shape.[9] In view of these developments, narrating the history of Africanist scholarship seemed like a valuable and straightforward project. After all, no such comprehensive study yet existed. Instead, the few historiographic articles available fragmented the field by genre (classical/traditional versus modern/contemporary art), discipline (art history versus anthropology), and date (pre-1960 and post-1960 with the recognition of African art as an established subfield in [American] art history departments as a turning point).[10] As it happened, my other book projects forcefully pushed the historiographic venture to the side, and only recently was I able to return to it. Resuming the literature research, I realized that over the last decade not much has changed. With the exception of an article by Sidney Kasfir, no article—let alone book—exists that recounts in full the development of the field from the beginning to the present.[11]

The finding astonishes. Given the by then widely accepted need to open up and "decolonize" art history, one would have expected to see manifold efforts focusing on the field of historiography, with new African modes of historiographic self-writing emerging simultaneously in the realm of African art.[12] The fact that this did not occur, or only very sporadically, begs the question, Why? What has led to this curious absence of retrospective self-reflection and self-accounting among African art scholars, and what would such a self-accounting look like?

Let me begin to explain my take on the question by looking at the relationship between objects and fields.[13] Conventionally, objects constitute fields. Reliquaries and stained glass windows from the tenth century, for instance, allowed for, and in a sense formed, the study of medieval art just as Italian paintings and frescos from the fifteenth century allowed for and formed the study of Renaissance art. However, the same applies conversely: fields constitute (i.e., create and define) objects just as much as objects constitute fields. The academic field of African art studies instantiates this principle. When the field emerged in the mid- to late nineteenth century—that is, during the zenith of the Christian-colonial project—objects were experienced, investigated, and interpreted not in the places where they had been made but where missionaries, explorers, ethnographers, traders, soldiers, and a whole slew of other people had sent them, that is, in museums. The objects thus found themselves "strangers in a strange land," dropped into a world alien to the world in which they had been made and greeted by people very different from those who had made them. Surely the same distance between the purposes for which objects were made and the way in which they came to be understood and used by another culture is not unique to the colonial context. The appropriation, exchange, and collection of foreign items are not a distinctive feature of Western societies. Among members of the elite in Swahili port cities along the East African coast, for instance, the possession and display of decorative objects from faraway places was a sign of status and sophistication, an aesthetic practice that stretches back to the fourteenth and fifteenth centuries.[14] While the display is reminiscent of Renaissance art chambers, Swahili royalty did not turn this interest in the "other" into a calculated massive extraction of cultural objects.

Indeed, it may be argued that the peculiar dialectic of ruthless violence and subjugation on the one hand and bitter remorse and self-critique on the other that came to inform the history of African art scholarship is a distinctly Western feature that seems to have its roots in the age of imperial expansion.

How does one write historiography under these circumstances? How to explain the dynamics of canon building within a field like African art studies? Michael Baxandall once explained the job of art historians (and historiographers) by stating, "We do not explain pictures. We explain remarks about pictures—or rather, we explain pictures only in so far as we have to consider them under some verbal description or specification."[15] Obviously, the application of this method to the history of African art studies is problematic. After all, who is we? The question recalls the proverb the Nigerian novelist Chinua Achebe once invoked in an interview for the *Paris Review*: "Until the lions have their own historians, the history of the hunt will always glorify the hunter."[16] For Achebe, the proverb captured his early conviction to become a "historian of the lion." Still, Achebe chose to write in English, the language of the hunters. As he came to realize, the historians of the lions and those of the hunters are inexorably intertwined.[17]

Let me come back then to Baxandall's language-driven approach. For Baxandall, the focus was about the historical interpretation of a painting or a sculpture. How can we "explain" an artwork, or rather an object designated an artwork? The question is as simple as it is profound. At stake is the inadequacy between image and word, perception and translation, or, if you will, experience and meaning. The relationship between the two is key to my project. Let me explain my premise in simple terms. Experience refers to the perception and responses to an artwork's subject and formal properties—its color, shape, volume, texture, motion, time, and so forth. The work may evoke emotions such as joy, disgust, or fear. Yet while these affective qualities quite literally have *sense*, they are devoid of *meaning* in terms of being able to be communicated and debated with others through language. Thus, to move from experience to meaning, we need to translate experience into words, words that may be the result not just of one but multiple translations. Obviously, this does not absolve us from questioning which experiences we are discussing and whose words we use. And surely, language does not exhaust experience; hence, disputes and conflicts over interpretation are bound to happen. The fact remains, however: as a matter of meaning, art exists only in the realm of language.[18]

As these remarks suggest, this book rests on a fundamentally action-oriented argument. What I propose is to understand (art) objects not primarily as aesthetic but as social objects. For the history of African art studies, this requires employing a relational perspective that focuses less on the artwork and its specific "artness" than on the social relations in which the work is entangled and that it constitutes. The aim of this book is to trace and study these processes within the field of African art studies. The focus is on the Global North as—up to now—still the primary location of the field. The clarification is crucial, for it echoes the book's intention. Thus, I do not offer an affirmative answer as to what African art was or is. Nor do I explore the "local" or "African" meanings and aesthetic qualities of (art) objects. Rather, I am interested in how the works labeled as "African art" figure in the historical processes and social interactions that constitute the Africanist art world.[19]

The Narrative

Where then does this book begin? The question is not merely rhetorical. After all, beginnings have consequences.[20] They decree. Beginning in late nineteenth-century Europe, as I do, defines an entry point into the debate that both enables and excludes. What it excludes are alternative beginnings, such as those whose objects came to be the subject of the field. What it authorizes are the academic texts that have come to constitute the field of African art studies. Given the lasting efforts to "decolonize" the field, the approach requires an explanation. Surely, Africanist scholars have long criticized the absence of African voices and narratives in the Euro-American writing of African history.[21] And yes, there are numerous successful attempts to recover these voices from vernacular and colonial archives.[22] But the purpose of the book is not so much to critique the subject with counterhistories but to show how the need and demand for these counterhistories emerged. In other words the book aims to explain both the formation of the field as well as the emergence of the continuous efforts to remake it and write it anew.

To account for the heterogeneity of parallel events and discourses, I have chosen a tripartite structure that I invite readers to read and see like a three-channel video installation. That is, each of the three parts discusses different developments, often happening simultaneously and often competing with one another, thus making each part a complex set of crisscrossing ideas and arguments.

The first part of this book covers the period from the late nineteenth century up to the time of World War II, when African art emerged as a field of study, a market, and an object of critique. Chapter 1, "Forming a Field: Colonial Collecting, Racial Omissions, and National Rivalries," focuses on the newly founded ethnographic museums. At the center of the discussion stands the process of collecting and the ways in which early anthropologists and art historians imbued the collected objects with new meanings and values that spoke to the scientific debates about the evolution and diffusion of culture prominent at the time. Chapter 2, "Celebrating Form: From Primitive to Primitivism," shifts the discussion from the world of curators and scholars to that of artists and critics. Ethnographic museums turned into contact zones where artists encountered sculptures and masks from Africa and the Pacific. The popular reception of these works as primitive, savage, or crude both enhanced their attractiveness to certain artists and provided models for experimentation and critique of the received European tradition. Chapter 3, "Creating Visibility and Value: Photography and Its Effects," investigates the effects of this artistic valuation of African sculpture on the research into African artifacts and their museal display. As I argue in this chapter, the extensive production and consumption of photographic images had far-reaching consequences with respect to style, value, and fieldwork.

The second part of the book spans the postwar period to the study of Black Atlantic traditions in the 1970s and 1980s. As World War II and colonialism gradually came to an end, the center of research shifted from Europe to the new imperial superpower, the US. Chapter 4, "Discovering the African Artist: Tradition and Tribality in the Cold War Era," discusses Africanist research under the conditions of Cold War politics and postcolonial nation building. The rapidly modernizing environment not only altered categories (from "primitive" and "tribe" to "tradition" and "artist") but also gave rise to the academic institutionalization of African art history as a recognized subfield in (American) art history departments. As I argue, interest in the "traditional" artist as the new leitmotif in postwar, postcolonial Africanist research was really driven by the presence of the modern/contemporary artist, attributes that tellingly come up in conjunction with the category of tradition. Chapter 5, "Acknowledging the Contemporary: New Forms, New Actors," therefore, investigates how modern African art developed and finally won legitimacy among the Euro-American academic art world. A critical turning point was the *Premier Festival Mondial des Arts Nègres* (translated into English at the time as First World Festival of African Negro Arts) 1966 in Dakar, Senegal. Just as the festival provided African contemporary art a prominent forum and platform, it also allowed the field to expand to the Americas. Chapter 6, "Extending the Horizon: Africa in the Americas," studies this redirection. As it turned out, the newly developed interest in modern/contemporary African art had no lasting effect. Parallel to and informed by the Black Power movement in the US, research returned to the study of traditional/indigenous art in Africa but now widening it to embrace continuities of black artistic traditions in the Americas.

The third and final part of the book examines the postmodern and postcolonial reconfiguration of the field from the rise of postcolonial theory and revived interest in contemporary art in the late 1980s and early 1990s to current debates on the dynamics of modernism, decoloniality, and the question of heritage. Chapter 7, "Intervening the Canon: The Postmodern, the Popular, and the Authentic," discusses the "crisis of representation" when hitherto largely unquestioned concepts and classifications became the subject of rigorous critique. The chapter focuses mainly on exhibitions and curatorial strategies exemplified by three major shows: *"Primitivism" in 20th Century Art* at the Museum of Modern Art in New York in 1984, *Magiciens de la terre* at the Centre Georges Pompidou and the Grande Halle de la Villette in Paris in 1989, and *Africa Explores* at the Center for African Art and the New Museum for Contemporary Art in New York in 1991. Chapter 8, "Challenging Representation: Postcolonial Critique and Curation," traces the process whereby, from the early 1990s onward, "the other" began to speak back. Informed by postcolonial theory, a new generation of black artists, critics, and curators began to challenge the "burden of representation" by using prominent international venues like the Venice Biennale or the Documenta in Kassel as effective platforms. Chapter 9, "Undoing the Empire: Duress, Defiance, and Decolonial Futures," discusses the frustrations about the lack of progress in building a more just (art) world. With debates ranging from the interest in modernism and modes of "delinking" from Western modernity to the toppling of monuments and the building of new museums, the result is an ongoing politicization of the field. Its future depends on the prospects of overcoming "the rock" of slavery and colonialism.

Linearity and Limits

The tripartite structure of the book reifies the shifting perspectives and attitudes of the several generations that make up the field of African art studies and that, every twenty to thirty years, reconfigure it.[23] Across these generations, the field has undergone three different phases that I understand as the making, remaking, and unmaking of the field. This last term, *unmaking,* may seem provocative, but I do not mean to suggest that the field is about to dissolve. What I call unmaking is rather like the unweaving of a piece of cloth or a tapestry—all the threads remain to be rewoven in a different pattern. So, too, the unmaking of African art studies does not signify an annulment or "end" of the field but rather a sense of indeterminacy shaped by shifting relations of authority, power, and influence—particularly relations between the Global South and the Global North—that will be reconfigured by coming generations.

The linear organization that structures my narrative may also raise eyebrows in some quarters. Indeed, in view of the diagnosed unmaking of the field, clinging to a linear model might seem odd. Recent debates about globalism and the problem of periodization in (art) history have highlighted and recalled the flaws of linearity. Categories such as medieval or modernism echo the assumption that the past can be organized into a succession of periods that entail distinct expressions of social experience, Baxandall's famous "period eye."[24] However, the geographical and cultural reach of these categories is limited. They cannot be easily translated into other spaces. In the African context, for instance, the period of modernism coincided with the period of colonialism and its politics of racial segregation, which meant that for many African artists the experience of modernism was not one of rupture, innovation, and progress but of exclusion and denigration.[25]

But the problem of linearity is not only one of representation. It is also a problem of narrativity. Historiography explains historical developments by turning them into narratives that in turn conform to certain rules or conventions of explanation, such as chronological progression, causal connection, and rituals of closure. Needless to say, history is more complex than such conventions allow. Scholars have struggled with these discrepancies repeatedly. Ernst Bloch's famous phrase about "the simultaneity of the non-simultaneous," coined, appropriately, in an effort to capture the "Heritage in our Times," is just one of many examples.[26] In the present context, this means keeping in mind that while the field has moved away from its previously exclusive interest in what was once "primitive," then "tribal," and nowadays "indigenous," "historical," or "vernacular" art, the corresponding shift toward modern and contemporary art is not a simple singular progression. Instead, what we find is a kind of palimpsest, a multilayered discourse consisting of different texts that crisscross, superimpose, and partially efface earlier writings. Classical Ife and Benin court art that once captivated the interest of early twentieth-century writers still engages scholars today. New research on the history of trans-Saharan exchange has deepened the temporal depth of African art history and allowed for a better understanding of the dynamics of global trade networks long before the rise of European imperialism.[27] Equally dynamic is the ongoing research on masks, masking, and masked performances, another long-established feature of the field (fig. I.4).

Contemporary masked ensembles and figurative sculptures continue to be important modes of engaging with the world and thus continue

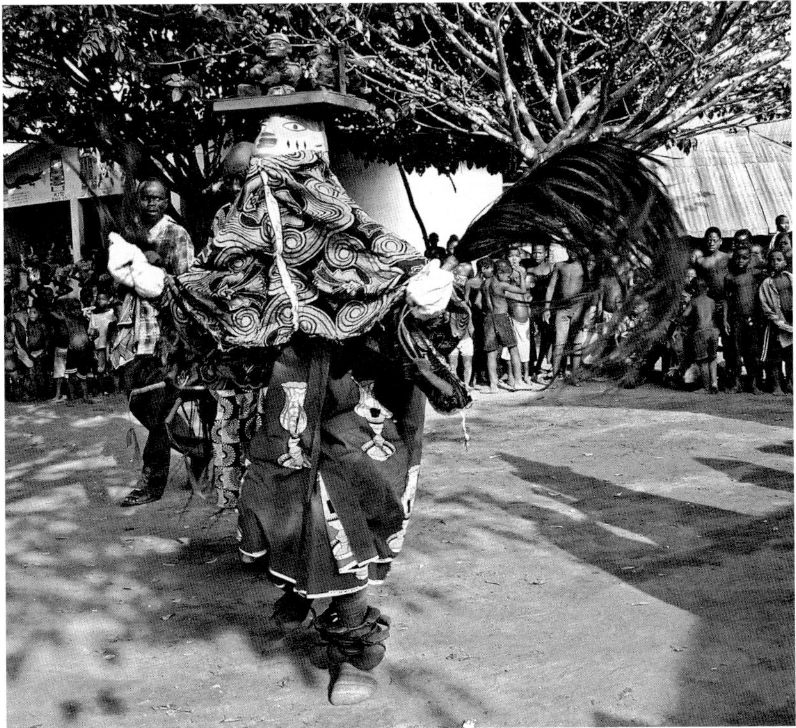

I.4 Gelede masked performance, Cové, Republic of Benin, 2006. Photo: Grete Howard. Public Domain.

to generate research well beyond the conventional focus on sub-Saharan Africa.[28] In fact, with its expansions into North Africa and the recognition of an African diasporic presence outside the continent, the field is now effectively conceived as the arts of Global Africa.[29] Equally ensuring the continuous research and interest in indigenous African art is the institutional and professional landscape. For graduates pursuing a PhD in African art studies—either in art history or anthropology—there are two primary employment tracks: university teaching and museum curation. While the former is precarious, the latter remains comparatively stable. Big encyclopedic museums but at times also (American) university galleries often have collections of African art objects that continue to require curation. However, what curation actually means has changed. A new public awareness of the manifold legacies of slavery and racism has reenergized the debate on the provenance of objects and the epistemologies that justify their presence in Western institutions.[30] Last but not least, there is the so-called tribal art market with special books, fairs, and journals addressing the interests of dealers and collectors. Even though the intellectual center of gravity of the academic portion of the field has clearly turned toward the contemporary, the "tribal" museum/market complex remains a bastion for the presence and visibility of the "traditional." In fact, the bastion itself has remained to be a steady subject of scholarly interest.[31]

To adequately capture this contemporaneity and heterogeneity would have meant to write a different book. My intention is to provide a guide through the history of the field, how it started and changed from its (contested) beginnings until the present. To do so one must construct a narrative, a decision that entails accepting the flaws of narrativity and taking responsibility for the numerous omissions resulting from it (the omission of architecture arguably being the most serious).[32] As I have noted, this book grew out of my teaching. Hence, the primary space I envision for its future life is the classroom. I invite students and instructors to fill the gaps and identify the continuities of past debates. As much as I acknowledge the book's shortcomings, it is my hope that they will prompt other, alternative and rival studies complementing, correcting, and advancing the picture I have painted here. After all, ideas, and especially an idea like "African art," resemble persons. They have their own identities and carry their own biographies/histories. When we use them we invoke their lives, they show themselves to us. But what we see depends on where we stand.[33] Consequently, I do not expect that others share my reading of the history of African art scholarship. Readers will invoke the idea from different vantage points. What I trust and believe in is the ensuing debate that results from these diverse positions.

PART I

Forming a Field

COLONIAL COLLECTING, RACIAL OMISSIONS, AND NATIONAL RIVALRIES

We took up our spades, our picks, and our crowbars and spent the light of day in seeking for the treasure there, where the moaning of the night had whispered in our ears the promise of success. And the voice of Africa was heard, saying: "Let there be light!"

LEO FROBENIUS, *Und Afrika Sprach*, 1912

Introduction

On October 16, 1910, the German ethnographer and cultural historian Leo Frobenius arrived in Lagos, Nigeria, to shed light on the history of Africa by collecting ethnographic and archaeological artifacts for German museums. By then Lagos had developed from a swampy slave post to a busy cosmopolitan port city, referred to by the colonial public at the time as the "Liverpool of West Africa."[1] As a British colony and the capital of the British Protectorate of Southern Nigeria, Lagos had well over one hundred thousand inhabitants. The climate, both physical and political, though, posed challenges. Nationalism was in the air. The local population resented the colonial administration.[2] Experiences of exclusion, inequality, unjust taxation, and misrepresentation were the subject of heated discourse. Criticism was especially sharp from the local elite. Members ranged from merchants and medical doctors to lawyers and clergymen whose wealth and interest allowed for an urban modernity with local newspapers, studio photographers, painters, and art patrons.

As someone distinctly interested in artistic practices, Frobenius could have visited the studios and written about the local art scene.

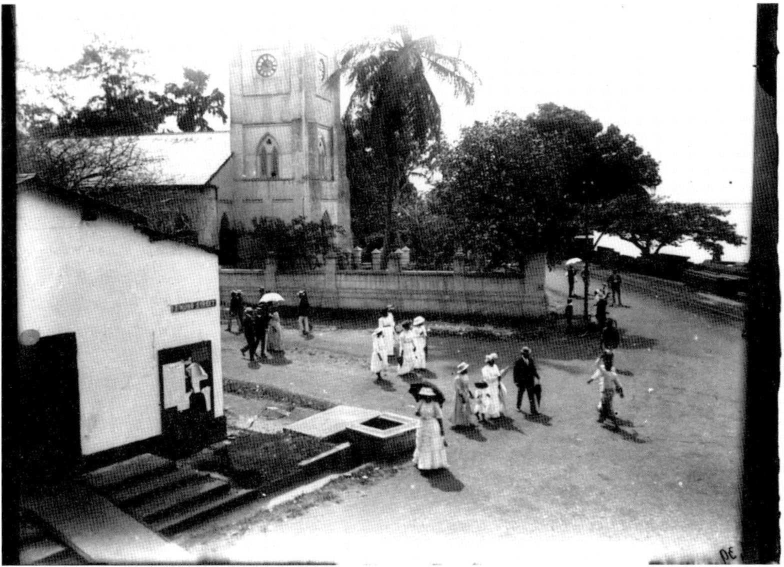

1.1 Church visit in Lagos near the harbor, around 1910. © Bildarchiv der Deutschen Ko-
lonialgesellschaft, Universitätsbibliothek Frankfurt am Main.

But his reaction to Lagos's colonial modernity was one of disbelief and
disappointment (fig. 1.1).

> A walk through the streets on a Sunday evening is all that is wanted
> to give one a correct notion of what goes on. The people pour in and
> out of numerous buildings like music-halls, glaring with electric light.
> They come on bicycles, swagger canes in their hands, cigarettes be-
> tween their lips and top-hats on their heads. They can be seen from the
> outside, sitting in tightly packed crowds, singing for hours together.
> They display all the outward signs of advanced European civilization,
> from patent leather boots to the single eye-glass; and every other in-
> dividual wear either spectacles or eye-glasses of gold. And then the
> ladies! Good gracious me! The picture hats! The stoles! The frocks of
> silk!—These temples of vanity, blazing with illuminations like Variety
> theatres, are—Christian churches![3]

For Frobenius, Lagos offered nothing worth seeing or studying. It was
a place filled with "trouser negroes" (*Hosenneger*) who had traded their
cultural dignity for a false sense of European modernity. What mattered
to Frobenius was the past, not the present. Only four days after his arrival in Lagos, Frobenius left for Ibadan some seventy miles to the north
(fig. 1.2).

He and the members of his team had come to collect artifacts for ethnological museums in Germany. Clearly, the venture was a commercial one: Frobenius made his living from the expeditions he conducted.[4] But it was also a personal mission: he aimed to rehabilitate the "dark continent" in the European imagination by throwing light onto its hidden past. Hence, the epigraph at the beginning of his Nigerian travelogue: *Fiat lux*—Let there be light. Collecting objects alone was not enough. Early on while he was studying museum collections, Frobenius had learned that objects were not simply found but rather are made or, as we would say today, "constructed" or "animated" by virtue of being placed into meaningful contexts or "frames."[5]

The purpose of this chapter is to show how this "animation" of objects actually happened and how it provided the basis for the study of African art as a scholarly subject in the Western academy. To trace this process, the chapter is divided into three parts. In the first part I will first discuss the evolution of the museum and the dynamics of colonial collecting. The "Scramble for Africa" in European imperial politics triggered a flood of objects into the colonial centers where newly built ethnographic and ethnological museums became de facto research laboratories for the study of the history of culture. In the second part I will explain the discrepancy

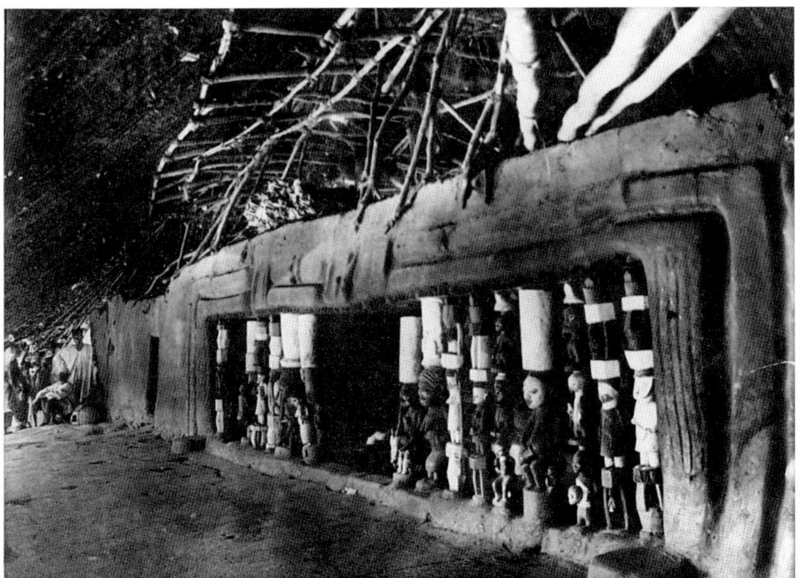

1.2 Screen of figural posts at the entrance to the shrine for Shango, the Yoruba deity of thunder and lightning in Ibadan, photographed by Frobenius in 1910. © Frobenius Institut, Universität Frankfurt am Main.

between the steadily increasing quantity of African artifacts in museum collections on the one hand and the conspicuously marginal role African objects played in the wider theoretical debates about the evolution of art and aesthetics on the other. In the third part I will come back to the issue of collecting and address the shifts in political context and the colonial rivalries that shaped Africanist research and the debate on Benin and Ife, arguably the two most prominent examples of so-called classical African art.

Accumulation and Animation

The history of African art studies begins with the massive extraction of cultural objects. In fact the "Scramble for Africa" was not only a rush to secure and explore new markets on the African continent for the rapidly industrializing colonial powers in Europe but also a "scramble" for artifacts in the hope of advancing equally rapid developments in the realm of the sciences, arts, and humanities. The extraction of natural and cultural resources went hand in hand; the growth of the African collection at the Royal Ethnological Museum in Berlin is a case in point.[6] In 1873, when the museum was founded, the Africa collection consisted of 875 objects. In 1886, only one year after the infamous Berlin Conference that regulated the colonial partition of Africa, the inventory already listed ten thousand objects. Thirteen years later, in 1899, the number had increased to 25,105 objects, which constituted 48.8 percent of the whole ethnographic collection. By 1914, the start of World War I, the size of the collection had more than doubled again to 55,079 objects.[7]

As rapid as the increase was, the colonial accumulation of objects happened throughout a long history of contacts and interactions between Africa and the West. The expansion of Islam and the emergence of long-range trade networks among Africa, Europe, and Asia during early medieval times had made Africa part of a global network of exchanges early on.[8] However, it was only with the beginning of Europe's imperial expansion—which eventually resulted in transatlantic slavery and the establishment of forts and trading posts along the African coast, effectively starting in the sixteenth century—that African objects entered Europe in a sustained way. Their status ranged from curiosities to luxury goods, and they served as media of exchange among the African and European nobility. For the latter, the objects signified the astonishing variety of Christian creation that had become visible in the course of imperial expansion and exploration. The world had become a stage for the play of European power and imagination—by collecting artifacts from around the world, patrons brought that world into their homes while also exercising control over it. Neither aesthetic appreciation nor the desire to learn and preserve played much part in this collecting. The situation changed only in the nineteenth century, when colonialism and Christianization joined forces with industrialization, nationalism, and the emphatic belief in science and progress. The result was an assemblage of heterogeneous hopes and ideas in which romantic resentments toward the costs of progress and the revival of old Enlightenment debates about the universality of mankind stood side by side with concepts of human evolution, cultural diffusion, and racial superiority. Together, these justified colonialism as a necessary civilizational project whose aim was to uplift African peoples from the "darkness" of savagery and ignorance.

Ethnological museums played an important role in this social milieu. For Adolf Bastian, for instance, the first director of the Ethnological Museum in Berlin and a leading figure in German ethnology, the basic premise of museum work was the "psychic unity of mankind." As he saw it, different geographical provinces gave rise to different "folk ideas" (*Völkergedanken*) that expressed themselves in material artifacts.[9] As a science whose subject was defined by the destructive onslaught of "progress," ethnology had a duty to salvage and study these artifacts and the ideas they entailed before their disappearance. In this, the size and comprehensiveness of a collection was key. The approach was inductive rather than deductive. The theoretical paradigm was not biology but philology, which meant that an ethnographic artifact was studied as a kind of text or text fragment. Seen in this way, collections functioned like libraries. The more items they contained, the better. Hence, the "richness" of the collections.

The sources of the collections varied. Some objects came from military and colonial officers, some from missionaries, some from planters, and some from professional collectors. In fact the scramble for objects among ethnological museums had generated a new breed of collector/ethnographer/entrepreneur, like the Hungarian Emil Torday or the abovementioned German Leo Frobenius. Colonial power relations and violence defined these interactions. The sources are unequivocal; ruthless expropriations formed an integral part of the business. Respective colonial testimonies abound and range from extensive coverage of the looting of Benin bronzes during the infamous "punitive expedition" of British troops to Benin city in 1897 (see below) to the private notes of anthropologists who shamefully confessed practices of extortion and the threat of physical force in their "desire" to acquire secret ritual objects in what was then "French Sudan" for the advancement of science.[10] The picture is bitter, and the costs to Africa of European extraction of its natural and cultural resources remains a crime. The picture also shows calculated local responses to the colonial greed and violence. By the late nineteenth to the early twentieth century, the demand for African artifacts had created a viable market situation that resulted in exchanges and straightforward sales, often mediated through middlemen. Masks, sculptures, spears, pots, and other decorated artifacts of daily use were often produced at workshops for exchange or sale to collectors. Local production responded to Western taste and aesthetic preferences.[11] Accordingly, the style of the objects changed.

A prominent example are the so-called *byeri* reliquaries of the Fang (or Pangwe/Pahouin in late nineteenth/early twentieth-century terminology) peoples in Gabon, Congo, Equatorial Guinea, and southern Cameroon. The name *byeri* signifies a wooden human figure attached to a bark barrel containing the skull of the deceased (fig. 1.3). From the early

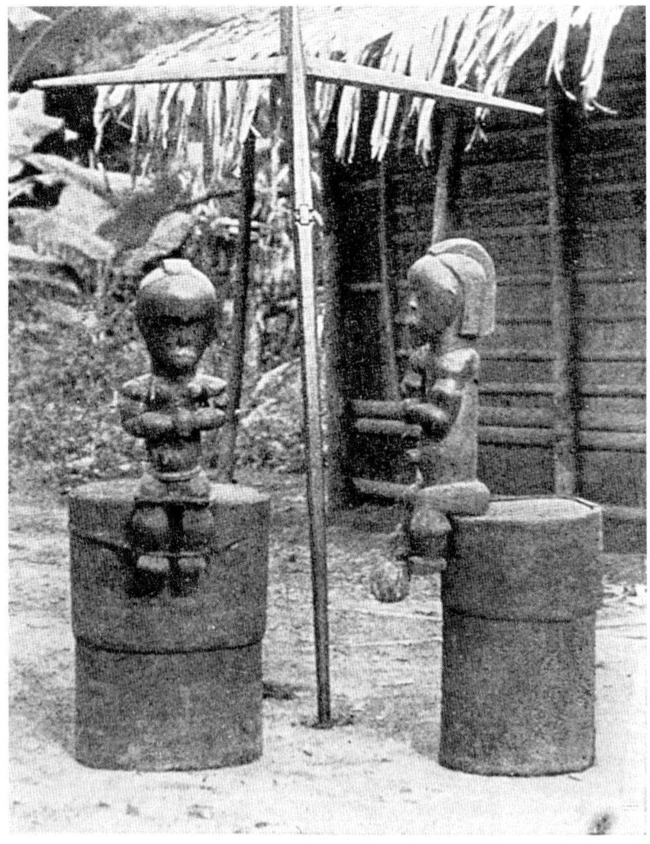

1.3 Fang reliquaries with *byeri* ancestor guardian figures sitting on top, ca. 1913. Karl Zimmermann, *Die Grenzgebiete Kameruns im Süden und im Osten* (Berlin: Mittler und Sohn, 1914). Photo: Hans Gehne. Ross Archive, Yale University.

twentieth century onward, *byeri* had attracted the attention of critics and artists in Europe and the US who considered them timeless representations of authentic "primitive" art (see chap. 2). However, by the time the figures reached Europe, *byeri* were already commodities produced for the Western market. As the German ethnographer Günther Tessmann, who lived in southern Cameroon as a plantation farmer, noted in 1913,

> The Pangwe sell these "idols," highly valued to Europeans, often without precondition, and even offer to sell them in areas influenced by the whites. . . . In contrast, it is probably impossible to sell the containers and their contents for high sums. The figures come in different forms. The oldest seem to be a simple head stuck on the container with a short or long stem. . . . Later, half figures . . . and lastly entire figures were made, on the backs of which were points that stuck into the skull container so that the figure appeared to sit on the edge. The two early forms now already appear very rarely and are only to be found in untouched parts of the Pangwe region, while the entire figures are found much more frequently. As the Fang themselves say, the "newest form" of this development is the self-standing figure, independent of the container, most of which are significantly larger (up to one meter).[12]

Tellingly, Tessmann discussed the *byeri* reliquaries as expressions of ritual and religion, not as the result of an artistic impulse. The classification followed the standard anthropological manuals at the time. We need to recall that anthropology, or ethnology as the field was called in Germany and France, was still first and foremost "museum anthropology," or what later became known as "armchair" anthropology.[13] Fieldwork was not yet part of the discipline's methodological repertoire. Or rather, the field was the museum collection. In general curators did not themselves collect but "outsourced" the job to traders like Tessmann, missionaries, or professional collectors. To get the information they sought, museums and anthropological institutes published collecting manuals, explicating what collectors were to do in the field. While the actual content differed, all shared the same ranking of categories: physical features came first, followed by the recording of material culture; notes on religious beliefs and social practices came last. Part two of the British *Notes and Queries* from 1884, for instance, a widely used handbook published by the British Royal Anthropological Society, started with clothing, personal ornaments, weaving, basketwork, string, leatherwork, pottery, metallurgy, and a whole list of other entries.[14] Only toward the end of the list is there a section on sculpture. The order expressed the subordinate status of objects, especially statues, masks, and other "fetish" figures. As carriers of "primitive beliefs and functions," they belonged to the realm of religion and worldview. Questions of aesthetic or artistic value did not form part of this rubric. Art did not exist as a separate category but was subsumed either under intangible heritage or tools and technologies where it was acknowledged as industrial arts.

Ornaments and Omissions

Where was this classification coming from? A key factor was the experience of rapid industrialization and mechanization. The shift from rural, manual work to industrial, mechanical labor and the corresponding transition from traditional building materials like mud, wood, and stone to steel, glass, and machine manufacturing had created a heightened interest in handmade, preindustrial decorative arts and the world of ornaments. In the context of colonialism and the dominating scientific paradigm of evolutionism, this meant widening the perspective from the medieval period, with its illustrated manuscripts and elaborate tapestries, to the study of ornaments outside Europe. Examining and comparing ornaments thus emerged as a prominent method with which to gain insights into the development of art and culture as a whole.

A prominent figure in this context was the German architect and historian Gottfried Semper. In his 1860 book *Style in the Technical and Tectonic Arts*, Semper argued for a "practical aesthetic" that focused on the natural or intrinsic logic of materials instead of situating aesthetics in the realm of ideas and perception.[15] For Semper, the form of an ornament was not the result of an aesthetic idea or capacity originating from the maker but rather the effect of specific materials, tools, and techniques, like wickerwork or weaving, the maker employed to create it. In other words, the study of ornaments allowed for an understanding of "the relation between the form and the history of its creation."[16]

Semper's interest in ornaments and "practical aesthetics" was widely influential. In England, prominent examples of his scholarly influence were Augustus Henry Lane Fox Pitt Rivers and Charles Balfour.[17] Pitt Rivers was an antiquarian and former military officer. In 1884 he donated his collection of twenty-four thousand anthropological artifacts to the University of Oxford, which turned them into a museum. Together with the museum curator, Charles Balfour, Pitt Rivers organized and presented the collection not according to the objects' provenance but according to "type."[18] While Pitt Rivers was an amateur scholar, Balfour was trained in the natural sciences. With a specialization in animal morphology, he followed Darwin's typological model and focused on the development of forms and surface designs.[19] Basing his ideas mostly on objects from Melanesia, Polynesia, and East Asia, he distinguished among three stages: the "appreciative stage," when objects were valued on the basis of natural peculiarities; the "adaptive stage," when such peculiarities were artificially accentuated; and the "creative stage," when art forms were created from scratch, based on copying nature, and then produced at will. For Balfour, copying was the main agent responsible for producing variation in designs. Copying led to degeneration as well as innovation, and meanings could be lost over time, leaving design "survivals" from an earlier cultural stage.

From the late nineteenth century onward, with the rapid increase of objects from the colonies, the architectural and anthropological debate about ornaments turned into the wider interdisciplinary debate on "World Art."[20] Initiated mostly by art historians and psychologists who aimed to identify general, scientific principles of art, the concept of World Art both advanced and superseded Semper's materialistic understanding of the origins of art and ornament and gave way to more relativistic and historical approaches that distanced themselves from evolutionist and materialistic conjectures. In 1893, for instance, the Austrian art historian and curator Alois Riegl traced the development of different ornamental motifs from Egyptian to Early Islamic and Ottoman styles and argued for the existence of an innate aesthetic drive, something he would later call *Kunstwollen*.[21] A year later the ethnologist and collector of East Asian art Ernst Grosse published his widely noted treatise on *The Beginnings of Art*.[22] Grosse's comparative approach softened the strict distinction between low/primitive and high/civilized art and emphasized the need for what we would today call "context." Still, contrary to its name, "World Art" did not aim to come up with a "global" model. Its purpose was primarily to complement the art history of Europe with the histories of the colonial other. In other words, "World Art" was first and foremost a study of the art of the Rest as opposed to the art of the West, and even within this residual category there were serious omissions.

A case in point is the absence of African examples. As detailed and extensive as the debate on ornaments was, African materials were hardly ever mentioned. Certainly, there were exceptions, such as Georg Schweinfurth's *Artes Africanae: Illustrations and Descriptions of Productions of the Industrial Arts of Central African Tribes*, published in 1875 in both German and English.[23] The English translation rendered the German *Kunstfleiss* somewhat clumsily as "industrial arts," but the term prefigures Riegl's *Kunstwollen* in terms of an innate artistic will or drive that manifests itself in aesthetic expression. Schweinfurth undoubtedly apprehended and was moved by that drive; he praised the elegant form of the Azande harps, conceded a distinct sense of architecture in the Mangbetu, and marveled at the tasteful decorations of Bongo pots. Despite the positive reception of Schweinfurth's work, his observations did not trigger any major interest in African materials in the debate on ornaments. In 1896, twenty years after Schweinfurth, Frobenius still felt compelled to refer to Africa as a "seemingly sterile region" when it came to the study of ornaments.[24] In fact those engaged in the new debate on "World Art" did not pay much attention to African examples. The neglect is puzzling given that the rising colonial interest in the continent had yielded a growing number of rich and informative accounts.

The answer to this riddle echoes the power of a deep-rooted, multifaceted history of racism. First, there was the theologically charged image of blackness as being categorically inferior to whiteness. Early medieval writers had started to associate dark skin color with the biblical story of Ham, the son of Noah whose descendants were condemned to servitude as punishment for having seen his father nude at sleep. From the sixteenth century onward, European imperial powers invoked this negatively charged notion of darkness to justify practices of slavery and colonization.[25]

Second, there was the mental and religious stigma of fetishism. In the sixteenth century, the Portuguese called the objects their West African trading partners used to ensure the validity of trades *feitiço* and compared them with Catholic rosaries and other Christian objects. Local middlemen picked up the term and changed it to *fetisso*, which formed the basis for European travel reports about fetish worship. Soon, reports about the practice shifted from quasi-ethnographic documentation to reflections on the psychology of natives and the difficulty of establishing a healthy and morally sound commerce based on the natural, that is, mercantile, value of objects.[26] Over the course of the seventeenth century, in line with the expansion of capitalist market activities, the notion of "fetishism" emerged, and by the eighteenth century, it had come to signify the antithesis of everything for which the Enlightenment stood: a dark, unenlightened, antirational world dominated by superstition, moral corruption, and capricious fancy. As the German philosopher Georg Wilhelm Friedrich Hegel elaborated in his influential lectures on *Philosophy of History* from the mid-1820s, history and religion required consciousness in terms of acknowledging the objective existence of a world outside the subject. Since "the negroes" had not (yet) attained consciousness, they had neither history nor religion. Instead, they exhibited man in the first state of nature, "completely wild and untamed" and still "enveloped in the dark mantle of night."[27] Accordingly, instead of "a higher being" and religion proper, what one finds is the belief in the power of the "fetich":

What they conceive of as the power in question is . . . nothing really objective, having a substantial being and different from themselves, but the first thing that comes in their way. This, taken quite indiscriminately, they exalt to the dignity of a "Genius"; it may be an animal, a tree, a stone, or a wooden figure. This is their *Fetich*—a word to which the Portuguese first gave currency. . . . Such a fetich has no independence as an object of religious worship; still less has it aesthetic independence as a work of art; it is merely a creation that expresses the arbitrary choice of its maker, and which always remains in his hands.[28]

Last not least, there was the problem of likeness. Following the aesthetic norms of ancient Greece and Rome, art was judged on the basis of its capacity to accurately reproduce the human figure. Deviations from that norm were seen either as "degenerative" or "primitive." The reigning Eurocentric paradigm also determined the cultural geography of Africa in terms of a tripartite organization: "European Africa," the territory north of the Sahara; "the river region of the Nile," which connects Africa with Asia; and "Africa proper," the region south of the Sahara, that is, black Africa.[29] Given this classification, objects that lived up to the Greek standards but were found in "proper Africa" defied the paradigm and thus had to be somehow relocated. It is here that we can see aesthetics and politics intermeshing.

A prominent example is the reception of Kuba sculpture in what is now the Democratic Republic of the Congo, thus Hegel's "Africa proper." In 1883 the Belgian King Leopold II manned an expedition to explore the Southern Kongo Basin with the intention of establishing a private colony, the Congo Free State. A critical part of the expedition was to travel on the Kasai River into the area of the Kuba, then a flourishing kingdom with an effective system of patronage and a highly developed court art that ranged from ornamented boxes and drinking cups to sophisticated raffia textiles and emblematic portraits of Kuba kings (fig. 1.4). Deeply impressed, a member of the Belgian Congo expedition described the Kuba as a "superior civilization" whose art descended from the Pharaonic Egyptians.[30] Thus elevated by the Egyptian connection, Kuba art became an object of interest to the Belgian authorities who exhibited Kuba works at the first Belgian World's Fair 1885 in Antwerp.[31] By then, Leopold II had just established his private Congo fiefdom, and the fair provided a platform to show off Belgium's new status as a colonial power. However, the number of works on display was still few. Twelve years later the situation had changed. In 1897 Belgium organized it's second World's Fair, and this time it was all about Leopold's Congo Free State. A newly

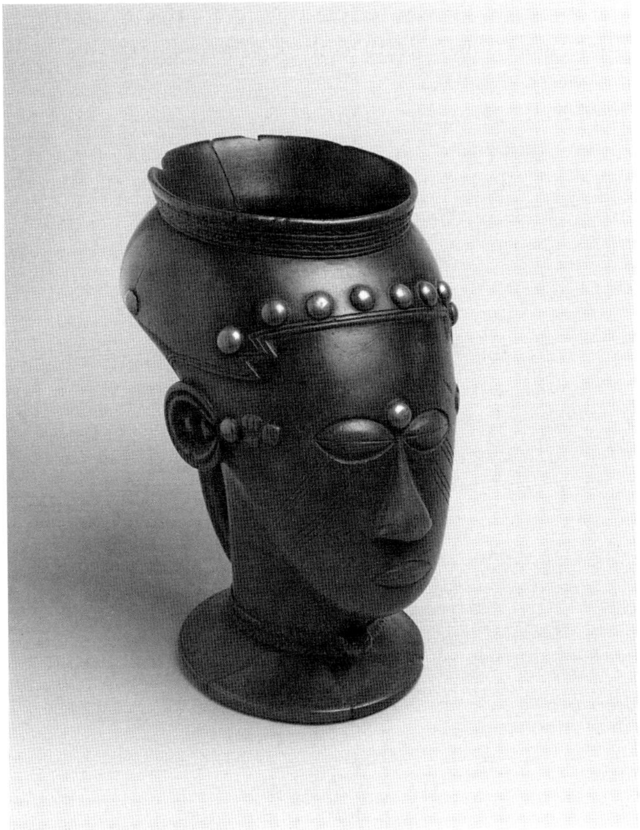

1.4 Unidentified artist, Kuba. Palm wine cup (*Mbwoongntey*), nineteenth century. Wood, copper alloy, 17.1 × 10.2 × 13 cm. Brooklyn Museum, Museum Expedition 1922, Robert B. Woodward Memorial Fund, 22.1487.

built tram line brought visitors from Brussels to the fair's colonial section, housed at a royal estate at Tervuren, outside the Belgian capital of Brussels. At the neoclassical Palace of the Colonies, organizers displayed examples of Congolese art and culture, flora and fauna, as well as export products such as coffee, cacao, and tobacco. In the adjacent park visitors could stroll through a replica of an "African village," complete with 267 Congolese who had been brought over for the duration of the exhibition from May to November. The museum guide celebrated the compositions of Kuba design as a source of inspiration for the decorative style of art nouveau popular at the time in Belgium.[32] Ethnographic information on local use and geographical origin was absent; the focus was on form not on content. In fact the arrangement and layout of objects within various exhibition rooms was an ornament in itself. Carefully arranged metal weapons and tools were put on the wall in a strict symmetrical design that allowed the foreign objects to absorb the aesthetic quality of the favorite local design (fig. 1.5).

The exhibition design invoked not only the flowery designs of the arts and crafts movement but also the movement's distinct interest in preservation. By the late nineteenth century, it had become clear that Christian-colonial modernity not only meant progress but also violence, irreversible loss, and widespread destruction, an awareness that prompted preservation campaigns to counter the negative effects of modernity. Indeed, preservation came to be seen as an obligation and mark of civilization that distinguished "modern" nations from the "primitive" peoples inhabiting the colonies. The recognition of the value of objects and their stewardship was seen as an intrinsic responsibility of civilization itself. Thus, one year after the 1897 World's Exhibition, the temporary exposition in Tervuren became the basis for the Royal Museum for Central Africa.

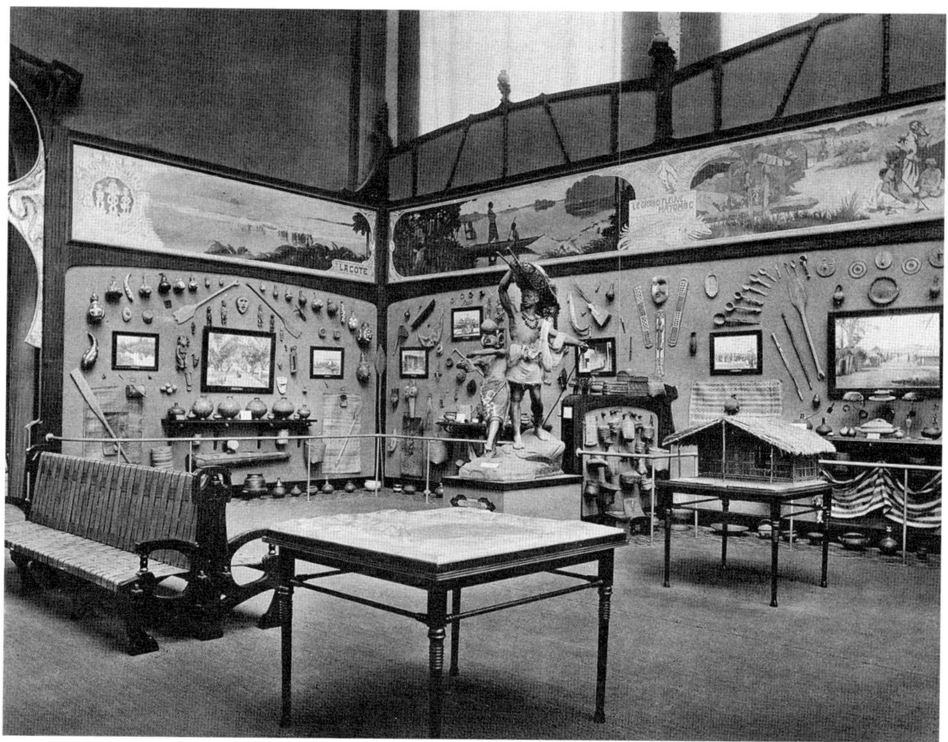

1.5 Installation view of the Salon des Grandes Cultures, Museum Tervuren, 1898. Wellcome Collection.

African Antiquities and European Rivalries

As widespread as the care and preservation model became in the art world, it also became a bone of contention. The German-English dispute over the Benin and Ife bronzes is a well-known case in point. Europeans had known of the Benin Empire in what is now South East Nigeria since the late fifteenth century, when Benin established diplomatic relations with Portugal. Benin's elaborate court art continued to impress the European public right into the twentieth century[33]—in particular, the sophisticated mastery of ivory carving and the technique of lost-wax casting, which had resulted in numerous figurative bronze and brass sculptures, many of them in the form of busts and statuettes, or as relief plaques depicting historical events and fixed on the wooden columns of an audience chamber in the king's palace. With the arrival of Britain as a colonial power in the second half of the nineteenth century, a number of these court art objects had entered England. In 1890, for instance, Pitt Rivers published a catalog of 228 Benin pieces he had purchased. While he called the works art of a "rather advanced stage," he rejected the idea of an African origin.[34] Given the continent's assumed position in the ladder of cultural evolution, an outside, most likely European, influence had to be taken for granted.

Things changed, though, after the so-called punitive raid of British forces on Benin in 1897, which, in effect, meant burning down Benin city and looting its court art.[35] Photographs depict British soldiers proudly presenting and sorting through the loot, which ranged from commemorative ivory tusks and brass heads to palace brass plaques (fig. 1.6). While the former had been ripped from altars, the latter were taken from a sort of store house where they were lying on the ground, having already been dismantled/removed from their original location. In total, the war booty entailed over two thousand objects. Some were shared among the members of the raid as trophies or souvenirs. The majority were auctioned off by the British Admiralty to defray the cost of the expedition. The rest were given to the British Museum, where they landed in the medieval department. Within months the curators published a catalog of the *Antiquities from the City of Benin* and organized an exhibition to show a representative sample to the public.[36] Displayed in a gallery that also housed Assyrian art, the exhibition was celebrated in the London *Times* as "remarkable," evidencing "exceptional skill," "leav[ing] but little to desire."[37] The praise prompted the question of origin. While some speculated about "wandering Egyptians,"[38] others pointed to "the Portuguese,"[39] who had not only provided the copper for the metal works but were also depicted in some of the plaques and sculptures. The mystery caused the

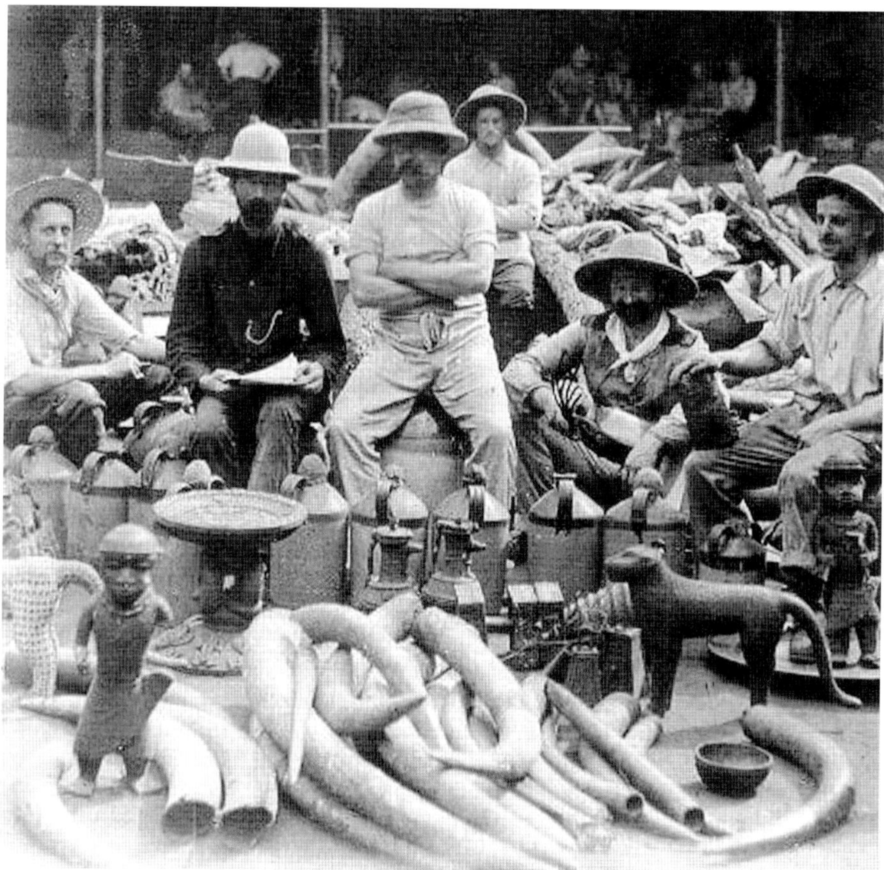

1.6 Members of the British punitive raid posing in front of their loot. Benin, 1897.
CPA Media Pte Ltd / Alamy Stock Photo.

market prices for Benin bronzes to increase. In 1898 a large ivory tusk with plaited carvings went for thirty-one pounds, a bronze headpiece for fourteen pounds, and a brass bell for thirteen pounds. In the next years the prices doubled and tripled, especially when Benin bronzes became sought-after trophies for museums in Europe.[40]

The most potent buyer was the Royal Ethnological Museum in Berlin. In 1897 the museum's deputy director, Felix von Luschan, had read about the bronzes in the newspapers and immediately traveled to London to participate in the auctions. Subsequent travels followed, eventually resulting in a collection of Benin works that was even bigger than London's. In contrast to his English colleagues, von Luschan rejected the argument of foreign influences and insisted on the local origin of the works: "The style of the works is purely African, absolutely and exclusively African;

to talk about Phoenician or Assyrian forms here would simply show that one knows nothing of either of these, nor of modern African art."[41] With respect to the argument posited by British art historians that representations of the Portuguese proved Portuguese origins, he wrote, "I cannot accept these objections as justified. In the same manner, one could pick the representation of a Dutch admiral on an ancient Japanese lacquer box and infer from it that the Japanese lacquer technique came from Holland."[42] The passionate character of the origins argument also informs the detailed description of the bronzes (fig. 1.7). In reference to a plaque von Luschan described as "Benin, European, Warrior with crossbow and pitchfork," he wrote,

> For purely artistic and academic reasons it is important that all of the relief sculptures from Benin be dated with certainty. This is almost impossible for the plates depicting natives, so it is that much more pleasing that in addition to these there are sixty-five plates depicting Europeans that can be dated without doubt. The clothing of the Europeans has been misinterpreted in such a way that the details are not always clear, but for the most part it can be seen with certainty that the clothing comes from the time of Kaiser Maximillian I, Albrecht Dürer, Hans Burgkmair, and Hans Schäufelein, around the end of the fifteenth and beginning of the sixteenth century. Right around this time there were already active relations between the West Coast of Africa and Western Europe.[43]

Ultimately, for von Luschan, the question of origin needed to be settled in order to turn one's attention to the really significant issues: historical content and cultural meaning. In his eyes, the works were not only "great art." They also provided a unique insight into the history and stylistic development of Benin art.

I will return to von Luschan's interpretation of the Benin bronzes in chapter 3 when I discuss his monumental *Die Altertümer von Benin* (Benin Antiquities), published posthumously in 1919. But for the moment, the political dimension of the bronzes merits attention. Two decades after the "Benin raid," the Royal Ethnological Museum in Berlin had amassed 580 Benin bronzes, more than double the collection of the British Museum. For the German authorities that funded von Luschan's "hunting expedition," the acquisitions were both a cultural as well as a political and propaganda project. In 1898 Hans Meyer, patron of ethnology and head of a large publishing house in Leipzig, wrote to von Luschan concerning some bronzes he had acquired: "It is actually a riddle to me, that the English let such things go. Either they have too many of them already or

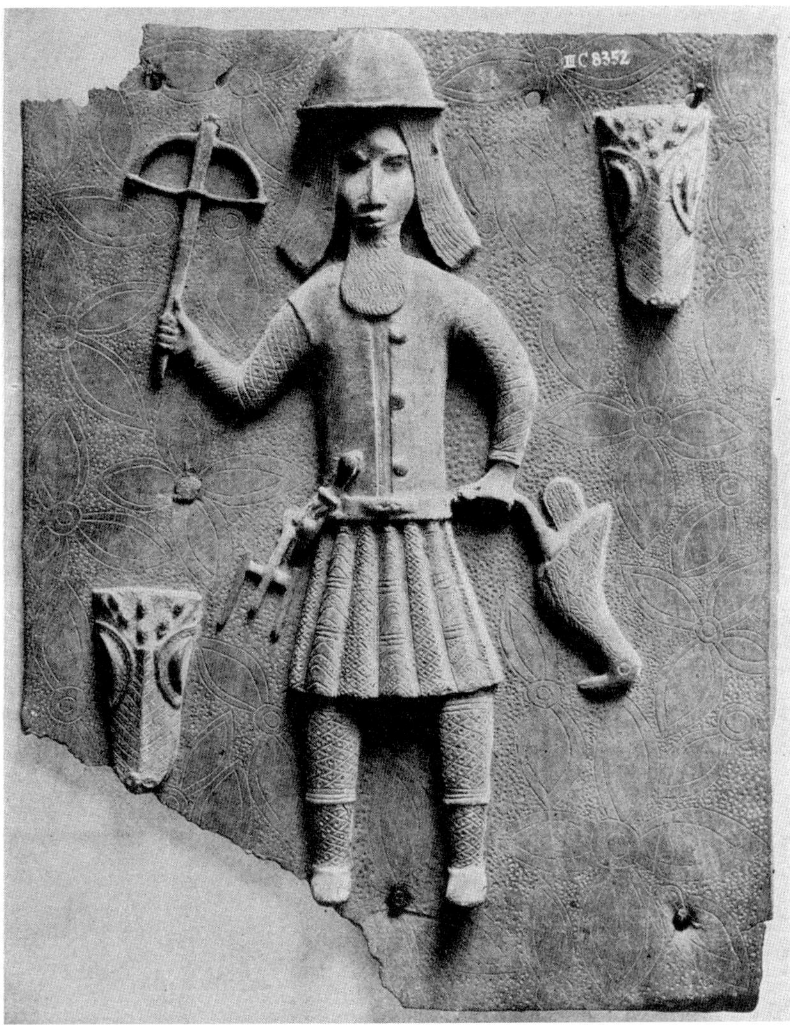

1.7 Unidentified artist, Benin plaque depicting a Portuguese warrior with crossbow and pitchfork, sixteenth century. Copper alloy, 38.5 × 29.5 × 3.8 cm). Felix von Luschan, *Die Alterthümer von Benin*, Berlin: Reimer, 1919. Ross Archive, Yale University. Photo: Ethnologisches Museum Berlin, Art Resource, NY.

they have no idea what these things mean for ethnology, cultural history and art history."[44] Two decades later, Luschan proudly stated that, with 48,845 objects, "the Berlin collection is seven times as large as the ethnographic department of the British museum."[45] The bragging was fueled by nationalistic sentiments. The German government considered itself the superior colonial power—more understanding, benevolent, and just than its rivals France and England. German newspapers heavily criticized the British government for neglecting the ethnographic artifacts kept in British museums and for not properly taking care of its colonies. As they argued, colonialism was threatening the cultural traditions of the colonized. It was thus the duty of the colonizing nation to research, document, and save these traditions before they disappeared altogether—a duty that Germany was performing better than the other colonial powers.

As it happened, this national rivalry also framed Frobenius's research in Nigeria referred to at the beginning of this chapter. Given his quest to throw light on Africa's past, Frobenius's interest was primarily in antiquities. He had heard about the splendor and glory of Ife, the religious and political center of the Yoruba peoples, in his earlier travels in West Africa. At his arrival in early December 1910, Ife still conveyed an aura of power, but the city was visibly marked by the effects of an internal civil war and the pressures of colonial rule.[46] Accordingly, Frobenius's chapters on Ife recount heated disputes over money, ownership, legitimacy, truth, and defalcation—many of which resulted from his public announcement that he was searching for antiquities and was willing to pay for them. With the (apparent) approval of the Oni, or king, of Ife, he swiftly accumulated a series of objects, ranging from ancient glass beads and stone sculpture to terra cotta tiles and terra cotta heads, that documented the former might of the city. The most spectacular acquisition, however, was a bronze head of the ancient sea deity Olokun, which Frobenius describes as follows (fig. 1.8):

> It is cast in what we call "à cire perdue" or hollow cast, and very finely chased indeed, like the finest Roman examples. It cannot be said to be "negro" in countenance, although it is covered with quite fine tattooed lines, which at once contradicts any suggestion of its having been brought from abroad. The setting of the lips, the shape of the ears, the contour of the face, all prove, if separately examined, the perfection of a work of true art, which the whole of it obviously is. The diadem surrounding the head is especially remarkable. There is a flower in its center, behind which rises an entwined staff, ending in a button. . . . I do not think there can be the least doubt but that we are faced with a form of local art whose perfection is absolutely astounding.[47]

In his travelogue Frobenius narrates at length how he managed to persuade the aged guardian of the Olokun grove to sell him the bronze for six pounds sterling. He also notes that the old man and his sons had second thoughts, fearing penalties or repercussions from the British resident and the Oni of Ife. Around mid-December 1910, obviously anticipating con-

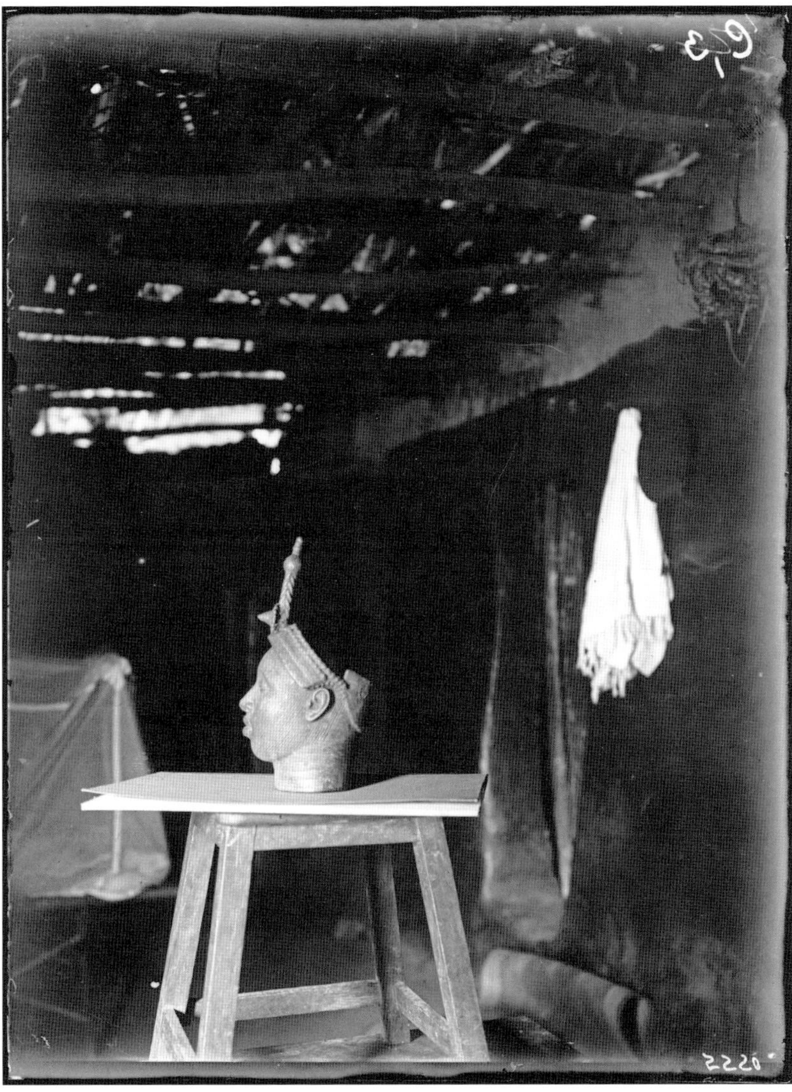

1.8 Unidentified artist, Ife Olokun Head, ca. thirteenth century, copper alloy, on display in Frobenius's tent in Ife, 1911. © Frobenius Institut, Universität Frankfurt am Main.

flicts, Frobenius left Ife in haste. And indeed, on his way back to Ibadan, the British resident, Charles Partridge, stopped him and forced him and his entourage to return to the city. The next chapter offers a long and detailed account of the allegedly biased, rude, and unjust manner in which Partridge investigated Frobenius's Ife collection.[48] We learn that shortly after Christmas 1910, as soon as the "collision" was over, Frobenius finally traveled to Lagos, where he complained about the incident to the German consul, who in turn informed the colonial office in Berlin.

Attached to the complaint is a short report in which Frobenius explains the relevance and value of his finds. As he states, his quest to illuminate the continent's precolonial past had finally been crowned with success. Eager to justify the expenses to his sponsors in Berlin as well as to attract attention to the finds, he presented the Olokun, as well as seven terra cotta heads, as testimonies to an outpost of classical antiquity. This outpost once reached the shores of the West Atlantic Ocean until it mysteriously disappeared, leaving behind only the legend of "Atlantis." The news spread fast. On January 29, 1911, the *New York Times* reported,

> German discovers Atlantis in Africa. Leo Frobenius, author, leader of the German Inner-African Exploration Expedition, sent word from the hinterland of Togo [*sic*], according to information reaching the *New York Times* correspondent, that he has discovered indisputable proof of the existence of Plato's legendary continent of Atlantis. He places Atlantis, which he declares was not an island, in the northwestern section of Africa, in territory close to the equator. The explorer bases his assertions principally on the discovery of an ancient bronze, the head of a man. It is a work of high artistic merit, he says, and dates back to the period ages before the days of Solon.[49]

Two months later, Charles Hercules Read of the British Museum in London rejected Frobenius's "discovery" as "wild speculation."[50] Read's short article also includes a photograph of the Olokun priest together with the Olokun head. It is the last photograph of the bronze head taken during the investigation into Frobenius's collection. Shortly after, the head went missing. How it happened and where the head ended up, whether it was stolen or buried again at an unknown place, has remained a mystery.[51] What remains are the photographs and drawings in Frobenius's travelogue, which he published in 1912. Therein, he also explains the head's importance as evidence for the existence of the legendary Atlantis he claimed to have found. His theory is a mix of ethnographic remarks on Yoruba impluvium architecture and cosmology, archeological findings of Etruscan masks in Sardinia, and ancient reports about seafaring peoples attacking Egypt. Taken together, they paint the diffusionist picture of a pre-Indo-European Atlantic culture that once stretched from the Mediterranean all the way to the shores of West Africa, where it gave rise to ancient Ife: "The culture of Yoruba is the crystallization of that mighty stream of Western civilization which, in its Euro-African form, flowed from Europe into Africa, and, when it sank in volume, left behind it the Etruscans as its cognate and equally symphonic exponents."[52]

Frobenius's book reflected his characteristic promotionalism. His sensationalism, the heroic adventurism, and the nationalist attacks on the English were all clearly calculated to boost book sales and thus generate enough revenue to finance his next research project. However, part of Frobenius's aim was to exploit the romantic potential of African art—its ability to provoke revolt against the West's self-righteous ethnocentrism.[53] In 1912, the same year he published his scientific travelogue *The Voice of Africa*, Frobenius wrote a small piece on "Ancient and Recent African Art" for the journal *Die Kunstwelt* (The Artworld). Turning the argument for cultural flow from north to south upside down, he noted, "the peaks of cultural achievement shifted from the South to the North. It seems that the darker people were the bearers of the first higher culture, which was then transmitted to us and further developed in the northern idiom."[54]

*   *   *

Frobenius's remark was not meant to change the colonial logic of domination and exploitation that enabled his position. The remark was strategic. It aimed to generate attention toward Frobenius's own activities as both a scholar and entrepreneur. In fact as much as he challenged the popular colonial image of Africa as a "dark continent" devoid of history and culture, he also profited from it. Filling the void allowed him to engage in his own animation of Africa. After all, it was not enough to collect artifacts. Rather, they had to be brought to life by lending them with significance and meaning.

The purpose of this chapter was to show the different conceptual and institutional contexts in which this animation happened. Race, violence, and national rivalries between the colonial powers shaped the endeavor. The result was the emergence of a network of relations in which the notion of "African art" gradually took shape. The media and genres of this notion varied. Yet they all gravitated and conformed to the prominence of the figural, sculptural traditions of the West, thereby excluding other art forms such as textiles, ceramics, or beading. As the case of the Fang reliquaries showed, local subjects were not just passive figures in this process. Rather, they often actively responded to the new interest in their material culture by producing works that met the taste and preferences in the colonial metropoles. But having agency does not mean having authority and control over meaning and value.

As we have seen, the aesthetic appreciation of African objects was initially directed toward racially grounded practices of ignorance, omission, and denigration. The interest was an interest in form and the origins of art. It was not to overcome colonial rule, hence the distinction between "Art" and "World Art" as the art of the West versus the art of the Rest. Still, the distinction took time. It did not happen overnight. Interest and recognition by scholars were not enough. What turned the recognition of aesthetic value into a matter of wider public and commercial interest was the involvement of artists and critics.

CHAPTER 2

Celebrating Form

FROM PRIMITIVE TO PRIMITIVISM

*One wonders how African art would have fared if it had not been labeled
"primitive."*

MICHEL LEIRIS, *Afrique Noire,* 1967

Introduction

In the spring of 1936, the Museum of Modern Art in New York hosted
an exhibition called *Cubism and Abstract Art.*[1] For the dust jacket of the
exhibition catalog, the graphic designer had altered a simple hand-drawn
chart made by Alfred Barr, the first director of the Museum of Modern
Art, representing "the origins and influences" of modern art by way of
a complex array of arrows, half circles, and rectangles edged by vertical
columns of dates running from 1890 to 1935 on either side (fig. 2.1).

This depiction of the historical development of abstract art also vi-
sualized a remarkable cultural transformation. Over the course of four
decades, the objects colonialism had extracted from West and Central
Africa into the ethnological and anthropological museums in Paris, London, and Berlin had changed their meaning. What had once been condemned and stigmatized as "crude," "grotesque," and "hideous" was now
celebrated as the "life-giving-sperm" that had revitalized the spiritual and
artistic life of the West.[2] In 1936, the results of this revitalization occupied
all four floors of MoMA gallery space at 11 West 53rd Street: nearly four
hundred paintings, sculptures, installations, photographs, films, and so
forth, mixed with a handful of African objects placed strategically next to
works by Picasso, Lipchitz, Stieglitz, and others to illustrate the influence
of African art on modern art in the West.

The masks and sculptures were a visual reminder of an exhibit the

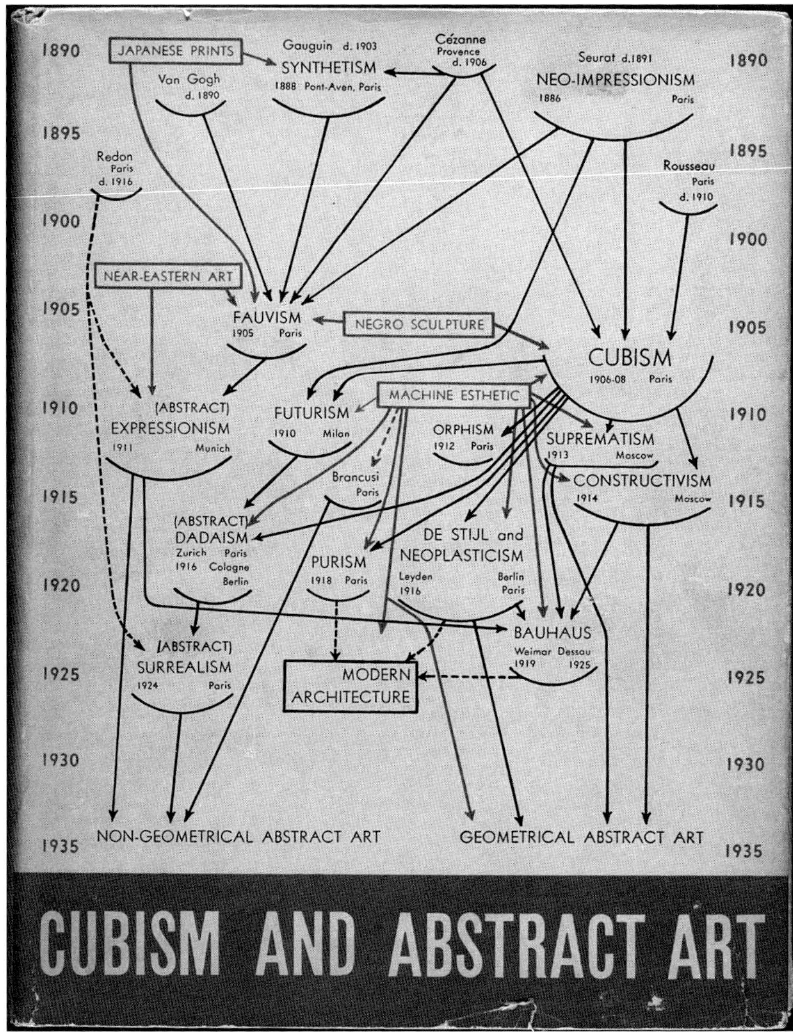

2.1 Dust jacket with chart prepared by Alfred H. Barr Jr. of the exhibition catalog *Cubism and Abstract Art*, by Alfred H. Barr Jr., 1936. Digital Image © The Museum of Modern Art / Licensed by SCALA / Art Resource, NY.

museum had mounted a year before, in the spring of 1935, titled *African Negro Art*. Attracting nearly fifty thousand visitors, it was one of the most successful exhibitions the museum had organized since its opening in 1929.[3] Practically all the six hundred objects on display came from collections in Europe. James Johnson Sweeney, the curator of the show, had traveled to France, Belgium, Germany, and England to identify the best works. Ethnographic or historical considerations did not matter for the selection: the criteria were purely formal. As Sweeney explained in the catalog:

> It is the vitality of the forms of Negro art that should speak to us, the simplification without impoverishment, the unerring emphasis on the essential, the consistent, three-dimensional organization of structural planes in architectonic sequences, the uncompromising truth to material with a seemingly intuitive adaptation of it, and the tension achieved between the idea or emotion to be expressed through representation and the abstract principles of sculpture. The art of Negro Africa is a sculptor's art. As a sculptural tradition in the last century, it has had no rival. It is as sculpture art we should approach it.[4]

Sweeney's manifesto-like passage represents the high point in the new modernist attitude toward African objects. What was once "primitive" had become "primitivism," a modernist category that Sweeney's assistant in the *African Negro Art* show, Robert Goldwater, had introduced in his book *Primitivism and Modern Art*.[5] While late nineteenth-century Europe rejected African objects as expressions of superstition, savagery, and cultural benightedness, early twentieth-century artists, critics, and collectors embraced them as emblems of a lost wholeness, an unblocked immediacy and direct access to the wellsprings of creativity (figs. 2.2, 2.3).

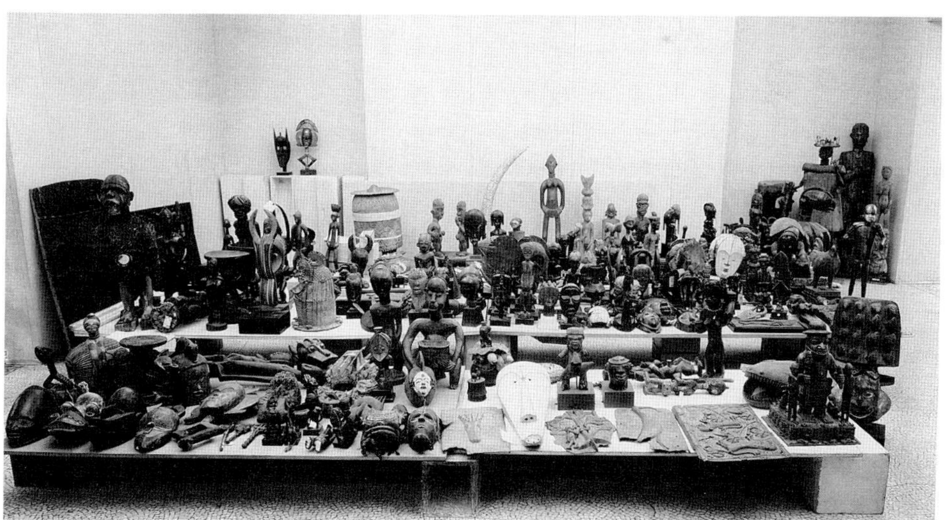

2.2 Assemblage of objects included in the exhibition *African Negro Art*, March 18, 1935, through May 19, 1935, at the Museum of Modern Art, New York. Photo: Soichi Sunami. Digital Image © The Museum of Modern Art / Licensed by SCALA / Art Resource, NY.

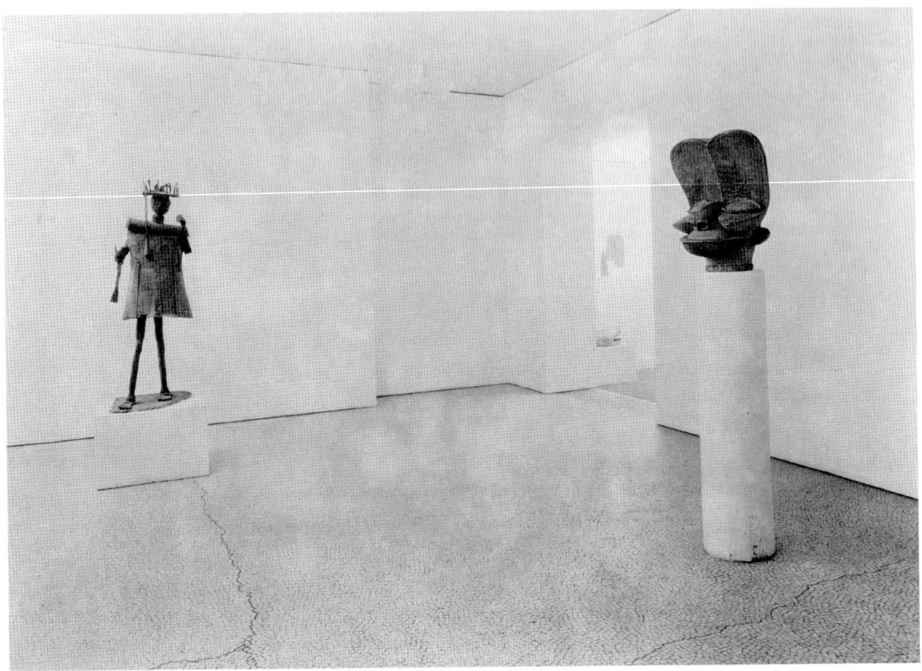

2.3 Installation view of the exhibition *African Negro Art*, March 18, 1935, through May 19, 1935. Metal warrior figure, Fon, Dahomey (see also figs. 3.7, 3.8), situated vis-à-vis a wooden crest mask, Bamileke peoples, Cameroon. Photo: Soichi Sunami. Digital Image © The Museum of Modern Art / Licensed by SCALA / Art Resource, NY.

In the following, I will discuss the various stages and places of this development as a process of purification by which objects were stripped of their relationships with the environment in which they were produced, thereby allowing them to be experienced and understood from a purely formal or, as Sweeney put it, a "sculptural" perspective.[6] However, as the chapter will show, the experience differed for different audiences. For white artists, critics, and collectors, purification meant something different than for their black counterparts. Whereas the former pushed for the purification of form, for the latter purification also aimed to counter, if not overcome, the filter of whiteness through which black subjects had come to learn about African art.

Encounters and Exorcisms

With its red and black arrows, dotted lines, half circles and rectangles, the cover design of *Cubism and Abstract Art* shows an odd affinity with military maps and the maps of colonial exploration. And indeed, comparing the accounts of nineteenth-century explorers with those of early twentieth-century artists reveals remarkable parallels. Both quarreled about the question of who "discovered" African art first. Both bragged about the bravado and courage it took to reach their destination. And both showed a mix of distance and desire in their attitude toward their subject-object.[7]

The most famous example of this attitude is Pablo Picasso's account of his visit to the Ethnographic Museum of the Trocadéro in Paris some time in 1906/1907:

> When I went to the Trocadéro it was disgusting. The flea market. The smell. I was all alone. I wanted to get away. But I did not leave. I stayed. I stayed. I understood something very important: something was happening to me, wasn't it? . . . I kept looking at the fetishes. I understood. . . . I understood what the purpose of the sculpture was for the Negroes. . . . They were weapons. To help people stop being dominated by spirits, to become independent. Tools. If we give form to the spirits, we become independent of them. The spirits, the unconscious (which wasn't yet much spoken of then), emotions, it's the same thing. I understood why I was a painter. All alone in that awful museum, the masks, the red Indian dolls, the dusty mannequins. Les Demoiselles d'Avignon must have come to me that day, but not at all because of the forms: but because it was my first canvas of exorcism— yes, absolutely![8]

Picasso's "exorcism" signified the urge to leave behind centuries-old conventions of representation and "to break out of the circle the realists have locked us into," as Picasso's colleague Derain put it,[9] which soon generated a wide-ranging movement that transcended national boundaries while as the same time acquiring distinct national inflections.

In the US, the movement arrived in the form of a short article published in May 1910, in which the American writer, artist, and critic Gelett Burgess reported on the revolt of a group of young Parisian artists against the artistic establishment in France.[10] Titled "The Wild Men of Paris," the article described and recounted interviews with the main protagonists, providing photographs of their works. The ironic tone of the article conveyed Burgess's skepticism and ambivalence regarding his encounter with the modernist revolt. But while he ridiculed the "ugliness" and "monstrosity" of the works, he also acknowledged that they moved him to undertake a "radical reconstruction" of his own "views on art" (fig. 2.4).[11]

One of the first in the "New World" to follow up on Burgess's lead was the Mexican artist and gallerist Marius de Zayas. De Zayas had arrived

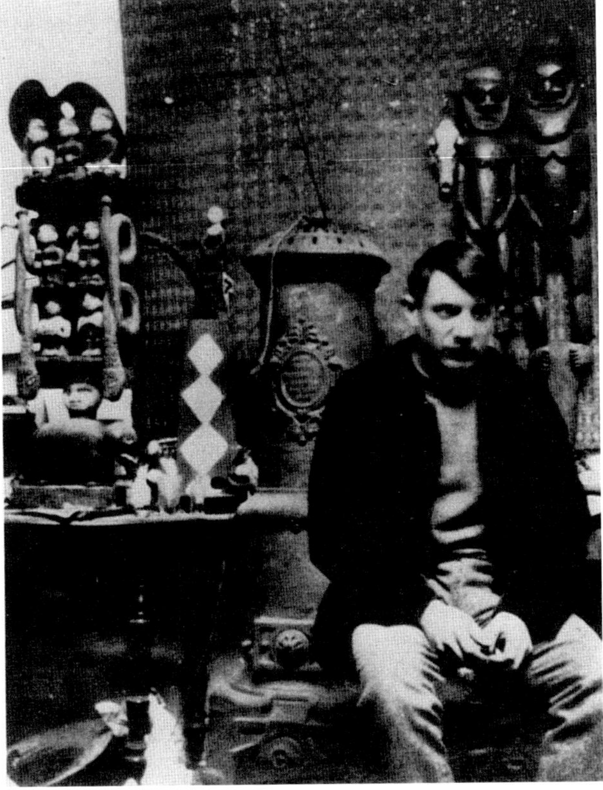

2.4 Pablo Picasso in his studio at Bateau-Lavoir, 1908. Photo: Frank
Gelett Burgess. © 2020 Estate of Pablo Picasso / Artists Rights So-
ciety (ARS), New York. Digital Image © RMN-Grand Palais / Art
Resource, NY

in New York in 1906 and quickly became acquainted with members of
the avant-garde, among them the photographer and gallery owner Alfred
Stieglitz, who offered him work as a trend scout and partner of his gallery 291. De Zayas accepted, and in October 1910, four months after Burgess's article, he traveled to Paris to establish contact with the "wild men"
about whom Burgess had written. During the subsequent three years, de
Zayas organized exhibitions of Picasso, Brancusi, and other avant-garde
Parisian artists at Stieglitz's gallery in New York. It was during this time
that he also realized the economic potential of the new interest in African
sculpture. Accordingly, in 1914, he proposed to Stieglitz that they show a
selection of works from the collection of Paul Guillaume. Though only in
his early twenties, Guillaume had already managed to become a leading
figure in the new art trade in African objects.[12] The exhibition project

worked for both sides: for Guillaume, it meant opening a potential new market in the US and thus evading the negative effects of the outbreak of World War I on his European business; for de Zayas, it meant consolidating the status of gallery 291 as New York's prime venue for everything new and exciting (fig. 2.5).

In the absence of African colonies and only a few ethnographic museums, the American audience was largely unfamiliar with Africa, let alone with African sculpture. With the single exception of the Washington Square Gallery, owned and run by American painter Robert Coady, only the Natural History Museum in New York had previously shown African artifacts[13]—all of them from Congo because of the interest aroused by the alleged Egyptian connection of Kuba art (discussed in chap. 1). As in European museums, the exhibition was densely packed and followed the conventional typological model that denied objects their individuality. *Statuary in Wood by African Savages: The Root of Modern Art*, the show that opened on November 3, 1914, was different.[14] With its deliberately provocative title, the exhibition aimed to demonstrate the new modernist

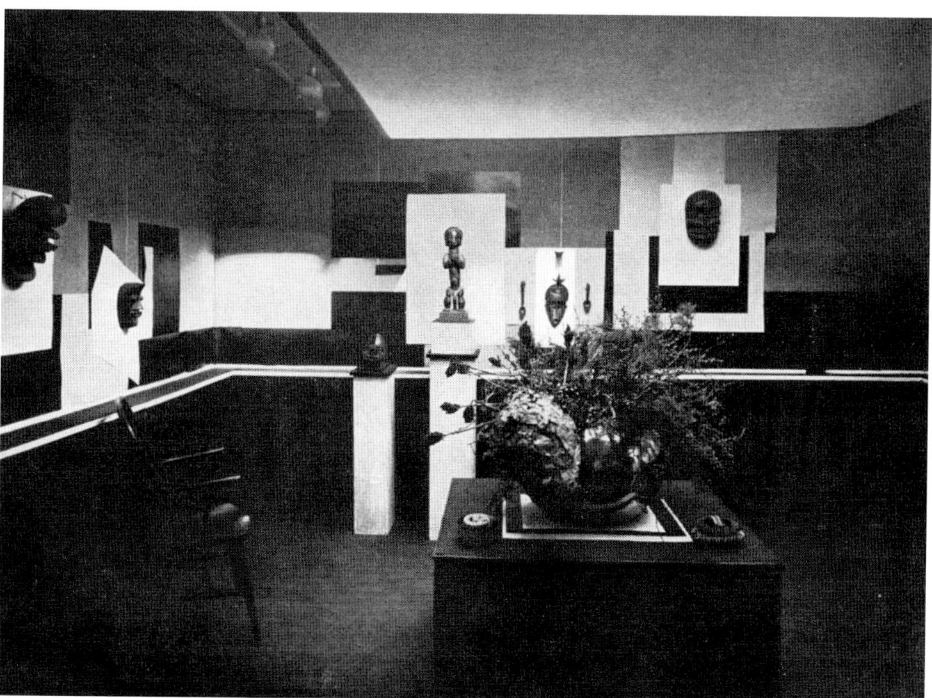

2.5 Alfred Stieglitz, View of the exhibition *Statuary in Wood by African Savages: The Root of Modern Art*, printed in *Camera Work*, no. 48 (October 1916). © The Metropolitan Museum of Art, Art Resource, NY.

appreciation of African sculpture. On display were the highlights of Guillaume's collection: Fang and Kota reliquary figures from Gabon, a Dan mask from Liberia, Baule carvings from Côte d'Ivoire, and other works from West and Central Africa. Some were placed on pedestals, others were mounted on the wall in front of sheets of colored paper. The exhibition design by photographer and painter Edward Steichen allowed for a formalist way of seeing. As such it focused on the "sculptural" aspects of the works or what Matisse and others called the "values of volume."

"Negro Art" in Theory

"Values of volume"—the concept signified not only an artistic and practical but also an art-theoretical interest in what had come to be known as *art nègre* in French or *Negerkunst* in German. Both terms emerged in the first and second decades of the twentieth century and began to shift the debate on African art from anthropology and geography to art criticism and art history. Notions of rupture and rebellion were in the air. The general feeling was that Western culture had run out of steam, that social, moral, and artistic progress had exhausted its energies and devolved into a dead end. To overcome the state of enervation, it was deemed necessary to break with both the customs of bourgeois society and its norms of representation. As the poet Guillaume Apollinaire, an energetic promoter of the young Spanish artist Pablo Picasso, noted, "You cannot carry around the corpse of your father on your back. You must leave it with the other dead."[15]

The causes fueling this iconoclastic sentiment were numerous. Besides being repelled by the signs of decrepitude in European civilization, artists, like members of the general public, were shocked by the violence perpetrated by that civilization abroad. Especially disturbing was the news about the atrocities committed by Belgium's King Leopold II in his Congo Free State. To meet the rapidly growing demand for rubber in Europe's industries, Leopold had established a local police force, the notorious *Force Publique*, whose members perpetrated acts of gruesome brutality, such as cutting off the hands and feet of those who did not reach the required production quota in the rubber plantations of the Anglo-Belgian India Rubber Company, King Leopold's private enterprise. Photographs documenting the atrocities reached the US and Europe around 1905–1906, the same time French and German artists were developing an interest in "primitive Negro art." We know that initially, at least some of the "wild men" Burgess met in Paris were actively involved in anticolonial campaigns.[16] By 1910, however, the year Burgess conducted his interviews, public protest had seemingly calmed down. Discussions among the city's "wild men" focused on concepts like "simplicity," "harmony of volume," and "architectural values."[17] The aim was to go beyond the visible, or rather, to leave the centuries-old imitation of the visible world behind in favor of a new approach. Artists and their promoters (critics, gallerists, and dealers) began to conceive of art less as a representation of reality and more as a sovereign, autonomous system, hence the ambition to identify and master the distinct "signs" of which the system consists. In other words, art was thought to function like a language or writing system with basic geometric shapes taking the role of letters and words acting as signs or building blocks of meaning. From that perspective, art appeared as an analytical, and quasi-semiotic/architectural enterprise. Daniel-Henry Kahnweiler, the art dealer who had Picasso under contract, called the new style "conceptual painting" (*peinture conceptuelle*).[18] The turn to *art nègre* was thus driven by the search for a new visual language that African sculptors were thought to have mastered. As Kahnweiler put it, "The negro artist always shows us what he *knows*, not what he *sees*."[19]

A key author exploring this notion was the writer and critic Carl Einstein. Born in Germany in 1885, Einstein had left his provincial home early in order to study in Berlin. He never finished his studies, though, and instead decided to become a writer. In 1907, he traveled to Paris. As a writer, he was fascinated by the cubist rejection of a linear perspective, an approach he tried to translate into his novel *Bebuquin oder die Dilettanten des Wunders*,[20] which met with limited critical success. What put Einstein on the map of the art world was instead his second book, *Negerplastik* (Negro Sculpture).[21]

Published in 1915, *Negerplastik* is a short text of just twenty-two pages followed by a long appendix of 119 untitled photographs of African figures. The title cites an exhibition from 1913 in Berlin that presented Picasso's works in dialogue with African sculptures (fig. 2.6). Einstein's *Negerplastik* followed up. All the pictures came from the Paris-based art dealer Joseph Brummer, who also sponsored the publication of *Negerplastik*, a fact that might explain why the photographs represent only works for which there was a steady supply (wooden carvings from West and Central Africa) and nothing—with the exception of one Benin Queen Mother bronze—from Ife, Benin, and other rare sources.[22] The text and the images are completely separated; there are no references in the text to the individual objects in the appendix. While this strict division seems to have been the result of an accident—Einstein was injured in World War I, and the publisher did not receive the captions Einstein had sent to him in time—the layout inadvertently underscored the intention of the work: to theorize African sculpture from a purely artistic perspective that prioritized form over any idea of context and meaning. For Einstein,

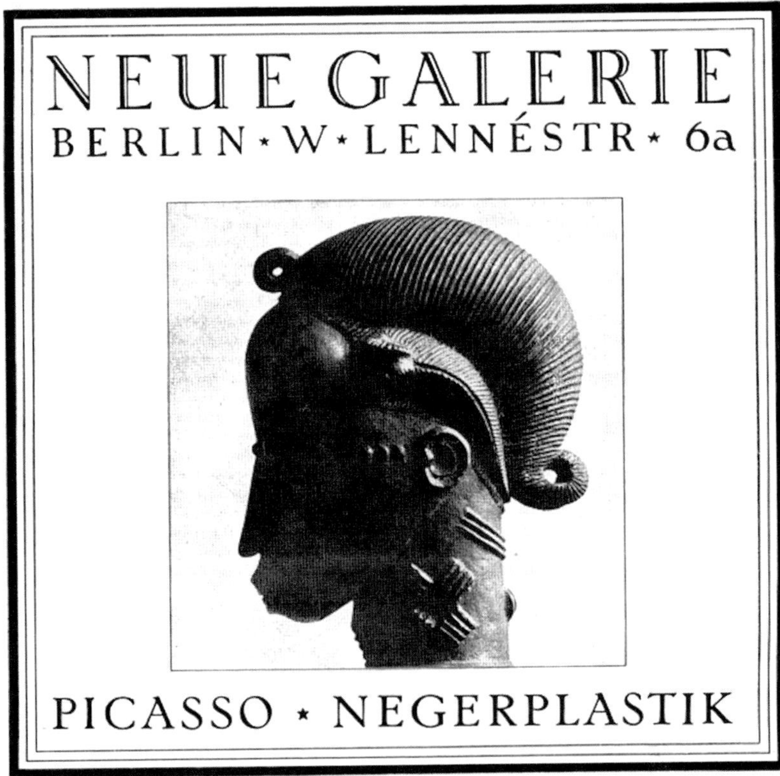

2.6 Catalog cover for the exhibition *Picasso—Negerplastik* at the Neue Galerie, Berlin, 1913. Ross Archive, Yale University.

the purpose of (African) art was not the depiction of an object but the structuring of a way of seeing. Accordingly, Einstein starts the essay with introductory remarks on method wherein he vehemently criticized both the racist and the romantic distortion of the subject. In their stead, he pushed for a strictly formal analysis. As he argued, African sculpture had to be understood and discussed as a unique response to the problem of form and the way in which the spectator sees and experiences the world. Einstein's elaboration of this point is dense, often hermetic, and full of allusions to early twentieth-century German debates about visibility, art theory, and the challenge of sculpture.[23]

Einstein's argument may be outlined as follows: art is not mimetic; its objects do not exist in the world but are constituted for the first time in the act of seeing. Likewise, the act of seeing is not natural but culturally trained. Since the Renaissance, Western art involved the development of perspective to the detriment of the three-dimensionality of space. For the act of looking at sculpture, this meant that the spectator succumbed to the artist's personal stamp and learned to see sculpture from a frontal perspective instead of experiencing its cubic space. The recent encounter with African sculpture, however, has led to a reappraisal of the way in which space is structured. What the study of African sculpture thus offers is a lesson in the "cubic intuition of space" (*kubische Raumanschauung*) (fig. 2.7). Instead of the frontal perspective characteristic of Western, perspectival art, African sculpture works with formal distortions that allow for a simultaneity of multiple perspectives, all apprehended in a single act of perception. What looks to the Western eye like an inability to master proportion is rather a necessity resulting from the distinct worldview of the "Negro."[24] This distinct worldview, Einstein maintained, is conditioned by the supernatural forces under which Africans operate. Recalling Hegel's assumption of the "Negro's" inability to distinguish between subject and object (cf. chap. 1), Einstein argued that totality, immediacy, and ecstasy characterize both the artist's and audience's relationship with the transcendent. The result is a distinct mode

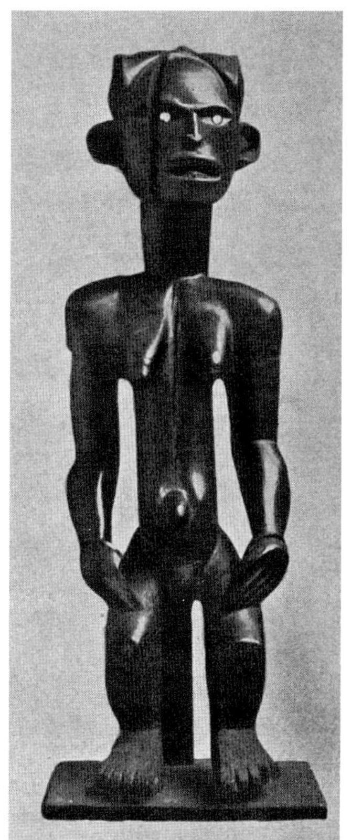

2.7 Unspecified illustration in Carl Einstein's *Negerplasik*, 1915, Plate 36, (identified as Fang *byeri* reliquary figure). Galerie Ernest & Joseph Brummer, Paris. Ross Archive, Yale University.

of seeing and experiencing sculpture—one that extinguishes distance. It consumes the viewer, transforming them from spectator into worshipper (*adorant*):

> To this transcendence corresponds a spatial vision that precludes every function of the beholder; a completely exhaustive, total, and unfragmented space must be given and guaranteed. Here the isolation of the space does mean abstraction but is rather unmediated sensation. The self-completeness of the work is guaranteed only if a cubic space is fully realized, such that nothing further can be added. The activity of the beholder is out of question. (In the case of religious painting, then the image will be entirely confined to the picture surface so as to produce a similar effect. This kind of painting cannot be achieved by a decorative or ornamental approach; those qualities are merely by-products.)[25]

As noted above, *Negerplastik* appeared in 1915, one year after the outbreak of World War I. Three years after the war ended, Einstein published *Afrikanische Plastik* (African sculpture, 1921). The change from "Negro" (*Neger*) to "African" (*Afrikanisch*) signaled not only a terminological shift but also a different approach to the study of African sculpture. In *Afrikanische Plastik*, Einstein pushed for recognition of the proper cultural and historical context of sculpture. Complementary to the formal perspective he had pursued earlier, he now wanted to "open the door to specialized research addressing the history of sculpture and painting."[26]

What caused this change? One reason was the war. After an injury in 1915, Einstein was no longer able to engage in active combat. In 1916, he was therefore transferred to Brussels in occupied Belgium, where he worked in the colonial department of the civil administration, a position that allowed him access to the library and exhibition of the Congo Museum at Tervuren. The resulting direct encounter with the richness of the material had a sobering effect on Einstein. In the introduction to *Afrikanische Plastik*, he remarks on the difficulty of grouping figurative works according to ethnicity, style, and history. He finds himself confronted with a messy territory in which things do not conform to simple tribe and style equations and where it is not the rule but the exception that seems to dictate the research. Despite all odds, he insists on the "stylistic unity of African art."[27] Accordingly, what *Afrikanische Plastik* aspires to be is an introduction to Frobenius's category "West African Culture Circle," which Einstein presents on the basis of selected annotated examples from Nigeria, Gabon, Angola, Congo, and Zimbabwe.

Einstein evinced ambivalence about his project, shifting between self-doubt and self-confidence, in the opening line of the book. It reads, "Exoticism is often unproductive romanticism. Geographical Alexandrinism. Awkwardly, the unoriginal negrifies."[28] The line can be understood as an implicit self-criticism of Einstein's own previous study, especially with regard to his positing the totality of African religion. Yet the neologism *negrify* may also refer to Leo Frobenius's shameless exclamation, "I am African,"[29] in his travelogue *The Voice of Africa*, a book that Einstein knew well and used extensively. But finally, the line may be read as a critique of the blatant exoticism and commodification of all things black, a result of the enthusiastic artistic reception African sculpture had generated. Among the European bourgeoisie, black African culture had changed within only one decade from the object of racist disregard and colonial ignorance to one of fashion, curiosity, profit, and amusement. Besides the avant-garde appreciation of African sculpture, a key factor driving this change of reception was the market. In fact, the artistic elevation of the objects had created a booming art market in African objects with gallerists and collectors sharing the stage with critics and artists.[30] *L'art nègre* was the *dernier cri*. Fetish had become fashion, embraced by both the establishment and the antiestablishment.[31]

Einstein realized that his own work was deeply entangled in these developments. In his *Art of the Twentieth Century* (1926), he notes,

> For the European, longing for the past and the faraway, primitive cultures served as an often misused means of rethinking his own history. This tendency grew, too, out of the struggle against Enlightenment rationality. Reason was only the tip of the iceberg; beneath it lay other forces: dream, instinct, feeling. Among primitive peoples you could still find mystical forces, a hierarchy of instincts suppressed in Europe, the tyranny of dream and ecstatic rite. Not arrogant individualism, not standardizing community, but miracles were regarded as the highest, the most extreme occurrences. Here the European found a mysticism that was actually experienced and given visible form in ceremonial, color, totem, dance, and mask. He misappropriated these cultic and mystical forces for his aesthetic purposes by tearing them apart from their cultural context. In this way, a surrogate religion was established.[32]

The tone of disappointment and disillusionment that pervades Einstein's critical diagnosis of the postwar situation still echoes the hopes he invested in "primitive culture." In the course of its transition from avant-garde to mainstream, blackness had evolved into an emblem of exotic otherness.

"What is Africa to Me?" Ambivalence and Agency

The move did not go unnoticed. Numerous projects commented on the new Western fascination of *art nègre* (fig. 2.8).[33] However, none of the avant-garde journals—like *Documents* (1931–1933) and its more art-oriented sequel *Minotaure* (1933–1939)—that cherished the revolutionary potential of black art published articles by black authors even though their voices were beginning to be heard in other quarters.

In March 1935, for instance, Aimé Césaire, Léopold Senghor, and Léon Damas started the literary review *L'étudiant noir* (The black student). All three were students from the French colonies—Césaire from Martinique, Damas from French Guiana, and Senghor from Senegal. Senghor, the oldest of the three, had arrived in Paris in 1927. While he described Paris as "the greatest museum of Negro-African art,"[34] he also realized that the celebration did nothing to alter colonial policy. In fact, both belonged together. They were part of "colonial humanism's double bind" in France, as Gary Wilder has put it.[35] That is, moral universalism and ethnic particularism formed an alliance to protect and justify France's claim of civilizational leadership and superiority. To tackle this "double bind," Damas and Césaire—less so Senghor—turned to the ideas of Marxism, Pan-Africanism, and the Harlem Renaissance. In early summer 1935, in an angry article titled "Racial Consciousness and Social Revolution," Césaire noted,

> Before making the revolution and in order to make the revolution the true one—a devastating groundswell, not the mere shaking of surfaces, one condition is essential: to break up the mechanical identification of the races, tear up superficial values, apprehend in ourselves the immanent Negro, plant our *négritude* [emphasis mine] like a beautiful tree until it bears its most authentic fruits.[36]

The notion of *négritude*, here used by Césaire for the first time, would later signify a powerful cultural movement that would transform the transnational black public sphere in Africa and its (French) diaspora. In 1935, however, Césaire was only twenty-two years old, a student at the École Normale Supérieure in Paris collecting material for a thesis on the subject of the south in African American literature.[37] The interest in the US was well founded; parallel to the spread of primitivism, black activists and intellectuals on both sides of the Atlantic had forged ties. Both shared similar experiences. Just as (most of) the French avant-garde did not align with African students in Paris, neither did its American counterpart affiliate itself with African American artists in Harlem.[38] Absence

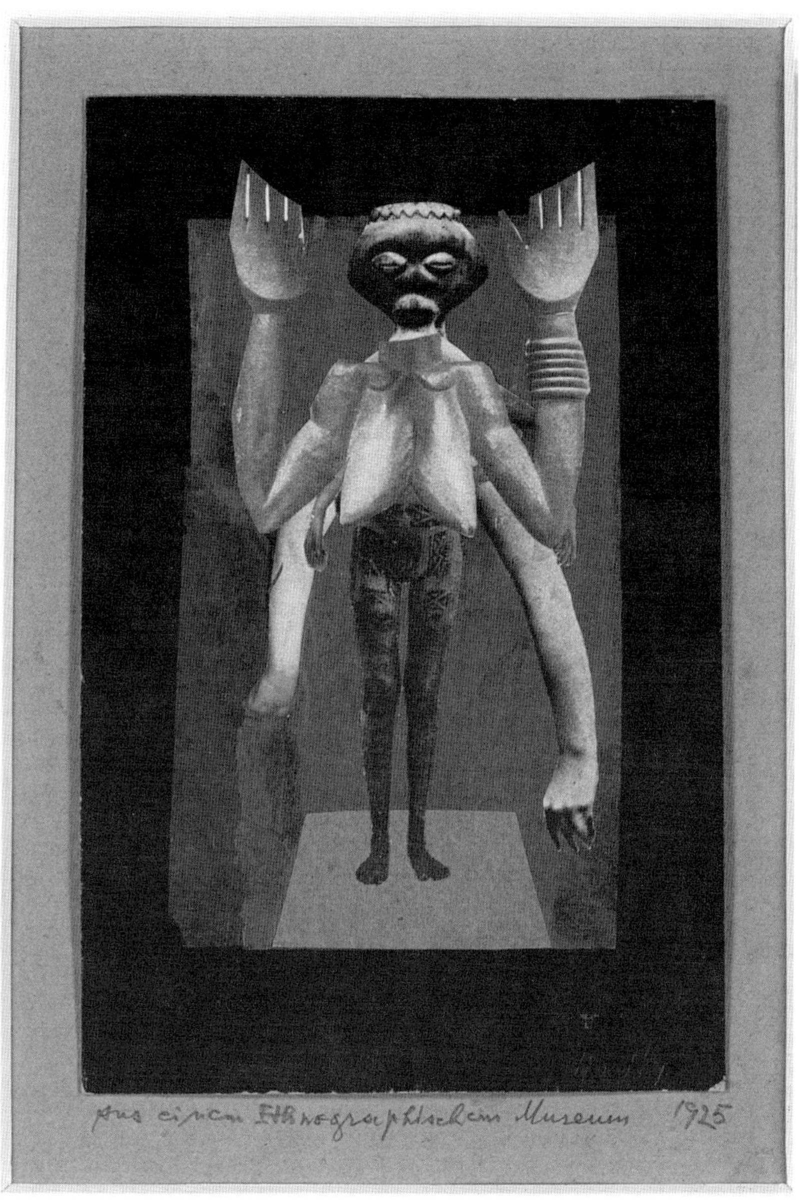

2.8 Hannah Höch, *Trauer* (Sorrow), from the series *Aus einem Ethnographischen Museum* (From an Ethnographic Museum), 1925. Photomontage, 17.6 × 11.5 cm. Using the new technique of photomontage, Höch's series commented critically on the male gaze driving and shaping the Negrophilia of her time. Photo: bpk-Bildagentur / Kupferstichkabinett, Staatliche Museen, Berlin, Germany / Jörg P. Anders / Art Resource, NY. © Artists Rights Society (ARS), New York / VG Bild-Kunst Bonn.

and invisibility characterized the role of African Americans during the early stages of (white) America's interest in "Negro Art."[39] As W. E. B. Du Bois put it in 1926, during the Harlem Renaissance, "We can go on stage, we can play all the sordid parts that America likes to assign to negroes, but for anything else there is still small space for us."[40] Accordingly, he regarded art as a means of politics:

> All art is propaganda and ever must be, despite the wailing of the purists. I stand in utter shamelessness and say that whatever art I have for writing has been used always for propaganda for gaining the right of black folk to love and enjoy. I do not care a damn for any art that is not used for propaganda. But I do care when propaganda is confined to one side while the other is stripped and silent.[41]

Du Bois's remarks point to the fact that the early African American encounter with art in general and African sculpture in particular was predominantly mediated through Euro-American individuals and institutions, which meant that the encounter was conditioned by the experience of racism, segregation, and institutionalized inequality. A key and complex figure with regard to the mediated nature of African art was the American businessman Albert C. Barnes. Barnes had begun to collect European, primarily French, avant-garde art in 1912 after a trip to Paris. His interest in artists such as Matisse, Braque, and Picasso soon led him to collect African art as well, which he started to buy from Paul Guillaume in Paris. From the start, Barnes's intent was to turn his private collection into an educational institution to promote social progress and moral reform through the encounter with beauty.[42] Accordingly, in 1922, he established the Barnes Foundation and immediately developed plans to use his African art collection as a means to fight racial inequality.

Barnes's ideas focused on the power of form. Realizing the quality of an artwork, he reasoned, would counter any racial verdict on cultural and mental inferiority. However, in the climate of the nascent Harlem Renaissance, many African Americans viewed Barnes's initiative with suspicion and ambivalence. After all, Harlem had become the American version of the French's obsession with *art nègre*. As Sonia Delgado-Tall noted, "Any term evocative of Africa was highly fashionable in Harlem's nightlife: Beale Street was known as Jungle Alley, artificial palm trees decorated the Cotton Club and enhanced the prefabricated exoticism of the stage and performances."[43] Thus, with primitivism prevailing on both sides of the Atlantic, African Americans found themselves in a problematic position. How could they advance and participate in the progressive modernist agenda—with its interest in "savage" and "primitive" African art—while being themselves considered descendants of the "primitive"? Not surprisingly, the attitudes of African American artists and writers toward the new white primitivist interest in African art was divided.

Among the African Americans who realized the positive potential of the primitivist movement was the philosopher and critic Alain Locke. By reaching out to Barnes, he engaged in a kind of "diasporic ancestralism," as Kobena Mercer has put it.[44] Locke had first met Barnes in December 1923 at Paul Guillaume's gallery of African art in Paris, one year after Barnes had established his foundation at his home base in Merion, near Philadelphia.[45] By that time, Locke was teaching at Howard University in Washington, DC, as chair of Howard's philosophy department. Barnes's aesthetic creed appealed to Locke. Upon his return to the US, he invited Barnes to a dinner meeting in New York with leading representatives of the emerging black cultural movement at which Barnes gave a short talk on the quality and purpose of his collection of African sculpture. He explained, "When art is recognized, the step to social justice should not be so big if backed by the trained minds of the negroes who have devoted their lives to that cause."[46] In a letter to Charles S. Johnson, editor of *Opportunity: A Journal of Negro Life,* a journal focusing on civil rights and economic self-reliance for African Americans, he followed up:

> The Barnes Foundation has ready a crack between the eyes for the so-called authorities in antique art. It consists in showing the masterpieces of Negro sculpture side by side with finer pieces of ancient Greek and Egyptian sculpture than can be found in the Metropolitan Museum of Art. It may be left to us to apply scientific method to make known that Negro art is in just that highest class of creations.[47]

Encouraged by Alain Locke, Johnson decided to publish a special issue of *Opportunity* solely devoted to the importance of Barnes's collection and foundation for the "negro cause."

Locke was the mastermind of the venture and acted as the issue's de facto editor. Titled "A Note on African Art," Locke's own contribution approached the subject from the perspective of "comparative aesthetics" in accordance with his cosmopolitan background. Having studied at Harvard, Oxford, and Berlin, he knew the European debates on the formal values of aesthetics broadly, with a concentrated focus on these topics in African art. Much of the article is therefore a review of these various positions. At the end, though, he shifts the perspective from formal discussions to the "cultural significance" of African art:

Since African art has had such a vitalizing influence in modern European painting, sculpture, poetry, and music it becomes finally an important and natural question as to what artistic and cultural effect it can or will have upon the life of the American Negro. It does not necessarily follow that it should have any such influence. Today even in its own homeland it is a stagnant and decadent tradition, almost a lost art, certainly as far as technical mastery goes. The sensitive artistic minds among us have just begun to be attracted toward it, but with an intimate and ardent concern. Because of our Europeanized conventions, the key to the proper understanding and appreciation of it will in all probability first come from appreciation of its influence on contemporary French art, but we must believe that there still slumbers in the blood something which once stirred and will react with peculiar emotional intensity toward it. If by nothing more mystical than the sense of being ethnically related, some of us will feel its influence at least as keenly as those who have already made it recognized and famous. Nothing is more galvanizing than the sense of a cultural past.[48]

The special issue of *Opportunity* followed an issue of the journal *Survey Graphic* on "Harlem: Mecca of the New Negro," which formed the core of the anthology *The New Negro*. Edited by Alain Locke, *The New Negro* exemplified the new black cultural and political "awakening" after the great migration from the land of Jim Crow in the South to the opportunities available in the rapidly industrializing North (fig. 2.9).

For Locke, the Harlem "awakening" was the result of the local mixing of different types of black experience that allowed for the recognition of the "legacy of ancestral (African) arts."[49] For Locke, the "legacy" meant to acknowledge the impossibility to retrieve or reclaim the ancestral past. Instead, the recognition of value in ancestral forms was meant to allow for the ability to form a new Black American modernist-diasporic subjectivity that was able to blend and combine Africa, Europe, and America into something new and different.[50] It was a political position he was eager to convey through visual means. Besides using photographs from Barnes's collection, Locke commissioned the German immigrant artist Winold Reiss to do the book's graphic design and the young African American artist Aaron Douglas to provide the illustrations.[51] Certainly, Locke was aware that Douglas was Reiss's student, but that seemed to have been exactly the point. It was the translation, transformation, and adaption of the "ancestral art" that was of interest to Locke, not the "ancestral" itself.

Not everybody shared Locke's position though. In fact the anthology presented different takes on the idea of the "New Negro." Countee Cullen's seminal poem "Heritage" articulated the deep ambivalence that the

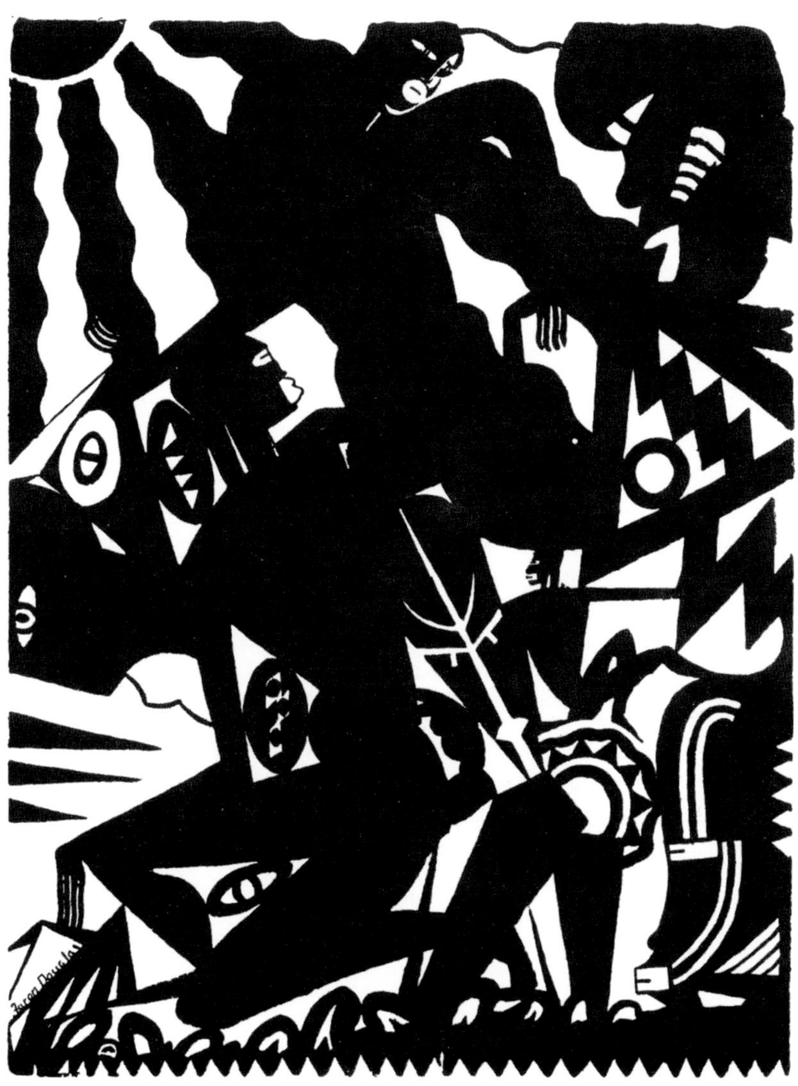

2.9 Aaron Douglas, *Awakening*, 1925. Print. © 2021 Heirs of Aaron Douglas, Licensed by VAGA at Artists Rights Society (ARS), New York. Digital image from *The New Negro* by Alain Locke. Copyright © 1925 by Albert & Charles Boni, Inc., introduction copyright © 1992 by Macmillan Publishing Company. Reprinted with the permission of Touchstone, a division of Simon & Schuster, Inc. All rights reserved.

invocation of an African past occasioned in many African American artists, and this ambivalence made them shun the subject.[52] Accompanied
by two photographs of Barnes's African art collection, a Dogon couple
and a Baule mask, erroneously labeled "Bushongo," Cullen's poem poses
the insistent, only partially answered question, "What is Africa to me?"
as it follows the writer on his journey-like reflections from his disturbing
bewilderment over the belief in "Quaint, outlandish heathen gods" to the
final recognition that "They and I are civilized."

For Barnes, the matter was less complicated. Using gospel music as his
illustrative case in point, he emphasized the ways the "American Negro"
maintained essential Africanness in the "New World":

> The Negro has kept nearer to the ideal of man's harmony with nature
> and that, his blessing, has made him a vagrant in our arid, practical
> American life. But his art is so deeply rooted in his nature that it has
> thrived in a foreign soil where the traditions and practices tend to
> stamp out and starve out both the plant and its flowers. It has lived
> because it was an achievement, not an indulgence. It has been his hap-
> piness through that mere self-expression which is its own immediate
> and rich reward. Its power converted adverse material conditions into
> nutriment for his soul and it made a new world in which his soul has
> been free. Adversity has always been his lot but he converted it into a
> thing of beauty in his songs. When he was the abject, down-trodden
> slave, he burst forth into songs which constitute America's only great
> music—the spirituals. These wild chants are the natural, naïve, un-
> tutored, spontaneous utterance of the suffering, yearning, prayerful
> human soul. In their mighty roll, there is a nobility truly superb. Idea
> and emotion are so fused in an art which ranks with the Psalms and
> the songs of Zion in their compelling, universal appeal.[53]

Given this position, Barnes understood his collection of African sculpture as a precious archive that would allow both black and white Americans to see and acknowledge the "original gifts" that were "Negro" culture's legacy. A hidden reference in Barnes's portrayal of this legacy was
Du Bois's treatise *The Gift of Black Folk*, published just a year before.[54]
Not surprisingly, Barnes does not mention the book, but it is worth
identifying the reference for it shows Barnes's geographical and political reframing of blackness. Thus, while Du Bois conceived "Negro Art"
from a politically charged Pan-Africanist perspective that meant the inclusion of Egypt as a quintessentially black culture, Barnes considered it
from the perspective of his collection and hence reduced "Negro Art" to
sub-Saharan Africa.[55] The difference illustrates Barnes's self-fashioning

as the patron(izing) guardian of the *Gift of Black Folk,* a position that entailed—in Barnes's view—both the right and the obligation to grant access to the gifts to whoever was in need of them.

In view of Barnes's educational agenda, this meant especially American Negro artists, among the first of whom was Aaron Douglas, whom Barnes had already met in 1924 at the dinner with leading figures of the Harlem Renaissance in New York. Two years later, after the publication of the *New Negro,* which Douglas had helped to illustrate, Barnes invited him to see his collection. In April 1926, Douglas wrote a letter thanking Barnes for the educational experience:

> My enthusiasm for the paintings was displaced by awe, almost terror at sight, of the collection of African negro sculpture—amazingly powerful, moving, mystic. Thus far, the "new consciousness" among negroes has produced nothing of value in the plastic arts. This is mainly due to the three hundred years of bondage separating the Negro from the roots of his native traditions and culture, and, to the substitution of alien culture and ideals, which, even among those to the manor born have never proven, especially fertile for the cultivation of the arts. Nevertheless, it seems now only a matter of time before the American Negro will again learn to express himself in plastic forms original and enduring.[56]

It can be taken for granted that Douglas returned to New York with a small present from Barnes in the form of the catalog *Primitive Negro Sculpture,* which presented and explained Barnes's collection to a wider public.[57] In line with the educational mission of the foundation, the aim was to produce a text for art appreciation. Besides the organization of the pieces into distinct style and culture areas, this meant, first and foremost, an appreciation of the formal qualities of each work.

* * *

Barnes financed and published *Primitive Negro Sculpture* in 1926, twenty years after French and German artists first encountered these works. This chapter has discussed the interim time as a process of purification that stripped artifacts from Europe's colonies of their local contexts and histories and allowed them to enter new contexts and assume new meanings. Surely, the process was not new. Disentanglements had happened before and, undoubtedly, also in the African context. After all, objects travel. Reinterpretations and appropriations by new users are part of their life. Still, the colonial purification was different. The shift from museum to gallery meant a shift from "primitive" to primitivism. The new celebration of form elevated the artifacts and lent them value. Depending on the party involved in this process, the value differed and frequently overlapped. With dealers, critics, artists, scholars, poets, and other personnel, the spectrum ranged from aesthetic and commercial to political appreciations. Accordingly, our discussion started with Alfred Barr's genealogy of modern art in Europe and ended with Albert Barnes's African art collection and Alain Locke's proclamation of a new black modernist subjectivity in terms of a diasporic ancestralism. As varied as the development was, the presence of photography turned out to be a crucial constant. In fact, it was the ubiquity of photographs that allowed for the celebration of form. It is therefore the relationship of visibility and value to which we need to pay attention.

CHAPTER 3

Creating Visibility and Value

PHOTOGRAPHY AND ITS EFFECTS

Photographs! Photographs! In our work one can never have enough.
BERNARD BERENSON, *Italian Pictures of the Renaissance*, 1932

Introduction

By the first decades of the twentieth century, the conventions of display prevailing in ethnographic museums in the early twentieth century had begun to clash with the aesthetic sensibility that had been generated by the encounter between European artists and African sculpture. In 1921, the German art critic Karl Scheffler scoffed at the crammed conditions in the Royal Ethnological Museum in Berlin (fig. 3.1):

> Not even the largest of toy warehouses, the most jumbled of antique vaults, the most tightly packed of natural history collections, could be more confusing, mustier, or more like a storeroom. Incredible riches, their value running into the billions, priceless rarities—all placed next to, behind, in front of, or on top of one another with such a lack of concern that one almost begins to despise them. One cannot view anything individually. Everything is crammed together so tightly that only a seasoned ethnologist could keep his composure. Many exhibits include hundreds of objects. Row upon row of grotesque gods; national costumes hanging in showcases like off-the-rack dresses. . . . Slowly making one's way through the collections is like perusing an encyclopedia for hours on end.[1]

Scheffler's critique was informed by his knowledge of the recent interest in the formal qualities of African sculpture. In 1913, he had celebrated the

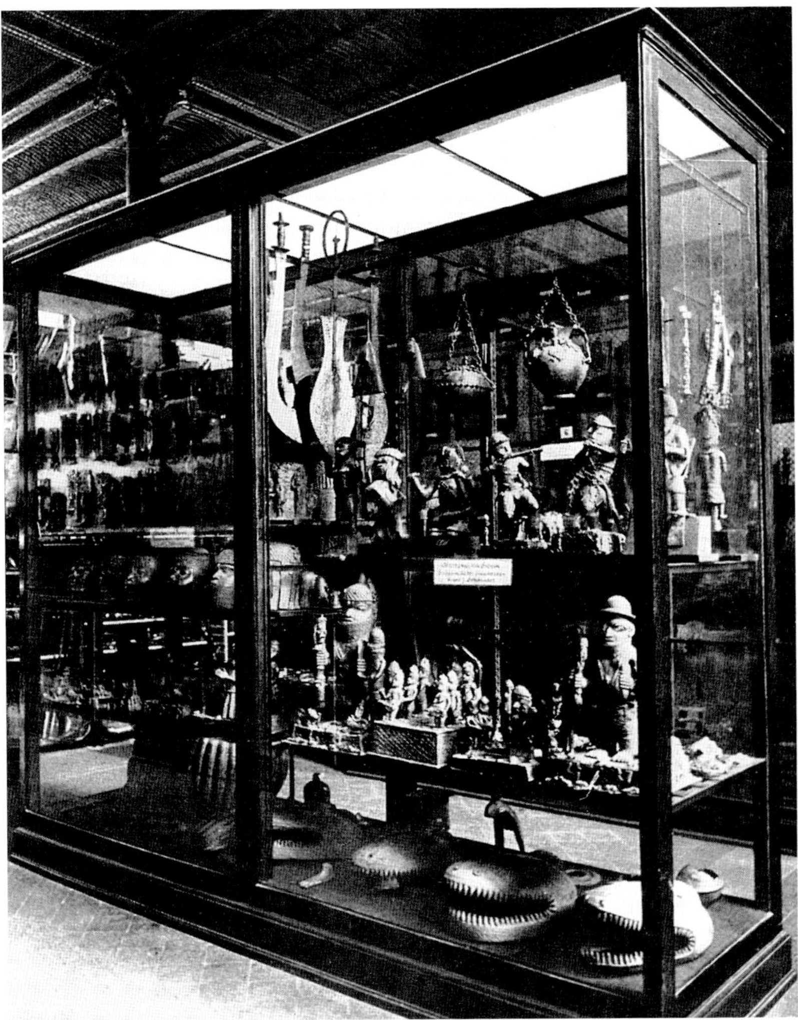

3.1 Museum cabinet displaying Benin bronzes in the Royal Ethnological Museum in Berlin before 1914. © Ethnological Museum Berlin, Art Resource, NY.

first Picasso exhibition in Berlin (see fig. 2.6). He was aware of the growing importance of "Negro Art" and had read Einstein's study on the subject. In line with this position, he pushed for a reorganization of the Berlin museum landscape and argued that the assembled objects should be displayed from an aesthetic rather than an anthropological or ethnological perspective. The curators of the Ethnological Museum pushed back and insisted on the value of a context-bound approach, jeeringly speculating that "perhaps the time is not far that Scheffler and his followers will be bowled over by the hordes of sentimentalists for primitive art."[2] However, the response was to no avail. From the early 1920s onward museum displays changed. Open spaces with selected objects began to replace the crammed showcases. The new arrangement still focused on the cultural context of the displayed objects, but the openness allowed and encouraged the visitor to see and experience the aesthetic quality of the objects, thereby acknowledging their autonomy as discreet art objects (fig. 3.2).

As we will see in the following, much of this change can be attributed to the ubiquity of photography. With the rise of photography and the new possibilities of reproduction, images began to circulate much faster than before, allowing for new ways of seeing and studying. In a real sense, photography not only gave things a new visibility, it enabled their existence. In fact, it can be argued that the new field of African art would not have emerged without photography. Thus, it is no coincidence that the mass reproduction and circulation of photographic pictures in the late nineteenth and early twentieth centuries correlated with the art-historical debate on the notion of "style."[3] The new technique not only compensated for the problem pertaining to museum displays, making it

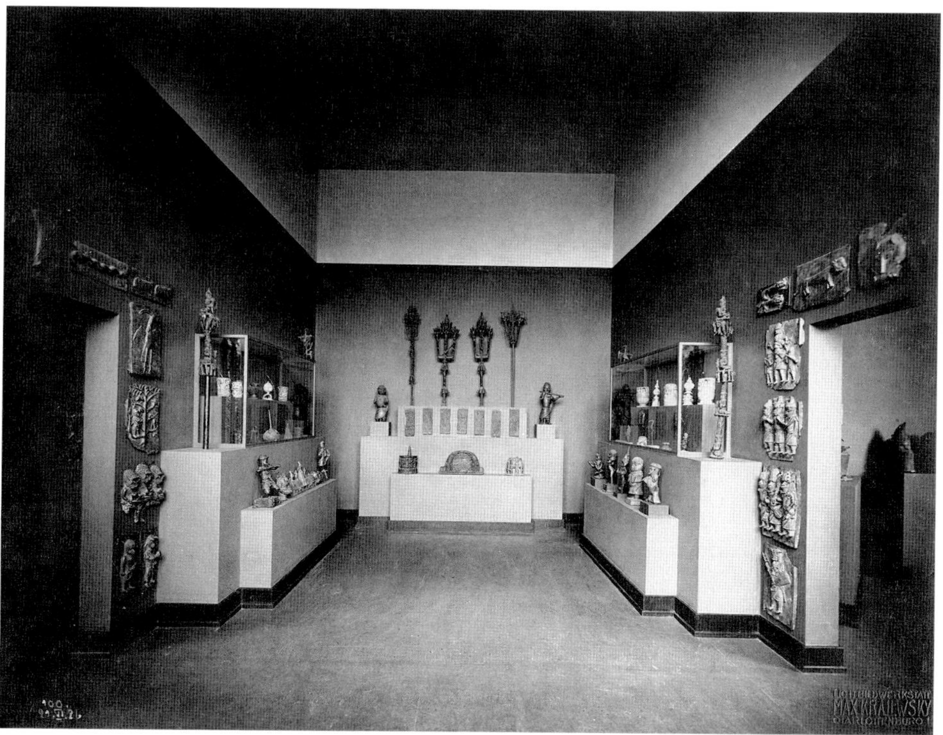

3.2 New Benin Gallery in the Ethnological Museum Berlin, 1926. © Ethnological Museum Berlin, Art Resource, NY.

possible "to view things individually," as Scheffler had demanded; it also allowed for the formation of canons. That is, it allowed for the identification, (e)valuation, comparison, marketing, and sale of objects, all crucial for the scholarly—and commercial—viability of the field.[4] As such, photography was part and parcel of the process of aesthetic purification discussed in the previous chapter on the primitivist celebration of form. Framing, background, close-ups, light, tone, texture —all the various techniques and compositional elements of photography allowed for the disentanglement of objects from their cultural context.[5]

But what about the colonial context? How to account for colonialism's "scopic regime"? A lot has been written about the use of photography as an integral element of colonial power.[6] Clearly, the aesthetic purification of objects and the identification of tribal styles went hand in hand with the identification of racial types. How to assess the quality of this relationship? Was the aesthetic purification of the object a liberation from the colonial gaze, or was it part of it? The colonial camera worked in different directions. Just as photography allowed for denials of recognition and contemporaneity, it also generated curiosity and the desire to reconnect the represented with its representation, the signifier with the signified: who are the artists who created the works now shown in museums and galleries? What is the artistic process that produced them? In other words, just as photography allowed for processes of disentanglement, it also generated research that aimed to resituate or reentangle the objects with the culture in which they originated.

In the following, I will discuss this dialectic in terms of three equations according to which photography changed and informed the newly emerging field of African art: equating style with tribe, equating aesthetic with commercial value, and equating form with fieldwork.

Conditions of Style

Much of the early twentieth-century critique of the congested and overstocked cabinets of the Berlin Ethnological Museum targeted the display of Benin art (see chap. 1). Because of von Luschan's successful "hunt" of Benin bronzes and ivories, the number of Benin works had increased radically while the space to show them had not. Von Luschan realized the limitations.[7] Unable to properly show the Benin collection, he concentrated on compiling a massive photographic archive and card index, the famous *Corpus antiquatum beninensum*. It contained all the visual and textual information available at that time on Benin and provided the basis for his three-volume *Antiquities of Benin*.[8] The work has become a classic, not the least because of its systematic use of the photographic archive. In fact, what allowed von Luschan to identify stylistic shifts in the history of Benin court art were not the artworks themselves but rather the availability of their photographic reproduction.

Written between 1911 and 1916, but published only after the war, *Antiquities of Benin* was a massive undertaking. Borrowing the methodology of art history and deploying altogether 889 illustrations, the focus was on questions of stylistic development. At that time, the discipline basically offered two well-established style models. One derived from Giorgio Vasari, a sixteenth-century Italian artist, architect, and historian who, in line with the Renaissance's humanistic and anthropocentric ideals, conceived the history of art as a history of masterly individuals.[9] Vasari's compilation of artist biographies contrasts with the second model: Johann Joachim Winckelmann's *The History of Art in Antiquity*, which appeared some two hundred years later, in 1764, during the European Enlightenment.[10] Winkelmann was an archaeologist and antiquarian who was interested in Greek and Roman art, particularly sculpture, which he studied in Italy. Given the paucity of information about individual artists of antiquity, Winkelmann focused on the history of collective styles, which he understood to develop organically in cycles of growth, maturity, and decline. Both models were influential in the nineteenth-century formation of art history as an academic subject. More recent approaches had come to offer technical (Semper) and formal (Riegl, Wölfflin) alternatives (see the debate on ornaments in chap. 1). Structurally, though, Winkelmann's model prevailed, as it allowed art historians to turn art history into a national project by identifying historical periods with national identities and distinct national styles. Hence, it was this model that also informed von Luschan's stylistic history of Benin art.

As noted in chapter 1, von Luschan insisted on the "purely African" style of the works in question. He emphasized the superb technical skill of lost-wax casting and compared the Benin bronzes to European master artists like Benvenuto Cellini.[11] But instead of correlating the variable quality of particular artworks with specific artists, he correlated it with the political history of the Benin court, tracing the rise and fall of the art, from elegance and naturalistic beauty to a gradual degeneration. Von Luschan's aesthetic verdicts focused largely on the shaping of the human figure and especially the depiction of the human face: the closer the correspondence to the European norms of Greco-Roman naturalism, the more laudable the achievement—the greater the deviation, the more lamentable the decline. But let us look more closely.

Von Luschan's Benin art history begins with ancient bronze bells from what he called an "archaic period" (twelfth through fourteenth century), which he regarded as shrouded in mystery. Frobenius's unearthing of bronzes in neighboring Ife and the obvious question of possible linkages between the two empires did not matter for him.[12] Much richer in information and material was the "great period" from the sixteenth to the seventeenth century (fig. 3.3). During this time, Benin art flourished, and casting reached its peak. Bronze and brass plaques, memorial heads, royal animals, and many other forms of court art emerged. The "late period" (eighteenth and nineteenth centuries) marked the "decline" of Benin art, characterized by the increasing size of the memorial heads and changing facial expressions. The rings of coral beads around the neck became lon-

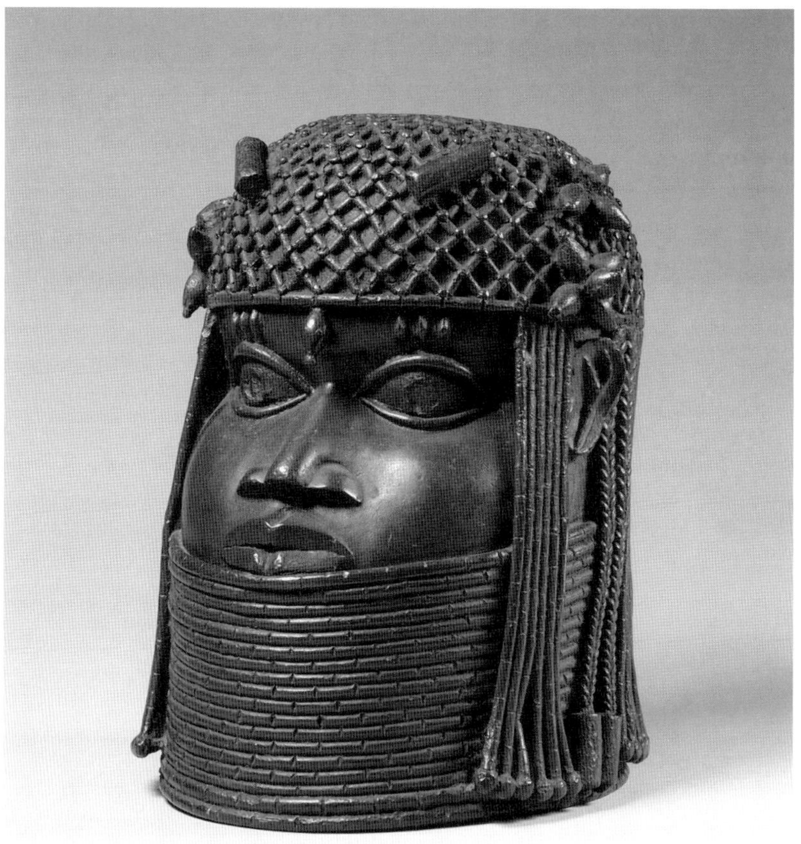

3.3 Unidentified artist, Commemorative Head of an Oba (King), Benin, 1550–1680. Copper alloy, 27.3 × 21.3 × 21.9 cm. Metropolitan Museum of Art. The Michael C. Rockefeller Memorial Collection, Bequest of Nelson A. Rockefeller, 1979. Public Domain.

ger and the crowns more elaborate. The earlier serene facial expressions were replaced with more compact faces, fuller lips, and blank eyes without the iron inlays, a distinctive feature of the earlier period. For von Luschan, the change must have been realized in Benin itself. For him, the stylistic change reflected social and political changes. Thus, the fact that the British troops found the plaques taken down and kept in storage when entering the city in 1897 seemed to indicate that Benin's glory had already come to an end before the raid. In any event, the raid marked a watershed. Even though brass casting continued into the twentieth century, von Luschan and his British colleagues declared post-1897 Benin art dead.

Because of the ephemerality of material—most of the artifacts in ethnological museum collections were made of wood—periodizations such as von Luschan's Benin chronology remained a rare exception. What dominated the field of African art studies were stylistic/morphological and geographical clusters or centers, with photography functioning as a tool of interpretation rather than documentation and identification. French and German studies dominated. In their short treatise *L'art nègre et l'art océanien*, the Parisian curator Henri Clouzot and the art dealer André Level used Gothic art as a model of interpretation and aesthetic value.[13] Seen from that perspective, the naturalism they identified in the ethnic diversity and economic intensity of the Guinea coast was analogous to "our Mediterranean's Gulf of Lion," while the abstract refinement of French Guinea was said to be the African version of Île-de-France. In his *L'art nègre*, colonial administrator Georges Hardy employed a psycho-geographical approach.[14] Emphasizing the influence of climate and vegetation on culture, he distinguished between the "optics and symbolism of the savannah" and the "realism of the forest zone."[15] While Hardy despised the abstract forms in French Sudan, Clouzot and Level praised them, a bias also found in Barnes's *Primitive Negro Sculpture* from 1926 (see chap. 2), which distinguished between "major" (Sudan, Côte d'Ivoire, Gabon, and Congo) and "minor" (Benin, Dahomey, and Guinea) artistic traditions (fig. 3.4).

In 1928, The German art historian Eckart von Sydow proposed a different model. As a contemporary of Carl Einstein—both were born in the same year, 1885—von Sydow had developed an expertise in African art via his interest in German Romanticism and Expressionism.[16] For him, a useful starting point was ancient Ife and Benin. Unlike von Luschan, he pointed to the connections between the two and commented on the oral traditions of both Ife and Benin, according to which Ife is recognized as the originator of bronze casting. In the "slim" but "sinewy" wood carvings of the Yoruba, von Sydow recognized the artistic afterlife

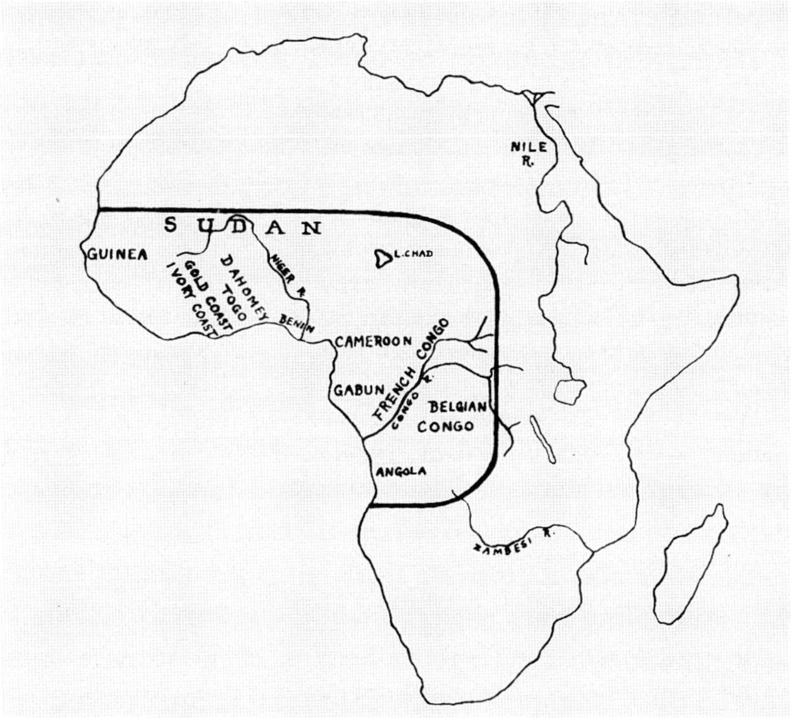

3.4 "The Country of Negro Art" from Paul Guillaume and Thomas Munro *African Negro Art*, 1926.

of ancient Ife: "All Yoruban work makes a clean cut, refined impression, and is full of dignity."[17] With notable exceptions such as the Baule/Guro, the Mende/Vai and the Bamana, Malinke, Dogon, and Senufo art zones, he declared that "artistic power" weakens the more one goes toward the West and North. Here, too, there are multiple subcenters, like the Cameroon Grasslands and the vast, multicentered zone of the Congo.

> Taking African sculpture as a whole, we find that the elaborated type of form prevails in a broad strip of land, which roughly extending westwards in a wide track from the northern end of Lake Tanganyika to Lake Bangweolo, with offshoots to the south, reaches the Atlantic Ocean, then leads up to the Cameroons in a narrow strip, and stretching along the Upper Guinea coast to Sierra Leone, finally occupies in a wide crescent the western part of West Sudan. In this crescent, which extends from the Rivieres du Sud to the Habe and Mossi, art is dominated by an over-strong tendency to cover with ornament, while elsewhere West African art is distinguished by a just proportion of natu-

ralistic and decorative styles. Sandwiched between the double lines of the southern, western, and north-western districts of elaborated form, we have in the northern part of Congo and East and Central Sudan a continuous region of extremely simple art which also appears in East Africa, in a few places in South Africa and in Madagascar.[18]

The various style distributions hark back to the work of Frobenius. On the basis of a morphological comparison of the growing museum collections, Frobenius had distinguished three basic areas or "circles": Upper Guinea, Lower Guinea and the Congo region, and Southwest Africa, all of them encompassing a wider "Atlantic culture." Museum curators, collectors, and critics quickly picked up the model and developed it further with a focus on distinct regional and tribal styles. Aided by photographic handbooks, it became the basis of an internationally accepted and widely used "tribe and style" model that equated each tribe with a particular style and area.[19]

From Visibility to Value

I will return to these handbooks shortly. For the moment, let me dwell on the relationship between modernist primitivism and the ubiquity of photography. We know by now that Picasso's groundbreaking innovations in the realm of painting were not only derived from his encounter with three-dimensional sculptures at the Trocadéro—they were also indebted to his collection of photographic postcards.[20] Between 1903 and 1908, Picasso compiled a collection of at least forty postcards from the Dakar-based French photographer Edmond Fortier. As these postcards show, Africa appeared in Picasso's work not just in the form of statues and masks but also in the form of people. By the early twentieth century, postcards had become a popular way for the French to learn about the landscape, architecture, and people of their colonies, particularly the various ethnic and "racial types" living there. Picasso collected primarily portraits of women, with legends such as "Malinké Girl," "Bambara Woman," or "Sudan: Types of Women." The interest was mainly formal, however. Indeed, the similarities to his own early work are striking. Some poses and compositions Picasso used during his "African period" seem to have been taken directly from Fortier's postcards.

Artists like Picasso were not the only ones using photographs. In the early 1910s the Latvian artist Vladimir Markov visited several ethnographic museums in Europe where he analyzed the principles of African sculpture through his camera lens.[21] With the help of close-ups he showed that hip and torso, knee and calf, leg and foot are often treated independently as autonomous elements, instead of conveying them anatomically and correctly as one integral unit. Markov's analysis recalls Einstein's study but was written independently. Focusing on the "formation" and "movement of mass" as specific features of African sculpture he wrote,

> The Negro loves free and independent masses. . . . He combines parts of the body into one mass and receives in this manner an inspiring heaviness, juxtaposing it by contrast with other weighty masses, he achieves mighty rhythms, planes, and lines. I must emphasize the basic feature of this play of massiveness and weight: the masses that represent the part of the body are linked arbitrarily, with no connection to the articulation of the actual human organism. These works give the sense of being architectural constructions with only a mechanical linkage. We notice a piling on of masses, an application to or surrounding of one mass by another in which each mass retains its autonomy.[22]

Just as photography became an important tool for artists and critics, it also became essential for dealers, gallerists, and collectors. In fact, photography made possible the commercial success of *art nègre*, which in turn shaped the new field of African art studies in profound ways. An early and prominent example is the linkage between the Paris-based art dealer Paul Guillaume and the American photographer Alfred Stieglitz. As we have seen in the previous chapter, in 1914, Stieglitz and his Mexican business partner Marius de Zayas showed Paul Guillaume's collection of African art in Stieglitz's gallery 291 in New York. The exhibition design by the photographer and painter Edward Steichen carefully choreographed the *Statuary in Wood* for both the human eye and the eye of the camera. Quite literally, the approach "worked." Through Stieglitz's photographic journal, *Camera Work*, the show's aesthetic ennobling of the objects reached a wide audience and thus opened the door for other such collaborations. In 1918, de Zayas commissioned the painter and photographer Charles Sheeler to photograph the objects de Zayas was showing in his Modern Gallery in New York under the title *African Negro Sculpture*.[23] In 1909, Sheeler had traveled to Paris, where he learned about the newly emerging interest in *art nègre* and the cubist turn to abstraction. For De Zayas, Sheeler carefully staged the objects of the exhibition in order to visualize the aesthetic connection between cubism and African sculpture. By placing the objects in front of artificial light, he created a composition whose sharp shadows emphasized the geometric volume of the piece and turned the photograph into a work of art in itself (fig. 3.5).

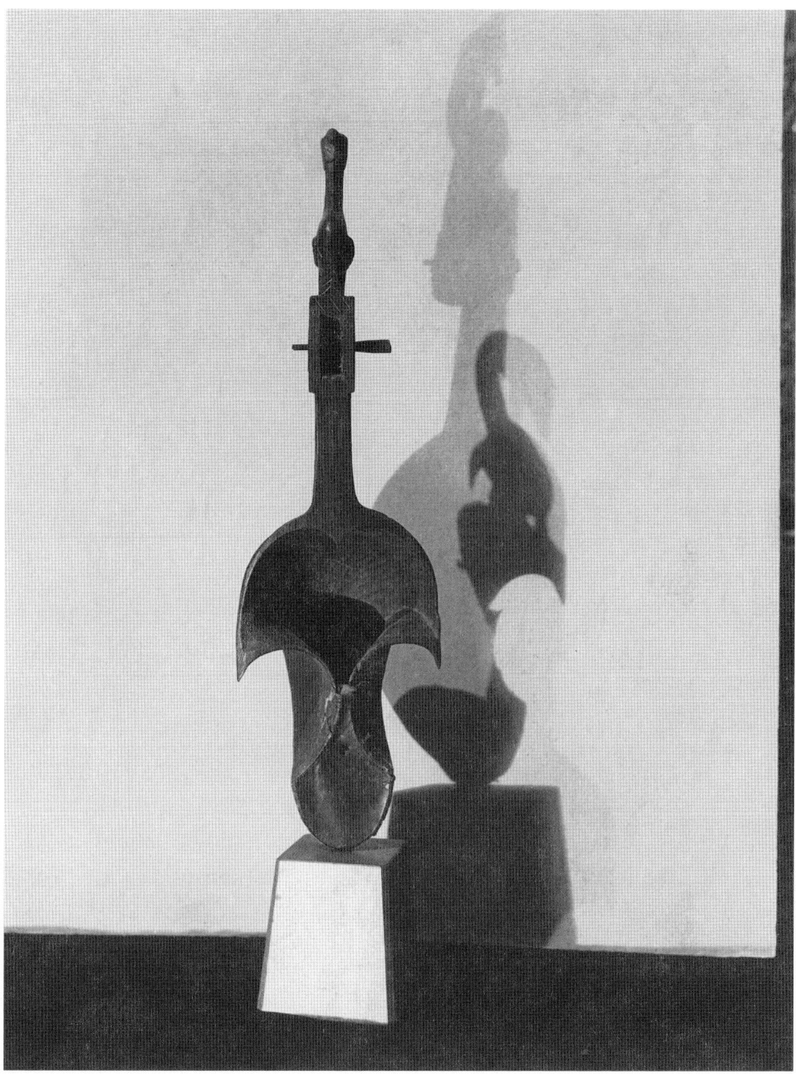

3.5 Charles Sheeler, *African Instrument*. Photograph, 1918. J. Paul Getty Museum Los Angeles.

Back in France, Paul Guillaume hired the American Man Ray to photograph masks from his collection shortly after Ray had arrived in Paris in 1921.[24] Like Sheeler, Ray had started off as a painter before venturing into photography. His interest in Dada and Surrealism, which had crossed the Atlantic in 1913 with the *Armory Show* in New York, brought him to France, where he befriended members of the Parisian avant-garde. Short of money, he made passport photos and product advertisements but also

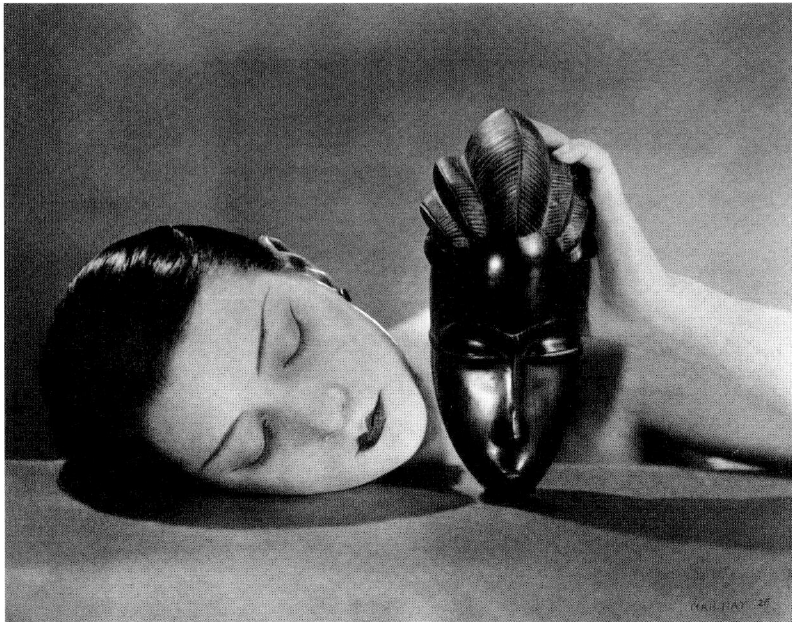

3.6 Man Ray, *Noire et blanche*, 1926. © 2015 Man Ray Trust / Artist Right Society (ARS), NY / ADAGP, Paris 2021.

worked for fashion magazines and art dealers like Guillaume. Ray's photographs of Guillaume's collection have been lost, yet we can assume that Albert Barnes must have seen them when he bought Guillaume's collection for his newly established Barnes Foundation in Merion, Pennsylvania. Still, in 1923 it was Sheeler and not Man Ray to whom Barnes offered the opportunity to photograph his entire collection, anticipating a "big demand" for "photos and exhibitions."[25]

As it happened, when the book came out in 1926, it coincided with the publication of one of Man Ray's—now—best-known photographs, which he made for the French fashion magazine *Vogue*: *Noire et blanche* (fig. 3.6).[26] *Noire et blanche* capitalized on the commodification of *art nègre*. What was once a sign of avant-garde distinction had become reduced to an attribute of fashion, an edgy signifier of exotic otherness (see chap. 2). As such, "African Negro art" had entered the mainstream and been absorbed by consumer culture. It is thus fitting that the black convex Baule mask that Man Ray's model Kiki was holding next to her white face was an inferior carving, obviously made for the European market. Still, it served the purpose, at least for *Vogue*. Whether Barnes ever saw the photograph is not known. The picture achieved its iconic status only after Barnes's death in 1951. If he did, we can assume that he would have strongly disapproved of it. For one, the bodily intimacy of the composition openly alluded to an erotic/sexual dimension of the black "fetish," an association the very location of the picture strengthened and underscored. Secondly, and closer to Barnes's self-understanding as a connoisseur, was the all too smooth, tight, and inexpressive features of the mask, which identified the object as made for the European market, thus lacking the authenticity and sensuality Barnes's considered essential for a genuine aesthetic and educational experience.[27]

Like Barnes, Alfred Barr, the director of MoMA, realized photography's cultural and political importance. Influenced by Barnes's ambition to make African art available to African Americans, Barr approached the general education board of the Rockefeller Foundation to fund a photographic record of the objects shown in the exhibition. The purpose of the documentation was to offer sets of photographs to black colleges so that students and teachers could learn about their "ancestral pasts," as Alain Locke had put it. The application was successful, and in April 1935 the museum issued the following public announcement:

> About 450 objects will be photographed, the more important of them from two or three different angles. The collection, which will be known as the Photographic Corpus of African Negro Art, will be composed of 500 photographs and a catalog of labels and indices. The Museum will distribute six sets of the Corpus to Negro colleges and one set to the 135th Street Branch of the New York Public Library. One set will be retained in the Library of the Museum of Modern Art. Five sets will go at a nominal fee to museums and universities; two of these have already been subscribed.[28]

The museum engaged Walker Evans for the photographic project. Evans had already made himself a name through his documentary photographs of the recent Cuban revolt and his photographic record of nineteenth-century American houses, of which the MoMA had a collection. His approach to photographing African art was markedly different from that of Sheeler and Man Ray. For the MoMA project, Evans employed a frontal perspective and close-ups, resulting in images that look as if he "squeezed" the object into the frame, thus imposing the presence of the object on the viewer with an almost physical force.[29]

A particularly arresting example is Evans's close-up of a Fon warrior figure from Dahomey, a Fon kingdom in what is now the Republic of Benin and once a key player in the North Atlantic slave trade (fig. 3.7). In

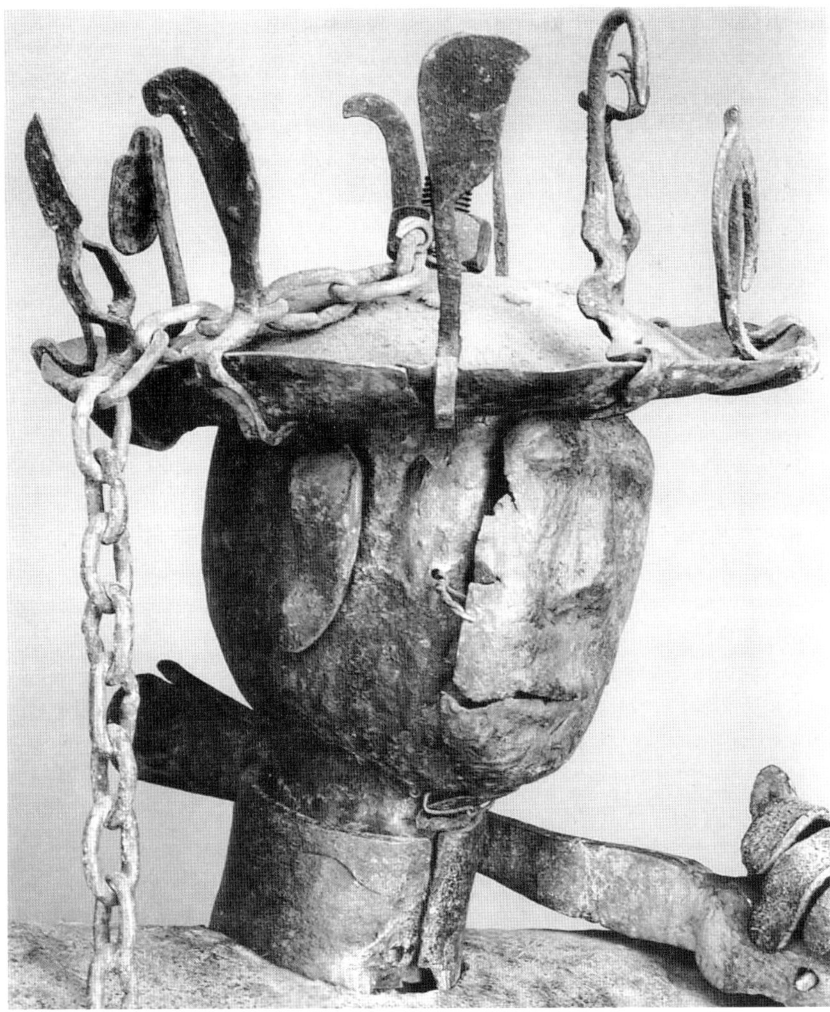

3.7 Walker Evans, Head of Akati Ekplékendo's metal sculpture of the Fon warrior deity
Gou. 23.5 × 18.4 cm, 1935. © Walker Evans Archive, Metropolitan Museum of Art.

the MoMA exhibition, the life-size metal sculpture was placed at some
distance from other objects to ensure its arresting presence (see fig. 2.3).
Evans's close-up focused on the sculpture's head, on which the artist had
placed a crown-like hat encircled with iron tools and weapons. Standing upright, the head slightly bent to the side, and holding a sword in
each hand, the figure was the work of Akati Ekplékendo, a Yoruba war
prisoner, who had created it in 1858 at Abomey, the capital of Dahomey.
Representing the Fon warrior deity of Gou, the figure had been commis-

sioned by King Glele and dedicated to Glele's father, King Guezo. After French troops seized the palace in Abomey in late nineteenth century, the figure was turned into a French war trophy and brought to Dahomey's former slave port Ouidah, from where it was shipped to France. It arrived there in 1898 and was subsequently donated to the Ethnographic Museum of the Trocadéro in Paris, where Picasso saw the figure during his legendary museum visit in 1906–1907 (fig. 3.8).[30] Given Picasso's ambition to move away from the Western conventions of representation, the figure's assemblage technique—composed of found metal objects and forged iron parts—would have been particularly appealing to him. While the figure had a specific cultural significance in its original context (it was carried onto the battlefield to bring luck), what attracted Picasso and his fellow artists was the reduction of the human form into discrete shapes, a technique MoMA praised and celebrated (see chap. 2).

The aim of the various photographic enterprises we have discussed was to capture the aesthetic value or "essence" of African sculpture. Questions of origin were still marginal to the photographic project. Gradually, however, the interest widened from the individual object to "tribal styles," which the individual object represented. A sequel to von Sydow's abovementioned style distribution was the four-volume *Centres du styles de la sculpture nègre africaine*, written and published between 1935–1938 by the Danish collector Carl Kjersmeier.[31]

A lawyer by vocation, Kjersmeier began collecting in 1918. By the mid-1930s he had assembled more than 1,400 objects of different genres and mediums. In line with other collection catalogs at the time, the photographs in Kjersmeier's "style centers" intentionally dramatized the works' formal features and thus endowed them with a heightened presence. Most of the pictures are credited to the Danish fashion photographer Vagn Guldbrandsen. However, a few were also made by Man Ray.[32] As important as photography was, the four volumes don't constitute a collection catalog in the conventional sense; the idea was to authenticate originals and build a canon.[33] Only about half of the objects presented in the four volumes are from Kjersmeier's own collection. The rest are reproductions of photographs found in the available literature. Based on this corpus, the images were meant to illustrate the various "tribal styles" dominating the four "style centers" the volumes covered: (1) French West Africa, (2) Portuguese Guinea, Sierra Leone, Liberia, and the Ivory Coast, (3) Belgian Congo, and (4) Cameroon, French Equatorial Africa, Angola, Tanganyika, and Rhodesia (fig. 3.9).

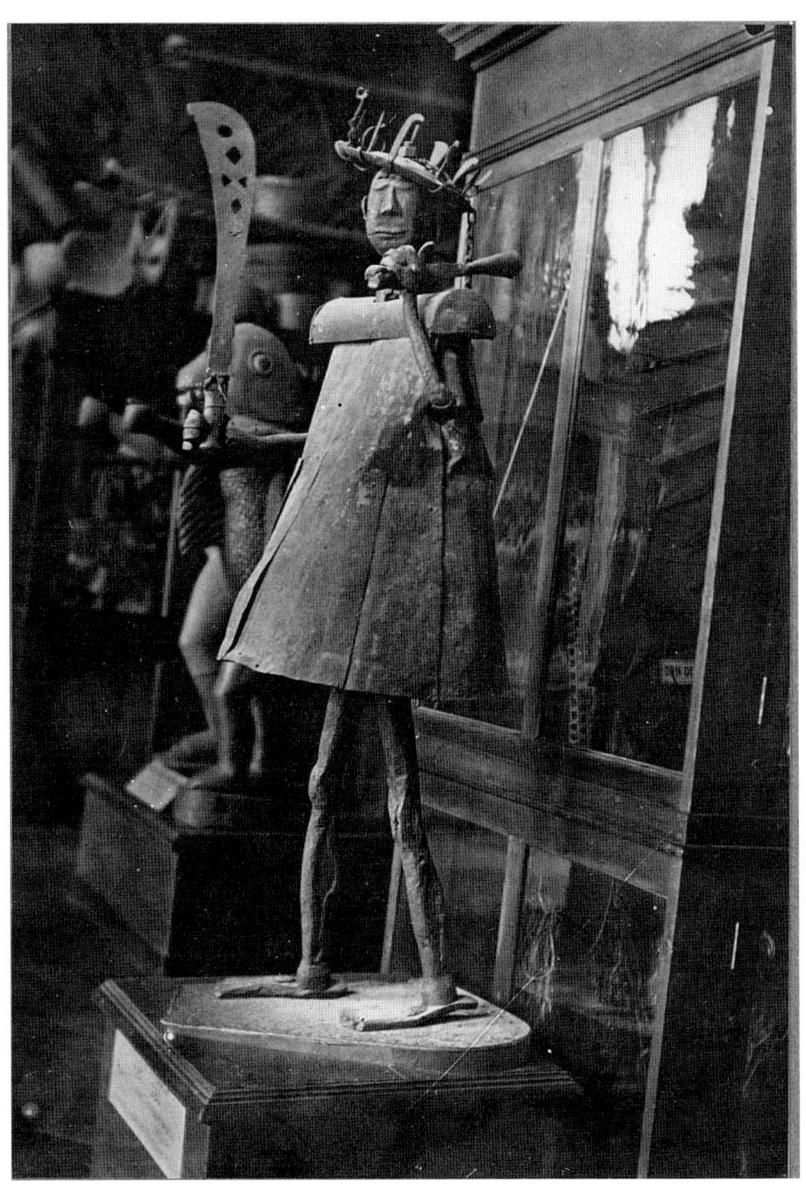

3.8 Akati Ekplékendo's metal sculpture of the Fon warrior deity Gou in the Ethnographic Museum at the Trocadéro, Paris, shown at *African Negro Art* in New York (see also fig. 2.3). Height 165 cm. © Musée du Quai Branly—Jacques Chirac, Dist. RMN-Grand Palais / Art Resource NY.

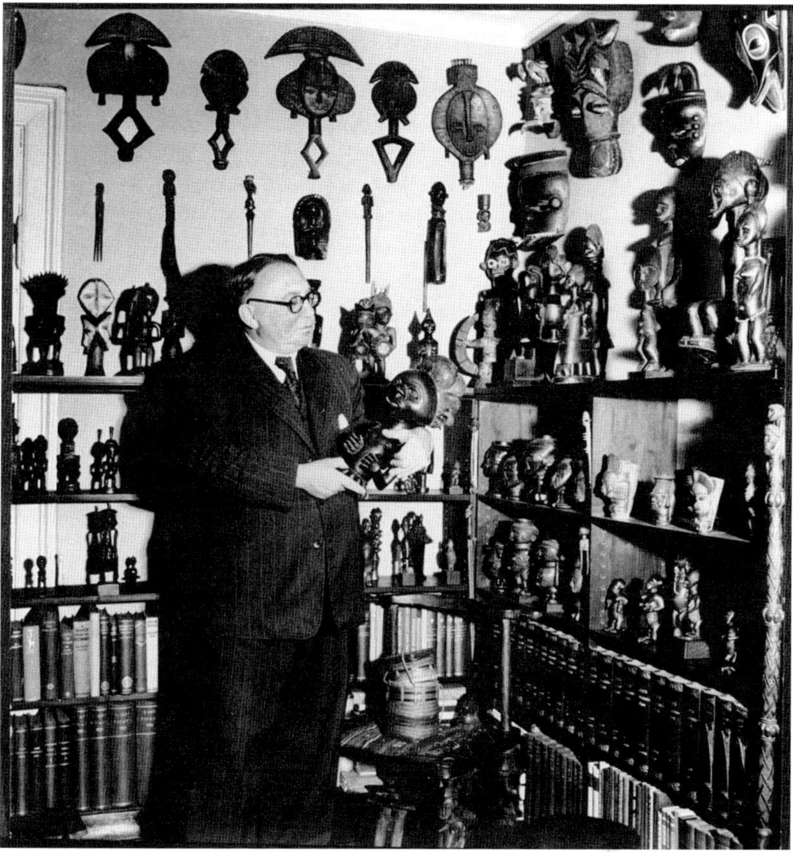

3.9 Carl Kjersmeier with his private collection of African art, ca. 1933. National Museum of Denmark. Public Domain.

Colonial Concerns and Curiosity

Kjersmeier's photographic affirmation of distinct "tribal styles" can be seen as a response to a period when colonial administrations in Africa were grappling to create order out of a seemingly incoherent cultural terrain. That is to say, the experience of fragmentation, dissolution, and distraction that characterized the aesthetic debate about modernity in late nineteenth-century Europe correlated with the discourse about the dangers of "detribalization" and the emergence of "trouser negroes" (Frobenius) in early twentieth-century African colonial modernity. In both cases, scholars invoked the concept of "style" in their search for unity, clarity, and coherence in a field perceived to be characterized by disintegration and dissolution.[34] While in European art history, "style" came to be understood as a "visual grammar"[35] based on limited aesthetic "principles,"[36] in the colonial context, "style" came to mean a specific set of aesthetic features or motifs associated with each "tribe" that served to bring order into, what seemed to Europeans, a complex and unruly patchwork of tribal groups and subgroups.

A key institution for fostering field research in Africa was the London-based International African Institute for the Study of Languages and Cultures. Founded in 1926 as a kind of colonial think tank, the institute provided research grants that aimed to generate practical ideas for countering the dangers of "detribalization" and social "disintegration" resulting from the introduction of a money economy, taxation, urbanization, and labor migration.[37] The following passage from 1932 expressed the respective concerns and proposed measures to counter the negative effects of colonial modernity.

> The fundamental problem arising from the permeation of African life by the ideas and economic forces that are entering the continent may bring about its complete disintegration, the results of which must be calamitous for the individuals who compose it and at the same time render it impossible to achieve an orderly evolution of the community. It is proposed, therefore, that the inquiries fostered by the Institute should be directed towards bringing about a better understanding of the factors of social cohesion in African society, the ways in which these are being affected by the new influences, tendencies towards new groupings and the formation of new social bonds and forms of co-operation between African societies and Western civilization.[38]

Many of these concerns stemmed from observations in the realm of the arts. At the end of his abovementioned survey article on African sculpture from 1928, Eckart von Sydow had said, "A survey of the primitive art of Africa, however cursory, in the end necessarily leads to the practical question: how can the ancient art of the African native tribes be preserved and revitalized?"[39] To gather firsthand information on the matter, von Sydow successfully applied for a research grant from the institute. In 1936, and again in 1939, he traveled to Nigeria, Cameroon, and Ghana. The results were published in a short report from 1938 titled "Ancient and Modern Benin Art" and a posthumously published travelogue of Nigeria and Cameroon.[40]

Von Sydow's findings contradicted popular assumptions about the decline of Benin art. In contrast to von Luschan and his contemporaries, who had declared Benin art practically dead, he found Benin art "in a highly flourishing condition; the wood-carvers, in particular, were fully occupied. Again and again, I came across altars for ancestor worship, images, carved doors, &c., which have been made during the last few score years. . . . One has the impression that Benin is determined to make good the colossal damage that was done to it."[41] Oddly enough, the reader does not learn about the people who account for the vitality of Benin art. In both von Sydow's research report and travelogue the artists of the objects he describes remain mostly invisible and anonymous. In fact, the texts convey a distinct sense of racial distance and disengagement. For von Sydow, interest in African art did not mean interest in the people making it.

A more complicated case was von Sydow's student Hans Himmelheber. In the early 1930s, Himmelheber had gone to Berlin to study under von Sydow because of his own commercial trade in African and Oceanic art. His business activities triggered his interest in the individuals who made the objects he bought and sold. Therefore, in 1933, at the age of twenty-five, he traveled to Côte d'Ivoire in what was then still French West Africa to collect and do fieldwork among Guro and Baule sculptors. The pictures show him in colonial white attire selecting pieces and negotiating prices with Guro and Baule men (fig. 3.10). The racial hierarchy the photographs exemplify are one matter. Himmelheber's PhD

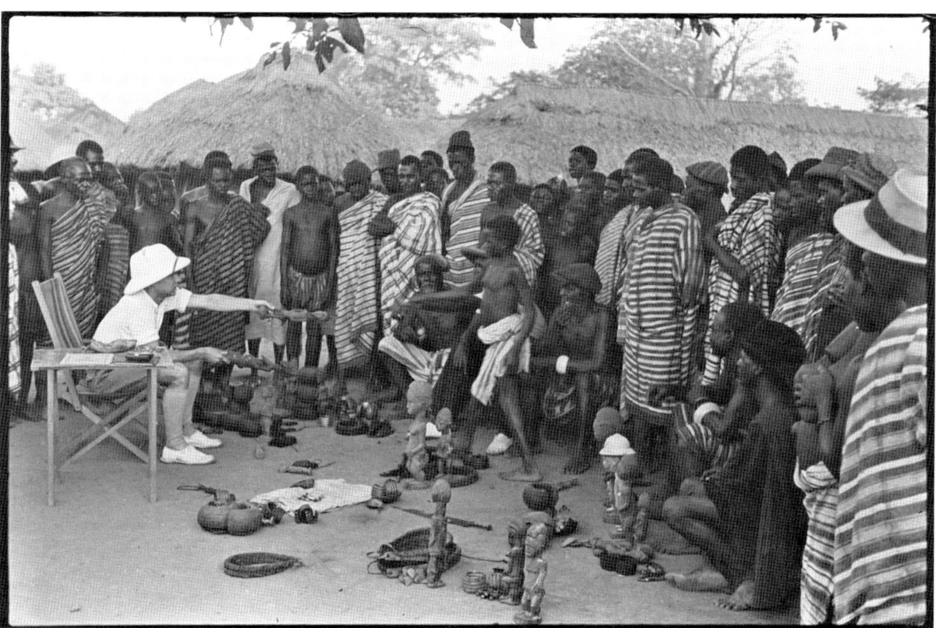

3.10 Hans Himmelheber assessing objects for purchase in the Baule village of Saundi, Côte d'Ivoire, 1934. © Museum Rietberg, Zürich.

dissertation is another. Published in 1935 under the title *Negerkünstler: Ethnographische Studien über den Schnitzkünstler bei den Stämmen der Atutu und Guro* (Negro artists: Ethnographic studies on the carver artist among the Atutu and Guro tribes), the study aims to get an understanding of the "carver artist" and the local aesthetics informing his work.[42] The eighty-page-long study is structured in four chapters, ranging from the artists' biographies and the use of materials and techniques to criteria of aesthetic value and the role of the audience. By far the most thorough discussion is devoted to what is framed as the relationship between (precolonial) tradition and (colonial) modernity. Does the idea of the autonomy of art in terms of *l'art pour l'art* exist among these peoples? How much individual leeway do artists have in the carving of an object? How do local aesthetic concepts inform the shape and function of a carving? When does local conformity conflict with individual creativity?

Himmelheber's questions and methodology were novel and innovative for the new field of African art. Up to that point, the assumption was that (a) the art/artist concept is alien to African society, (b) African sculptures are not the product of individuals but of tribal collectives, and (c) all carved objects are deeply enmeshed in religious beliefs and practices. Himmelheber's study broke with these ideas. Through empirical research, interviews, photos, and films, he conveyed a different picture of African art, one that entailed not just forms and shapes but human beings with individual personalities, distinct styles, and creative ambitions.

*　*　*

There are good reasons to maintain that photography was deeply involved in this shift. As I have argued in this chapter, photography played multiple roles—often simultaneously. While politically it worked as an instrument of domination and submission, aesthetically it freed the object and allowed for the latter's formal appreciation. Of course, one can ask, Did the aesthetic recognition really counter the colonial gaze, or was it not simply part of it? Fact is, it was the presence of photography that helped the aesthetic alignment of modernism and colonialism in which "African art" as both an economic and artistic category emerged. Once brought into being, it developed its own dynamic. Part of it was curiosity. That is, with the ubiquity of photographs came the quest to know more about the works private individuals and public museums collected and displayed. In other words, photography not only pushed decontextualization, it also triggered recontextualization.

Himmelheber's early research is a key element in this dialectic; by the time his book on African artists appeared in 1935, the Nazi regime had left its effects on the African art market. The artistic milieu that had created the market was decreed as "degenerate." With the passing of the Nuremberg laws, Jewish critics and collectors saw themselves forced into either leaving the country or being sent into concentration camps, which usually meant dying in gas chambers. It was in view of this situation that Himmelheber decided to travel to the US to present his work and establish contacts with American museums and universities.[43] While he eventually returned to Germany, his move to the US was indicative of the development of the field as a whole. With the beginning of World War II in 1939, the European dominance in African studies came to a close. A decade later, not only the political but also the academic landscape had changed. With the US, a new imperial power had taken over.

PART II

Discovering the African Artist

TRADITION AND TRIBALITY
IN THE COLD WAR ERA

The suddenness with which Africa has emerged onto the world scene is one of the striking happenings of our day. Nowhere has the recognition of Africa's importance been more rapid than in the United States.

MELVILLE HERSKOVITS AND WILLIAM BASCOM,
The Problem of Stability and Change in African Culture, 1959

Introduction

In 1965, the University of California at Los Angeles organized a lecture series called Individual Creativity and Tribal Norms. Given by anthropologists, the talks were part of a series of events celebrating the gift of thirty thousand African and Oceanic artifacts from the collection of the American-British pharmaceutical entrepreneur Henry Wellcome. Housed in the basement of Haines Hall, the recently opened Museum and Laboratories of Ethnic Arts and Technology exhibited a selection of objects from the collection praising the works as masterpieces of African art.[1]

Wellcome had amassed his collection during the late nineteenth and early twentieth centuries, in the heyday of colonialism. By the time the objects arrived in Los Angeles, the political landscape had changed. Formally, colonialism had come to an end, and most former colonies were now independent. The lecture series focused on this new political reality and the shift in attitudes accompanying it. While up to the 1940s modernity had been seen as a deadly contagion that caused "primitive" societies to die, and therefore required salvage-mission-style collecting operations, modernity was now considered to be a necessity: something that could be planned, implemented, and engineered to generate development and progress. What was once "primitive" had become "tradition," or rather, the problem of tradition. The main question in this debate between the 1960s and 1970s was the role of tradition in a modernizing society.[2] Does tradition hinder development and nation building, or does it have a positive effect by providing orientation and stability in a rapidly changing environment?

Postwar research on African art was preoccupied with these same questions. By then, the center of scholarship had shifted from Europe to the US. In view of the changing political conditions, particular attention was given to the relationship between "individual creativity" on the one hand and "tribal norms" on the other. Or, as the anthropologist Daniel Biebuyck put it, "How can we deal with individual taste, skills, and temperament in communities that focus heavily on corporate solidarity?"[3] The question marked a shift in perspective. For a long time, African society had been seen as an agglomeration of tribes whose members remained largely faceless. The way to independence had shown a different society though, one not ruled by tradition and norms but by flesh and blood individuals with ambitions and aspirations (fig. 4.1).

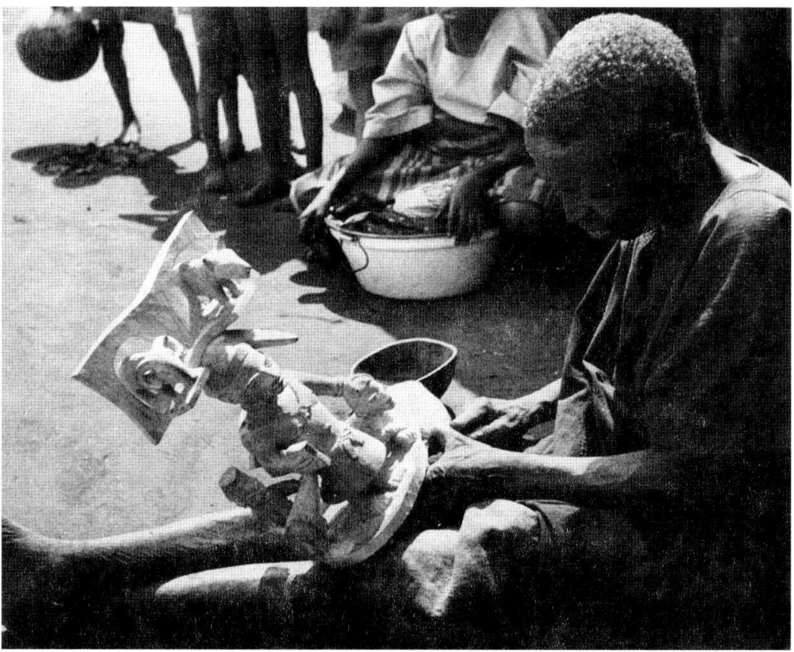

4.1 "Yoruba Master Carver: Duka of Meko." Photo by William Bascom, early 1950s. From *The Traditional Artist in African Society* (Indiana University Press, 1973).

In the following, I shall trace some of the relevant transformations that were happening in "the long 1960s." During the Cold War that followed World War II, the US was eager to gain and maintain power in the new postwar and postcolonial landscape. To this end, the American government started to fund so-called area studies to provide in-depth information in politically sensitive places. Africa was the subject of the first of these new research units, which allowed specialists from different fields to work together on one region.[4] Art and artists were part of the new research agenda.[5] Anthropologists argued that concepts like "tribal style" or "tribal art" were too simplistic and raised more questions than they answered, glossing over complex internal dynamics and ignoring the fact that, all too often, specific styles are representative not of whole societies or tribes but of specific institutions *within* them.[6]

The conceptual critique correlated with the emergence of African art as a new subfield of art history (in the US). In fact, anthropologists, political scientists, and economists were not the only ones profiting from the new public interest in Africa. The access to research grants also allowed for the rise of African art history at American universities.[7] Given how small the entire field was, the relationship between anthropology and African art history was one of free exchange and reciprocity. Still, African art historians had their own distinct profile: what mattered to them were not only the aesthetic ideas and practices in the "field" but also the objects in the increasing number of private collections. Imitating the collecting taste and practices in Europe, the founders and heirs of economic empires in the US had started to amass objects of "primitive art"—usually encompassing African, Oceanic, and pre-Columbian art—from the 1920s onward, and it was their collections that provided the "field research" for art historians. Some of the themes, such as the question of style, simply resurfaced from under the rubble of World War II. Others, however, such as the relationship between the traditional/tribal and the modern/contemporary artist were genuinely new.

Finally, I will explore the internal tensions that arose within the new subfield from the clash between the conventional, object-and-collection-centered approach to the study of art on the one hand and a more holistic, performative approach emerging from fieldwork on the other. Increasingly, though, and not least as a result of the American Peace Corps Program starting in 1962, actual fieldwork gained in importance. Students who had spent a year on the continent came back and applied to art history PhD programs to pursue a research project in the country in which they had worked as volunteers. The numbers were still small, but the newness of the field fostered a sense of its distinct identity apart from the mainstream. Given the political conditions at the time (the Vietnam war, student uprisings, the Black Power movement), many early students and specialists brought to the field an ambition to develop an alternative art history—one less conservative, less preoccupied with "high art," more critical of the status quo, and more open to the margins of society.

The Rise of African Studies

Of crucial importance in the landscape of new Cold War American research on Africa was the African Studies Program at Northwestern University in Evanston, Illinois. Established in 1948, it became the first area studies program in the country and for more than a decade the prime academic forge for Africanists. At its center was Melville Herskovits, the founder and director of the program. In fact, the boom of studies on African art in American anthropology in the 1960s and 1970s can be credited directly to Herskovits and his students.

Herskovits had studied under the founding father of American anthropology, Franz Boas, at Columbia. Herskovits was deeply influenced by Boas's vehement rejection of racial explanations for the differences between "primitive" and "Western" art.[8] His own research focused primarily on the history and variability of black culture, for which he carried out research in South America (Suriname 1928–1929 and Brazil 1941–1942), West Africa (Dahomey, Ghana, and Nigeria 1931), and the Caribbean (Haiti 1934 and Trinidad 1939). Interested mostly in hard social issues, he left the "soft" areas such as visual arts, folklore, dance, and music to his wife Frances, his partner in fieldwork. Yet he admonished his many students not to overlook the importance of art and aesthetics as a crucial key to understanding a foreign culture. His own understanding of art was very much informed by Boas, who in turn was indebted to Riegl's notion of *Kunstwollen* in terms of an innate aesthetic drive. Consequently, Herskovits's own musing on the question sounded very much like Riegl's: "We may say, then, that in all societies the aesthetic impulse finds expression in terms of the standards of beauty laid down in the traditions of the people. . . . No art, that is, is haphazarded or inchoate."[9]

A clear boundary between anthropological and art-historical approaches to African art did not yet exist. In fact, the first PhD in African art history was awarded only in 1957, the very year the African Studies Center at Northwestern became the country's first government-funded area studies program. The recipient was Roy Sieber at the University of Iowa. Initially trained in studio art, he shifted his focus to art history and concentrated in medieval art before developing an interest in African art. For Sieber, the move was plausible. Not only did he see parallels between the two fields from a conceptual point of view, he also believed both fields invited a joint approach.[10] Sieber's dissertation on "African Tribal Sculpture" was still only a rough survey of the relevant literature. He subsequently filled in the gaps in his knowledge by reaching out to Herskovits and his students in an effort to engage with the deeper, contextual understanding of the works included in his dissertation.

I will come back to Sieber later in this chapter. For now, let me remain with Herskovits's students. The list is long and ranges from William Bascom and Katherine Dunham to James Fernandez and Simon Ottenberg, to name only a few. Together, they formed a powerful and influential American tradition of art-related Africanist research. Each one of them made important contributions to the study of African art, with W. R. Bascom's finding of another series of Ife bronzes being perhaps the most spectacular one (figs. 4.2, 4.3).[11] Most research topics were approached from both an anthropological and art-historical perspective, as in the case of anthropologist James Fernandez's work on one of the most cherished and prominent objects in the Western interest in African art: the *eyema-o-byeri*, or, in short, *byeri* reliquary figures of the Fang. Between 1957 and 1959, Fernandez did fieldwork among the Southern Fang in Gabon. His PhD on acculturation and religious change echoed his advisor's research agenda, however, owing to Herskovits's insistence on attentiveness to artistic expressions. Fernandez also produced a series of articles on Fang sculpture.[12]

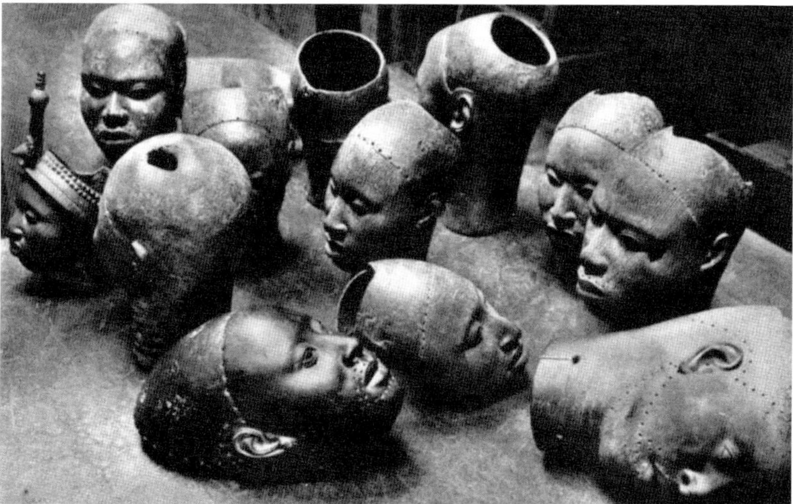

4.2 Ife copper alloy heads and masks, thirteenth to fifteenth century, uncovered in 1938 near the palace of the Ooni of Ife. A year later, when on display at the British Museum in London, the heads prompted *Illustrated London News* to run an article titled "The Legacy of an Unknown Nigerian Donatello."

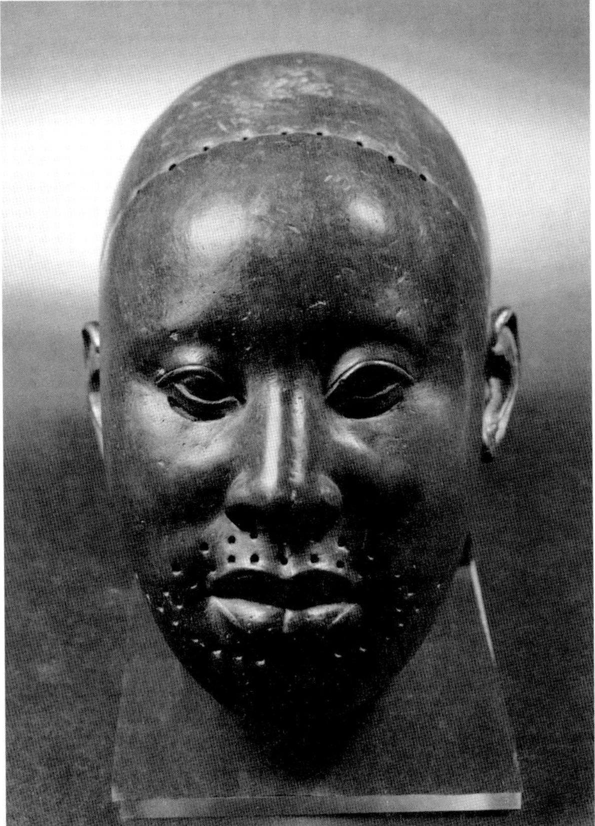

4.3 Unidentified artist, Mask of Obalufon, an early ruler of Ife associated with bronze casting in Ife, thirteenth to fifteenth century. Copper, height 29.5 cm. © National Museum Nigeria / Licensed by SCALA / Art Resource, NY.

The Fang had migrated into southern Cameroon and Gabon during the nineteenth century, resulting in various subgroups. Each extended family possessed a cylindrical bark box containing the skulls of its ancestors. Attached were wooden heads and figures whose task was to protect the relics from malevolent forces. The sculptures were thought to watch over the relics, just as the ancestors watch over their living descendants. To maintain these bonds, Fang regularly "fed" the figures by anointing them with palm oil. However, over time things changed. From the late nineteenth century onward, a growing number of *byeri* figures ended up in Europe as curios, where their atomized bulging limbs and distinct muscular form attracted the interest of critics and avant-garde artists, which, as we saw in chapters 2 and 3, in turn triggered a commercial interest. Frequently photographed, *byeri* became a valuable commodity that dealers, such as Guillaume and Brummer in France, sold to collectors and gallerists, such as Barnes and de Zayas in the US According to Tessmann's account, Fernandez explained the high number of *byeri* figures in the African art market as indicative of growing pressure from Christian missionaries, who considered *byeri* pagan and tried to eliminate their use, that led to their sale to European middlemen (see chap. 1). By the time Fernandez arrived in the late 1950s, most of the Fang had stopped using *byeri* figures. The few remaining ones were all full figures; the sole head figures, seen by writers like Tessmann some fifty years earlier, had disappeared. Fernandez, therefore, speculated that the shift from head to full-body figure might have been a result of Christian images of Mary and Jesus and other full-body figures coming from the Vili in the south, where the contact with Christianity was stronger. Despite these changes, the new sculptural productions continued to be the subject of passionate debates among the Fang about the aesthetic value, mastery, or relative failure of the works. These discussions were restricted to men and happened in the men's house, where Fernandez followed them. Commenting on the Fang's aesthetic conventions and notions of representational truth, he writes,

> The Fang often argue that these figures and masks constitute traditional photographs. Part of the qualitative reaction of the observers is based upon the degree to which the carver has been able to reproduce the human form in accordance with those expectations set by stylistic criteria—very short and flexed limbs, long thin torso, and large head. . . . That what is reproduced is very far from a reproduction of the human form is quite clear to a European. We have in this reference to "our photographs" an indication of the degree to which culture can persuade, if not impose a perception upon the senses. This indicated the degree to which artistic conventions can become a reality of their own, symbolizing greater truths than are iconically represented.[13]

According to Fernandez, Fang fully understood that the proportions of the figures were not the proportions of living people. As he argued, to Fang, *byeri* represented a cultural truth informed by the main Fang principle of vitality. At the center of this principle was the notion of balance, or more precisely, the capacity to hold opposites in balance. Full figures had to convey this balance by playing with carefully balanced opposites: atomized limbs versus full body, the big head of an infant versus the bulging muscles of an adult, the rebellious tension of youth versus the somber wisdom of the elders, flexing energy versus static symmetry, and so forth

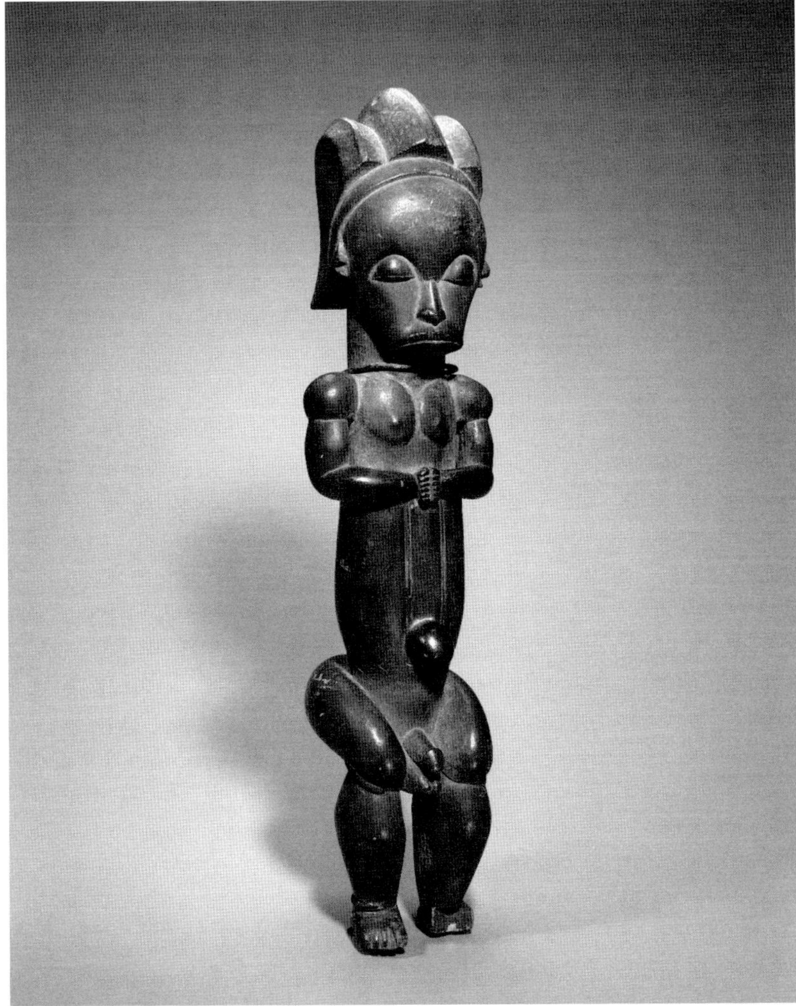

4.4 Unidentified artist, Fang Reliquary Guardian figure (*Eyema-o-Byeri*), mid-eighteenth to mid-nineteenth century. Wood and iron, 58.4 × 14.6 × 12.7 cm. Brooklyn Museum of Art, Frank L. Babbott Fund, 51.3.

(fig. 4.4). In view of these criteria, Fernandez quoted a Fang elder who stressed that Fang reliquary figures were idealized and generalized, not individual portraits of the deceased:

> The figure represents no ancestor. There are many skulls in the reliquary. Who should we choose to represent? And who would be satisfied with the choice if his own grandfather should be ignored? The

figures were made to warn others that this was "the box of skulls" and they made to represent all ancestors within. What causes us satisfaction in seeing the *eyima* [ancestor] atop the *byeri* is that we see disclosed our ancestors. Their faces are strong, quiet, and reflective. They are thinking about our problems and how to help us. We see what they see.[14]

In Fernandez's view, the task of the Fang carver was to make the invisible world visible. His work conveyed to the onlooker that the world of the ancestors, the unseen world, does not pose a threat; that things in the invisible world are in order, that complementarity, equilibrium, and tranquility triumph over conflict, fission, and aggression. In short, artists were expected to convey a sense of order and harmony—values that contrasted with the real world of everyday life, which was dominated, as Fernandez argued, by villages' disputes, lineage fissions, and a high degree of competitive individualism. In short, the sculptural aesthetics of *byeri* represented an antidote to the centrifugal forces of Fang society.

The functionalist tone of this argument was characteristic of much of the anthropological research devoted to African art from the 1950s all the way to the 1980s when the tradition-creativity model was giving way to a culture-agency perspective. Art was seen as a window that facilitated insights into larger cultural issues. Topics varied from masking and masquerades, leadership and power, to cosmology and religious ideas. Within this larger framework, there were national variants in research interests. For example, American anthropology tended to be more interested in the relationship between culture and personality, that is, the individual, while British and French anthropology tended to focus on social structures. In practice, however, research on artistic practices and artists often ran counter to both theoretical frameworks.

Postwar research on African art was thus highly heterogeneous. What unified the diverging approaches and interests was the focus on what was once "primitive" and was now "traditional art." Modern art, even though it was very much part of independence, was largely considered a nonsubject by anthropologists—and most African art historians—until the 1990s.[15]

Tribality and the Identification of the African Artist

For anthropologists, ethnographic fieldwork was a defining feature of the profession. It meant going to Africa for at least a year if not longer, living with the subject ethnic group, learning the language and engaging in so-called participant observation. In other words, the "field" was in Africa,

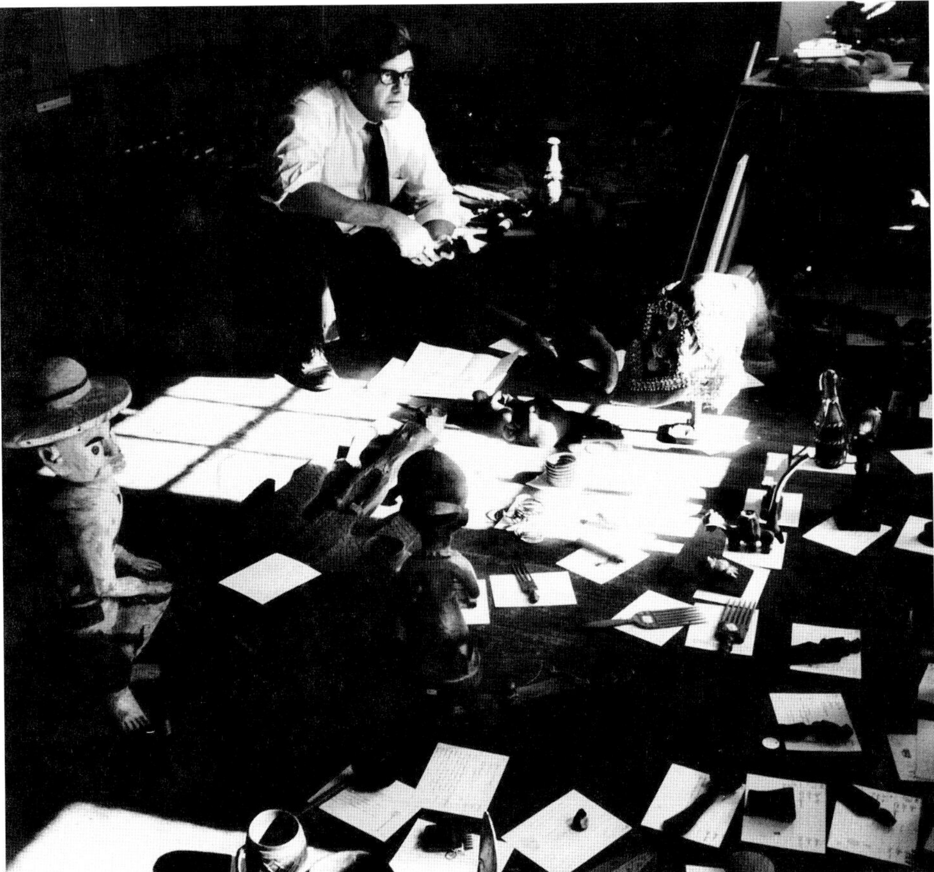

4.5 Roy Sieber examines objects of the Sheppard collection at the Hampton College Museum, 1965. Photo: Reuben Burrell. Hampton Museum. Courtesy of Roslyn A. Walker.

and the objective was to immerse oneself within it in order to understand the world from a local perspective. But what was the "field" for the newly minted African art historians graduating from American art history departments, with Roy Sieber's department at Indiana University, institutionally, holding the foremost importance?

Even though art historians recognized the importance of anthropological fieldwork, for them the "field" was constituted more by objects than by people. To do fieldwork, then, one did not necessarily have to leave the country; the "field" might be the collections of public museums and private individuals (fig. 4.5). In fact, the work with collections came to be a distinctive feature that defined and differentiated art-historical from anthropological research on African art. The postwar situation in the US was favorable in this respect: while European economies were suffering from the effects of the war, the US economy was flourishing, which allowed the heirs of the wealth amassed during America's Gilded Age to engage in collecting and museum projects.

A case in point is the Museum of Primitive Art in New York. The MPA, as it was called, opened in 1957 and housed Nelson Rockefeller's private collection of African, Oceanic, and pre-Columbian art. Institutionally, it was de facto an outgrowth of the Museum of Modern Art.[16] With its parent institution, it shared not only its location—it was situated across from the MoMA on 15 West 54th Street—but its leadership: the cofounders were Nelson Rockefeller, president of MoMA, and René d'Harnoncourt, the director of MoMA. Robert Goldwater, who had been influential in organizing MoMA's *African Negro Art* exhibit in 1935, and who was by then professor of art history at New York University, was the director of the MPA.

Goldwater was responsible for the quality of the collection and for garnering public recognition of the museum. No doubt Rockefeller's wealth helped. In 1958, for instance, just one year after its opening, the museum acquired the Benin pendant ivory mask, once looted by the British in the infamous punitive raid, for $56,000—at that time the highest price ever paid for an object of "primitive art" (fig. 4.6).[17] In a letter to Rockefeller from December 1957 in which he referred to an almost identical mask at the British Museum in London, Goldwater explained the rationale of the purchase as follows:

> I believe this mask surpasses it [the BM mask] in delicacy of workmanship and penetration of expression. It is thus the best object of its kind known, nor will any others ever turn up. . . . The purchase of this mask would give the Museum a permanent, primary attraction—a popular masterpiece. It is one of those objects that "has to be seen" by scholars, art lovers, and the public alike.[18]

Given this public attention, Rockefeller himself understood the museum and its collection as a tool of foreign policy. In September 1960, he led the US delegation to Nigeria to attend the official festivities celebrating Nigeria's independence.[19] Upon his return, the MPA organized an exhibition of *The Traditional Arts of Africa's New Nations*, which featured one hundred works from sixteen newly independent African countries, all of whose UN representatives were invited. The foreign policy objective was to demonstrate US recognition of African culture and stabilize the fragile young states by boosting their pride in their cultural and artistic achievements (fig. 4.7). The fact that the objects on display had colonial baggage with often dubious provenance did not seem to matter.

In spite of Rockefeller's objectives, Goldwater and his superiors were most invested in the aesthetic and formal properties of the objects on display. As MPA curator and specialist for Oceanic art Douglas Newton put it, "We look for quality within each element—the best of everything."[20] To find "the best," Newton and his colleagues relied both on photography

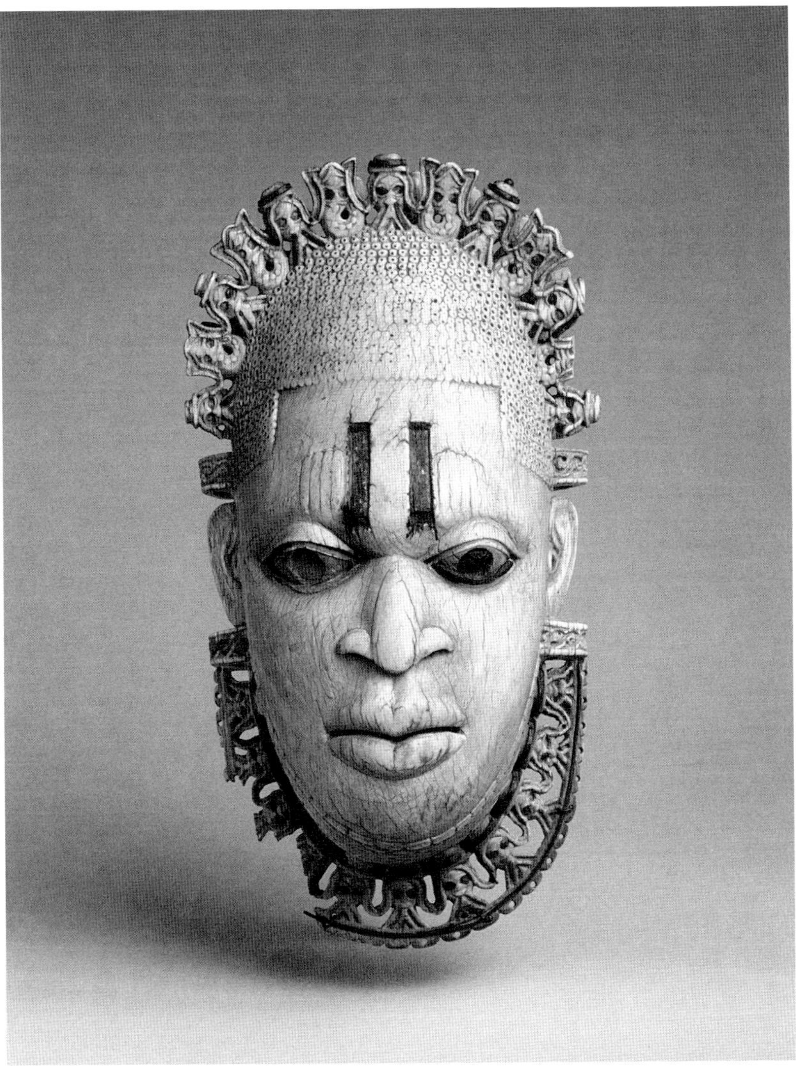

4.6 Unidentified artist, Pendant mask of Queen Mother (*Iyoba*). Edo peoples, Court of Benin, Nigeria, sixteenth century. Bone and ivory, 23.8 × 12.7 × 8.3 cm. Metropolitan Museum New York, The Michael C. Rockefeller Memorial Collection. Gift of Nelson A. Rockefeller, 1972.

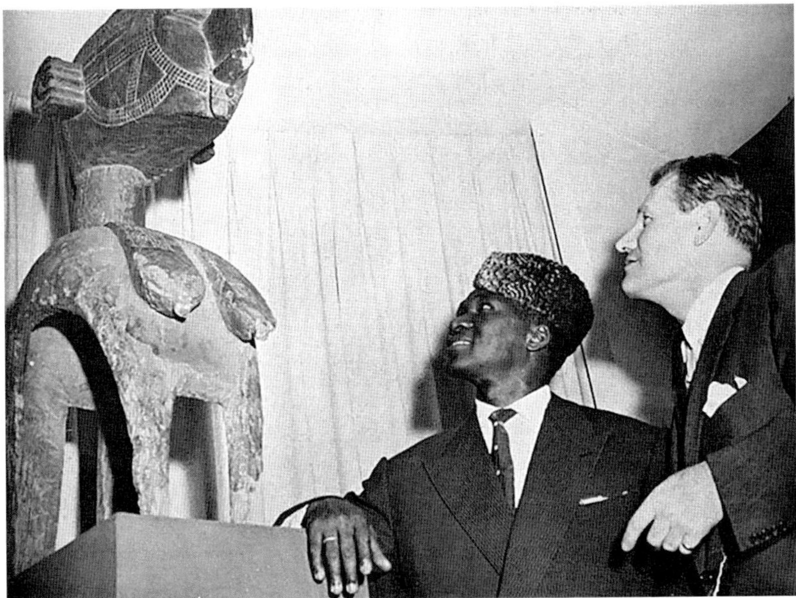

4.7 Ahmed Sékou Touré, president of Guinea, and Nelson Rockefeller in front of a Baga female bust and mask (d'mba) in the Museum of Primitive Art in New York, 1959. Photo: Bob Wands. © Rockefeller Archive Center.

and connoisseurship (see chap. 3). Thus, *Sculpture of Northern Nigeria,* which the MPA showed in 1961, resulted from a series of photographs the young Roy Sieber had sent to Goldwater and Newton after his return from a Ford funded "expedition" to the Benue River region in Nigeria.[21] The MPA's uncompromising belief in superior quality and connoisseurship left an impression on Sieber, as he later developed his own expertise and authority in the newly emerging field of African art studies.

Given the focus on connoisseurship, the museum regularly hosted lectures by scholars like Herskovits and Himmelheber. Some of them also acted as "consulting fellows" whose expertise helped to identify artists, illuminate the historical and cultural context of the works in the collection, and at times, prompt acquisitions. A particularly influential "consulting fellow" of the MPA was William Fagg, the former Keeper of Ethnology at the British Museum in London. In the 1960s and 1970s, Fagg was an eminent figure in the field of African art and was closely connected to important collectors, artists, dealers, and auction houses. His knowledge of museums and private collections was legendary. While his knowledge extended across the whole of sub-Saharan Africa, his own primary field of expertise was the art of Nigeria, where he traveled in the late 1940s and 1950s. Like Himmelheber, Fagg saw African sculptures as the works of individual artists who could be identified by a combination of documentation, fieldwork, and connoisseurship.

Fagg's expertise relied mostly on the so-called Morellian method. Named after the Italian physician and art critic Giovanni Morelli, the method aimed to identify the unconscious "signature" of an artwork by looking closely at the way the artist shaped particular anatomical details such as hands, mouths, ears, or noses. If they were identical, then it was seen as proof that they stemmed from the same "hand." In the mid-1940s, the director of the Museum of the Congo Free State in Tervuren, Belgium, Frans Olbrechts, used this method to identify distinct style regions and individual workshops in the museum's extensive Congo collection.[22] Fagg employed the "Belgian method," as it was called by then, when he worked on the collections of the British Museum. He and Olbrechts were thus instrumental in changing the popular perception of African art as the product of anonymous tribal makers by assigning works of art to individual "masters," such as the "Master of the Aquiline Profiles" for a medieval Ife caster of bronze heads, or the "Master of Buli" (a location name) for the maker of morphologically distinct nineteenth-century Luba caryatid stools and figural diviner's bowls (fig. 4.8).

Unlike his American colleagues, Fagg held on to the term *tribal* vis-á-vis the postwar category of "traditional" art. For Fagg, "traditional" missed the holistic quality of "tribal" art in terms of its self-referentiality:

> Every tribe is, from the point of view of art, a universe to itself . . . an "exclusive in-group" which uses art among many means to express its internal solidarity and self-sufficiency, and conversely its difference from others. . . . Tribal art, then, is "functional" within the tribe, but not outside it. . . . It is of the people, by the people and for the people.[23]

The quote is from the exhibition *Tribes and Forms in African Art*, which was shown in 1964 at the Congress Hall in West Berlin, Germany.[24] The division of the city into a western and eastern part represented the Cold War politics of the time, articulating Western modernism and consumer capitalism, promoted by the US, as an attractive countermodel to the totalitarian system the East, namely the Soviet Union.[25] The CIA was part of this endeavor. A covert CIA organization by the name of the Congress for Cultural Freedom sponsored cultural activities of liberal but anticommunist intellectuals around the world.[26] Among the events was also Fagg's *Tribes and Forms*. For the US, West Berlin was an international showcase for demonstrating the West's intellectual curiosity and open-mindedness vis-á-vis other cultures. Therefore, in the late 1950s, the US

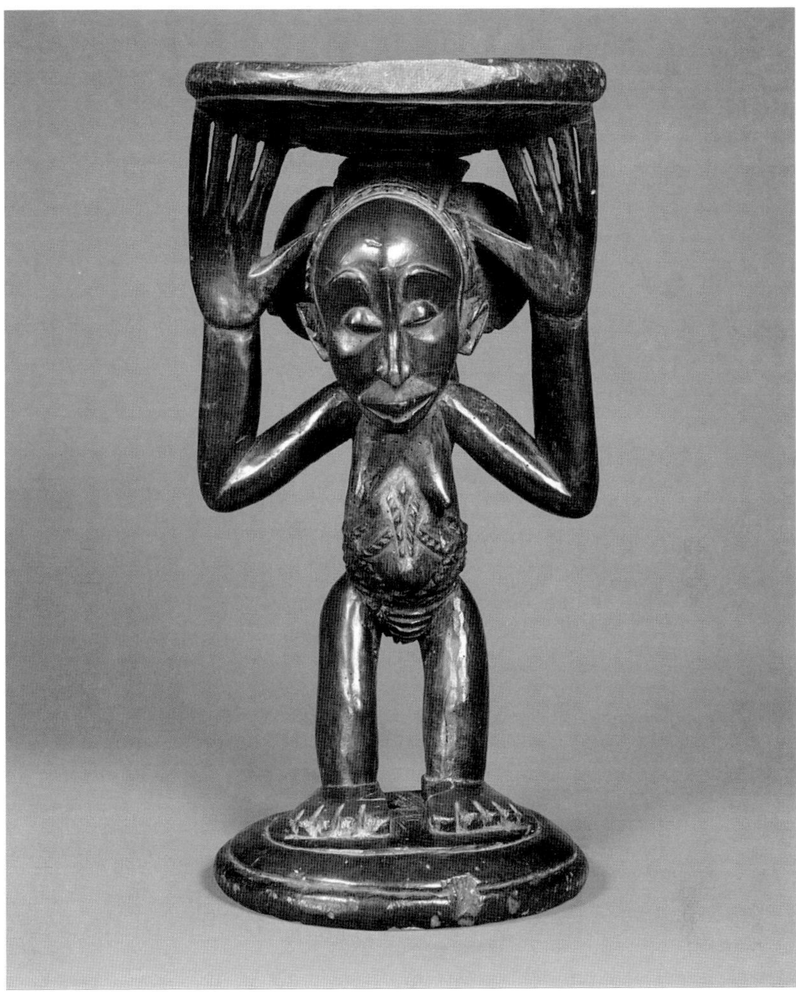

4.8 Royal Seat, female caryatid, "Master of Buli," Luba/Hemba, Congo, nineteenth century. Wood, 61 × 27.9 × 27.9 cm. Metropolitan Museum of Art, Purchase, Buckeye Trust and Charles B. Benenson Gifts, Rogers Fund, and funds from various donors, 1979.

government built a modernist Congress Hall and presented it to the City of Berlin as a present.[27] The artistic program of the opening ceremony reflected the Congress Hall's future program: combining theater, symposia, and concerts, it brought together prominent artists, scientists, and politicians engaged in an international dialogue between the New and Old Worlds. Fagg's rationale aligned with this agenda:

If Africa is able to act as a leaven in the art of the world, it is of utmost importance that African intellectuals—who have acquired bias towards the dominance of the intellect—should come to know and admire the qualities of the dying tribal arts of their past and if possible preserve them for the world.[28]

The argument clearly echoes the colonial fears of "detribalization" of the 1930s, ideologically fostering cultural alienation and leading to new social structures that would be difficult to govern or control. It is hardly surprising, then, that Fagg insisted on the need to focus on the "real" African artist, a category he defined as follows:

> By the African artist, I mean the traditional carver in wood, ivory, and stone, the metal-caster or the artist in pottery working in the context of the tribal system for the members of his own tribe and expressing the religious and artistic values of his community. Many such artists still exist and, though they are undoubtedly on the way out (such is the destructive force of westernization) they will not disappear completely for a long time to come.[29]

Ironically, the "destructive force" worked also within Fagg's own conceptualization of the field. In order to defend his idea of "tribal art," he excluded what he saw as corruptions of the true "African" artist:

> I exclude from the definition three classes of artists, real or so-called. The first of these is the contemporary African artist and, although many are true artists, they are not truly African artists, although of African race, because they have been trained in art schools in the Western romantic tradition and conform unmistakenly to the international style, whereas their patrons are almost exclusively not African. The weaker brethren of this class tend to slide into the second class, the makers of tourist art which, of course, is not art in any proper sense, but more or less mechanically produced *Kitsch*, or trashy souvenirs, for the less sophisticated traveller. . . . The third class, and the most dangerous to our correct appreciation of the real African artist is the forgers, who make and carefully age imitations and fantastications of the traditional works of their own or of neighboring tribes. Their work is addressed . . . to the international art market, and therefore is both commercially oriented and intended to deceive.[30]

Fagg's rant echoes the profound transformations both African societies as well as the field of African art studies were undergoing. By the late 1960s, many tribal designations had already been subject to serious revisions. Those scholars who challenged the "tribe and style" model pointed to its oversimplification and ahistoricity, given the stark discrepancy between the fluidity of group identities, the mobility of objects, and the rigidity of tribal names, which were all too often the invention of colonial authorities in an effort to govern and tax an unruly area.[31] Gradually, the field expanded and matured, incorporating not only nonsculptural genres such as textiles[32] and architecture,[33] but also critical voices opposing the focus on style and the "tyranny of the object."[34]

Performance versus the "Tyranny of the Object"

African art historians' focus on objects and questions of style was motivated in part by an effort to conform to the discipline's standards in the interest of establishing the relatively new subfield's bona fides within the mother discipline. A key figure in that effort was Roy Sieber. As noted earlier, Sieber was the first art historian awarded a PhD in African art history in 1957. In 1962, after a few years of teaching at the University of Iowa, he moved to the University of Indiana, where he helped to grow the university's newly established African Studies Program. Within a few years, Sieber turned Bloomington, Indiana, into the foremost American institution for African art history that also regularly attracted African graduate students.[35] Sieber understood that the arts in Africa did not form bounded genres like theater, music, or visual arts but had to be studied in terms of their entanglement. But he also realized that in order to grow and become respected, the new field of African art had to have a fair share in the art market. Rather than engaging in debates about new concepts and theories, he insisted on the established skills of close looking and the primacy of the object.[36]

Given the student and civil rights movements that shaped the political climate at American universities in the late 1960s, critique and pushback was to be expected. In 1968 Arnold Rubin, a student of Sieber, organized a seminar at UCLA on "Frontiers in Art History: The African Area."[37] The purpose was to probe and push the critical potential of African art history. One of papers presented at the seminar was "Art as a Verb in Iboland" by Herbert Cole, by then a young assistant professor at the University of California Santa Barbara.[38] Invoking the African American poet LeRoi Jones, a.k.a. Amiri Baraka, Cole reminded his readers that "hunting is not those heads on the wall," that is, art is not an object but an action, a process, and performance.[39] As Cole argued, the disciplinary fixation on artist and object obscures researchers' perceptions of the ground truth that art is less about the object than about the communal experience of creating and living alongside the art.

Cole's critique of the formalist approach was based on his research

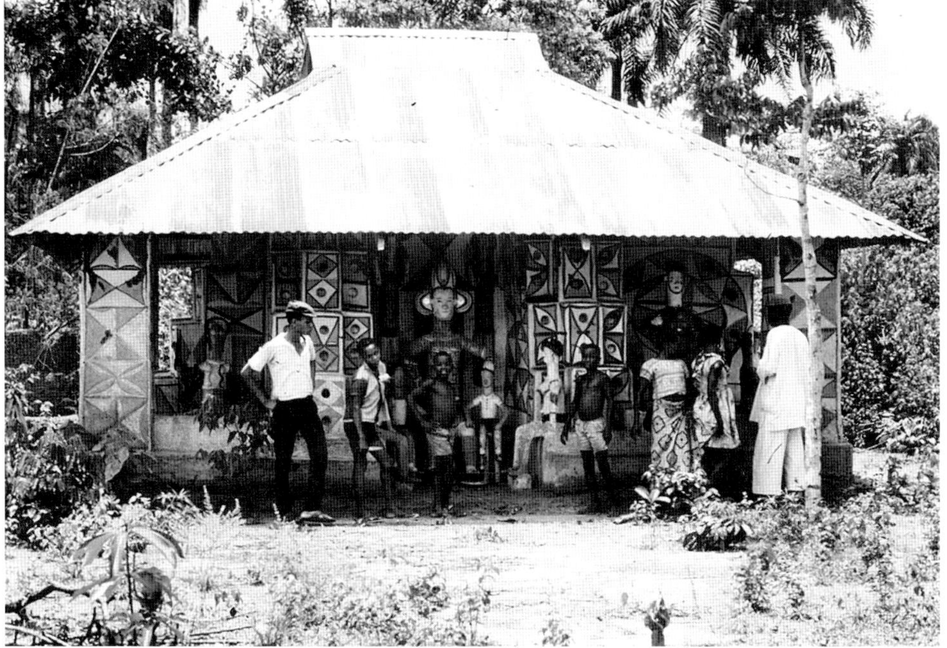

4.9 Mbari shrine to Igbo deity *Ala* in Umugote Orishaeze, Imo State, Nigeria, 1966. Photo: Herbert M. Cole.

among the Igbo in South East Nigeria. Among collectors, Igbo were famous for their masks and altar figures. Archaeologists marveled over the finding of beads and elaborate bronze works testifying to the existence of an ancient civilization dating back to the ninth century, which allowed for speculations regarding possible links to Ife and Benin.[40] Of particular interest to Cole, however, were the *mbari* spirit houses (fig. 4.9). Built in times of crisis, like famine or plague, *mbari* were mud structures containing sculptures of Igbo spirits, deities, animals, people, and other elements of village life, all grouped around the earth goddess *Ala*. According to colonial reports from the 1930s, some *mbari* houses contained up to two hundred figures. Building the houses, creating the figures, and erecting them in the completed *mbari* were communal affairs organized by gender. Including dancing, singing, drumming, painting, and many other activities, the process of *mbari* construction could take over a year to complete. Despite the sustained efforts, the result was ephemeral. The houses were meant to be left to deteriorate only to be built anew elsewhere. In the first half of the twentieth century, this circle of decay and renewal came to an end. Christianization, modernization, and nationalist politics gradually eroded the cultural foundations of *mbari*. By the late

1950s, things had begun to "fall apart."[41] The ultimate culmination of this decline was a bloody civil war fought between 1967 and 1970 over the secession of Igbo (Biafra) land from Nigeria. Hence, in the late 1960s, when Cole started to publish the results of his fieldwork, part of what he described no longer existed. Yet the changed situation on the ground did not weaken the power of the argument:

> That master artists are known and revered in Africa I do not doubt, but that the majority of African art, if the Ibo provide a characteristic sample, stems from communal activity I do not doubt either. . . . The tyranny of the object, our blinded attention to the carved head, causes us to miss a considerable portion of the art/ritual drama. . . . Forms, such as masks and figures, are imbedded in a large, pervasive artistic ambience and thus tend to lack autonomy or isolation. The spirit "face" is part of a costume, the whole "spirit" moves and relates to others, and so forth. Critics of this position will argue against its implication that in Africa art may often be equated with ritual. Yet ritual takes on the character of art when various objects and artistic media are combined and programmed into a stylized activity akin to the dance. Like myth, ritual formally reenacts a story, activity, or drama somehow crucial to the continuity of life in the village or tribe. Like ritual, art lifts such experience from the everyday world, giving shape to those abstract truths which cannot be otherwise expressed.[42]

In 1970, Cole's emphasis on the temporal and performative dimension of Igbo art, or its life process in time and space, resulted in an exhibition at the art galleries of the University of California, Santa Barbara. Titled *African Arts of Transformation*, the exhibition widened the Igbo lessons to other African masking traditions.[43] Slides, music recordings, films of dance performances, and artists at work aimed to capture the sensual, bodily experience of African arts as a kind *Gesamtkunstwerk* (total work of art), as Cole put it in the small but seminal catalog that accompanied the show.

Four years after Cole's *African Arts of Transformation*, Robert Farris Thompson followed up with *African Art in Motion*.[44] After Roy Sieber in 1957, Thompson was the second American art historian to earn a PhD in African art. His dissertation, submitted and defended at Yale in 1965, was based on research among the Yoruba in Nigeria and discussed Yoruba dance and sculpture.[45] Praised as "a true collaboration between collector and scholar,"[46] *African Art in Motion* took place at the University of California, Los Angeles, thus at the very same institution that had shown *Masterpieces from the Sir Henry Wellcome Collection* some ten years earlier.

This time, though, the exhibition was not at the Museum and Laboratories of Arts and Technology but in the new Wight Art Gallery, which had opened up just a year before, in 1973, and that now held and displayed the African art collection of Katherine Coryton White.[47]

The proximity to Cole's show in Santa Barbara was not just spatial but also conceptual. The poem White contributed to the catalog as a leitmotif of the study—"Africa is a verb to me / The vitality that comes from the ground is an awakening"—invoked Cole's reference to Baraka's poem "hunting is not those heads on the wall." Like Cole, Thompson insisted on the performative nature of African art. In the preface to the volume, he noted, "Africa thus introduces a different art history, a history of danced art, defined in the blending of movement and sculpture, textiles and other forms, bringing into being their own inherent goodness and vitality."[48] While he acknowledged that his discussion of "African art" really dealt with only a fraction of the continent, Thompson defended the totalizing signifier by referring to the "fame unity" of West and Central African performance. Three chapters structure his catalog text. The first focuses on the language of motion, which he understands as a knowledge of certain criteria both performers and audiences share. Accordingly, he is eager to explain his findings in a language used by musicians and dancers. The writing thus constantly switches from technical terms like "polymetry" and "antiphony," to jazzy words and phrases like "swing," "looking smart," or "cool." For Thompson, all the different criteria make up a kind of genetic "matrix" that survived the "middle passage" to inform the Afro-American culture of "black America."[49] The second chapter applies these aesthetic principles to the objects White collected in order to identify a series of "icons," which she determined based on motifs in bodily positions and gestures represented in African anthropomorphic sculptures. Arguing that the sculpted body works as a metaphor for social ethics, Thompson discussed six different sculptural "leitmotivs"[50]: standing, sitting, riding, balancing, kneeling, and supporting. The concluding chapter consists of six case studies of masked performances that Thompson argues conjoin "icon" and "act." All were based on Thompson's own fieldwork in Cameroon (Ejagham and Banyang), Liberia (Dan), and Nigeria (Yoruba). In an appendix titled "Texts of Artistic Criticism of the Dance in Tropical Africa," Thompson finally listed local comments on the aesthetics of sculpture and dance he recorded during his field research. To enforce the argument, the layout of the book complemented the snippets of text with stills of video films Thompson had shot in the field. The same method was used in the actual exhibition space. Following the innovative exhibition design of Cole's *African Arts of Transformation*, the curator Gerald Nordland used life-size photomurals, video projections, and textiles to counter and subvert the austerity of the conventional "white cube." The spaces were darkened. Spotlights picked out individual pieces. Some were placed inside vitrines; others rested on pedestals in front of the murals. The whole design aimed to position the body of the performer in relation to the objects of the collection.[51]

* * *

Thompson's colleagues responded to the catalog and exhibition with reticence.[52] The bold attempt to delineate a cultural nucleus or essence of a field that was just about to establish itself was seen as courageous, yet it also prompted anxieties. As we have seen, with the beginning of the Cold War, the research and market for African art shifted from Europe to the US The spatial shift also meant a shift of values. Whereas before World War II, the defining values were artistic and historical questions, now it was about politics and development. With the end of colonialism, the question now was, What is the role of art and the individual artist in the process of postcolonial nation building? Does tradition hinder or foster this process? New funding structures allowed for intensive research in which anthropology profited. Yet the new American interest in Africa also allowed for the rise of the new subdiscipline of African art history. It was a new beginning for the field with the focus now on the individual artist reflecting the political climate at the time. Yet, as energetic as the new research was, the basic framework remained the same. In fact, in many ways the new research strengthened the racial and conceptual disparities inherent in the field. Thus, the new introduction of area studies marginalized historically black colleges in the US whose scholarly output was deemed insufficient to receive government funding.[53] Funding did not reach the new universities in Africa either; the rationale was to do research on, not with, Africa. As a result, the field remained almost exclusively white. The canon remained equally unchanged. The image of African art was still defined by sculptures and masks from West and Central Africa, poured into Europe and North America by way of colonialism. Consequently, the idea of the African artist was first and foremost the idea of an artist working along the forms, media, and styles found in Western museums and collections. Increasingly, however, the difference with the situation on the ground caused tensions. One debate focused on the role of performance and the vision of a different, alternative art history that was more in tune with the racial and political situation in the US I will discuss this argument further in chapter 6, where I will follow up on Thompson's work in relation to the field's expansion from Africa to the Americas. The other issue revolved around the role of the modern or contemporary African artist. How to situate him (hardly ever her) in the field? What to do with the works coming out of art colleges and art departments in postindependence Africa? It is these questions I will tackle in the next chapter.

CHAPTER 5

Acknowledging the Contemporary

NEW FORMS, NEW ACTORS

The terms African Negro Art, African Traditional Art, Primitive Art, Tribal Art, and all such aesthetic clichés which have become the currency of aesthetic evaluation of works of African Art must now be reconsidered in the light of the present African view.

ODINIGWE BENEDICT CHUKWUKADIBIA ENWONWU,
The African View of Art and Some Problems Facing the African Artist Today, 1968

Introduction

In September 1956, the Nigerian painter and sculptor Odinigwe Benedict Chukwukadibia Enwonwu, better known as Ben Enwonwu, attended the First International Congress of Black Writers and Artists in Paris (fig. 5.1).[1] Organized by the founders of the Paris-based journal *Présence Africaine*, the aim of the conference was to announce an African "presence" to the public at large. The title of Enwonwu's talk in Paris was "Problems of the African Artist Today." Published months later in *Présence Africaine*, the piece spoke to the exclusions and "humiliations" Africans suffered in a world dominated by colonial rule. Enwonwu countered this experience by challenging the authority of the non-African critic:

I am not saying that the European authority whoever he may be, is not sometimes kind enough to offer a commission to an African artist, but the fact is that the African artist must be humble enough to apply for or receive from the benevolent European something that belongs to the African. The emotional strife involved under such conditions can be a hindrance to free creative energy being directed into its right channel.

This regrettable factor has thrown the field of African Art open to the monopoly of the powers that be, and sometimes to the Philistines, as well as to fallacious standardisation on foreign basis an art that is best known and understood by the people who create it. While Europeans are the best judges of their own art, and no one argues about this fact, the African does not even have a chance to play an equally important part in judging his art, let alone his justifiable claim if he chooses to make one, that he is the best judge of his own art.[2]

Enwonwu's indignant intervention marks the other side of the debate about the "traditional" or "tribal" African artist discussed in the previous chapter. Initially, anthropologists and African art historians hardly acknowledged the subjectivity of the African artist, and if they did it was generally by way of exclusion, as in the case of William Fagg, who, as we have seen, denied the modern African artist his African identity. And yet it was the "modern"/"contemporary" artist—the two attributes were still used interchangeably—who drove the interest in the "traditional" artist.

The argument rests on the historical simultaneity and close entanglement of colonialism and modernism. Both share the same time span, so

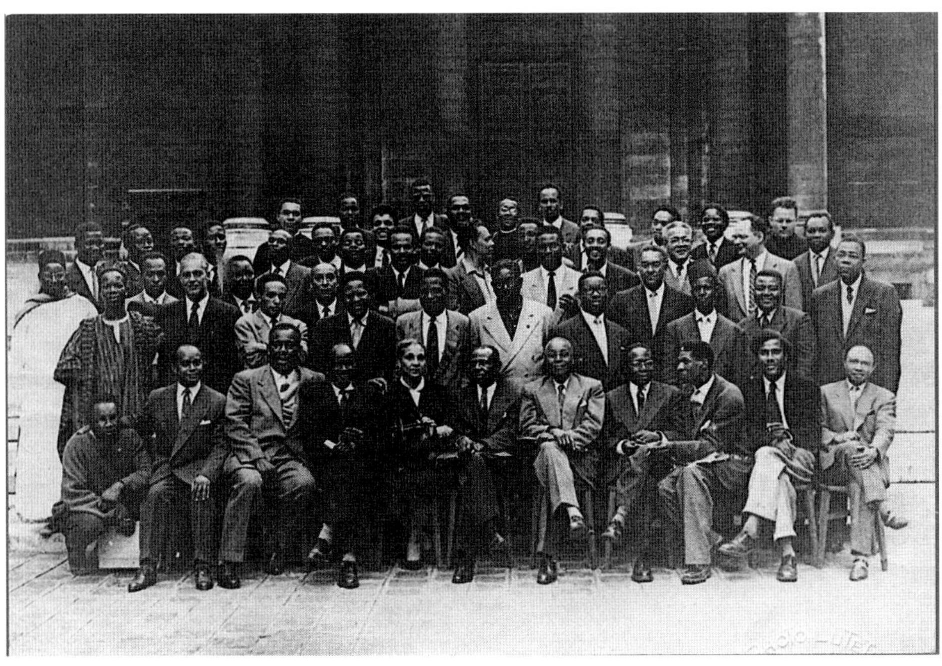

5.1 Participants of the First International Congress of Black Writers and Artists in Paris, 1956. Ben Enwonwu kneeling at the far left. *Présence Africaine*, nos. 8–10 (1956).

mutual influences are to be expected. As we have seen in the previous chapters, the encounter with African sculpture played a crucial role in the emergence of modern art in Europe and the US Critics like Burgess portrayed "The Wild Men of Paris" as explorers who ventured into new territories of artistic representations. Provocation was part of the agenda, but provocation had its colonial limits. At stake were the normative values of modernism, particularly the concept of the institutional autonomy of art.[3] *Autonomous*, in this sense, meant the emancipation of the artistic field from the domains of the market, the judiciary, and the realm of religion; it meant acknowledging that art should be free from political interference and censorship, allowing art to aspire toward its innovative potential that in turn allowed for a programmatic break with the past. It was this wider societal, agnostic configuration of modernism where artists became credited with the role of quasi-societal scouts (avant-garde) who explore society's future-oriented path toward progress.

While the modernist idea of the (institutional) autonomy of art became a contested yet defining feature of the West, in the colonies it faced a racial barrier. The notion that art and artists inhabited a separate terrain independent of government control did not align with the colonial realities of power. To curtail the cultural effects of (European) modernism and maintain the difference between colonizer and colonized, colonial authorities denied the colonized the capacity to make art, declaring it a sole feature of the colonizer.[4] Consequently, colonial policies on the ground precluded the indigenous population from art education and academic art training, deeming such pursuits alien to the interests and capabilities of the colonial subject. Eventually, however, the racial bastion of singularity weakened. A new colonial modernism emerged; from the 1920s onward, new colonial art worlds and infrastructures emerged with Western-style art studios, workshops, art colleges, art education, art galleries, and so forth, that introduced not only new media and techniques but also a disentanglement of genres evidenced in the conceptual and institutional separation of visual arts and performing arts such as music, theater, and dance. Granted, these developments hinged on the differences between various colonial policies. The British policy of indirect rule, for instance, allowed for a decentralized artistic landscape, whereas the direct policy in French colonies fostered a centralized system. Still, the growing visibility of modern art increasingly demanded that the Western art world acknowledge their existence.

To trace and document this visibility, I have organized the chapter into three parts. The first part briefly looks at Aina Onabolu, Kenneth Murray, and Ben Enwonwu, three key figures in the emergence of modern art in colonial Nigeria. Admittedly, the brief discussion of the Nigerian case does justice neither to the complexity of the Nigerian artistic landscape at the time nor to the manifold developments elsewhere on the continent. As noted above, the colonial conditions varied, and analyzing the differences would have exceeded the limits of this chapter. Yet the discussion of the developments in Nigeria should suffice to understand the main fault lines in the emergence of African modernism(s). The second part looks at the wider Pan-African effects of this process. At the center stand the transnational debates over decolonization, which culminated in the *Premier Festival Mondial des Arts Nègres* (back then translated in English as First World Festival of African Negro Arts) 1966, in Dakar, Senegal. The festival was a powerful celebration of blackness as advocated by Senegal's president Léopold Sédar Senghor in his notion of Négritude. The third and final part, therefore, looks at the reception of the new art forms in the Western public, whose members started to acknowledge the new forms of contemporary African artists as part of a new postcolonial reality.

Access and Aesthetics

The notion of "African art" that Euro-American scholars, dealers, and collectors created during the late nineteenth and early twentieth centuries did not include canvas and easel painting. Even though artists in the colonies picked up the technique from the 1900s onward, the results remained hidden to the Western public; they did not appear in the reports of Western travelers and collectors responsible for disseminating knowledge about African art. These artists were part of what Frobenius called "trouser negroes" (see chap. 1). Authors ignored them. Members of the colonial administration, however, did not. For them, the presence of the "modern" artist demanded attention as a sign of resistance.

The story of Aina Onabolu is a case in point.[5] Born in 1882, Onabolu was a portrait painter catering to the small local elite among whom he was known as "Mr. Perspective," reflecting Onabolu's interest in and mastery of European academic art. Since arts education initially had no place in the colonial curriculum, he trained himself by copying from books and magazines and acquiring tools from members of the Nigerian elite, namely J. K. Randle, a medical practitioner and political activist, who acted as Onabolu's patron.[6] Gradually, Onabolu made himself a name and was able to establish a studio, though he continued to rely on income generated from his position as a clerk in the Marine and Customs Department in Lagos.

Around 1915, he began lobbying for art education to be added into the curriculum of schools in Lagos and applied—unsuccessfully—for a teaching position in the colonial administration. Rationalizing that a Western arts education would help his cause, he worked toward getting formal arts training in Europe. In 1920, his paintings finally won him a scholarship, allowing him to further his study of painting at St. John's Wood College in London and the Académie Julien in Paris. Shortly before his departure from Nigeria, on the occasion of an exhibition of his work, he published a small pamphlet titled *A Short Discourse on Art*. The text is an interesting document. Meant to be a primer in art appreciation addressed to the local elite, it testified to political, anticolonial subjectivity.

> The word picture in this catalogue is used to denote the representation of objects as they would appear from an assumed point of sight. This definition would at once suggest to the mind of my reader the idea of perspective and of focus; now perspective being a compound of the Latin words per, through, and specto, to view; i.e. to see through; therefore perspective is the art of drawing several objects as they would appear if traced upon a glass or transparent plane; and here a line may be drawn between perspective and geometry; perspective shows objects as they appear and geometry shows them as they are in reality; and focus means a point of concentration. Now no picture should pass as a good one that is totally void of either focus or perspective. . . . It is not the object of this discourse, however, to do more than to draw the attention of those of my readers who feel their incapability to distinguish a good picture from a bad one and who may want to know the use of it. I cannot here dilate upon the subject, but it must be borne in mind that to be able to realize and appreciate a good picture one must learn something about art, just as it is that to be able to enjoy music one must know something about music.[7]

Clearly, Onabolu judged the quality of art according to the standards of European academicism. But he was also aware of the political implications of translating, appropriating, and mastering the colonizer's standard. He was the first black student at St. John's Wood Art School in London. Shortly after his enrollment, he executed a highly praised oil portrait of Rembrandt. The rationale was clear: if the colonizer defined good and proper art as a particular technique of easel painting, the colonized subject could counter the experience of exclusion by demonstrating mastery of just this technique and in so doing disprove the assertions of racial inferiority on which the colonial structure depended. Accordingly, members of the political and cultural elite like Herbert Macaulay, a journalist and prominent socialite in Lagos, praised Onabolu as a "clear, marvelous

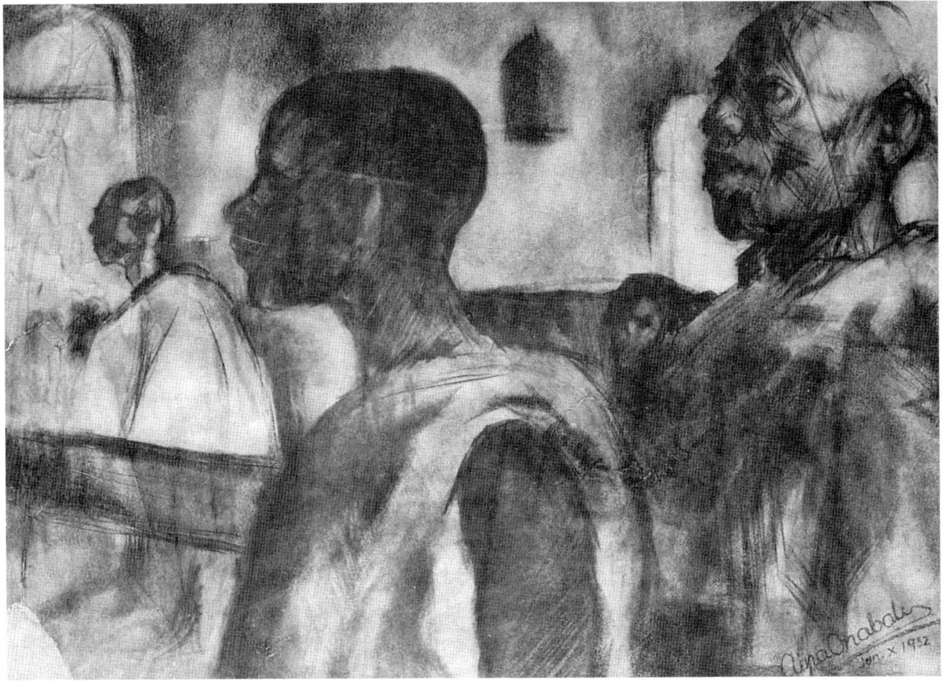

5.2 Aina Onabolu, *Awaiting the Verdict*, 1932. Charcoal on paper, 60 × 75 cm. Courtesy of Yemisi Shyllon Museum of Art, Lagos.

vindication of our struggle—a manifestation of our much-repeated feelings that Africans are capable politically, intellectually and creatively."[8]

Indeed, Onabolu's training in Europe earned him recognition and respectability (fig. 5.2). Upon his return to Nigeria in 1922, he was given permission to teach art in schools. Up until then, education was based on the British Education Code from 1887. The code entailed a rather unspecified "hand and eye" training, introduced at schools in British West Africa in 1908, with a distinct focus on industrial training. Onabolu widened the spectrum and designed a syllabus that was geared toward learning the technical aspects of studio art. Respective courses ranged from Color Theory and Principles of Perspective Drawing to Anatomical Studies and Imaginative Composition.[9] Parallel to his teaching, he also leveraged his position to lobby for more art teachers, a cause supported by Christian missionaries who saw the fine arts as an effective vehicle to fight paganism. Eventually, the Colonial Office in London and the Education Department in Lagos gave in, approving the appointment of a second art teacher, the British artist Kenneth Murray.

Murray was twenty years younger than Onabolu, and unlike Onabolu, he did not come from a personal experience of exclusion. Accordingly, his agenda differed from Onabolu's, eventually causing frictions between the two. Observing the decline of interest in local art forms relative to the celebration of *art nègre* and "primitive art" in Europe and the US, Murray's rationale was to preserve local craftsmanship by countering the negative self-image among large numbers of his students with a respect for their own artistic traditions.[10] In order to receive continuous funding for his curriculum, Murray had to demonstrate its success. To that end, he organized exhibitions, first in Lagos and subsequently in London and Glasgow. The selected works ranged from murals and sculptures in terracotta and wood to watercolor paintings with village scenes and flora and fauna as prominent subject matters. According to Murray, his students' work testified to the need to support and appreciate modern African art. As he saw it, art allowed for the production of self-confident colonial subjects who were able to creatively digest the rapid changes colonialism triggered.[11]

Ben Enwonwu was Murray's star student. After graduation he was employed as an art teacher at various government schools in Southern Nigeria. The presentation of his works at the exhibitions Murray organized soon attracted attention and earned him a scholarship to England, where he studied fine arts at Goldsmith College and the Slade School in London. The time in England from 1944 to 1949 propelled his career and allowed him to have a full professional art practice parallel to his studies. The British cultural establishment embraced him and provided opportunities to participate in prominent exhibitions abroad. Yet the international exposure also made him more political. He cofounded the African writers and artists club and participated in debates about decolonization and Négritude. Senghor's ideas about a Pan-African aesthetic appealed to him. Thus, he conceived his own art practice as a statement that aimed to convey African ideas and aesthetics. In view of his international success, the Nigerian government made him an official "arts advisor" (fig. 5.3). Besides producing portraits for the Nigerian elite and foreign dignitaries, such as Queen Elizabeth, he was tasked with creating a new visual language for the arts that would reflect the country's upcoming new status as a sovereign, independent nation-state. The task included public artworks such as the life-size bronze sculpture named *Anyanwu*, "the sun," which Enwonwu created for Lagos's new National Museum in 1957 (fig. 5.4). Denoting the dawn of independence and mounted at the museum entrance, it featured Enwonwu's signature style: a slim, elongated female captured in a poetic bend, recalling Senghor's emphasis on rhythm and dance as prime features of African artistic expression.

Remaining faithful to this aesthetic position, Enwonwu never warmed

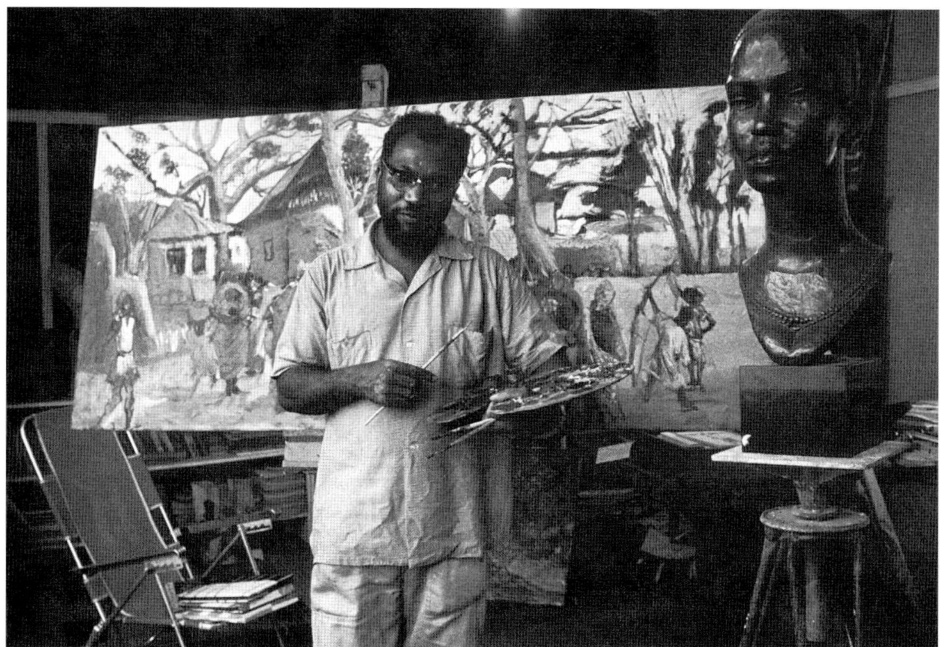

5.3 Ben Enwonwu in his art studio in Ikoyi, Lagos, 1959. Photo: Eliot Elisofon. © Eliot Elisofon Photographic Archive, National Museum of African Art, Smithsonian Institution.

up to the allures of abstraction as some of the younger, academically trained artists did after independence. In fact, he warned of the "jungle of abstract art" and considered it an aberration for the development of modern Nigerian art.[12]

I will come back to Enwonwu in chapter 9 when I discuss the recent surge of studies on African modernism. For now, let me turn to the transnational debates over decolonization and the aesthetics of blackness in which Enwonwu actively participated.

Decolonization and the New Presence of Blackness

Enwonwu's status as a quasi-state artist positioned him at the intersection between the old and the new, the tribal heritage and the modern nation. The question of the relationship between the two had already been the subject of discussion and discord at the 1956 First International Congress of Black Writers and Artists in Paris. Those who spoke out did so poetically and powerfully. Senghor insisted on the importance of "the spirit of African negro culture." As he saw it, this "spirit" had to be understood as defined by "rhythm, the architecture of the being, the internal

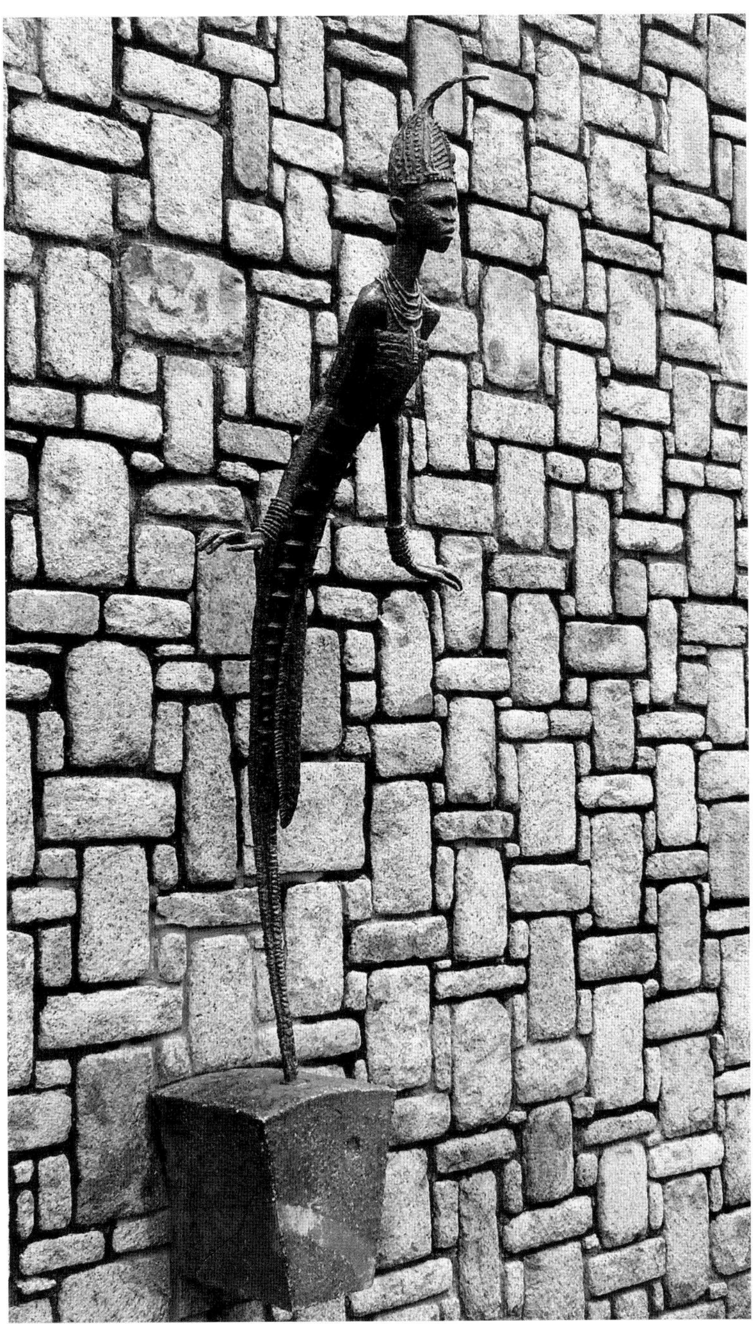

5.4 Ben Enwonwu, *Anyanwu*, installed 1957 at the façade of the National Museum of Nigeria, Lagos. Bronze, height 210 cm. Photo: the author. Courtesy of The Ben Enwonwu Foundation.

dynamism that gives him form, the system of waves that he emits in relation to Others, the pure expression of vital force."[13] Frantz Fanon, the physician and psychiatrist from Martinique and author of *Peau noire, masques blancs* (*Black Skin, White Masks*) and *Les damnés de la terre* (*The Wretched of the Earth*),[14] pushed back, arguing that Senghor's invocation of a Pan-African spiritual heritage was not compatible with decolonization. For Fanon, it only exemplified the fact that the colonial subject had fully internalized the logic of oppression and inferiorization:

> Because the inferiorized rediscovers a style that had once been devalorized, what he does is in fact to cultivate culture. . . . The oppressed goes into ecstasies over each rediscovery. The wonder is permanent. Having formerly emigrated from his culture, the native today explores it with ardor. It is a continual honeymoon. Formerly inferiorized, he is now in a state of grace.[15]

The Paris-based African American novelist Richard Wright dismissed both positions. Invoking Du Bois's notion of "double consciousness," he began by stating: "I am black. I am a man of the West."[16] Wright warned his listeners that unlike many of his predecessors, he would not engage in a "vehement and moral denunciation of Europe."[17] As a child of both slavery and the West, he regarded both Fanon's psychology of blackness and Senghor's rediscoveries of buried pasts as dead ends. The only way forward was to continue the European project of secularization and enlightenment. Only by embracing "science and industrialization" would it be possible to reach what he saw as the goal, intellectual freedom:

> The problem is freedom. How can Asians and Africans be free of their stultifying traditions and customs and become industrialized, and powerful, if you like, like the West? . . . The problem is freedom from a dead past and freedom to build a rational future. How much are we willing to risk for freedom? I say, let us risk everything. Freedom begets freedom.[18]

Wright's intervention was rejected by both Fanon and Senghor. Yet while Fanon came to the conclusion that resistance to colonialism had to follow a national agenda, Senghor favored a culturalist Pan-African option as the ultimately superior path to a decolonial future.

Given these grave philosophical differences, the only common denominator on which participants could agree was to widen the forum and begin an open debate about the future. The Martinique poet Aimé

Césaire envisioned a "reconciliation" of these divisions by way of a "synthesis" that transcends both old and new:

> In the culture that is yet to be born, there will be without any doubt both old and new. Which new elements? Which old? Here alone our ignorance begins. And in truth it is not for the individual to reply. . . . Today we are in a cultural chaos. Our part is to say: "Free the demiurge that alone can organize this chaos into a new synthesis, a synthesis that will deserve the name of culture, a synthesis that will be a reconciliation and an overstepping of both old and new." We are here to ask, nay to demand: "Let the people speak! Let the black people take their place upon the great stage of history."[19]

Ten years later, Césaire's call came to fruition at the *Premier Festival Mondial des Arts Nègres* (FESMAN) in Dakar, Senegal. The idea of organizing such a festival was essentially the brainchild of Léopold Senghor and his ally, Alioune Diop, founder of *Présence Africaine*. It had first arisen in 1959 at the second International Congress of Black Writers and Artists in Rome.[20] As such, the festival was meant to showcase the results of Senghor's national agenda to promote and teach Négritude and claim leadership in matters of cultural advancement. It was only in 1963, though, three years after Senghor had become president of Senegal, that he formally announced the decision to host the festival. Even then, the festival was delayed again two times, the first in 1964, and the second in 1965.

The reasons for the delay were partly political, partly organizational. The first five years of Senghor's tenure as president of Senegal were messy. Senghor's endeavor to promote a national identity and collective aesthetic informed by the lofty ideas of Négritude was met with strikes, riots, and political opposition. The idealization of blackness and the evocation of unity were critiqued as fabrications of a small political elite to cover up the lack of real material and political progress. In addition to the political unrest, Dakar lacked the infrastructure to host an event on the proposed scale. Funding had to be secured to build and finance a new airport, exhibition spaces, communication networks, and other improvements necessary to host the thousands of anticipated guests and participants. The festival finally occurred from April 1 to 24 in 1966. Over the course of three and a half weeks, more than 2,500 artists, musicians, writers, filmmakers, scholars, and politicians from three continents gathered in Dakar.[21]

In accordance with Senghor's holistic understanding of Négritude, the festival ranged from theater, literature, and poetry to dance, music, and the visual arts. The exhibitions and performances showcasing this celebration of blackness occurred at various places throughout the city. The high-profile events, though, were held at three separate venues: the newly built Theatre National Daniel Sorano in the administrative center of the city; the Palais de justice, a modernist structure, equally in the city center; and the new Musée dynamique, farther north, at the waterfront. Built by French architects in modernist, clear forms that cited the ancient Greek structure of a peristyle, the Musée dynamique spoke to Senghor's appreciation of what he called "classical" African art.[22] Senghor admired Frobenius and his passionate insistence on the importance of African cultural history.[23] Accordingly, he called the museums and the close to six hundred masks and figures on display "the real heart of the festival." The majority of objects stemmed from the collection of the French Institute of Black Africa, supplemented with works from public and private collections in Europe and the US. A group of seven African and European curators were in charge of the selection, led by Cameroonian Jesuit priest Engelbert Mveng and Swiss museologist Jean Gabus, the latter of whom was also responsible for the exhibition design. With its high ceilings and open rectangular hall, the structure conveyed an airy modernist flair.[24] The exhibition focused primarily on form: the objects were assembled over two floors in two parallel rows of glass cases, each with its own lighting system. The bigger pieces were presented either on plinths or hung on picture rails. The wall facing the entrance displayed a huge map of Africa, while the other wall held five large (2.5×5 m) black-and-white close-up shots, depicting the heads of some figures in the show (figs. 5.5, 5.6).[25]

Contemporary art, too, had a separate place. As noted above, the terms *contemporary* and *modern* were still used interchangeably. Both entailed allusions to a new political and aesthetic postcolonial reality informed by a sense of newness, freedom, and experimentation. Examples of this freedom were on display around the expansive atrium of the new Palais de justice. Curated by Iba N'Diaye and titled *Tendances et confrontations* (Tendencies and Confrontations), the exhibition comprised eight hundred works by two hundred artists from some twenty-five nations and three continents: Africa, Europe, and the Americas. The selection of artists and the presentation of their works were left to the participating countries to determine. Each country had a defined space marked by movable partition walls.[26] Even though Senghor praised the show as a demonstration of the unbroken vitality and creativity of black culture, the local newspapers did not cover the exhibition, and a catalog, though produced, was not distributed. There were multiple reasons for this neglect. Part of it had to do with the venue. For one, the venue lacked the

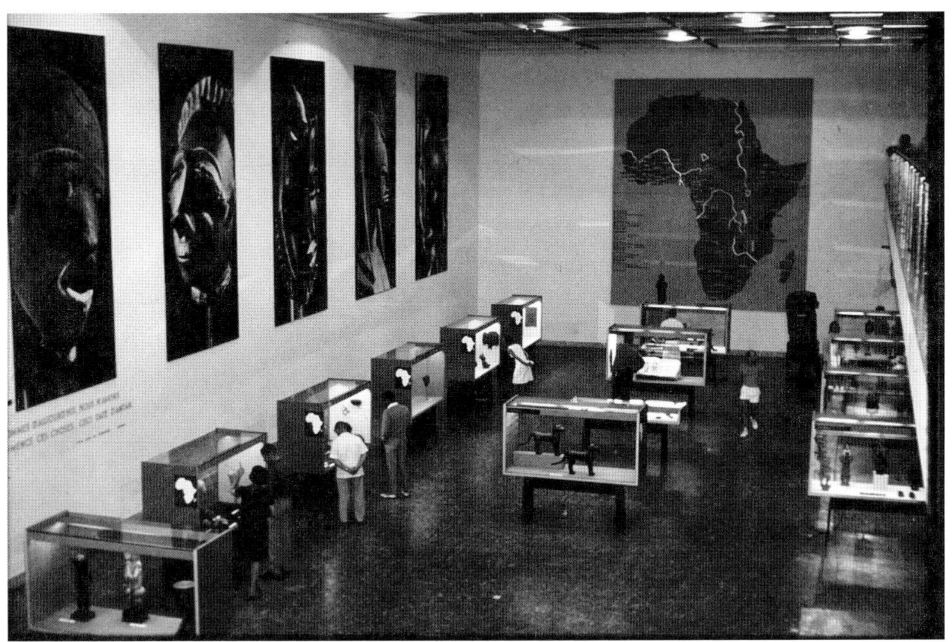

5.5 Installation view, *L'art nègre*, Musée Dynamique, Dakar, 1966. Photo: Fonds Roland Kaehr, PANAFEST. © Archives Musée du Quai Branly—Jacques Chirac, Fonds Panafest Archives (35AP).

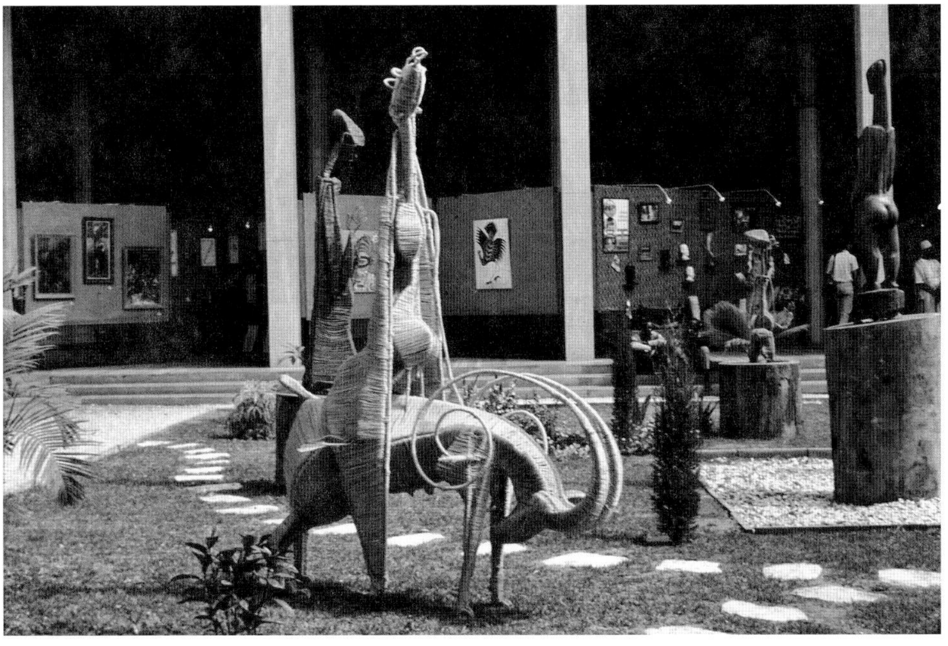

5.6 Christian Lattier, *Le bélier* (The Ram), installation view of *Tendances et confrontations*, Dakar, 1966. Lattier's rope-and-steel sculpture won the grand prize for visual arts at FESMAN. Photo: Roland Kaehr, PANAFEST. © Archives Musée du Quai Branly—Jacques Chirac, Fonds Panafest Archives (35AP).

wide-open spaces of the Musée dynamique and made it difficult to show the works in a visually attractive way. For another, with the artwork on display marked for sale, the show itself was rather like a fair. In fact, it was initially announced as a "salon" and only later changed into an "exhibition." Furthermore, there was the issue of the heterogeneity of the works on display. As the curator, Iba N'Diaye, later wrote,

> The prudent title given to this presentation of paintings and sculptures, "art contemporain, tendances et confrontations," corrected the overly ambitious intention declared by the organizers of the festival: to make it reflect "the unity and the originality of today's black world." In reality, Dakar's exhibition was characterized by a great heterogeneity whose source was regretfully not to be found in the originality of the various artistic currents of contemporary Africa.[27]

Last but not least, there was the participation of artists from North and Northeast Africa. The curatorial decision violated Senghor's preferred showcasing of "black" sub-Saharan Africa and the deviation from the official framing of the festival may have been a reason why *Tendances et confrontations*, unlike the main *L'art nègre* exhibition in the Musée dynamique, did not yield its own international colloquium and hence did not attract more public attention.

Funded by UNESCO and titled "Function and Significance of African Negro Art in the Life of the People and for the People," the colloquium took place from March 30 to April 8, 1966, at the beginning of the festival (fig. 5.7). Three main themes structured the program: "African Tradition," "The Meeting of Negro Art with the West," and "The Current Situation: The Problems of Modern African Art." The expertise of the participants—about half of whom came from Europe and the US—ranged from dance and theater to literature and film to the visual arts. As expected, there were diverse responses to the conference theme. In his opening contribution, Engelbert Mveng ended his welcoming remarks as follows:

> The future growth and renewal of African art ought to draw its inspiration from the function and significance of that art in the life of people. It should be the work of the African peoples and the responsibility for it should fall to the African elite and the governments of our countries.[28]

In his contribution, William Fagg challenged Mveng and the other organizers of the festival by asking whose lives they actually meant when

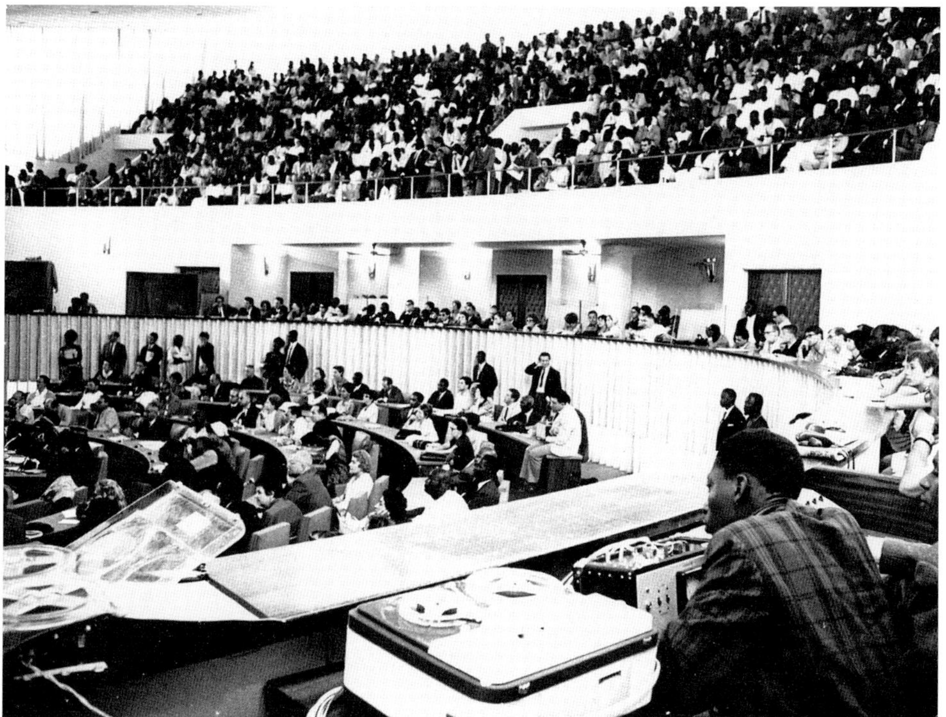

5.7 Scientific colloquium, *Festival mondial des arts nègres*, Dakar 1966. Photo: Roland Kaehr, PANAFEST. © Archives Musée du Quai Branly—Jacques Chirac, Fonds Panafest Archives (35AP).

they referred to "art in the life of people."[29] As he maintained, the encroachment of colonial modernity had created a growing rift between two, largely incompatible lifeworlds—that of the elite and that of the majority—which had implications for the meaning and function of art in society. In fact, the festival was a highly elitist event. Tellingly, to ensure that foreign guests were appropriately impressed by Dakar and Senegalese culture, the government ordered the military to clear the streets of beggars, the sick, and homeless people. Poor neighborhoods were cordoned off, and the university was closed to mute possible sources of protest.[30]

For Enwonwu, who led the Nigerian delegation, such concerns were a distraction. The real issue at stake concerned who exercised control over value and meaning. In a barely concealed reference to Fagg and the other Western scholars participating in the conference, Enwonwu restated the position he had articulated a decade before in Paris; namely, that Africans must claim authority over African art:

The terms African Negro Art, African Traditional Art, Primitive Art, Tribal Art, and all such aesthetic clichés which have become the currency of aesthetic evaluation of works of African Art must now be reconsidered in the light of the present African view. These clichés, together with the influences they exert on the critical mind, should now be regarded as part and parcel of the evangelical, educational, social, economic, and even the political chapters of the Colonial past. Art in present-day Africa is seeking a new role, and this role that must be given to it by Africans themselves, will determine the form that it should take as the mirror of the aspirations of Independent African peoples.[31]

As it happened, Enwonwu's critique coincided with an award William Fagg, one of the prime targets of Enwonwu's critique, received for his contributions to the understanding of African art. The inconsistency echoed the disconnect between political visions and political realities. Cold War interests and power plays informed the political dynamics in the postindependence political landscape. In 1967, shortly after Enwonwu returned to Nigeria, simmering ethnic tensions and the issue of control over the country's rich oil resources in the Niger Delta had led to a bloody three-year civil war in which the Southeast (unsuccessfully) attempted to secede and become independent as "Biafra." In 1966, the Ghanaian military—allegedly with the help of the CIA office in Accra—deposed the country's first president Kwame Nkrumah during his visit to North Vietnam and China. A year earlier, in the Republic of Congo, Mobutu Sese Seko had gained control over what he renamed the Democratic Republic of the Congo, thus filling the political vacuum that resulted from the assassination of Congo's first president, Patrice Lumumba, in 1961 by Belgian police officers, also with CIA assistance. In 1966, Uganda saw a constitutional crisis and power struggle between the country's president, Milton Obote, and the ruler of the powerful Buganda kingdom. The crisis resulted in a military coup and eight years of bloody dictatorship under General Idi Amin. Even in Senegal, where Senghor managed to remain in power until the 1980s, the political situation was tense: students were on strike and protesting government funding cuts. In short, the image presented during the festival did not match the reality. Nonetheless, the festival left a mark in the academy.

The Arrival in the Academy

Among the American visitors who attended the Dakar festival was John Povey, a professor of African literature who taught at the University of

California at Los Angeles. Upon his return from the Dakar festival, Povey wrote an extensive review of the event in the *Journal of the New African Literature and the Arts.*[32] While critiquing the basic conservativism of the festival, he acknowledged that it had revealed "the enormous potential" of contemporary art in Africa:

> A chance was missed to do something remarkable under the sun. What was done, however, at least gave more than a hint of the enormous potential of the developing arts of modern Africa—as the exposed peak of an iceberg implies its huge submarine bulk. There was far more to this festival than those colored pages of *Life* magazine suggested. Those of us who did not go seeking the local color and the confirmation of an expected prejudice saw, through all the limitations imposed by governmental caution, that a new African generation of artists was already present and articulate. That was the exciting thing about Dakar.[33]

In an effort to boost this "new African generation of artists," Povey teamed up with the former diplomat and lawyer Paul Proehl to launch the journal *African Arts.* With the inaugural 1967 issue, *African Arts* quickly became the flagship publication for the new academic field of African art studies, a legitimization of its existence, so to speak. Both Povey and Proehl conceived the new publication not as a scholarly journal but rather as a "magazine" covering "the graphic, plastic, performing, and literary arts of Africa, traditional and contemporary" (fig. 5.8).[34]

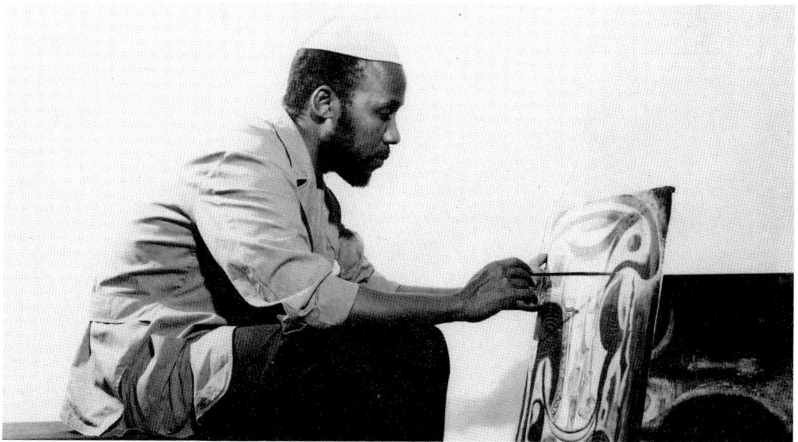

5.8 Ibrahim El-Salahi at his studio in Khartoum, ca. 1965. "Portfolio and Drawings," *African Arts* 1, no. 1 (1967). UCLA James S. Coleman African Studies Center. Reprinted courtesy of The MIT Press.

A notably large number of the contributors were nonacademics whose expertise was based on their work as critics, collectors, or curators. The composition echoed the fact that those who had pushed for the acknowledgment of modern art in Africa were not primarily scholars but European critics and culture brokers who lived and worked on the continent as expatriates, such as English artist and art teacher Frank McEwen.

McEwen had studied art and art history in Paris in the mid-1920s and was thus aware of the *art nègre* vogue. However, his own interest only developed in the mid-1950s when he was appointed head of the new Rhodes National Gallery in Harare, Zimbabwe, then still Salisbury, Northern Rhodesia. Like other white European critics of colonialism, McEwan felt complicit. As he saw it, colonialism had stultified and quenched the vitality and creativity of African artists. For McEwen, it was therefore necessary to "revitalize" African art by establishing independent art workshops and providing African artists with opportunities to show and sell their work both national and internationally.[35] An important event was the 1962 First International Congress of African Culture (ICAC) held at the National Gallery in Salisbury. Organized by McEwen, the congress brought together members of the newly emerging transcontinental African and Euro-American art world, among them Alfred Barr from New York, William Fagg from London, and Jean Laude from Paris, as well as contemporary African artists, including Ben Enwonwu from Lagos, Thomas Mukarobgwa, a "graduate" of McEwen's gallery workshop, and Malangatana Ngwenya from Maputo (fig. 5.9) The lectures and presentations by the participants took place within the gallery where McEwen had organized a massive exhibition that presented works of "tribal" African art together with works of both modern/contemporary African artists and European artists whose work was informed and inspired by their encounter with African sculpture.[36]

Though absent from the congress, a key figure in its planning process was the German Ulli Beier.[37] Born in 1922 in Germany, Beier had arrived in Nigeria in 1950 for what was supposed to be a short-term teaching position as an English lecturer at the University of Ibadan. Instead, the move proved to be the beginning of a long and highly influential career as a writer, critic, curator, and editor across the arts. At Ibadan, Beier switched from the English to the extramural department, which allowed him to travel widely and learn about Yoruba art, theater, and literature. It also enabled him to attend the First International Congress of Black Writers and Artists in 1956 in Paris, where he encountered Léopold Senghor, Frantz Fanon, Ben Enwonwu, Alioune Diop, Édouard Glissant, Richard Wright, and others. The Paris experience was transformative.[38] Back in Ibadan, he founded the literary journal *Black Orpheus*—named after a foreword

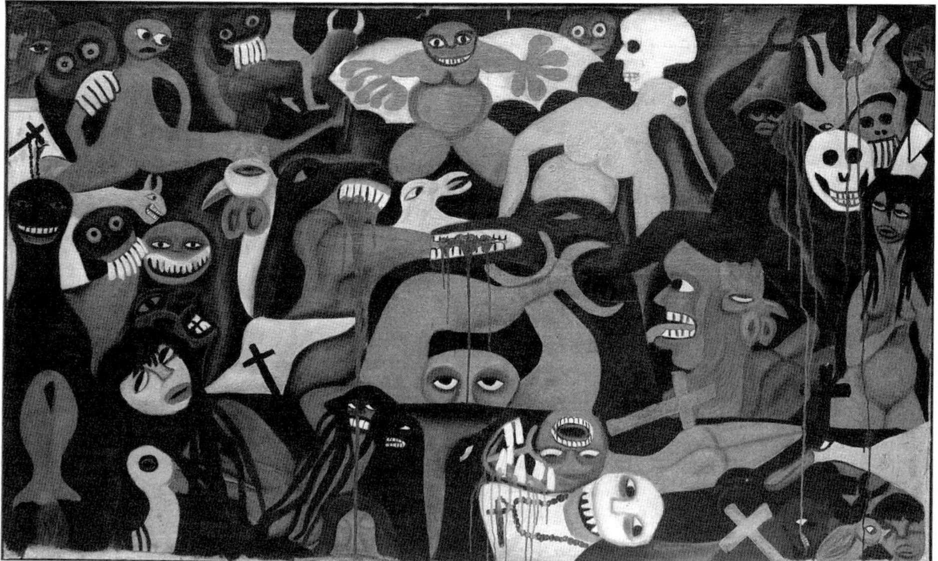

5.9 Malangatana Ngwenya, *Untitled*, 1961. Oil on canvas, 90 × 152 cm. The dense and disturbing presentation of grinning, monster-like creatures in the midst of dripping blood, crosses, and skulls speaks to the experience of violence and oppression under Portuguese colonial rule. Courtesy of Iwalewa Haus, Universität Bayreuth.

the French philosopher Jean-Paul Sartre wrote for an anthology of young African poetry edited by Léopold Senghor in 1948—that soon became the foremost African literary periodical in English. With writers and artists such as Chinua Achebe, Wole Soyinka, and Malangatana Ngwenya, the contributions ranged from poetry, art, and fiction to literary criticism and commentary. In 1961, four years after launching *Black Orpheus*, Beier cofounded the artists and writers club *Mbari*. Named after the Igbo spirit houses in South East Nigeria, *Mbari* functioned as a platform for readings, lectures, performances, and artistic exchanges about the question of what it meant to be "modern" in Nigeria. *Mbari* in Ibadan led to *Mbari Mbayo* in Osogbo, where Beier and his wife, the Austrian artist Susanne Wenger, had moved in 1958. Unlike Ibadan, Osogbo was in Nigeria's cultural hinterland. It had no university and no active literary life, but it was home to many artisans, a sizable middle class, and a lively religious and theater scene. It was here that Beier and Wenger teamed up with the local composer, playwright, and bar owner Duro Ladipo to establish an arts center and workshop (figs. 5.10, 5.11).[39]

The Osogbo workshops followed the interest in the seemingly "untrained, pure and uncorrupted eye" that informed the various European initiatives from the 1940s to the 1960s in an effort to acknowledge the

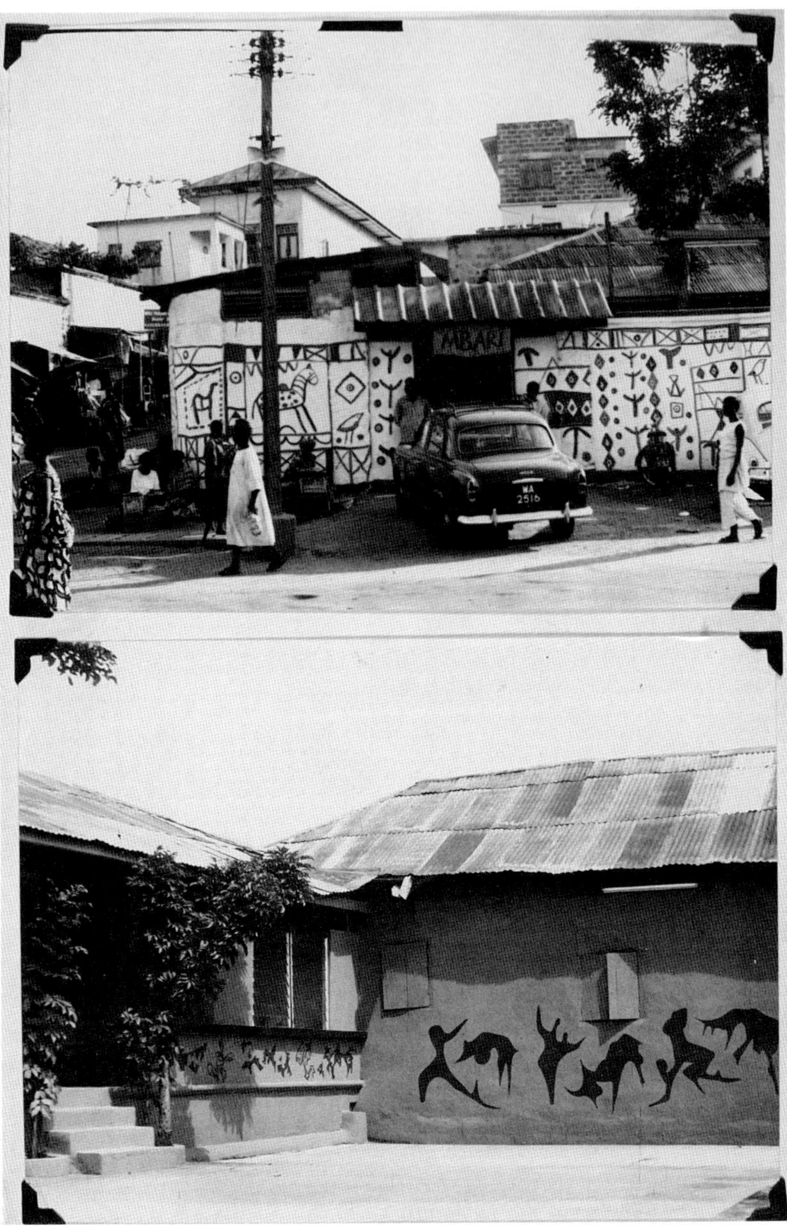

5.10 Mbari Artists and Writers Club, Ibadan, early 1960s. © Harry Ransom Center, The University of Texas at Austin.

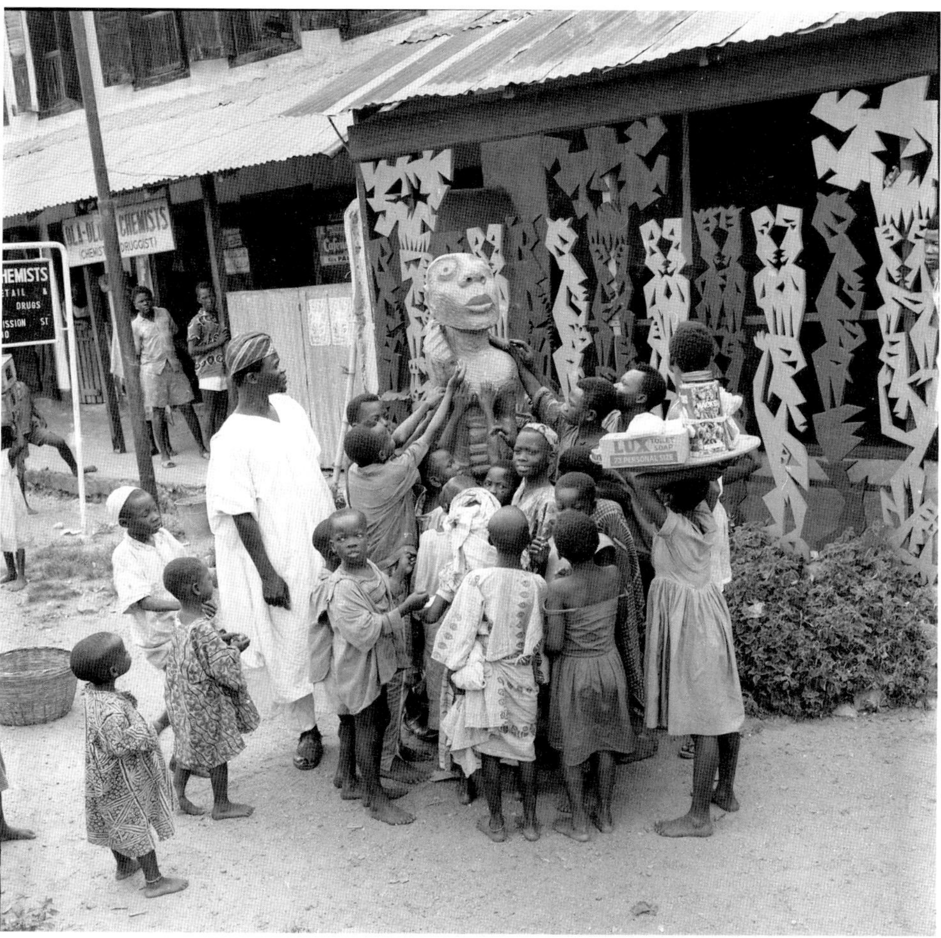

5.11 Ghanaian artist Vincent Kofi next to his sculpture *Drummer* in front of Mbari Mbayo in Osogbo, Nigeria. Cutouts from Susanne Wenger. Ca. 1963. Courtesy of Iwalewa Haus, Universität Bayreuth.

colonial debt and revitalize the supposed innate creative spirit of the African male (women artists did not figure into this idea). The methods employed to accomplish this goal ranged from Frank McEwen's nurturing encouragement of Shona sculpture in Rhodesia/Zimbabwe as a "return to origins"[40] to Beier and Wenger's iconoclastic efforts to combat colonial ideas of authenticity and uncontaminated cultural purity by celebrating the dynamics of cross-cultural contact as a sort of cultural hybridity avant la lettre.[41] A belief in art's responsibility to leave the walls of the museum, to go out into the public realm, and to become integrated into everyday life united the divergent viewpoints and served as a driving force. The rationale was no longer to (re)educate students by making them respect and value local cultures and local subject matters, that is, old images. In the spirit of independence and throwing off the yoke of colonialism, the motto was to create "new images" for a "changing society."[42]

Beier left Nigeria in 1966 shortly before the outbreak of the civil war between Nigeria and the southeastern part of the country attempting to secede as "Biafra." Two years later he published *Contemporary Art in Africa*, the first serious study of the new artistic landscape. There were precursors. One of the first appeared in the late 1950s, when the German journalist Rolf Italiaander wrote about *Neue Kunst in Afrika* (New Art in Africa) and Janheinz Jahn discussed "Neo-African" cultural expressions in the realm of Africa and the Americas.[43] Around the same time, the Harmon Foundation, a New York based nonprofit organization for the promotion of black artists, started to collect modern/contemporary African art that resulted in the 1961 exhibition *Art from Africa of Our Time*. Five years later, the foundation did a survey of contemporary, Neo-African artists at the occasion of FESMAN in Dakar.[44] However, most of these studies lacked analysis and context. As the title of Beier's book indicated, he rejected the notion that there is any specific "African" style of contemporary art. He did not believe in the various versions of a Pan-African ontological essence, nor did he share the pessimistic diagnosis of people such as William Fagg, for whom African art was on the verge of death. In contrast, Beier saw a positive future:

> A more optimistic picture of the Afro-European culture contact is emerging today. It is no longer possible to look at African art and see nothing but a continuous and rapid process of disintegration. We can now see that Africa has responded to the social and political upheavals that have taken place all over the continent. The African artist has refused to be fossilised. New types of artists give expression to new ideas, work for different clients, fulfill new functions. Accepting the challenge of Europe, the African artist does not hesitate to adopt new materials, be inspired by foreign art, look for a different role in society. New forms, new styles, and new personalities are emerging everywhere and this contemporary African art is rapidly becoming as rich and varied as were the more rigid artistic conventions of several generations ago.[45]

The signifier "contemporary" here, first and foremost, expressed new subjectivities;[46] the term had not yet acquired the reflexive, post-*histoire* implications it would assume in the 1990s. Rather it marked an

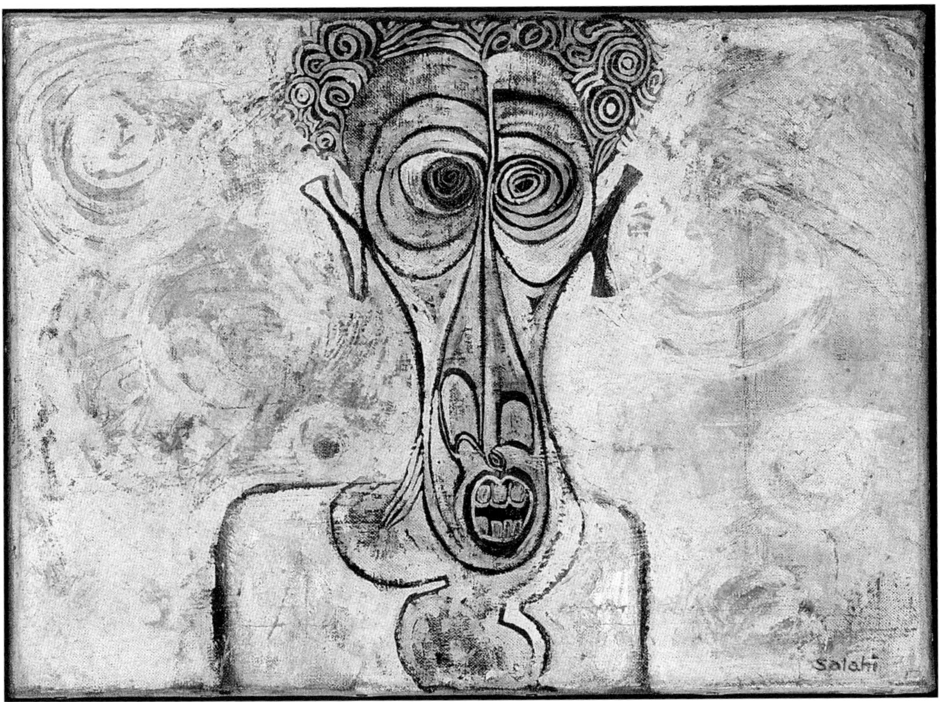

5.12 Ibrahim El-Salahi, *Self-Portrait of Suffering*, 1961. Oil on canvas, 30.5 × 40.5 cm. Painted after El-Salahi's return from England, the swirling lines are informed by his interest in Arabic calligraphy and local landscapes. Collection Iwalewa Haus, Universität Bayreuth. © 2021 Artists Rights Society (ARS), NY / DACS, London.

undetermined, transitional, open, "Neo-African" phase.[47] What Beier presented in his book *Contemporary Art in Africa* was a series of personal encounters with artists who represented the different facets of this Neo-African, contemporary moment. The spectrum he presented to the reader ranged from Uche Okeke in Nigeria, Vincent Kofi in Ghana, and Malangatana Ngwenya in Mozambique to Skunder Boghossian and Ibrahim El-Salahi in Sudan (fig. 5.12). Given all these new forms and actors, Beier questioned the usefulness of the category "African" and stressed the heterogeneity of the contemporary landscape:

I do not feel that one can theorize as yet about Neo-African art. The very variety and diversity of this art is one of its most exciting features. We can speak of modern art *in* [italics in original] Africa, but so far, these artists are too individualistic to be pigeon-holed as "African artists." Nor does it matter how we label them. Artists from different parts of Africa and from differing backgrounds are widening our vision and enriching our aesthetic experience. They are gaining recognition from critics in all quarters of the globe, and are beginning to make their impact felt in the international world of art.[48]

Five years later, Beier's assessment was shared by Marshall Mount's *African Art: The Years Since 1920*:

> The future of African painting and sculpture appears bright. The new art is still not well known outside the continent, but the situation is beginning to change. . . . Given the proper support, there is no reason why the talent and ideas evidenced by many of Africa's young artists should not continue to develop freely using elements from their own and other arts to describe the exciting and unique experience of life in modern Africa.[49]

Unlike Beier, who was very much writing as an active participant in the developments he discussed, Mount's perspective was that of a detached, (seemingly) neutral observer. His observations were based on research in the early 1960s, funded by the American Rockefeller Foundation. Leaving aside North and Lusophone Africa, Mount gave brief descriptions of the artists and art schools that had emerged before and after independence. Critical judgments were eschewed in favor of factual information. The intention was to provide a roadmap that allowed the reader to navigate the new landscape of contemporary art in Africa. Accordingly, the appendix listed eighty-seven names of artists and European patrons as a kind of "Who's Who" of modern African art.

*   *   *

As I have argued in this chapter, it was the appearance and growing visibility of the modern artist that drove the interest in the traditional African artist, discussed in the previous chapter. Colonialism coupled with modernism, resulting in a transnational colonial modernism that allowed for the emergence of a (post)colonial art world full of Western-style artist's studios, exhibitions, art education, art critics, journals, galleries, museums, and so forth. Eventually, a transnational public sphere emerged that found its culmination in 1966 at the Pan-African arts festival in Dakar. In the West, the event led to the founding of the journal *African Arts* one year later. Those who dominated the venture and wrote about modern African art and artists were critics and curators rather than university scholars. The excitement and euphoria surrounding the hopeful future of "Neo-African art" was palpable, and yet the new era of independence did not trigger lasting interest in the exploration and research of new African art worlds that had emerged with the dawn of colonialism. A decade after its inception, articles in the field's new flagship journal, *African Arts*, narrowed its scope to the coverage of mostly traditional arts—thus reverting to the field's focus before the journal had started. The art market in so-called classical African art prevailed. Surely, there continued to be contemporary art exhibitions here and there, but the momentum of the late 1960s did not last. Instead, the field got caught up in another political movement: the Civil Rights and Black Power movements' fights against racism as it had evolved from the aftermath of slavery in the US. As black students protested and demanded change on American university campuses, the field's focus shifted to the study of Africa in the Americas rather than the "new images" (Ulli Beier) produced by artists in the newly independent African countries. It is this expansion, from Africa to the Americas, that I will turn to next. For this, we need to come back to Melville Herskovits, Robert Farris Thompson, and the 1966 festival in Dakar, this time, however, from a different perspective.

Extending the Horizon

AFRICA IN THE AMERICAS

Say It Loud—I'm Black and I'm Proud!

JAMES BROWN, "Say It Loud," 1968

Introduction

On April 7, 1966, a Pan American charter flight left New York's Kennedy airport for Senegal. On board were 180 mostly African American passengers en route to Dakar, Senegal, to attend the First World Festival of Negro Arts as the English translation of the *Premier Festival Mondial des Arts Nègres* read at the time.[1] Both their tickets and accommodations in Dakar had been paid for by the American Society of African Culture (AMSAC). AMSAC's goal was to enable African Americans to reconnect with their African heritage. The spectrum of professions represented ranged from artists and educators to medical doctors and social workers. For many of them, it was their first visit to the African continent. Accordingly, the level of excitement was high.

Among the African American visitors was a filmmaker, William Greaves, who had arrived earlier with a film crew to shoot a documentary of the festival.[2] With shots of Dakar fishermen on the shores of the Atlantic and Langston Hughes walking along the beach, the film opens to Greaves's sonorous voice reciting Hughes's iconic poem "The Negro Speaks of Rivers" before shifting focus to Ife bronze and Nok terra cotta works of "classical" African art, seen on display in the Musée dynamique. Against the background of trombones in Duke Ellington's jazz orchestra, Greaves's voice-over asks: "Who am I? Look upon me. Look upon my images. Listen to my sounds. These are the gates through which you must pass if you are to know me" (fig. 6.1).

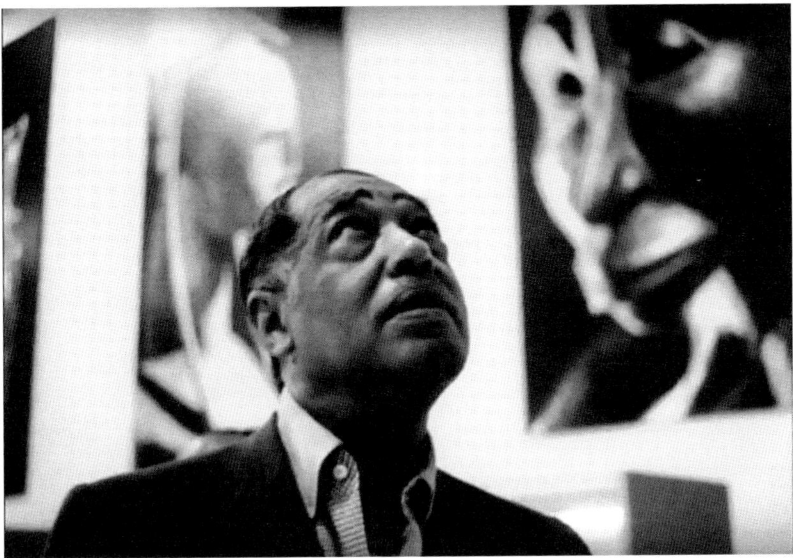

6.1 Duke Ellington at the Musée dynamique in Dakar, 1966. Still from "First World Festival of Negro Arts," by William Greaves and the United States Information Agency. New York: Distributed by William Greaves Productions, 2005.

Greaves's request marks the theme I am going to explore in this chapter: the expansion of the field of African art studies from Africa to the Americas. It was the time of the Cold War and the Civil Rights and the Black Power movements. The end of colonialism instigated competition between the West, namely the US, and the East, namely the Soviet Union, with the goal of gaining influence in the newly independent African nations. So, not surprisingly, the Soviet Union also had a film team documenting the Dakar festival.[3] While not much is known about the Soviet documentary, the agenda of Greaves's film was clear; commissioned by the United States Information Agency (USIA), a body created in 1953 to promote US interests overseas, the film focused on the close bond between the US and the African countries. Greaves's footage and Hughes's poem thus framed the Dakar festival as a cultural fusion of the African American idea of Pan-Africanism with Léopold Senghor's notion of Négritude, a synthesis that allayed the confrontational critique of Négritude formulated by black intellectuals before the festival.

As early as 1962, only two years after Senegal's independence, Senegalese filmmaker Ousmane Sembène had characterized Négritude as "an intellectual intoxicant used by the rising bourgeoisie."[4] An essay in the *New Yorker* appeared in the same year in which James Baldwin warned that a romantic identification with Africa would fail to solve the problems of blacks in the US.[5] A year later the sentiment was picked up by South African writer Es'kia Mphahlele:

> Who is so stupid as to deny the historical fact of Négritude as both a protest and a positive assertion of African cultural values? All this is valid. What I do not accept is the way in which too much of the poetry inspired by it romanticizes Africa—as a symbol of innocence, purity, and artless primitiveness. I feel insulted when some people imply that Africa is not also a violent continent. I am a violent person and proud of it because it is often a healthy human state of mind; some day I'm going to plunder, rape, set things on fire, I'm going to cut somebody's throat; I'm going to subvert a government; I'm going to organize a coup d'etat; yes, I'm going to oppress my own people; I'm going to hunt the rich fat black men who bully the small weak black men and destroy them; I'm going to become a capitalist, and woe to all who cross my path or who want to be my servants or chauffeurs and so on; I'm going to lead a breakaway church there is money in it; I'm going to attack the black bourgeoisie while I cultivate a garden, rear dogs and parrots; listen to jazz and classics, read "culture," and so on. Yes, I'm going to organize a strike. Don't you know that sometimes I kill to the rhythm of drums and cut the sinews of a baby to cure it of paralysis?[6]

Mphahlele's extended riff echoes the complex relationship between the demand for civil rights among African Americans in the US and the demand for independence among peoples on the African continent. Ideas of a Pan-African culture and consciousness had emerged toward the end of the nineteenth century among black writers and activists in the US and the Anglophone Caribbean islands, while Négritude started in Paris during the 1930s primarily as a poetic sentiment among black students from French colonies. Given these two movements, the Dakar festival—partly as a result of strategic political engineering on the side of the US—successfully performed a Pan-African culture that was able to tie the newly liberated African "homeland" to black people in the diaspora.[7]

For the newly established field of African art in the US, the result was both enriching and restrictive. On the one hand, the recognition of contemporary African art that had led to the field's first professional journal, *African Arts,* did not last long. The majority of scholars did not embrace contemporary art. Foundational interests in so-called traditional African art prevailed. On the other hand, the Dakar festival marked a decisive shift as it prompted the field to expand its horizon to the exploration of Africa's artistic and religious heritage in the black Americas.

In the following, I will trace the major steps in this expansion to the Americas. I begin in the 1930s and 1940s with the work of Melville Herskovits, a key figure in the study of "Africanisms"—that is, how elements of African cultures persisted in the Americas. The second section shifts the debate to the rediscovery and reclamation of African aesthetics among African American artists in the 1960s and 1970s. Finally, we close by coming back to the work of Robert Farris Thompson (see chap. 4). Informed and inspired by the political agenda of the Black Power movement, Thompson refashioned Herskovits's research on Africanism and effectively extended the perspective of the new field from Africa to the Americas.

Roots and Retentions

Two portrait photographs, two diverging perspectives (figs. 6.2, 6.3): one depicts the African American printmaker James Lesesne Wells, made in 1930 by James Allen. Allen was a portrait photographer in Harlem, New York, who worked for the Harmon Foundation, a philanthropic organization that helped African American artists gain visibility and public recognition. Allen's photograph depicts Wells looking down at the human face on a Kuba cup he holds in his hand. The carefully composed diagonal line spanning from the small Kuba face in the lower left to Wells's stern expression in the upper right frames the relationship between the two as a question of scale, distance, and hierarchy. Like the still lifes of African figures the artists' colleagues made, Wells's solemnly scrutinizing gaze toward the Kuba object conveys ambivalence. He seems to look at the cup with a sense of grief and mourning about the loss of the past but also with a curiosity regarding the meaning of the ancestral cup for advancing the cause of "the new negro" (Alain Locke).

Let us compare an anonymous photograph from 1928 of the anthropologist Melville Herskovits, in which he inspects a Maroon figure from Suriname in South America. Both photographs can be understood in dialogue with Countee Cullen's opening line, "What is Africa to me," in his famous 1925 poem "Heritage." Yet Herskovits's picture is strikingly different from Allen's. Notably, it lacks the intimacy and self-questioning imbued in Allen's photograph. The setting is laboratory-like; with the head of the Maroon figure on eye level with Herskovits, his pose conveys a sense of detachment, the sober gaze of the scientist. In fact, when, in 1925, Cullen first published his poem in Alain Locke's anthology *The New Negro*, Herskovits was still skeptical as to the "heritage" of African Americans. Born in 1895 to Jewish immigrants from Austria and Germany, Herskovits's early experience of difference and exclusion as a Jewish boy in rural America is said to have informed his interest in "Negro" culture.[8]

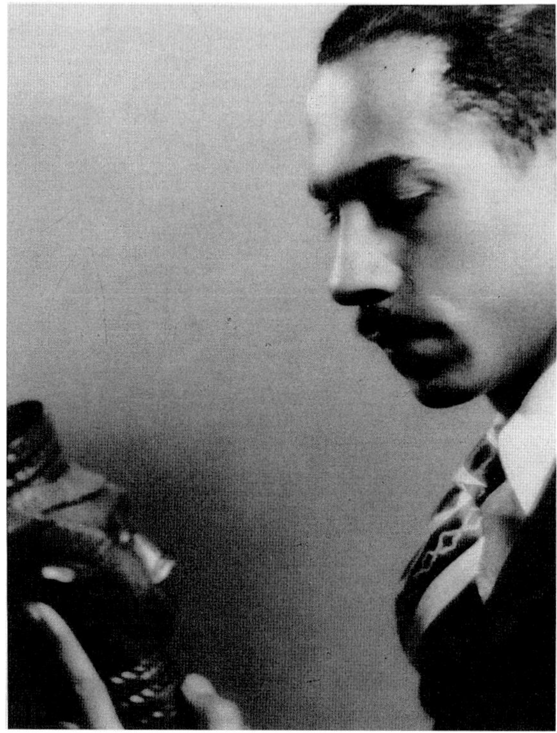

6.2 James L. Allen, Portrait of James Lesesne Wells, ca. 1930.
Courtesy of Moorland-Spingarn Research Center, Howard
University.

This interest deepened as a graduate student studying anthropology at
Columbia University in 1921, broadened as he experienced nearby Harlem, and developed as he read the works of W. E. B. Du Bois and Alain
Locke. In his article in Locke's anthology, he expressed skepticism that
African Americans retained cultural memories of their African origins,
citing the process of "complete acculturation."[9] Only three years later,
however, when the photograph was made, Herskovits had reversed that
position, and was now arguing for the retention of what he now recognized as traces of African ancestry.

Anthropological fieldwork led to this change. In 1927, he took a job
as assistant professor at Northwestern University near Chicago, where
private money from an affluent Columbia colleague—Elsie Clews Par-
sons—allowed him and his wife Francis to conduct research among
Saamaka Maroons, the descendants of runaway enslaved African subjects
in Suriname, then still Dutch Guiana.[10] The fieldwork he and his wife
conducted in 1928 and 1929 resulted in a different understanding of the

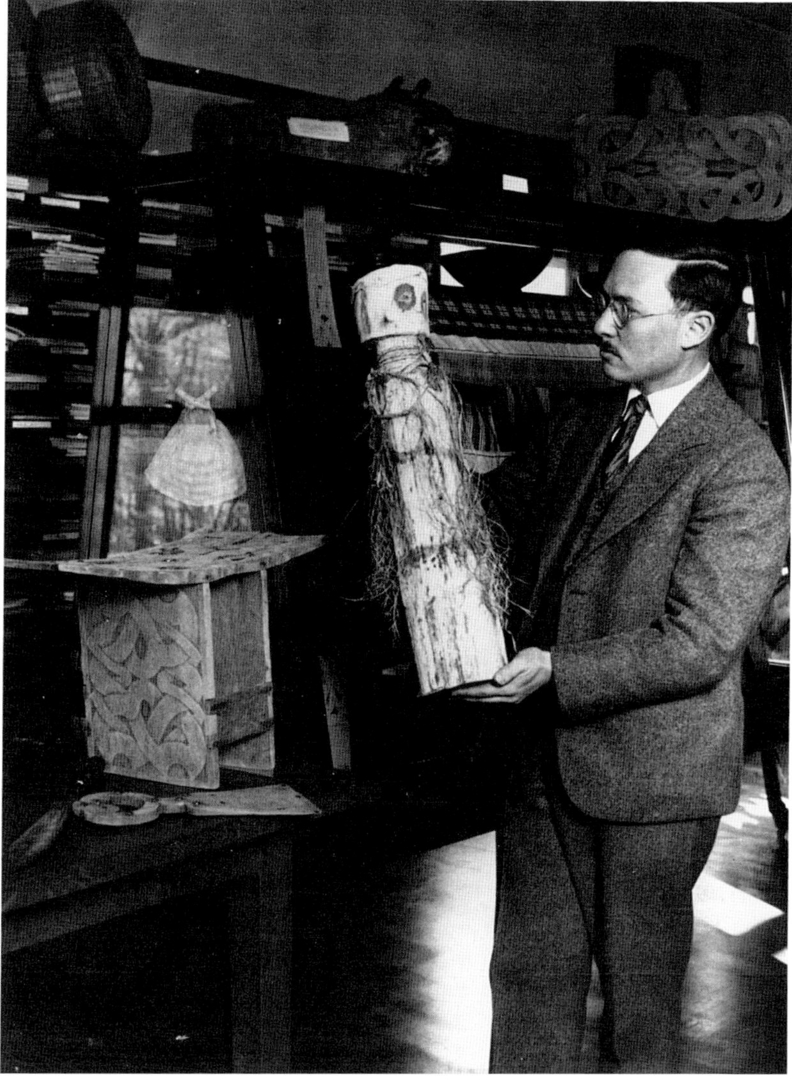

6.3 Melville Herskovits holding a Maroon figure from Suriname at Northwestern University, ca.1928. Courtesy of Northwestern University Archives.

"Negro in the World."[11] His research had brought to light a wide variety of examples showing that, instead of being culturally uprooted, African Americans had retained elements of African culture over generations via conscious preservation and unconscious imitation as body memory. Respective research in Dahomey, Ghana, and Nigeria focused on questions of history and folklore, whereas fieldwork in Haiti, Trinidad, and Brazil investigated the black reinterpretation of Catholicism along the lines of West (Yoruba, Fon) and Central (Kongo, Yombe) African religion.[12]

With the exception of his research in Suriname, none of Herskovits's fieldwork lasted very long. As Suzanne Blier noted in her discussion of Herskovits's work in Dahomey, Herskovits was "a man in a hurry"—more concerned with big ideas than with empirical proof and validity.[13] Still, his research amounted to a body of data that he finally (1941) presented in what would become his most famous book, *The Myth of the Negro Past*,[14] an odd mixture of Du Bois's "double consciousness" and Frobenius's motto *Fiat lux* (see chap. 1). Financed by the Carnegie Foundation, it was primarily a work of social policy. It revealed the limits of the official "melting pot" ideology the US had promulgated from the early twentieth century onward to assimilate the various waves of immigrants into American society.[15] The "myth" at which the book took aim was the popular notion that African Americans had lost their cultural identity during the "middle passage" and had arrived in the New World as a collective blank slate with no history or culture worthy of being preserved. Informed by Locke's interest in translation and transformation (see chap. 2), Herskovits countered that conception by maintaining the persistence of what he called "Africanisms," which allowed African Americans to be rooted in the African past while constantly moving, mixing, and adapting to the American present.[16] Still, racial segregation and systemic economic deprivation had made it exceedingly difficult for African Americans to find a place in US society.

The publication of Herskovits's study during the onset of US involvement in World War II prevented any immediate effect. However, with the rise of the Cold War, Herskovits's Africanist expertise turned out to be politically appealing and relevant. Oddly enough, even though the "middle passage" very much defined Herskovits's research, he consciously evaded its psychological effects. That is to say, he bypassed the experience of slavery, repression, and segregation as key elements in the African American experience. In his 1959 entry on "Afro-American Art" for the *World Encyclopedia of Art*, Herskovits simply ignored prominent black American artists like Aaron Douglas, Meta Warrick Fuller, or Jacob Lawrence and instead discussed the "retentions" of African forms he had identified in the work of sculptors during stays in Suriname, Haiti, and Brazil.[17]

Herskovits passed away in February 1963 after his return from Accra, Ghana, where he had given a keynote address on the history of African studies at the First International Congress of Africanists.[18] The venue was well chosen. As one of the first African countries, Ghana had claimed independence in 1957, adopting the name of the medieval African empire of Ghana, with Kwame Nkrumah forcefully pushing a Pan-African emancipation agenda. Western participants outnumbered Africans two to one. It was a postcolonial setting, however, and the tone of the opening addresses delivered by the local hosts and organizers echoed the new political conditions. In his address, Ghana's president Kwame Nkrumah made it clear that science had to be in the service of the nation and its people. For him, sociology was more attractive than anthropology. As he saw it, academics had a duty to help Africans "understand correctly the strains and stresses to which Africa is subjected, to appreciate objectively the changes taking place, and enable us to contribute fully in a truly African spirit for the benefit of all and for the peace and progress of the world."[19] Alioune Diop, editor of *Présence Africaine* and president elect of the congress, demanded greater representation of African voices, especially in the field of the arts: "The meaning attached to [African art] by Africans in ordinary life past and present will in future be a factor to be reckoned with in any appraisal of African art."[20] Kenneth Onwuka Dike, a highly respected historian at the University of Ibadan, Nigeria, and president elect of the congress, continued this line of reasoning. However, in his opening address, he also exhorted his African colleagues not to romanticize one's own history:

> Our newly acquired independence must be without meaning if it implies mere imitation of Western ways. Africa like every other continent in history must build on its past . . . [,] for it is no use inventing a romantic past which has no relation to reality; we must accept that our past like the past of the rest of the world has its good and bad aspects. We must accept the glories of Benin art with the human sacrifices, just as the Spaniard accepts the horrors and bigotries of the Inquisition with the achievements of EL Greco and Cervantes.[21]

The congress's postcolonial agenda to change the power dynamics in African studies had limited effects. Euro-American scholars remained the gatekeepers for funding and academic visibility. In fact, the 1960s were the heydays of African studies in the US (see chap. 4). This development can be seen as Herskovits's legacy. Yet his legacy also entailed a counterdevelopment that focused on (re)conceiving and (re)claiming African art from the perspective of the black American experience.

NATION Time: From Africa to Africana

At the end of the Africanist congress in Accra, delegates decided that the next meeting would take place three years later in Dakar, Senegal. As it happened, three years turned into four years, and the second congress, now focusing on the question of art, eventually became the academic segment of the *Premier Festival Mondial des Arts Nègres*. In preparation for the Dakar festival, the US government had instituted several committees that were responsible for identifying artists whose work would be shown at the festival. The head of the visual arts committee was Hale Woodruff, an African American artist from New York who was well known for his mural series, *The Art of the Negro*, which he did in the early 1950s at Atlanta University in Atlanta, Georgia. Informed by Aaron Douglas's *Aspects of Negro Life* from 1934, the work consists of six panels depicting the development of black art from the precolonial beginnings on the African continent to the emergence of African American art in the US. The first panel, titled "Native Forms," shows scenes of warriors, dancers, and rock art motifs grouped around a towering frontal figure in the upper center. The figure wore the double axe emblem of Shango, the Yoruba deity of thunder, lightning, and justice on its head (fig. 6.4).

Woodruff's visual citation of Shango signals the growing presence of African and African derived religions in certain corners of the American public sphere. Factors driving this development were partly demographic—an increase of immigrants from the Caribbean—and partly political—the realization that the end of colonialism in Africa did not correlate with the end of racism in the US. Though the Civil Rights Act from 1964 had officially ended racial segregation, it did not stop constitutional racist policy and practice. Social, economic, and political exclusion remained pervasive. Given these conditions, many African American artists felt that hope for change was no longer an option. Out of this disillusionment there emerged a new Black Arts Movement, which sought to combine the political with the artistic. Respectively, the old word *negro* was abandoned because of its associations with slavery, inferiority, and obedience. The language of oppression gave way to a celebration of blackness articulated in such slogans as Black Is Beautiful, in radical political movements such as Black Power, and in a turn to Islam and socialism as social countermodels. For instance, in 1965, after the assassination of Malcolm X, the African American writer LeRoi Jones renamed himself Amiri Baraka and founded, together with Larry Neal and Askia Touré, the Black Arts Repertory Theatre/School (BARTS) in New York, an institution that quickly became a model for the development of black cultural centers across the US.[22] In 1994, Baraka recalled,

> What seemed most important about the BARTS was that it was a living paradigm of what many people had come to feel was the direction

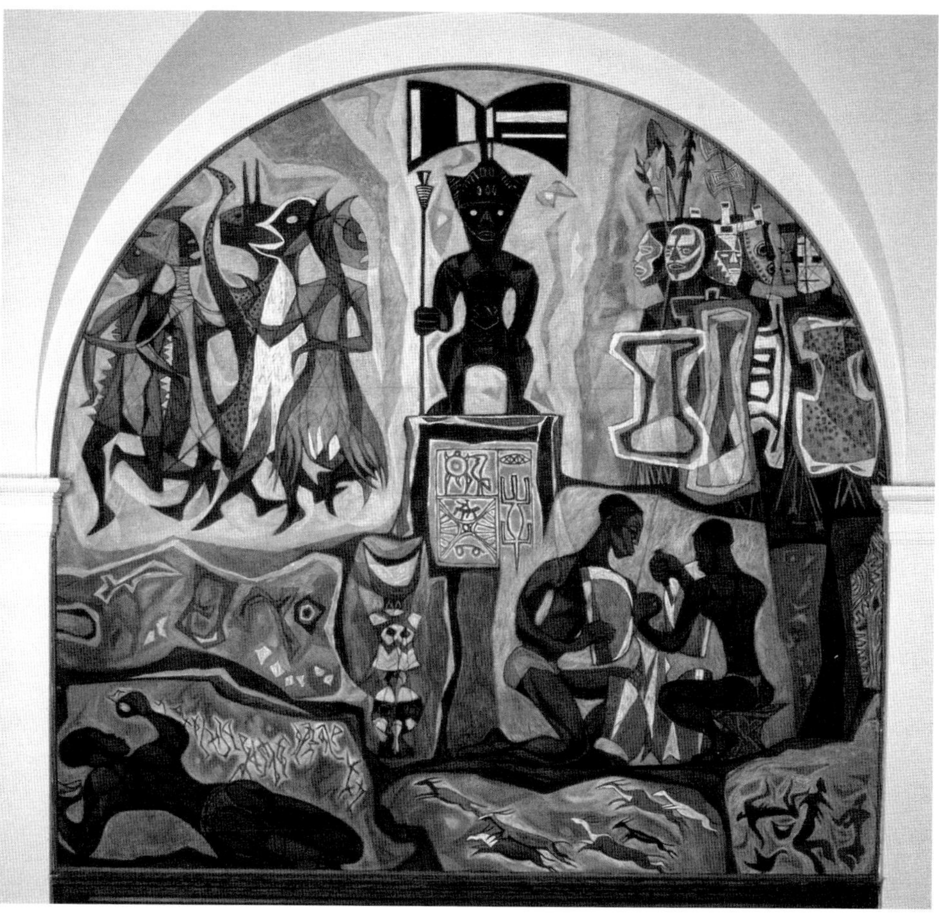

6.4 Hale Woodruff, *The Art of the Negro*, "Native Forms," 1951. 365.76 × 365.76 cm. Clark Atlanta University Art Collection. © 2021 Estate of Hale Woodruff / Licensed by VAGA at Artists Rights Society (ARS), NY.

that Afro-American artists and the art with which they expressed the particular culture they reflected had to go in. Fundamentally we must pursue what Du Bois called True Self-Consciousness and defeat its reverse, Double Consciousness. The Black Arts Movement raised this antagonistic contradiction once again, as part of the Cultural Revolution still necessary to raise and unite the consciousness of the oppressed Afro-American people, so that they better understand themselves as well as better resist their enemies. . . . The essence of our call and our work was to try to unite the Afro-American people by raising their consciousness, by attempting to raise our own consciousness and that of the Afro-American artists and intellectuals. We were new nationalists, older nationalists, and others, and that was the center of our loose front.[23]

One immediate outgrowth of BARTS was the Harlem artist collective WEUSI (Swahili for blackness), founded in 1965, which centered on a gallery named Nyumba Ya Sanaa ("House of Art" or "House of Form"). The borrowings from African languages were part of the effort to achieve "true self-consciousness" by aligning themselves not with American society but newly independent African nations like Ghana and Tanzania.[24] Tanzania, where president Nyerere had not only adopted key socialist ideas and programs but had also instituted Swahili as the national language, wielded particular influence. Inspired by Nyerere's agenda, Swahili—and, in a similar way, Islam—became an Afrocentric counter-model to white mainstream American society. This provided forms for both celebration and dissent, for example, in alternative holidays like Kwanzaa and Swahili-Arabic names like Amiri Baraka (figs. 6.5, 6.6).

A particularly prominent motif among artists associated with the Black Arts Movement became the double axe emblem of the Yoruba

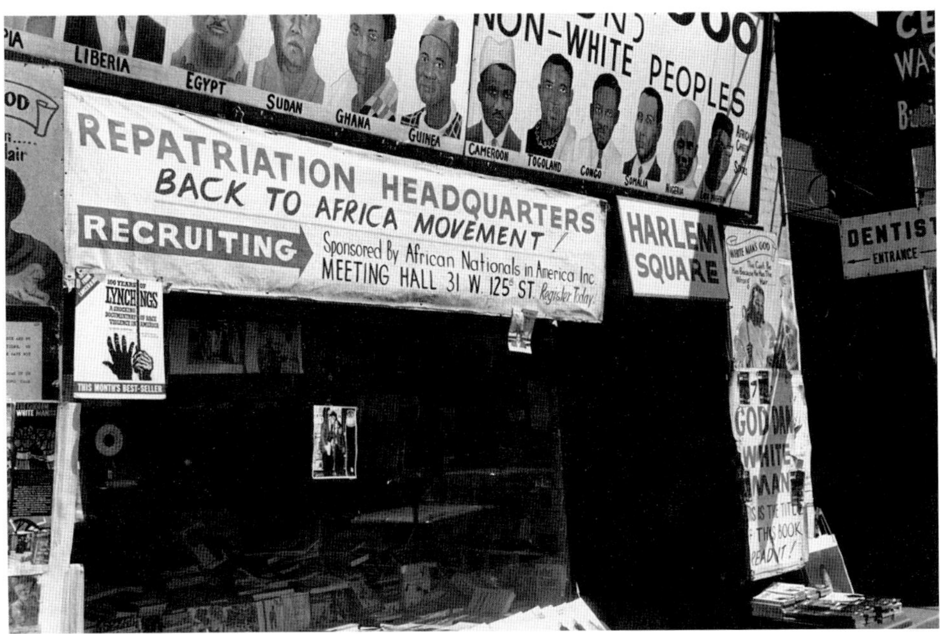

6.5 The National Memorial African Bookstore in Harlem Square, facing Seventh Avenue above West 125th Street, in Harlem, 1964. © Klytus Smith. Photographs and Prints Division, Schomburg Center for Research in Black Culture, The New York Public Library.

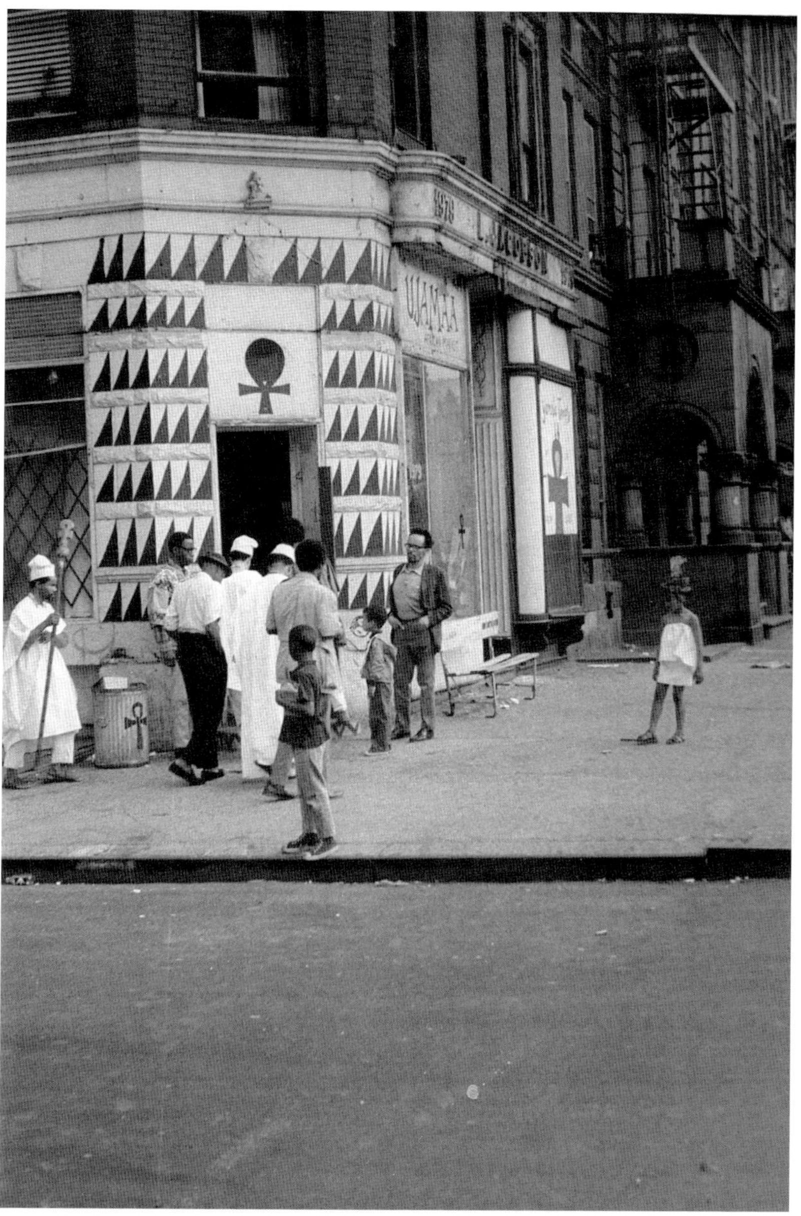

6.6 Yoruba Temple in Harlem with Ujamaa African market door next door, 1969. The
Egyptian hieroglyph *ankh* on the temple door and market front functioned as a symbol
of black cultural identity. © Klytus Smith. Photographs and Prints Division, Schomburg
Center for Research in Black Culture, The New York Public Library.

deity Shango. As noted above, in Yoruba iconography, the axe symbolizes Shango's power to wield thunder and lightning and to punish wrongdoing (see chap. 4, fig. 4.1). However, in the American context, Shango accrued additional meaning as a figure of moral vengeance, retaliating for the injustice of racism. In effect, the figure of Shango emerged as a popular symbol of empowerment and resistance in the black public sphere.[25] I have already mentioned Hale Woodruff's mural, "Native Forms" (1951), which showed a Shango figure dominating over a series of stylized African peoples, periods, and religious practices. Yet what really catalyzed the popularity of Shango as a symbol among Black Power artists was the assassination of Martin Luther King in 1968. In 1969, for example, Ademola Olugebefola, one of the founders of WEUSI, portrayed Shango's weapon in the form of a stylized, semiabstract double stone axe using Shango's ritual colors, white and red, against a bright blue background.[26] In the same year, Jeff Donaldson depicted the *Wives of Shango* wearing bandolier bullet belts, a mannerism popular among Black Liberation Movement members at the time (fig. 6.7).

Donaldson was a leading figure in the Black Arts and Liberation Movement. In the 1960s, after a BFA and MFA in studio art and design, he studied with the Yoruba and Ife scholar Frank Willet at Northwestern University with the idea of doing a PhD in African art. However, realizing that "all the literature was by non-Africans," he changed his topic to the study of black art and consciousness in the US supervised in part by the prominent black painter and collage artist Romare Bearden.[27] In Chicago, Donaldson teamed up with Wadsworth Jarrell, Jae Jarrell, Barbara Jones-Hogu, and Gerald William and founded COBRA, the Coalition of Black Revolutionary Artists, which, partly due to the homonymity with a European avant-garde movement active from 1948 to 1951, soon renamed itself AFRICOBRA, an acronym for African Commune of Bad Relevant Artists.[28]

As the title suggests, the political and artistic agenda of the group was directed against the mainstream American art establishment and in favor of a transcontinental African community, adopting what it conceived of as Pan-African aesthetics. The visual aesthetics combined poster art, lettering, and commercial art techniques with collage and fragment-like patterning. Unlike Hale Woodruff, Jacob Lawrence and other senior African American artists members of WEUSI and AFRICOBRA had not (yet) visited the "motherland." However, by the end of the 1960s, the joint effects of the American Civil Rights and African Liberation movements had revitalized the idea of a Pan-African nation that allowed for imaginary reconnections. On the occasion of a 1970 group exhibition

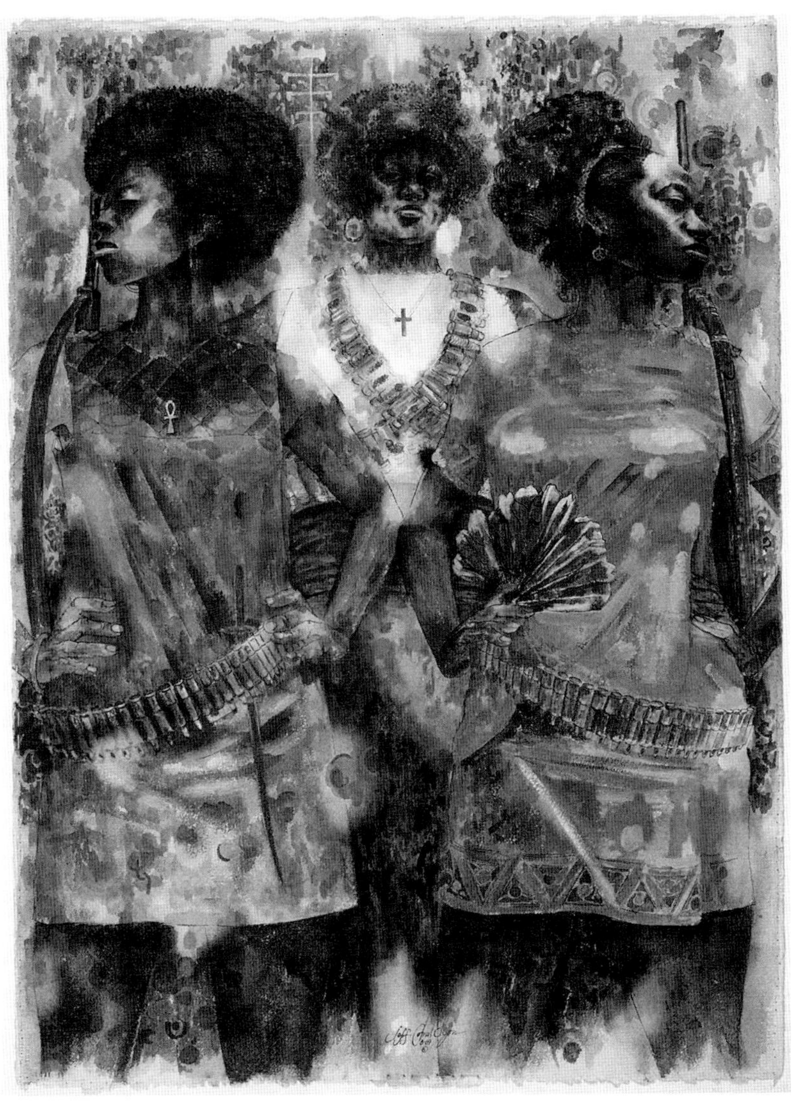

6.7 Jeff Donaldson, *Wives of Shango*, 1969. Matte, semigloss, and gold metallic paint with traces of pen and brown ink with scratching out over traces of graphite on thick, rough texture, hand-made wove paper, 76.2 × 55.9 cm. Brooklyn Museum of Art, Gift of R. M. Atwater, Anna Wolfrom Dove, Alice Fiebiger, Joseph Fiebiger, Belle Campbell Harriss, and Emma L. Hyde, by exchange. Designated Purchase Fund, Mary Smith Dorward Fund, Dick S. Ramsay Fund, and Carl H. de Silver Fund. © Estate of Jeff Donaldson.

at the Studio Museum in Harlem titled *Ten in Search of a Nation*, Donaldson wrote,

> It's NATION TIME and we are searching. Our guidelines are our people—the whole family of African people, the African family tree. And in this spirit of familyhood, we have carefully examined our roots and searched our branches for those visual qualities that are more expressive of our people/art. Our people are our standard for excellence. We strive for images inspired by African people—experience and images that African people can relate to directly without formal art training and/or experience. Art for people and not for critics whose peopleness is questionable. We try to create images that appeal to the senses—not to the intellect.[29]

By the time the show opened, Donaldson had accepted a position as chair of the art department and director of the art gallery at Howard University in Washington, DC. Responding to students' demands for an Afrocentric curriculum in line with the NATION TIME agenda, Donaldson reached out to Ben Enwonwu, then still the most prominent modern African artist, and offered him an exhibition and speaking tour. Enwonwu accepted and traveled to Washington in 1971. However, Enwonwu's position differed from that of his host and audience. In his address to members of the university, he was skeptical of the radical demands to topple the system of white domination. As he saw it, such policies would only increase the marginalization of African Americans in the US. Instead, he suggested changing the system from within.[30] Unsurprisingly, Enwonwu's advice was not well received. For Donaldson and the other members of AFRICOBRA, Enwonwu was a disappointment. Both politically as well as stylistically, the two positions did not match.

Like WEUSI, members of AFRICOBRA created bright, boldly colored pictures imbued with social messages. Reminiscent of Du Bois's activist understanding of art (see chap. 2), what dominated was a kind of agitprop—an art of agitation that spoke to black sentiments and aimed to stir political action. As Barbara Jones-Hogu stated in 1973,

A. The visual statement must be humanistic with the figure frontal and direct to stress strength, straight forwardness, profoundness, and proudness.

B. The subject matter must be completely understood by the viewer, therefore lettering would be used to extend and clarify the visual statement. The lettering was to be incorporated into the composition as a part of the visual statement and not as a headline.

    C. The visual statement must identify our problems and offer a solu-
tion, a pattern of behavior or attitude.

    D. The visual statement must educate, it must speak of our past, pres-
ent, or future.[31]

Abstract art was embraced only if it conveyed "aesthetic awesomeness" by using brilliant, high energy ("cool ade") colors, and dense, rhythmic design compositions.[32] With respect to the sensory appeal, another member of the group, Jones-Hogu, elaborated five "aesthetic principles" informing the work of the group:

> 1. free symmetry, the use of syncopated, rhythmic repetition that constantly changes in color, texture, shapes, form, pattern, movement, feature, etc. 2. mimesis at midpoint, design that marks the spot where the real and the unreal, the objective and the nonobjective, the plus and the minus meet. A point exactly between absolute abstractions and absolute naturalism. 3. visibility, clarity of form and line based on the interesting irregularity one senses in a freely drawn circle or organic object, the feeling for movement, growth, changes, and human touch. 4. luminosity, "shine," literal and figurative, as seen in the dress and personal grooming of shoes, hair (process or Afro), laminated furniture, face, knees, or skin. 5. color, cool-aid color, bright colors with sensibility and harmony.[33]

For Jones-Hogu, "These principles were drawn not only from the work of the artists in the group but also from our inheritable art forms as an African people (fig. 6.8)."[34] Encounters with these "inheritances" were festivals like the one in Dakar in 1966 and meetings with African artists like Skunder Boghossian, Papa Ibra Tall, and Bruce Onobrakpeya in the US.[35] But they also included books and articles coming out of the newly emerging field of African art history, and here especially the work of Robert Farris Thompson.

Mambology

In 1973, Robert Farris Thompson published his essay on "Yoruba Artistic Criticism."[36] Among the eight different criteria that Thompson deemed "common denominators of taste" were also the five "principles" of "inheritable art forms" that Jones-Hogu had listed as informing the work of AFRICOBRA artists. Jones-Hogu's adoption of Thompson's categories indicates the impact of his work on the formation of black aesthetics and the extension of African art history in the Americas.

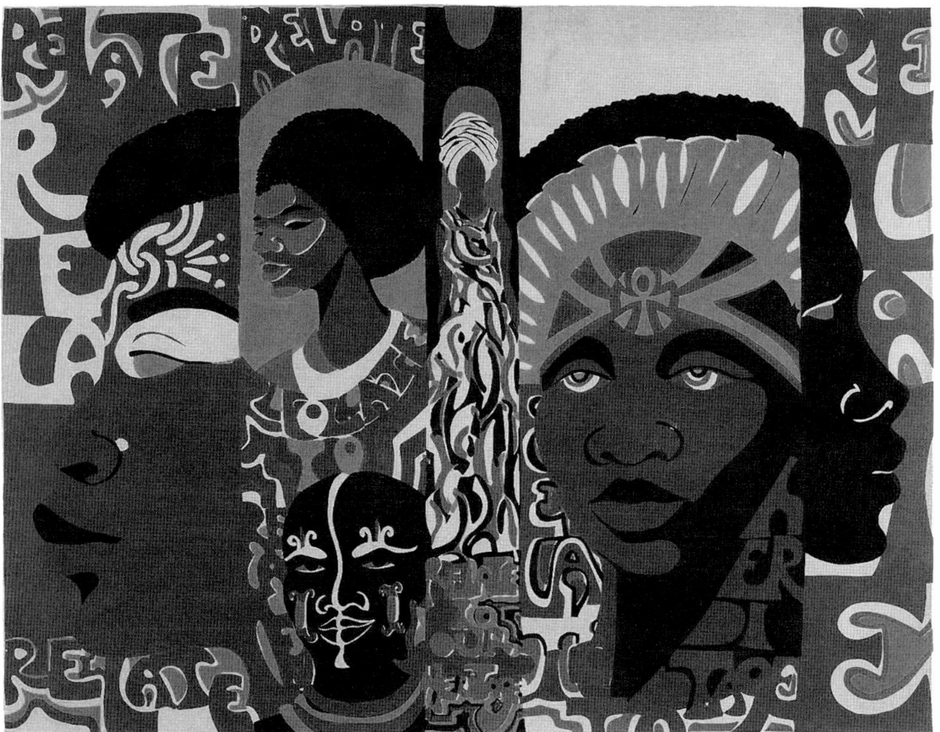

6.8 Barbara Jones-Hogu, *Relate to Your Heritage*, 1971. Color screenprint, 86.4 × 109.2 cm. Brooklyn Museum, Gift of R. M. Atwater, Anna Wolfrom Dove, Alice Fiebiger, Joseph Fiebiger, Belle Campbell Harriss, and Emma L. Hyde, by exchange. Designated Purchase Fund, Mary Smith Dorward Fund, Dick S. Ramsay Fund, and Carl H. de Silver Fund, 2012.80.26. © Estate of Barbara Jones-Hogu.

Thompson's research interests were similar to those of Melville Herskovits and his students: both were interested in the African presence in the Americas; both considered the role of the body key to understanding the African presence; and, interestingly, both grew up in El Paso, Texas, whose status as a border town between America and Mexico turned out to be formative for their scholarly careers. But Thompson, born in 1932, represented the next generation. When he earned his PhD at Yale in 1965, Herskovits had already passed away, and while Herskovits believed in the rules of proper scientific scholarship, Thompson flirted with their willful transgression, calling himself a "guerilla scholar."[37]

According to Thompson's self-fashioning, it was the musical milieu of El Paso in the 1940s that led to his interest in Afro-American culture.[38] In the early 1930s, mambo, an Afro-Cuban musical and dance genre, swept over from Cuba into Mexico and subsequently to the US, where Thompson encountered it as a youth in El Paso. Later, during his freshman year at Yale in 1952, he traveled to Cuba to experience Afro-Cuban music and dance firsthand. The trip resulted in regular weekend trips from New Haven to the Palladium and other dance halls in New York, where he saw Katherine Dunham's dance troupe and mambo legends like Tito Puente and Tito Rodriguez. During his military service from 1956 to 1958 in Germany, he visited the Musée de l'homme in Paris and met with Africanists like the ethnomusicologist Gilbert Rouget, from whom he learned about the role of music in African ritual and religion. Back in the US, he read the work of Herskovits and his collaborators and students. But it seems it was only in 1959, after a visit to Haiti, that he decided to pursue a PhD in African art history.

His advisor at Yale was George Kubler, a Mesoamericanist whose courses he had attended as an undergraduate. At the time, Kubler was working on his study *The Shape of Time: Remarks on the History of Things*,[39] which shared certain concerns with African art history, in particular, How does one write an art history of a people who have left no written records about their artists? Kubler's answer was to shift the focus from the (biographical and stylistic) history of artists to the (material and metaphorical) history of things, which resulted in a partial reversal of the conventional subject-object, artist-artwork relationship. Kubler's conceptual iconoclasm clearly had an impact on Thompson's own thinking, just as Thompson's interest in the dynamics of the Afro-Atlantic must have intrigued Kubler. But while Kubler's research was theoretical in nature, Thompson plunged into fieldwork in Nigeria and Benin. Following the leads derived from his interest in mambo, he decided to embark on research among the Yoruba in Nigeria, which resulted first in the dissertation on "African Dance Sculpture" (1965), and then in a junior position in Yale's art history department. It was here that Thompson's work gained an explicitly political dimension.

In the winter of 1968, the Black Student Alliance at Yale organized a symposium to discuss the need for an Afro-American studies program at Yale. Given the political climate at the time, the idea was to provide an "educational experience for professional educators" that would allow the participants to understand the arguments for instituting such a program.[40] About two hundred people attended the event, the majority of whom were white, which drew some bitter remarks on the part of black participants as to the viability of the symposium's central goal: to understand the black experience as informed by the history of slavery and everyday racism in the US. The discussions were heated and difficult.

Much of the debate centered on issues of academic freedom and the contrasting values of detachment and activism. The Cornell historian David Brion Davis summarized the different positions as follows:

> White scholars are convinced that universities, for all their overt and implicit racism, still embody priceless and hard-won values of universal worth. Black students may agree in principle, but their perception is different; they are understandably suspicious of trite claims to universality, which have demonstrably been used to justify slavery, enforced segregation, exploitation, and effacement of non-white, non-Western identities. The fundamental question is how these two quite valid and sincere perceptions can be brought into a working arrangement.[41]

Among the few white scholars who delivered a lecture was Robert Farris Thompson. At the time, he had just finished organizing the exhibition *African and Afro-American Art: The Transatlantic Tradition* in New York. With the help of 125 lantern slides, a thirty-minute film on the use of sculpture in dance, and demonstrations of praise drumming, Thompson demonstrated the "African Influences on the Art of the United States."[42] The focus was not on citations of prominent painters of African deities—like Shango in the work of Donaldson, Woodruff, and others—but on creations in the realm of "vernacular art." Like Herskovits, Thompson interpreted his examples as retentions of certain African aesthetic "traits," like "frozen faces" and "equilibrated gestures," and, like Herskovits, he explained them as lived, bodily experiences stored in "motor habits." These "motor habits," he expounded, are expressed in a wide range of media, from the design of grass baskets on the Gullah islands, to carved walking sticks with serpent motifs from Charleston, South Carolina, to Bible quilts with appliqued silhouettes of human figures and animals from the outskirts of Athens, Georgia.

Underlying these examples was a conceptual Pan-African folk model that Thompson labeled "An Aesthetic of the Cool."[43] Thompson developed his argument in two steps: the first focused primarily on basic principles of tropical, sub-Saharan African dance and music, while the second followed years later and moved from the analysis of performance to the lexicon of African languages. In essence, the argument can be summarized as follows: in much of tropical Africa, multimetric rhythms produce polysynchronic dances, demanding that a dancer learns to split his or her body into different parts, to compartmentalize him or herself, in order to follow the different pulses of the music (fig. 6.9). Mastery of this task requires a high degree of balance, control, and composure, qualities that also have a moral and spiritual dimension, often referred to as

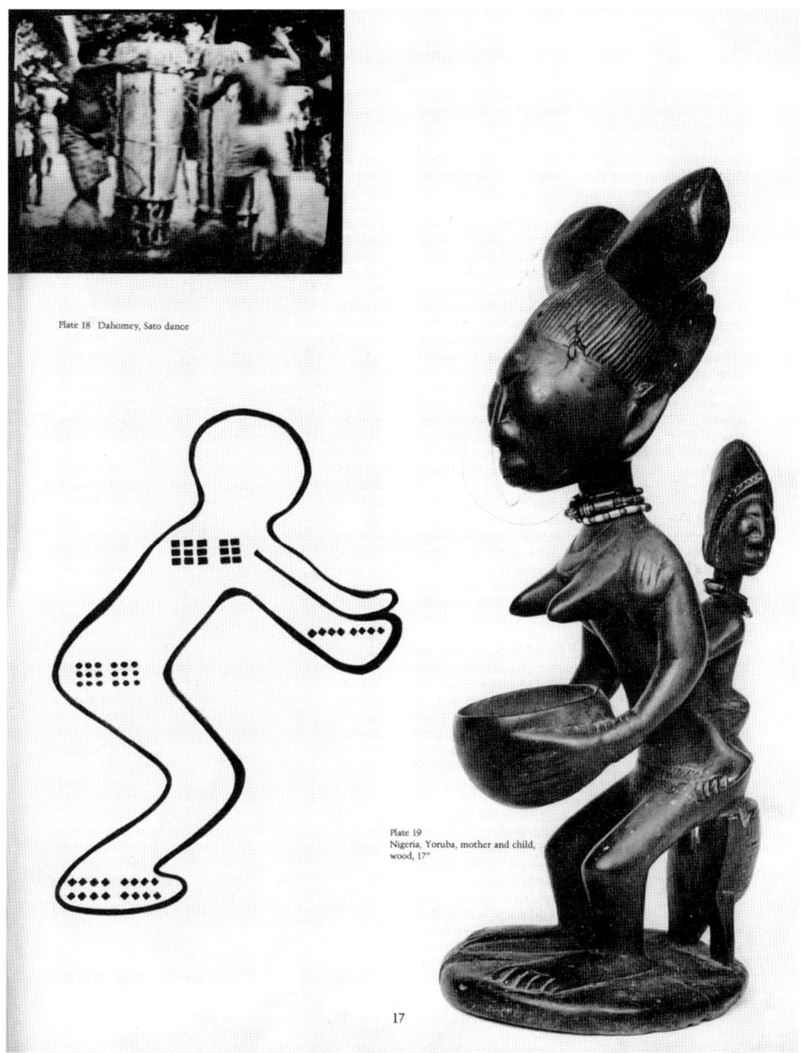

Plate 18 Dahomey, Sato dance

Plate 19
Nigeria, Yoruba, mother and child,
wood, 17"

17

6.9 The "two-part body system" from Robert Farris Thompson, *African Art in Motion* (Berkeley: University of California Press, 1974).

"cool," or in Yoruba, *tutu*. Based on a survey of thirty-five sub-Saharan African languages, Thompson aimed to show the antiquity and different "contexts of the cool," both on the African continent and in the Americas (Cuba, Haiti, Suriname). Examples ranged from the striking serenity in the facial expressions of thirteenth-century Ife bronze and brass heads to the use of chalk and the aesthetic connection with whiteness in rituals of healing, purification, and death (see chapter 4, figs. 4.2 and 4.3).

Thompson was certainly not the first to identify "coolness" as a key feature of African sculpture. As early as the late 1920s, the German art historian Eckart von Sydow had noted "the full force of calm, concentrated and compressed energy, a natural stability" that he saw emanating from African sculpture.[44] In 1934, von Sydow's student Hans Himmelheber noted the African carving practice of depicting a sleeping subject in portraiture.[45] The concept of coolness also echoes the famous distinction between "hot" and "cold" societies by the French anthropologist Claude Lévi-Strauss, whose work Thompson frequently praised.[46] Still, Thompson's analysis differed in terms of the early personal experiences that informed his findings. Referring to his experience of the mambo in New York dance halls, he later remarked: "What I was really doing was, in essence, glossing what I had learned at that point in Nigeria in terms of the Palladium insights."[47]

Driven and inspired by his insights into "an aesthetic of the cool," he boldly proclaimed "A Coming Golden Age of Afro-Americana."[48] And indeed, the late 1970s and 1980s saw a wave of works exploring the extension of Africa to the Americas; the hugely popular television adaption of Alex Haley's *Roots* and Nigeria's FESTAC (Pan African Festival of Arts and Culture), both in 1977, were arguably the most prominent events.[49] Thompson's work was an integral part of this celebratory climate. A real hit was *Flash of the Spirit: African and Afro-American Art and Philosophy*, which came out in 1983.[50] Unlike Thompson's previous books, *Flash of the Spirit* was not an exhibition catalog. Instead, it offered a comprehensive picture of his decade-long research into what he termed the "Black Atlantic Visual Tradition." The book's five chapters discuss different streams of this tradition: Yoruba deities, Kongo cosmograms, Mande textiles and architectures, and Ejagham sign communication. For Thompson, "These civilizations not only were impressive for their urban density, refinement, and complexity but were empowered by an inner momentum of conviction and poise that sent them spiraling out into the world."[51] The crux of the book is chapter 3, which focuses on Haitian vodun, explaining how it "reblended" African traditions, fusing and "creol[ing]" Yoruba and Bakongo religious elements with French Catholicism, resulting in an Ejagham-informed sign language called *veve*.

Taken together, the five chapters make a strong argument. Like his dissertation advisor Kubler, and in a similarly poetic style, Thompson reversed the hierarchy of scholarship and changed Africa from being an object to a subject that empowered black people in the diaspora with agency. Clearly, the empirical foundation of the argument was vague and vulnerable. What Thompson presented as fact was frequently no more than a hunch based on one or two questionable examples. In his endeavor to explain the "spiraling out" of African traditions, Thompson's approach resembles the black diaspora cultures he explored but only insofar as he cooked up an academic callaloo—a mixture of diffusionism and structuralism, cognition and comparison, music and art—all seasoned with a pinch of Merriam, Waterman, Kubler, Du Bois, Frobenius, Herskovits, Senghor, and others. The fact that the book's argument was mostly speculative and impressionistic only increased its impact. After all, the "flash" captured the bodily experience, not the reflective intellect. *Flash of the Spirit* became an instant hit. It was seen as a countermodel to conventional academic writing, a perception that Thompson consolidated by writing about rebel painters like Jean Michel Basquiat and rebel hip-hop musicians like Grandmaster Flash and Grandmaster Afrika Bambaataa.[52]

By the late 1980s and early 1990s, things had begun to change. In 1993, ten years after *Flash of the Spirit*, the Afro-English literary scholar Paul Gilroy published *The Black Atlantic: Modernity and Double Consciousness*.[53] Gilroy acknowledged Thompson as the originator of the concept of "the Black Atlantic,"[54] which he embraced as a countermodel, or rather a "counterculture," that challenged the politically dominant notion of modernity as a Western prerogative. Yet in contrast to Thompson, Gilroy—similar to Wright's intervention at the 1956 conference of black writers and artists in Paris (see chap. 5)—understood the phrase not as an affirmation of blackness but rather as a "desire to escape the restrictive bonds of ethnicity, national identification and sometimes even 'race' itself."[55] Thus, Gilroy's "Black Atlantic" advanced a transnational approach to black identity, one that focuses not only on African roots and cultural continuities but also on the routes, ruptures, and cross-cultural exchanges that are equally constitutive of the black diaspora.

Thompson himself responded to these arguments by stressing the creativity and flexibility of Black Atlantic traditions. Yet he also expressed concern about the growing rethinking and partial renunciation of hitherto widely accepted concepts and hierarchies of value, a critical position that had become known as "postmodern" (see chap. 7). In a short piece from 1991 titled "Afro-Modernism," he wrote,

At the dawn of what we hope will be a culturally democratic world, we are called, out of our name, post-modern. Can an oxymoron really serve as a slogan for potential richness and redemption? Can anything really be post-*now*? To me, the word "post-Modern" suggests another of those patricidal, patriarchal Western wars of intellect, the junking of one age in favor of another. This is particularly dangerous when we've not fully tabulated the wonders created during the Modern age among women and men of color beyond the West, to say nothing of within it. . . . My fear is that post-modernists don't really mean it. . . . Why use the word "post-Modern" when it may also mean "postblack."[56]

Thompson's fear of a postmodern, "postblack" world was also a fear that the field of African art studies seemed to have lost its compass.[57] At stake was the canon, an ironic situation given the fact that Thompson's own work always aimed to subvert the canon. "Postmodernism," in Thompson's sense, meant the loss of the binding ligature a canon provided. In fact, for the history of the study of African art, the late 1980s and early 1990s marked the time when the underlying premises and precepts the field had taken for granted began to fall apart. New actors with new subjectivities entered the scene and started to reconfigure the field.

*   *   *

Of course, the reconfiguration did not happen overnight. Respective shifts and reorientations had long been in the making. As we have seen in the previous chapters, the end of colonialism and the growing visibility of modern artists had left their mark on the field. Yet just as the new discipline was shaped by the developments in Africa, it was also shaped by the situation at home. In the US, where the center of the field had moved after World War II, the encounter with African art brought back the history of slavery. Expanding the field from Africa to the Americas was a way of acknowledging its cultural echoes. In terms of both politics and research, this meant unfinished business. Members of the Harlem Renaissance had started to address the meaning of Africa. The Civil Rights and Black Power movements pushed the exploration of the question further. The Cold War allowed for funding. Research designs ranged from Herskovits's idea of "retentions" to Thompson's "aesthetics of the cool." When the geopolitical landscape changed and the Cold War ended, the seemingly homogeneous notion of Africa cracked. As "modern" turned into "postmodern," the canon began to falter. The field responded by returning to the question of the contemporary and addressing the issue of representation. Who speaks, and on whose behalf? What had flickered at the dawn of the colonial era now became a central concern.

PART III

Intervening the Canon

THE POSTMODERN, THE POPULAR, AND THE AUTHENTIC

Now, in the closing years of the twentieth century, it is perhaps time to bring the canon into better alignment with the corpus.

SIDNEY KASFIR, *Art and Authenticity: A Text with a Shadow,* 1992

Introduction

In September 1987, on the occasion of its relocation to a new complex on the National Mall, the Smithsonian National Museum of African Art in Washington, DC, organized a symposium on the state of African art studies (fig. 7.1).[1] Among the speakers was Henry Drewal, who had made a name for himself through his fieldwork (much of it conducted jointly with his wife, Margaret Thompson), which focused on gender and masked performances among the Yoruba in Nigeria.[2] But Drewal did not use this lecture to delve into his Yoruba research. Instead, he alerted his colleagues to the "crisis of representation" that had been brought about in the humanities by the "age of postmodernism." Referring to the new critical discussion about the representation of subjects in disciplines such as anthropology, he noted

> Nowhere in African Art studies has this "crisis of representation" surfaced. I think this is partly true of our priorities. . . . In feeling a sense of urgency about simply documenting the vast array of art traditions across Africa and beyond, we have concerned ourselves primarily with the content of our writing, not its form and style. . . . Reflexivity about our own practices and products has not even begun.[3]

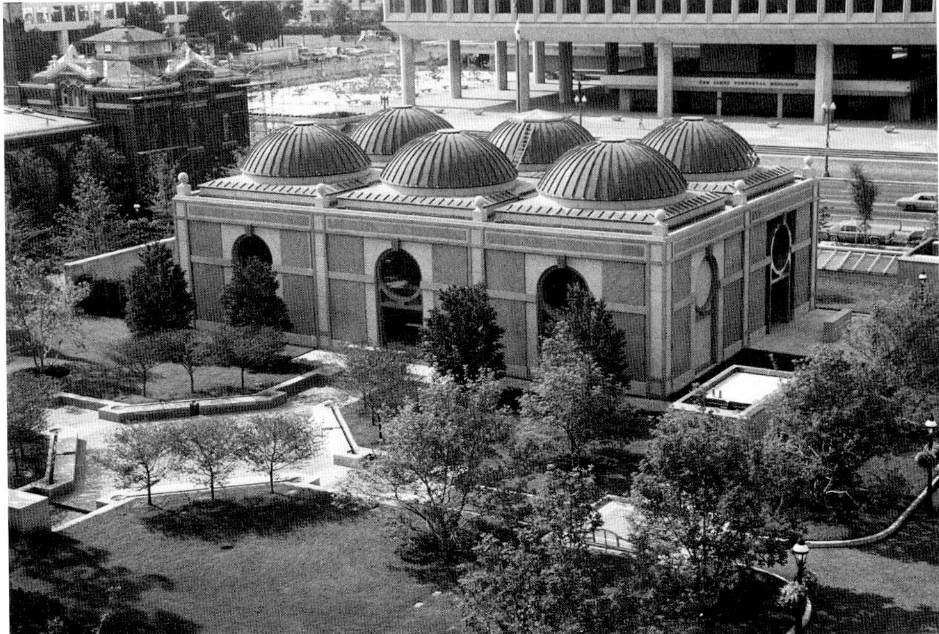

7.1 National Museum of African Art, viewed from the top of Smithsonian Institution building, 1987. Photo: Jeff Tinsley. Smithsonian Archives.

The "crisis of representation" Drewal observed refers to the history of the field; over the preceding century, museums and private individuals created collections, exhibitions, and catalog that now collectively defined both the canon and the market value of the new field of African art. Surely, the canon had always been questioned (see chap. 4). Yet in view of the profound political, social, and artistic changes both on the African continent and in the US, the very idea of a canon had become increasingly difficult to defend and maintain.[4] In the late 1980s and early 1990s, therefore, the hierarchy of values shifted toward the contemporary and gave way to a reconfiguration of the field.

A key element both informing and driving this process was the weakening and growing "exhaustion" of high modernism.[5] In the West, the historical demarcation between art and commodity not only granted artists an elitist, avant-garde status but also gave rise to the distinction between "real" progressive art and "cheap" consumer kitsch. From the 1950s onward, however, this binary began to show cracks. Pop artists like Andy Warhol explored techniques of seriality and challenged notions of originality, innovation, and authorship. Similar developments happened in music and literature. In 1969, the American literary critic Leslie Fiedler declared, provocatively in the men's lifestyle and erotic magazine *Play-boy*, that modernist literature was dead and called on cultural elites to "cross the border" and "close the gap" between high and low art.[6] A decade later, the French philosopher Jean-François Lyotard proclaimed the end of the explanatory power of modernity's great "master narratives" such as "progress" or "emancipation."[7] And in 1983, the German art historian Hans Belting asked whether the history of art (in terms of its representation of a linear progression) had not in fact come to an end.[8]

These provocations were flanked by an increasing postcolonial awareness of the techniques of representation by means of which the "West" had managed to construct its colonial "other." The term *postcolonial* meant more than just a historical signifier of the period after colonialism. Rather it entailed challenging a colonial mode of thinking about identity and cultural productions (see chap. 8) Formerly unquestioned models of representation were now identified and discussed as "dispositives" or configurations of power.[9] The effect was a "crisis of representation" that allowed for a critical deconstruction of the "other" in fields such as literature,[10] sociology,[11] and anthropology.[12] As Drewal put it in his lecture, "If anything characterizes this postmodern era it is the fundamental reorientation of power centers in the world that makes dialogue, not authoritarian pronouncement, a necessity."[13]

In hindsight, it is striking how quickly—roughly from the late 1980s to the early 1990s—the field of African art studies underwent a profound transformation, generated by the convergence of different and competing paradigms. Since these explorations into the new terrain of contestation played out largely in the arena of exhibitions, this chapter focuses on how American and European museums and curators in the "postmodern era" changed the way they presented Africa to their Western audiences. Setting the stage for the discussion is the dispute over the 1984 MoMA show *"Primitivism" in 20th Century Art*. I will then chronologically move from the 1989 *Magiciens de la terre* in Paris to the early 1990s exhibitions *Africa Explores* and *Fusion*, in New York and Venice respectively. The middle section of this chapter tackles the conceptual debates on authenticity, popular art, and the question of value that pushed the transformation of the field from within.

Primitivism Reconfigured

An important marker of the postmodern turn in African art studies was the debate that ensued over the exhibition *"Primitivism" in 20th Century Art*, which was shown from September 1984 to January 1985 at the Museum of Modern Art in New York. Conceived by MoMA curator William

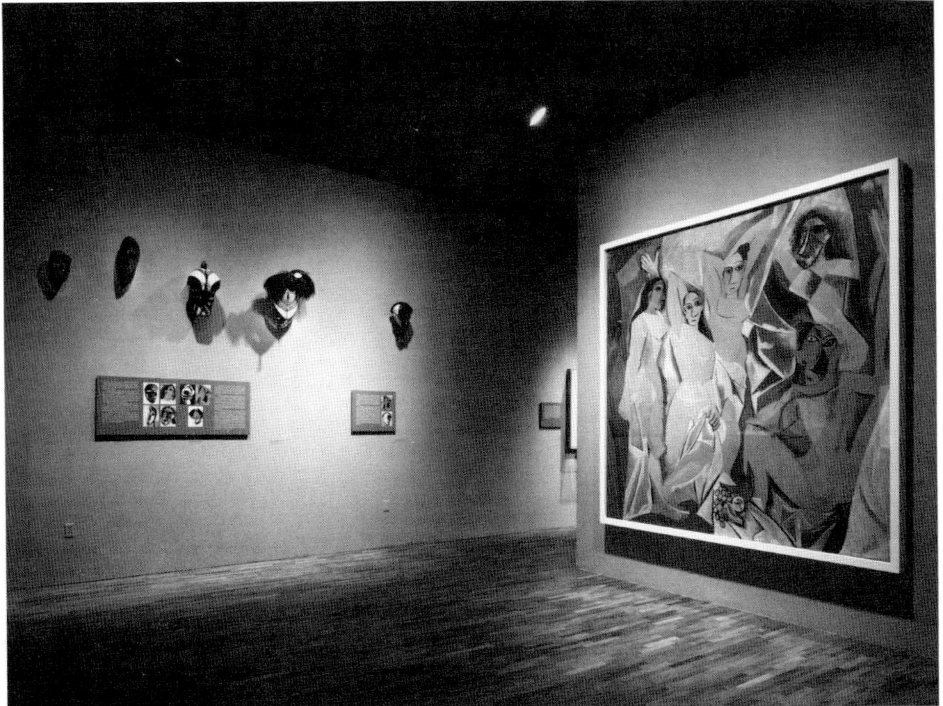

7.2 Installation view of *"Primitivism" in 20th Century Art* with Pablo Picasso's *Les demoiselles d'Avignon* on the right and African masks that inspired the painting on the left, Paris, 1989. Photo: Katherine Keller. Digital image © The Museum of Modern Art / Licensed by SCALA / Art Resource, NY.

Rubin and subtitled "Affinity between the Tribal and the Modern," the exhibition aimed both to defend and revive the critical energy of the modernist movement. For Rubin, "primitive" was not a derogatory term; it was not meant to evoke nineteenth-century notions of savagery and cultural darkness. Instead, by juxtaposing "tribal" sculptures from Africa, Oceania, and Mesoamerica with works of "modern" avant-garde European artists, Rubin sought to reclaim the revelatory truthfulness of "primitive" art in terms of its supposed authenticity and proximity to the wellsprings of creativity and spirituality (fig. 7.2).

Clearly, Rubin and his cocurator Kirk Varnedoe were very much aware of the complex and contested terrain within which the exhibition operated. After all, they had opted to put "primitivism" in quotation marks. Varnedoe rationalized this decision as a reference to the "political" and "dark side" of primitivism, which he called "primitivism per se."[14]

The idea of primitivism as flight from civilization, or of Primitive art as a wholly "outsider" challenge, is an offshoot of the Romantic notion that true progress, true revolution, indeed truth in its most irreducible sense is only accessible when we step outside the enchaining confines of culture. Modern ideas of the mind and of the constraints of language suggest that this fantasy of escape is never realized. Yet this need not mean that the power of primitivism lies only in delusion, or that we are prisoners of conventions that bar us from contact with anything beyond our ken, or kin. Modern thought and style are not only blinders but also powerful lenses. The history of modernism, primitivism, and the character of its best recent examples speak directly to the point. This is a process of revolution that begins and ends in modern culture, and because of that—not in spite of it—can continually expand and deepen our contact with that which is remote and different from us, and continually threaten, challenge, and reform our sense of self.[15]

One might well have expected to find these self-reflexive declarations at the beginning of the massive catalog that accompanied the exhibition. Instead, they come at the very end—a position that reifies the fact that the show bypassed the colonial context of its topic almost entirely, leaving the quotation marks in the title to appear as an empty gesture. As if nothing had happened since the 1920s and 1930s, the artifacts were displayed as timeless and nameless works, unaccompanied by label or wall texts, and thus reduced to mere prompts for the formalist appreciation of Euro-American modernism. Hardly surprisingly then, the exhibition became a major source of contention among critics. While some praised it as holding up the last lantern of modernism, others disparaged its attempt to revive a patient that had already long been declared dead.[16]

On the level of curation and exhibition, arguably the most prominent response to the *"Primitivism"* show in New York was *Magiciens de la terre* in Paris. From May to August 1989, the exhibition ran at the Centre Georges Pompidou and the Grande Halle de la Villette in Paris.[17] Organized by a curatorial team around the French art historian Jean Hubert Martin, the exhibition aimed to decentralize both the art world and its Western-oriented mindset by presenting works from contemporary European and American artists side by side with works by non-Western artists and ritual specialists from all five continents. To bridge the vast differences among all the 104 artists represented— seventeen from Africa and six from the African diaspora in Haiti, Brazil, and Cuba—Martin posited terming the artists "magicians" to provide a common denominator, openly alluding to Picasso's famous understanding of art as "a form of magic designed as mediator between this strange, hostile world and us."[18]

The main entrance to the exhibition was the French National Museum of Modern Art at the Centre Pompidou. Attracting attention and visibly marking the event was a huge carbon fiber and fiberglass globe by the New Zealand artist Neil Dawson suspended high up over the museum's industrial structure (fig. 7.3). Visitors entering the exhibition space encountered a big red billboard by the American artist Barbara Kruger, which addressed the theme of the show by asking *Qui sont les magiciens de la terre?* (Who are the magicians of the earth?) Right behind, next to the reverse side of the billboard, which stated *On n'a plus besoins de héros* (We no longer need heroes), stood a huge Ijele mask by the Nigerian Mike Chukwukelu, who constructed the mask right before the show out of five hundred objects he found in Paris. The visitors who passed the entrance saw themselves confronted with a perplexing array of comparisons and juxtapositions. In the Grande Hall, for instance, a huge circular wall painting (*Red Earth's Circle*) by the British artist Richard Long hung over a dream painting by a group of Aboriginal artists from Yuendumu in the Northern Territory of Australia, which was flanked by South African Esther Mahlangu's geometric Ndebele house designs and an ensemble of royal Abomey emblems and statues by Cyprien Tokoudagba from Benin (fig. 7.4). At each station, wall labels showed the artist's name and place of origin in the center of a globe image, thus conveying the unifying message of the exhibition in terms of breaking down hierarchies of genre, geography, status, and value.

While the show left many visitors with a sense of bewilderment, the catalog tied the diverse works together in a manifesto-like critique of how the West imaged "the other" as part of a "grand alibi" to exploit, appropriate, and dominate the world. The key piece was a collage of texts and photographs illustrating this thesis. Other contributions came from Martin and his collaborators (Francis, Solillou, Magnin, and Gaudinert) plus two external authors: the art critic Thomas McEvilley and the literary scholar Homi Bhabha. The latter reflected on postcolonial notions of hybridity and difference, while the former explained the exhibition as a postmodern antidote to the *"Primitivism"* show, which had ignored the contemporaneity of the "tribal" artist and penned them into a prehistorical cage. And yet, just like MoMA's *"Primitivism,"* Martin's *Magiciens* occasioned waves of mostly negative criticism.

The first wave came in a series of essays commissioned by *Cahiers du Musée national d'art,* then later translated into English for a special issue of the new journal *Third Text,* founded and edited by the artist, critic, and

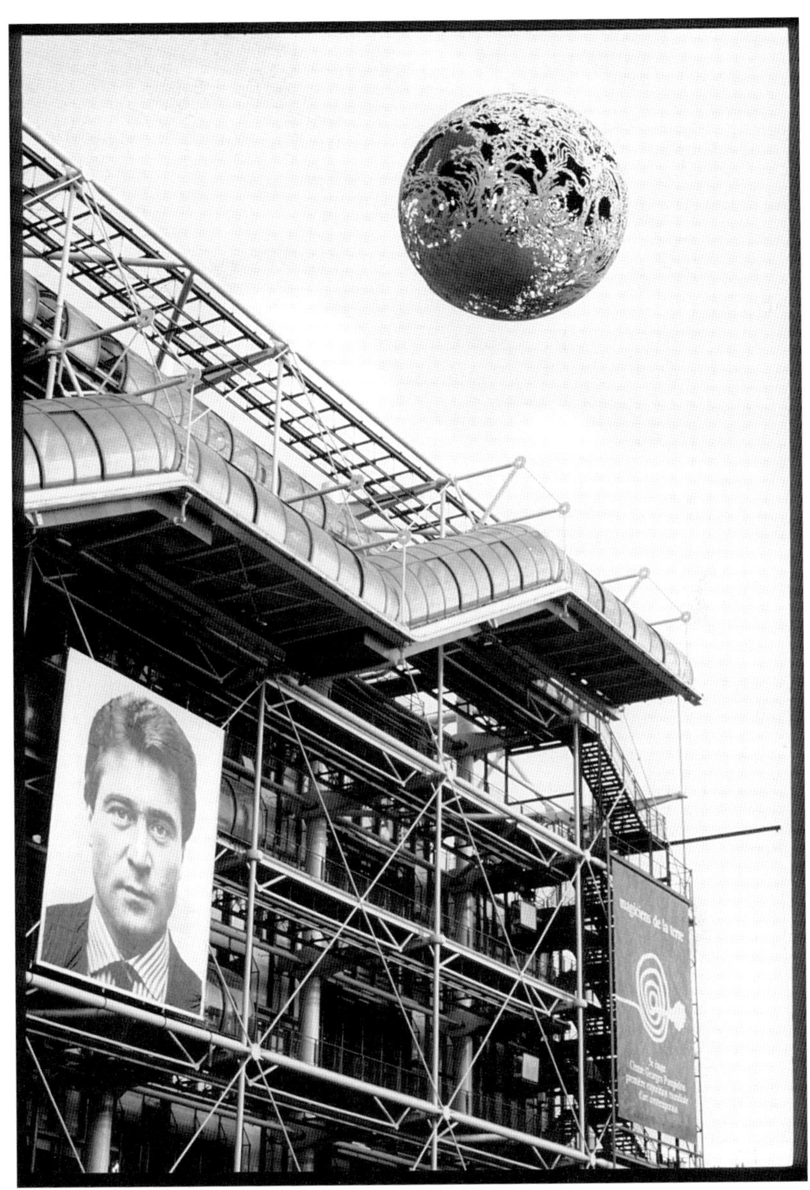

7.3 Neil Dawson, *Globe*, hanging over Centre Pompidou at the exhibition *Magiciens de la terre*, Paris, 1989. Photo: Béatrice Hatala. © CNAC/MNAM, Dist. RMN-Grand Palais, Art Resource, NY.

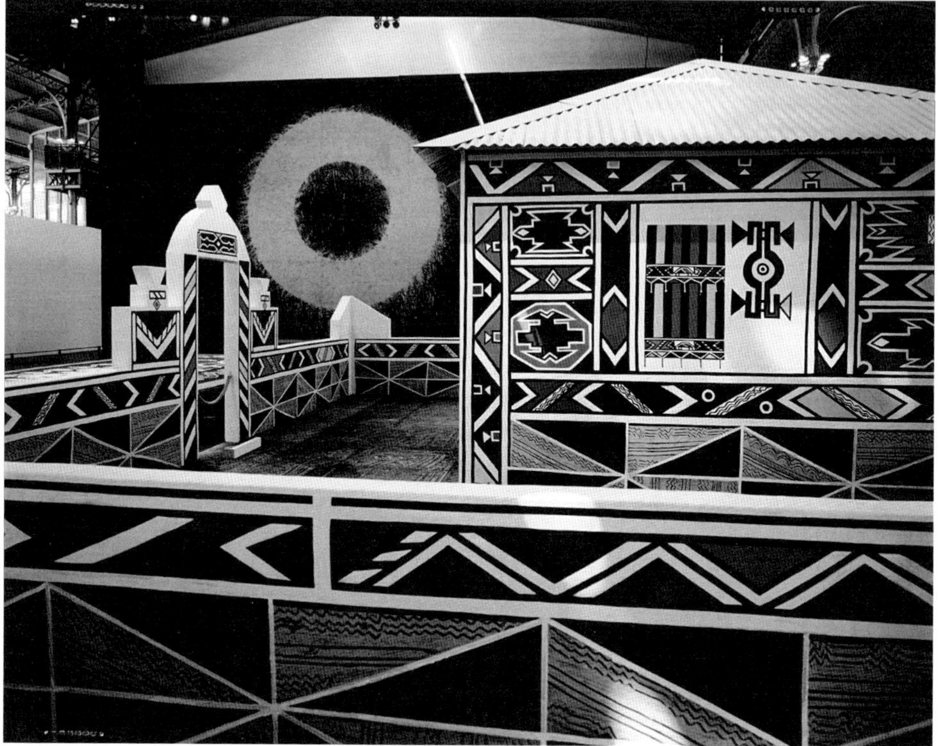

7.4 Installation view of *Magiciens de la terre* with Esther Mahlangu's Ndebele house designs in the fore and Richard Long's *Red Earth's Circle* in the back, Paris, 1989. Photo: Konstantinos Ignatiadis. © 2020. Richard Long. All Rights Reserved, DACS / London / ARS, NY.

participant of the Paris show Rasheed Araeen. Araeen displayed a series of his paintings in the 1989 Paris exhibition while also organizing his own show, *The Other Story: Asian, African and Caribbean Artists in Postwar Britain* at the Hayward Gallery in London.[19] In the introduction to the special issue of *Third Text*, he criticized Martin's show for its exoticizing focus on so-called folk artists to the complete exclusion of academically trained modern artists from Africa. Why did Martin feature artists like Chéri Samba and not Ben Enwonwu or Uzo Egonu, another London-based Nigerian modernist whose work Araeen had shown in *The Other Story* (fig. 7.5)? However, Araeen's critique went further, challenging the validity and parity of the exhibition's ostensible focus on folk, or popular art:

> If all things are equal and same, why was nobody sent to the villages of Europe? Is there no folk or traditional art in Europe? If the pur-

pose of the exhibition was to question distinctions between modern works of art and folk or traditional art, why was this not done also within or in relation to Western culture? It appears that the assumption is that Western culture alone passed from one historical period to another and its contemporary creativity is represented only by modern art. . . . Are we really breaking the distinctions or reinforcing the very same assumptions which divide the world into the West (modern/dynamic) and the "other" (traditional/static)? There is no point in repeating here that traditions do not necessarily represent static societies. The important point is that other cultures have already aspired to modernity, and as a result have produced modern works of art.[20]

In line with Araeen, other critics questioned whether the *Magiciens* exhibit succeeded in its purported aim to surpass the modernist instrumentalization of the "other" that informed the MoMA *"Primitivism"* show. In two probing interviews with Martin, art historian Benjamin Buchloh critiqued the seemingly neoprimitivist premise of the enterprise and questioned whether the show's inclusive approach was any better than the politics of exclusion it set out to overcome.[21] Martin admitted the impossibility of pure objectivity, explaining that his choice of artists was ultimately based purely on his own personal aesthetic sensibility and taste. This acknowledgment led the English critic Jean Fisher to discredit the show as Martin's personal *Wunderkammer*, designed to elicit a sense of wonder and excitement based not on quality but on a naive and misguided curiosity and exoticism.[22] In a similar vein, Sally Price pointed to the dubious authority of connoisseurship and the role of the collector in the long history of exhibiting "primitive art in civilized places."[23]

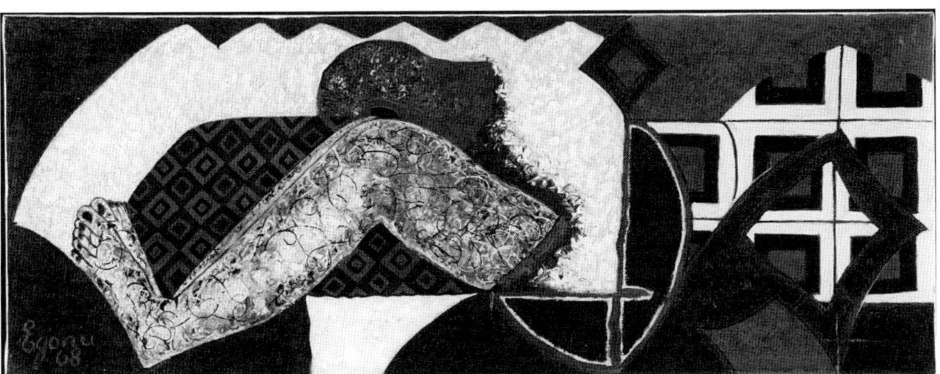

7.5 Uzo Egonu, *Woman in Grief*, 1968. Oil on canvas, 48.2 × 12 cm. The title refers to the casualties of the battle over Onitsha, Egonu's city of birth, during the Nigerian civil war (1967–1970). Digital image © Tate Gallery, London.

Yet despite all the outrage and protest, *Magiciens* did change the museum landscape and did increase the visibility of African artists. As Thomas McEvilley, one of the contributors to the catalog, noted one year after the show,

> "Magiciens" opened the door of the long-insular and hermetic Western art world to Third World artists. The question is not really whether the people who opened the door had gravy on their jackets, or slipped and fell as they were opening it. The question is this and only this: as we enter the global village of the 1990s would any of us really rather that the door remained closed?[24]

McEvilley's seemingly rhetorical question as to whether "we" would collectively choose to keep the door closed to "Third World" art hints at what became a heated debate about the definition of value, its relationship to authenticity, and its relevance to what the critics termed "popular art."

Fakes and Fictions

As exemplified by Kane Kwei's figurative wood coffins from Ghana, or Chéri Samba's urban genre paintings from the Democratic Republic of the Congo, African "popular" or "urban" art held a prominent presence in the *Magiciens* show. Like pop art in Europe and the US, it was tied to a new consumer and commodity culture and appealed particularly to youth. Unlike in Europe and the US, however, it was not taken up by academic artists but remained, as it were, in the streets, where it became an expression of the experience of colonial and urban modernity.

In terms of scholarship, among the first accounts of African popular art were those of Ulli Beier in the 1960s. Beier focused mostly on Nigeria's new visual cultures in commercial centers such as Onitsha in the southeast, where signwriters had produced paintings that drew on the tradition of cheap pamphlet market literature.[25] Beier's reports were followed by Johannes and Ilona Fabian's studies of popular painting in the mining towns of the Democratic Republic of the Congo, then still Zaire (fig. 7.6).[26] The subjects of these Congolese paintings ranged from political and historical events like the assassination of Congo's first president after independence Patrice Lumumba to supernatural presences like Mami Wata, a popular water spirit associated with modernity, sexuality, and dubious wealth, often depicted in the form of a seductive mermaid. As the Fabians pointed out, people valued these paintings not in terms of their formal and aesthetic features but for the stories they triggered. Paintings were thus interwoven, along with music and memories, into the fabric

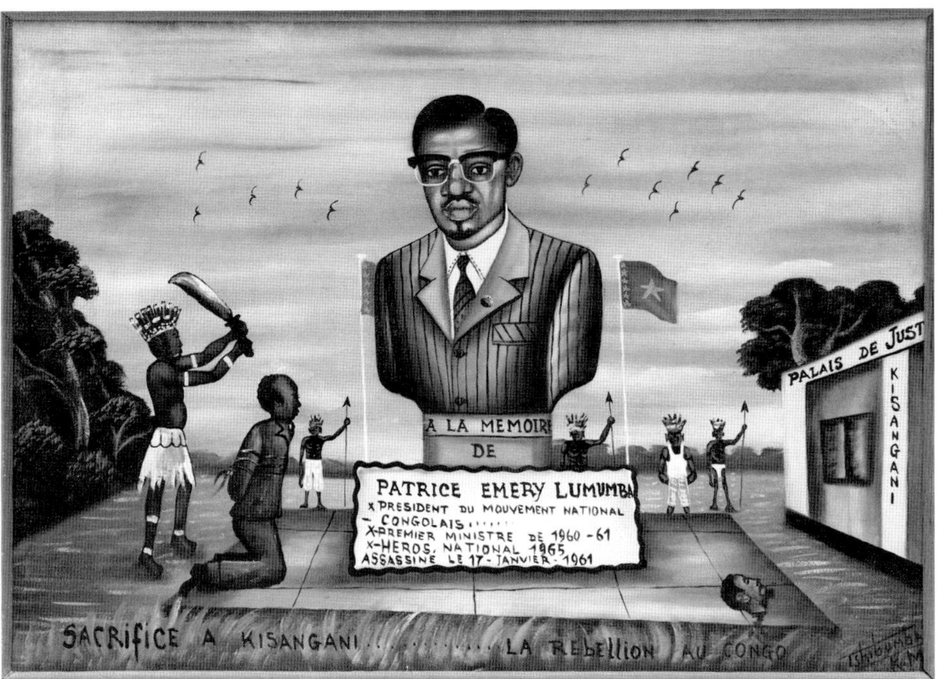

7.6 Tshibumba Kanda-Matulu, *Sacrifice a Kisangani . . . La Rebellion au Congo*, early 1960s. Oil on canvas, 40 × 60 cm. Courtesy of Iwalewa Haus, Universität Bayreuth.

of the community's cultural life in a way that preserved shared experiences and undergirded social interactions. As Fabian would later phrase it, the paintings "remember the present."[27] By the late 1980s, enough research on popular art had accumulated to warrant a special issue of *African Studies Review* devoted to the topic. In the lead article, Karin Barber acknowledged the fuzzy boundaries of the genre encompassing visual, literary, and performance arts.[28] What holds the various forms together, she argued, is their situatedness in the informal and unofficial realm that allows popular art to be unregulated and outside institutionalized control, either through the state or through traditional authorities.

Given the fluid character of popular art, it is no coincidence that its discovery and discussion fell together with a debate over authenticity and connoisseurship. In 1975, Father Joseph Cornet, then director of the National Museum of what was at that time Zaire, published "African Art and Authenticity."[29] In view of the museums' nation-building mission, Cornet asked how one distinguishes between authentic and inauthentic works in the documentation of the (stylistic) history of Central African art. For Cornet, the criterion of "tradition" or "tribal" was far too simplis-

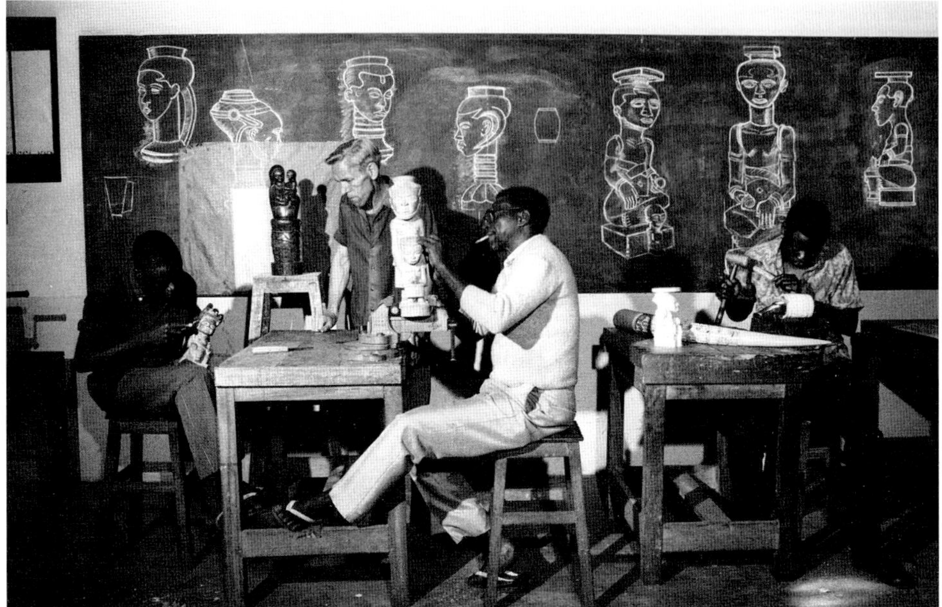

7.7 Mission School, Mushenge, Congo, 1972. Father Cyprien L. Herbers with students carving *ndop* statues. Photo: Eliot Elisofon. © Eliot Elisofon Photographic Archive, National Museum of African Art, Smithsonian Institution.

tic. Contrary to William Fagg—for whom a work was deemed authentic only if it had been produced by a traditional artist, for a traditional purpose, and in conformity with traditional forms (see chap. 4)—Cornet argued that the complexities of the field defied such a tidy definition. For instance, among the Kuba, the famous *ndop* royal portraits had ceased to be produced locally and were now manufactured in mission-led workshops whose participants hailed from non-Kuba areas (fig. 7.7). In other cases, such as that of a prominent type of Songye *tshifwebe* masks, new forms had been developed and performed, originating not in Songye society but in the aesthetic preferences of a European trader and his clients. In the light of these facts, Cornet wondered whether the whole question of authenticity was not "a false issue which exists only because it is characteristic of our time."[30]

The phrase "of our time" was a barely concealed reference to Zaire's nationalist policy of *authenticité,* introduced in the late 1960s by head of state Mobutu Sese Seko in order to counter unwelcome Western influences and silence internal critics.[31] As director of Zaire's national Museum, Cornet realized that Mobutu's political usage of authenticity had practically discredited the concept. Still, despite his ambivalence about the term, he ultimately upheld the value of authenticity as an indispensable feature of (art-)historical analysis, albeit by loosening and broadening its meaning from that posited by Fagg and others, to propose that a "work is authentic to the extent that it belongs to the space and time which fit the corresponding style."[32]

Cornet's article prompted John Povey, the editor of *African Arts*, to produce a special issue on *Fakes, Fakers, and Fakery*, which appeared one year later in April 1976. As the title indicates, the discussion was mostly about what was seen as intentional and straightforward fraud or deceit. Surely, fakes had been an issue from the very beginning of the field, but as the identities of certain individual "traditional artists" became known (see chap. 4), the issue took on an additional importance. Fakery was now discussed as an attack on the established canon and the authority of connoisseurship. At stake was the legitimacy of both the museum and the market as spaces for the negotiation of value. Marilyn Houlberg, for example, referred to her own research among the Yoruba in Nigeria, where Muslim and Christian parents of twins had come to use plastic dolls and photographs instead of wooden *ibeji* twin carvings to mark their distance from "pagan" Yoruba beliefs.[33] Her finding corresponded with Daniel Biebuyck's observation among the Lega people in the Democratic Republic of the Congo: whereas in the past initiates into the secret *bami* society had learned about the *bwami* codes using small handmade ivory figurines, Western-made Madonnas, dolls, and electric light bulbs had recently been substituted—apparently with no loss or detriment to cultural transmission.[34] Confronted with these real-world instances, Houlberg asked, "How do we decide what is authentic African art? Is it what we—the art historians, anthropologists, collectors, or museum curators—say is authentic, or does this decision rightfully belong to the art-producing culture itself?"[35]

In 1976, that question was more or less rhetorical; however, fifteen years later it came back with force. In 1990, when the study of African art had effectively entered the postmodern era, the editors of *African Arts* commissioned Sidney Kasfir to revisit and reexamine the concept of authenticity.[36] The choice of the author was well founded. Kasfir had a reputation as an innovative and iconoclastic thinker who, early on, had not only tackled new fields like contemporary art but had dismantled cherished notions like the "one style–one tribe" paradigm.[37] Titled "African Art and Authenticity: A Text with a Shadow," Kasfir's essay, published in *African Arts* in 1992, combined Cornet's reflections on authenticity from 1975 with the poststructuralist position of the French literary theorist Roland Barthes, who provided Kasfir's epigraph:

There are those who want a text (an art, a painting) without a shadow, without the "dominant ideology," but this is to want a text without fecundity, without productivity, a sterile text. The text needs its shadow: this shadow is a bit of ideology, a bit of representation, a bit of subject: ghosts, pockets, traces, necessary clouds: subversion must produce its own chiaroscuro.[38]

Following Barthes, Kasfir argued that the meaning of African art (the "text") cannot be separated from its reception (the "shadow"); it has to include the role of Western dealers, curators, and connoisseurs operating in a Western-dominated art market. Consequently, Kasfir maintained, the market's criteria for authenticity do not reflect local (African) perceptions and practices but are based on a number of "fictions" rooted in modern European capitalist history and the colonial appropriation of Africa. It was Europe's quest for an uncorrupted, premodern, noncommodified "other" that resulted in the notion of African art as a radical antipode to the European experience of (capitalist) modernity. To maintain this fiction, any European presence in African art had to be eliminated. As a result, African art was mystified as stemming from a "pure" time— that is, that African art existed before European contact—produced by homogenous tribes representing a timeless tribal past, expressing collective religious beliefs and attitudes, and embodying core cultural values. Aesthetic and political realities that contradicted these projections and instead expressed the modern character of African societies were generally excluded—with the result that museums ignored modern African art just as they excluded "tourist art" from their display cases. To support and illustrate her argument, Kasfir drew from her own extensive fieldwork in Uganda, Nigeria, and Kenya.[39]

The immediate reactions to Kasfir's essay were mixed. Verdicts in *African Arts* ranged from "provocative"[40] to "trendy"[41] and "pretentious."[42] Among museum respondents, a certain reluctance and nervousness as to the consequences of the arguments prevailed. At the same time, none of the points Kasfir raised were particularly new; all participants in the "authenticity" debate were aware that similar criticisms had been raised before. Moreover, Kasfir's argument had not altered the close proximity of market and scholarship. *African Arts,* the flagship journal of the field, remained replete with ads from dealers, galleries, and auction houses celebrating the very "fictions" Kasfir targeted. What was new and different, however, was the larger intellectual landscape in which Kasfir's argument landed. By the early 1990s, the primitivist spirit that had once created the study of African art had finally given way to fresh theoretical takes and a critical revision of the field.

Of particular importance were new studies on value and processes of valuation coming out of sociology and anthropology. In 1979, the French sociologist Pierre Bourdieu published the results of his extensive empirical research on questions of taste, class, and aesthetic judgments conducted in France.[43] As Bourdieu argued, people's position in a particular social field enables or restricts their access to and use of different sorts of capital (social, economic, and cultural or symbolic). Seen from this angle, taste functions as a form of social distinction. Rather than an individual and idiosyncratic sensation, taste informs, consolidates, and replicates social class differences. The English translation of Bourdieu's work was published in 1984. Two years later, the anthropologist Arjun Appadurai widened the debate on value by shifting the focus from the social fields of subjects to the social life of objects, or "the social life of things" as he called the edited volume.[44] The book grew out of a conference that aimed to understand commodities from a cultural perspective. Adopting that angle, Appadurai and his colleagues focused on processes of exchange and circulation. As the authors of the volume argued, the meaning and value of things are not fixed; instead, they are shaped by different "regimes" and "tournaments of value."[45] That is to say, it is by moving through processes of exchange that things acquire—or change— their particular value and status. What was once an ordinary commodity—a carpet or a painting, originally made to be sold for money or another medium of exchange—can become a precious and inalienable object intimately entwined with the identity of its possessor. But the same item can also lose its elevated status and "relapse," as it were, into a plain commodity. To understand these processes, the authors proposed to focus on the "cultural biographies" of objects. As one of the authors, Igor Kopytoff, explained, as we identify and study the "biographies" of things by tracing their way through different classifications and circulation spheres, both in time and space, new insights into the malleability of meaning and value emerge.[46]

The new scholarship on value and valuation not only informed Kasfir's essay on authenticity but also formed the line of demarcation between her critics and her supporters. Among the latter was Christopher Steiner, for whom Kasfir had shown that "authenticity is the *product* of art historical evaluation, not its determinant."[47] The verdict echoed Steiner's own anthropological fieldwork on the market of African art in Abidjan, the capital of Côte d'Ivoire.[48] Field studies on the African art market had been carried out before,[49] but Steiner's book differed in three decisive ways. First, it focused on a group hitherto ignored by researchers on African art: the local traders who act as middlemen between the artists and artisans on the one hand and the dealers and their clients (collectors and curators) on the other. Second, it traced the alteration of (art) objects (such as the removal of parts or the creation of an artificial patina) in the course of their global circulation from the local production sites in Abidjan's hinterland to the end-consumer in the US, thus providing deep ethnographic insights into the hidden rules and workings of the art market. Finally, it employed an effective theoretical model for analyzing both the dynamics of the circulation of objects and the lives of the people caught up in the circulation. In fact, it may be argued that it was primarily Steiner's ethnographic portrayal of the traders and their interactions with their clients that lay behind the book's success. In conjunction with a documentary film that focused on one of the traders, the book revealed what had been obscured by dealers, galleries, and auction houses.[50] Learning and seeing just how objects in the course of their travel from production to display change meaning, status—and price—made abstract phrases like "regimes of value" and "biography of things" real and concrete.[51]

Steiner's study reinforced many scholars' growing skepticism of the field's entanglement with the market. To finance the costly production of the field's main periodical, *African Arts*, editors relied on advertisements from African art galleries whose commercial interest and sensational images often oddly contradicted the critical arguments put forth by the articles in the journal. As Fabian had asked in response to Kasfir's authenticity essay, "What happens (does anything happen?) in cohabitation in *African Arts* between scholarly disquisitions and commercial advertisements that get almost equal space?"[52] Yet the fear of market corruption was not the only concern. There was also the increasing presence—or rather resurfacing—of contemporary art.

As we have seen in chapters 5 and 6, the late 1960s and early 1970s saw a recognition of "Neo-African," contemporary art forms. But the recognition did not last long. The field did not embrace modern art. A feeling of uncertainty prevailed. Most scholars felt ill equipped to assess and deal with these new forms of artistic expression. Those who had the expertise were largely outside the academy. It was an expertise gained by training and working with artists in their studios. Within the academy things were different. Because of its close connection to the "tribal art" market, what continued to dominate in one form or the other was Fagg's tribality model. Critical interventions allowed for modifications, but they did not question the model's validity and value. In fact, an alternative value system had not yet evolved. Auction houses were not interested.

Two decades later, the interest in the contemporary eventually resurfaced. In 1990, the Studio Museum in Harlem showed *Contemporary African Art: Changing Traditions*.[53] While public reception remained modest, the show nevertheless elicited an editorial in the journal of *African Arts*: "What are we going to do about contemporary African art?" John Povey, the founding editor of the journal, asked.[54] Twenty-three years earlier, Povey had written on Ibrahim El-Salahi in the journal's very first issue (see chap. 5). Looking back, he pondered the field's reluctance to accept contemporary art as a legitimate field of study. For Povey, the culprit was the canon that had evolved in Euro-America in the early decades of the twentieth century. Not only had it triggered the West's aesthetic interest in African sculpture but also it had also created a canon whose binary logic (art versus craft, modern versus traditional, autonomous versus functional, etc.) resisted any fundamental change. As Povey insisted, however, "the issue of contemporary art will not go away."[55]

His admonishment proved prophetic. Only one year later, in 1991, the Center for African Art in New York showed Susan Vogel's *Africa Explores: 20th Century African Art*, an exhibition that addressed both the contemporary and the contemporaneity question with contentious force.

Curating "Voices"

Susan Vogel, the curator and intellectual head of *Africa Explores*, was by then founding director of the center. Established in 1982, the center was a private institution on New York's Upper East Side, not far from the Metropolitan Museum of Art, where Vogel had formerly worked as an associate curator in the "primitive art" department.[56] As a student of Robert Goldwater with fieldwork experience among the Baule in Côte d'Ivoire, Vogel embodied the fusion of the canon-defending formalist/modernist art connoisseur with that of the unruly postmodern rebel, a position whose seeming contradictions she explored at the center.

Housed in an old townhouse, the center made up for its spatial limitations by exploring new approaches to exhibiting and thinking about African art. A key part of this practice was to work through issues of meaning and representation. In 1987, Vogel had organized *Perspectives: Angles of African Art*, for which she invited ten different "curators" (artists, writers, scholars, collectors) to choose ten different images from a body of a hundred photographs of objects and explain their choice. A year later, Vogel presented the much-noted show *ART/artifact* which discussed the distinction as a matter of framing.[57] That is, the categories and classifications echo "our" aesthetics; they don't reflect "theirs."

Africa Explores: 20th Century African Art pushed the debate further by stressing the contemporaneity of different genres, or "strains," as Vogel called them, existing side by side. Dispensing with fixation on the (seemingly lost) past, she demonstrated the creativity and diversity of African art in terms of its aesthetic acumen to digest and "explore" what is happening in the present:

> "Africa Explores" seeks to focus on Africa, its concerns, and its art and artists in their own contexts and in their own voices. Western perceptions of Africa, and Western uses of African art, are entirely secondary here, as are isolated African uses of Western ideologies.[58]

The "voices" consisted of 135 works from a variety of artists, each representing a different strain/genre exemplifying the heterogeneity and dynamics of an African modernity. As Vogel noted, the strains themselves were "conceptual tools rather than sequential or developmental phases, for they provide not a history of twentieth-century African art but an interpretation of it."[59] Thus, Dogon masks and Bamana marionettes represented "village-based, traditional" art. Kane Kwei's figurative coffins, Sunday Jack Akpan's human cement sculptures, as well as wholesale plastic Yoruba *ibeji* twin figures were said to exemplify "new functional art" (fig. 7.8). The genre paintings of Chéri Samba and his Congolese colleagues were presented as "urban art." Artists such as Paris-based

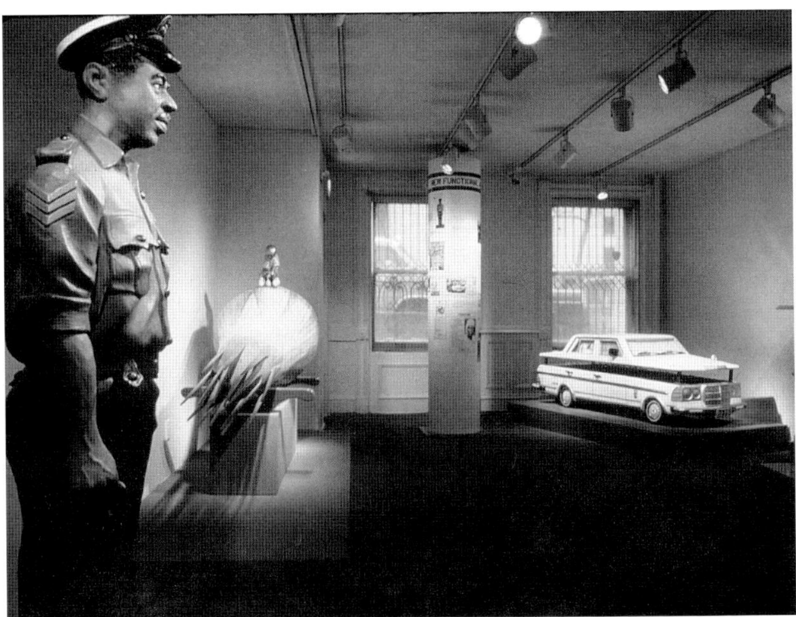

7.8 Installation view of *Africa Explores: 20th Century African Art* at the Center for African Art, New York City, 1991, with Sunday Jack Akpan's cement sculpture and Kane Kwei's figurative coffins. Center for African Art, courtesy of Susan Mullin Vogel.

Iba N'Diaye and London-based Sokari Douglas Camp were presented as creators of "international art," and emotionally as well as politically charged emblems of cultural identity like the ivory masks of the Benin Queen Mother, once looted by British forces and now in Western museums, were labeled "extinct art" (see chapter 4, fig. 4.6).

To expand the space, Vogel divided the exhibition between two locales: Vogel's Center for African Art on the Upper East Side and the New Modern Museum in Lower Manhattan.[60] Within both exhibition spaces, different wall colors marked the different genres the works were said to represent. Wall texts and labels were presented on round kiosks in each gallery, a design as well as an interpretative decision Vogel later explained as follows:

> We chose the kiosk because like a community bulletin board, it carried connotations of popular notices and posters, with their transience and informality, and implied that the information contained there might constantly change, and that it came from different people and could not be definite. We hoped that visitors would "read" these qualities into the messages without focusing particularly on the kiosk itself. Alongside all the other voices on each kiosk, the museums' voice appeared only in the heading and in a short, general text. Among the items posted were statements and letters from the artists, quotes from scholars and critics, photographs, clippings from African newspapers and even a cartoon. Because the conversation on contemporary African art is so new, and there is still so little consensus on major questions, this seemed a good way to present contradictory information and to convey the statement's contingent nature.[61]

The deliberate questioning of curatorial authority worked. Visitors responded positively to the attempt to convey the continent's artistic diversity and largely acknowledged the show's pioneering gesture. Within the field, however, the reception was different. While the show's ambition to expand the parameters of the field was recognized (studio photography, for instance, was recognized as an important art form; contemporary women artists, formerly practically absent, received visibility; globalism was acknowledged as a key part of the African art world), critics were quick to point out conceptual and curatorial flaws. Thus, Vogel's effort to let artists, or rather, their works, "speak" for themselves conflicted with her role as the show's organizer—that is, the one who selected and curated the "voices." The same applied to the strains Vogel identified as an organizational principle of the show. Despite her own admission that the strains were "interpretations," Vogel proclaimed that "Western perceptions" were "secondary." Not surprisingly, then, the exhibition became a focal point of contention from several directions.[62] The most trenchant critique came from the Nigerian American artist, critic, and scholar Olu Oguibe and focused on Vogel's curatorial authority as a self-described "intimate outsider."[63] In an incisive review, Oguibe especially took issue with the show's ambition to provide a new look at African art.[64] For him, what was presented as an opening was in fact a closure or, as he put it, a "thinly disguised colonial-ethnography-as-the-new-art-history."[65] For Oguibe, then, the takeaway was straightforward: "Africans must narrate themselves and must not be mere stagehands in a ventriloquist show."[66]

The demand echoed the "crisis of representation" I referred to at the beginning of this chapter. Questions of history, power, and legitimacy were at stake. Who speaks for whom, and on what grounds? While postmodern critique had allowed for the multicultural recognition of difference and otherness, the "others" were now beginning to speak back, a move that also affected Vogel's other venture into the contemporary.

In 1993, two years after *Africa Explores*, Vogel curated *Fusion* at the Venice Biennale, where she presented five artists from Senegal and Côte d'Ivoire. It was the second time the biennale had shown sub-Saharan African contemporary artists; three years earlier, Grace Stanislaus from the Studio Museum in Harlem, with support from the Rockefeller Foundation, presented a reduced version of *Contemporary African Art: Changing Traditions* (see above) in an "African countries pavilion" by focusing on artists from Nigeria and Zimbabwe. This time, though, the show did not just survey recent artworks from different nations but focused on notions of cultural hybridity and nomadism.

In the early 1990s, both were seen as postmodern phenomena generated by new global flows of capital, ideas, and people that were understood to have effectively changed the modern(ist) legacy of nation-states and bounded identities. Alluding to these ideas, Vogel explained the show's rationale as follows:

> The show is intended to contribute to a new understanding of "African art" that will remove it from the realm of the ethnographic, and place it firmly within the framework of the transcultural aesthetic that has become accepted practice among Western artists. The free-ranging references found in contemporary African work may come as a surprise to those who remember it as bound by Africa's great art of the past, or who expect it to be subservient to contemporary Western art. In their melding of cultural codes from their own ancient traditions and from the cacophonous present, contemporary African artists may have independently arrived at their own post-Modern aesthetic.[67]

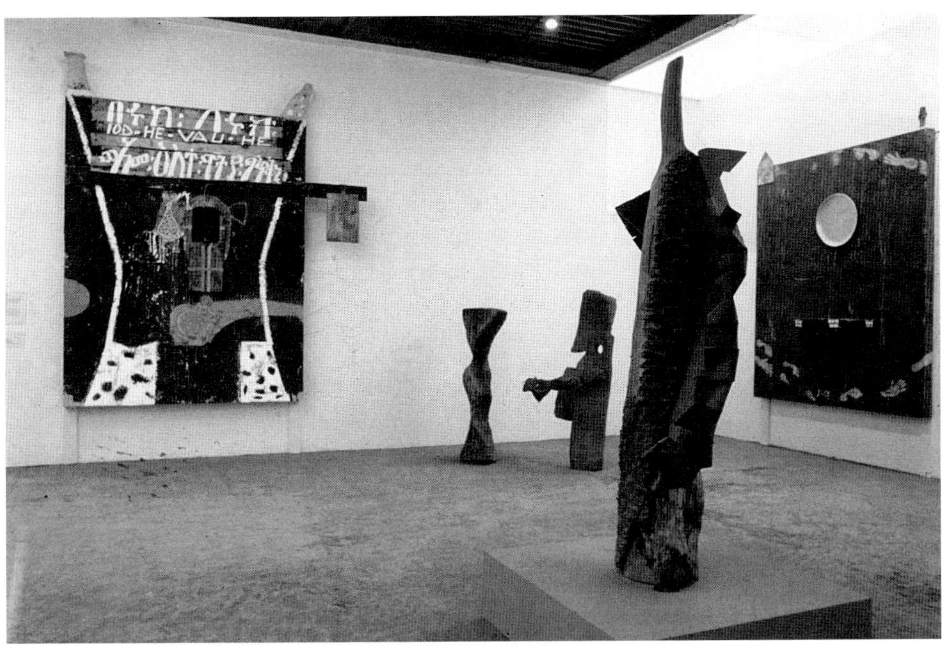

7.9 Installation view of *Fusion: African Artists at the Venice Biennale* (1993) showing two wall pieces from 1993 by Ouattara Watts (*Masada* and *Dance of the Spirit*) and sculptures by Moustapha Dimé, *Untitled* from 1993 and *La dame au long cou* from 1992. Photo: Jerry L. Thompson for the Museum for African Art, courtesy of Susan Mullin Vogel.

Showcasing this new African aesthetic, "nomadism," were Mor Faye, Moustapha Dimé, Tamesir Dia, Ouattara Watts, and Gerard Santoni (fig. 7.9).[68] The latter two had already participated in Vogel's *Africa Explores*, as had the critic Thomas McEvilley, whom Vogel commissioned to write the catalog for the new show. McEvilley seemed to be a good choice; a decade earlier, he had been among the fiercest critics of the "Primitivism" show in New York, chiding, in particular, the curators' "egotism":

> My real concern is that the exhibition shows Western egotism still as unbridled as in the centuries of colonialism and souvenirism. The Museum pretends to confront the Third World while really co-opting it and using it to consolidate Western notions of quality and feelings of superiority.[69]

The *Fusion* show's intentionality about redressing these failings was evident in two ways. The first was evident through the curators' carefully conducted interviews with the participating artists (Faye had already passed away); the second was made apparent by McEvilley's catalog essay "Fusion: Hot or Cold?" The title referred to the postmodern condition in terms of its (assumed) reconfiguration of identities. Do they boil up and result in "hot" identity-driven culture wars, or do they turn into a "cold" multicultural balance or negotiation of differences? McEvilley proposed seeing "the issue of identity" in the grand scheme of history. For this, he outlined a "four-stage-model" that paralleled the development of identity with the development of art. In premodern/precolonial times (stage 1) when identity was (seemingly) bestowed by the collective and unquestioned, art was primarily functional and communal, and society conceived artists as artisans. With the advent of the triad of modernism/nationalism/colonialism (stage 2), identity became a weapon. Colonizers dismissed the colonized people's artwork and culture by labeling it primitive and inferior. The colonized reacted by reversing the strategy (stage 3) and pursuing a nativistic and nationalistic agenda that celebrated national identities. Cultural hybridity and multiculturalism mark the postcolonial/postmodern era (stage 4) in which artists are able to balance multiple identities and reflect the competing forces that have shaped them, both as individuals and as members of a community. As McEvilley stressed, the four-stage model was "not a law of nature."[70] Yet, "Whether these African artists see themselves as post-modernists or not, the fact remains that it is the complex of changes called post-modernism that brought them to Venice."[71] In view of the history of these relations, he asked, "Can we—descendants of both colonizers and colonized— acknowledge the colonial karmic debt yet build from it into some more generous, less volatile geopolitical fusion?"

The answer came two years later. In another fierce critique, Olu Oguibe focused on the artist interviews McEvilley conducted for the exhibition catalog *Fusion*. Especially infuriating to Oguibe was the following passage between McEvilley (TM) and Ouattara Watts (O):

TM: Would you tell me a little about your family?

O: I prefer to talk about my work.

TM: I am interested in both your work and the background of your work. I hope you don't mind if I am trying to find out what kind of social and cultural conditions it comes from.

O: That's all coincident and accident. I could have been born in Russia, Canada or in Africa. But if you must know—it's a large family, with many sisters and brothers.

TM: How many?

O: That has nothing to do with my work, I'd rather not say.[72]

For Oguibe, McEvilley's insistence on the relevance of cultural background and identity revealed the flaws of McEvilley's postmodern invocation of "a more generous, less volatile geopolitical fusion." By refusing to yield to Ouattara's own criteria for self-definition, the interview still entailed the (colonial) differences of power:

> The construction of voices belongs squarely in the postmodernist tradition of American multiculturalism, false and appropriatory, pulling in the insider for use and sound bite. The invited insider is only a stranger in his own discourse, swamped and drowned out. It is the "intimate outsider" who truly is in charge.[73]

To overcome the differences, Oguibe argued, it is necessary to start by questioning the power of representation. Who speaks? Who defines? Who draws the boundaries?

* * *

On the face of it, Oguibe's questions were not all that different from the ones raised by Enwonwu roughly half a century earlier. When in 1956 he presented his lecture on the "Problems of the African Artist Today" at the First International Congress of Black Writers and Artists in Paris (see chap. 5), he, too, complained about the lack of control over representation and unequal dispositions of power. Back then, however, it was still the colonial era. Enwonwu argued from the position of a colonial subject residing in Nigeria. Some forty years later the situation had changed. The field was still controlled by Euro-American scholars and curators, but their unquestioned authority relating to the definition of quality and value was over. With new models of plurality and decentralization as well as the attack on notions of authenticity, the canon crumbled. In the course of these debates, interest in traditional art forms declined, and the question of the contemporary resurfaced. New voices pushed old demands. Unlike Enwonwu, Oguibe was born after independence. He belonged to a different generation. While Enwonwu sought to find an answer to what the historical equation and simultaneity of modernism and colonialism meant to an African artist, for Oguibe and his generation, the task was to translate postmodern critique into an appropriate critique of the postcolonial condition. It is the field's postcolonial reconfiguration that I turn to in chapter 8.

CHAPTER 8

Challenging Representation

POSTCOLONIAL CRITIQUE AND CURATION

I feel strongly that there is a difference between the representation of politics and the politics of representation.

YINKA SHONIBARE, *Of Hedonism, Masquerade, Carnivalesque and Power: A Conversation with Okwui Enwezor,* 2004

Introduction

In February 1994, the Centre 181 Gallery in London produced small posters to announce the exhibition of *Double Dutch,* an installation by the young British Nigerian artist Yinka Shonibare. Born in London in 1963 but raised in Lagos, Shonibare had returned to London in the mid-1980s, a time when Britain's conservative prime minister Margaret Thatcher advocated a return to "Victorian values." As an art student at Byam Shaw and Goldsmith College, Shonibare learned to respond to the country's imperial nostalgia by way of blending postcolonial arguments about hybridity and the politics of representation with an ironic play of images. After a few group shows, *Double Dutch* was his first solo exhibition. On the gallery poster, a sepia-brown photograph of a black male dressed in a white turban and an ornate brocaded eighteenth-century European coat appeared next to the following text in an elegant italic font:

Just imagine being a primitive; a proper primitive that is. A primitive that is beyond civilisation, a primitive in a state of perpetual indulgence, a primitive of excess. I think I would really enjoy that. Here too I can be a kind of back to nature cliché with a twist. Oh, how I long to be ethnic. I love paint, it's really sumptuous; yum. What is the meaning of the skirt? What did Lycra represent? What language does Doctor Martin speak? Who needs pinstripe? Let's have a goatee instead; perhaps not-pass! Double Dutch.

The text's invitation to imagination signaled Shonibare's playful engagement with viewers' perceptions and representations. Upon entering the gallery, visitors encountered a large pink rectangular panel studded with fifty aligned squares wrapped in cotton canvases of colorful "ethnic" fabrics overlaid with acrylic paint. Critics took some time to realize that the grid format did not point to the pure space of minimalism but was a subtle postcolonial comment on cultural hybridity. Against the national(istic) container model of culture, Shonibare conceived of culture as movement, mixture, and exchange. Thus, what looked like paint on quintessentially "authentic" African fabric was actually paint on so-called Dutch wax print, a textile resulting from of a nineteenth-century global economic network ranging from Holland to Indonesia, England, and West Africa that had prompted multiple translations (figs. 8.1, 8.2).[1]

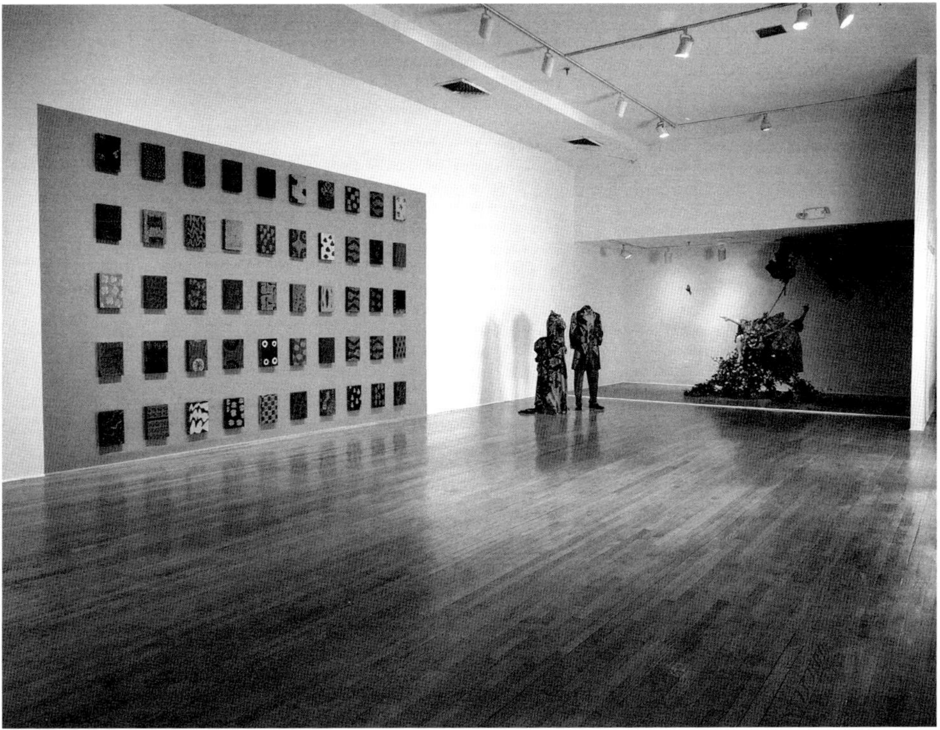

8.1 Yinka Shonibare, CBE, *Double Dutch*, installation view, 1994. Acrylic paint on wall, emulsion, and acrylic on fifty Dutch wax printed cotton canvases. Photo: Jean Young.

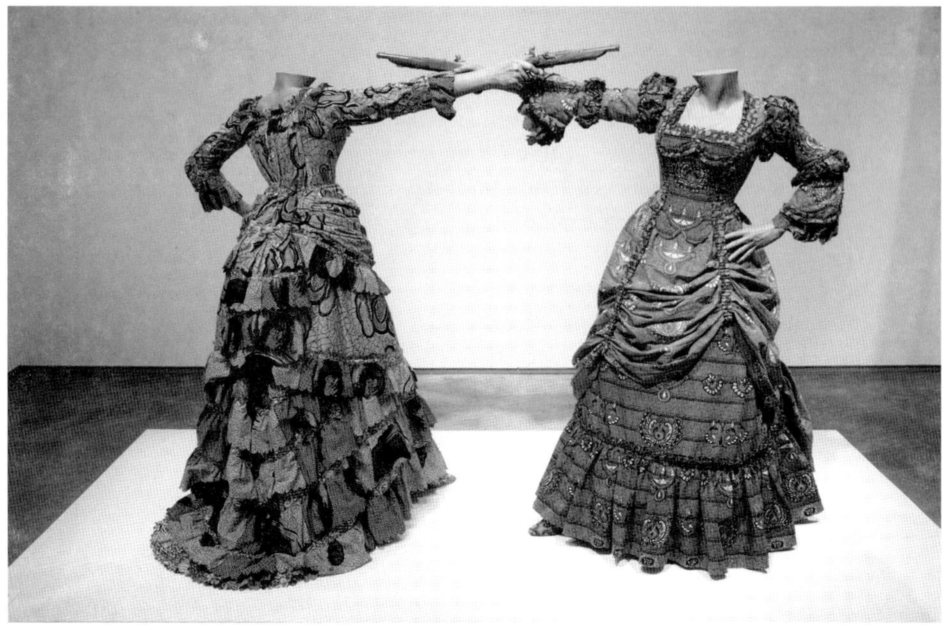

8.2 Yinka Shonibare, CBE, *How to Blow Up Two Heads at Once (Ladies)*, 2006. Two fiberglass mannequins, two prop guns, Dutch wax printed cotton textile, shoes, leather riding boots, plinth, 237.5 cm × 160 cm. Davis Museum at Wellesley College. © Yinka Shonibare CBE. All rights reserved, DACS / ARS, NY 2021.

Shonibare's *Double Dutch* has become emblematic of the postcolonial turn in contemporary art. As noted in the previous chapter, in the 1980s and 1990s, the term *postcolonial* had widened from a historical signifier in terms of after colonialism to a conceptual critique in terms of identifying and challenging the legacies of colonial modes of thinking and representation. The development informed and correlated with shifts in the art world. With shows like *The Other Story, Magiciens de la terre*, and *Fusion*, the late 1980s and early 1990s saw a reemergence of contemporary art in the field of African art studies. The postmodern arena of competing paradigms—ranging from multiculturalism to cultural, visual, and feminist studies—had cleared a space for the arrival of conceptual artists like Yinka Shonibare, who were keenly aware of postcolonial debates over diaspora, identity, and space. From the early 1990s onward, "the other" began to speak back. Writers like Homi Bhabha made it clear that the postmodern condition is very much a postcolonial condition, defined by migration and the experience of displacement, exile, and dislocation.[2] Living under these conditions meant living in a state of in-betweenness, or, in the words of Bhabha, it meant occupying "a third space," which allowed the postcolonial subject to acquire agency and disrupt the seemingly stable binaries that made up the modern/colonial era.

Theory mattered, but so did age. In fact, what connected many of the postcolonial protagonists was not only their hyphenated identities but their date of birth. Those who enacted the postcolonial turn in African art studies were born in the early and mid-1960s, when colonialism had formally ended. What persisted were more subtle forms of domination, experienced on a daily basis, which lingered in modes of thinking and working through regimes of representation. Scholars such as Stuart Hall (1932–2014) in England and Edward Said (1935–2003) in the US provided the theoretical space that allowed critics and artists of the next generation to confront, undermine, subvert, and unmask the "burden of representation."[3] In 1998, the British painter Chris Ofili won the prestigious Turner prize as "the first Black recipient" (Tate Gallery). In the same year, the Nigerian American artist and critic Olu Oguibe proclaimed,

> There is a silent wind blowing across the plains of African art studies. Though some would rather have a storm and others the stillness of the arrested moment, this wind is billowing nevertheless, sweeping away old ways, desires, and questionable obsessions, bringing with it new attitudes, positions, and visions. It will take us through this century and into the next, past the twilight of a phenomenal millennium and over the threshold to an unpredictable one. It is the wind of change, and it is here to stay.[4]

In the following, I examine three dimensions of this "postcolonial turn," as the period between the mid-1980s and the mid-2000s became known: first, the rise of new actors and platforms; second, the emergence of photography as the genre uniquely suited to the postcolonial agenda of representation, power, and identity; and third, the impact of that agenda in the realm of curation and the world of exhibitions.

New Critics, New Platforms

A few months after the exhibition of Shonibare's *Double Dutch* in England, four US-based African critics—Okwui Enwezor, Salah Hassan, Olu Oguibe, and Chika Okeke-Agulu—launched the new journal *Nka: Journal of Contemporary African Art*. The four were roughly the same age—Enwezor was born in 1963, Hassan and Oguibe in 1964, Okeke-Agulu in 1966—and came from similar backgrounds. All four had left their home countries (Nigeria in the case of Enwezor, Oguibe, and Okeke-Agulu; Sudan in the case of Hassan) to pursue a career in the art world of the US:

Enwezor as a poet and critic in New York, Hassan as an art historian at Cornell University, Oguibe—via London—as an artist and art historian at the University of Illinois at Chicago, and Okeke-Agulu, who arrived slightly later, as an artist and art historian pursuing a PhD at Emory University.

The choice of the journal's name was calculated: *Nka* means "form" or "art" among the Igbo-speaking people in South East Nigeria. In his presentation at the 1966 Dakar colloquium on "African Negro Art," Ben Enwonwu had elaborated on the performance-oriented meaning of *Nka* in his effort to promote an "African view of art" (see chap. 5).[5] The invocation of the term three decades later was thus meant to carry on Enwonwu's struggle and to change the discourse about contemporary African art. As Enwezor argued in the journal's inaugural editorial, while contemporary African art had managed to gain a certain presence in the Western art world, the artists themselves were still seen through the lens of exoticism. By focusing on nonacademic, popular artists, large-scale exhibitions like *Magiciens de la terre* (1989), *Africa Hoy* (1990), and *Africa Explores* (1991) had marginalized the role of African art schools and art academies. Enwezor's goal for the journal was to help African art shed the "unwieldy yoke of the other" as "a body estranged from and unfamiliar with modernity hovering at the margins of historical consciousness."[6] In practical terms, this meant gaining authority over the discourse on contemporary African art by distancing it from both postmodernism and anthropology. To this end, Enwezor appealed to the journal's readers, asking them to submit materials consistent with the journal's vision and goals: "We seek the kind of work that, out of necessity, seeks to violate, destabilize, dislocate and unseat all the deep-rooted prejudices, and rote assumptions that pass themselves off as contemporary African art history."[7] Showcasing now prominent artists such as Ghada Amer, Pascale Marthine Tayou, El Anatsui, or Yinka Shonibare, *Nka* soon became a major voice in the debate over contemporary African art.

Nka was not the only journal in the field pushing for a postcolonial contemporary agenda. In 1987 Rasheed Araeen founded *Third Text* as a platform for voices rethinking and challenging the Western idea of a "Third World." Also of note was *Transition*, the famous African literary journal, relaunched in 1991 by Henry Louis Gates as a magazine about race and culture with an emphasis on the African diaspora. Closest to *Nka*, though, was *Revue Noire*, founded in 1991 by a circle of French intellectuals centered on architect Jean Loup Pivin. Engendered by Pivin's frustration and anger over the flaws of the big *Magiciens* show, *Revue Noire* (published quarterly in both French and English) focused primarily on academic artists but also covered developments in African literature and the performing arts.[8]

Each issue of *Revue Noire* was devoted to a city, a country, or a particular question. The holistic approach echoed the editors' political agenda. Pivin and his coeditors—Simon Njami, Pascal Martin Saint Lóon, and Bruno Tilliette—realized the persistence of the continent's colonial division in the art world. Artists in Senegal, Mali, or the Democratic Republic of the Congo tended to work with different dealers and galleries than their colleagues in Nigeria or Ghana. The same applied to critics and scholars. Paris and Brussels, the centers of the francophone art world, engaged minimally with London and New York. While difference in language provided an obstacle, the more significant barrier was the (initial) reluctance among established French critics and scholars to engage in the postcolonial debates on which their Anglophone colleagues were focused. From a (white) French perspective, postcolonial and cultural studies were seen as outgrowths of Anglophone identity politics and multiculturalism, an "academic carnival" whose centrifugal dynamics were seen as detrimental to scholarship and the notion of Francophonie.[9]

Maneuvering this contested terrain, *Revue Noire* functioned first and foremost as a platform that covered the manifold of contemporary art being produced in Africa and its diaspora. From its inception in 1991, photography constituted a primary focus of interest of the *Revue*. The rapid dissemination of photography after its invention in France and England during the first decades of the nineteenth century, as well as the photo studios that emerged in port cities along the African coast—as early as the 1850s onward—were well-known phenomena. With few exceptions, hardly anything was known about the local use and practice of photography.[10] *Revue Noire* aimed to fill the gap by building an archive of black photography from its beginnings to the present (fig. 8.3). The first issue, for instance, introduced the work of the deceased British Nigerian photographer Rotimi Fani-Kayode as part of a report on Black British Artists in London. Other photographers, whom the magazine first presented to a wider Western audience, include Seydou Keïta and Malick Sidibé (Mali), Mama Casset (Senegal), Cornélius August Azaglo (Côte d'Ivoire), and Ricardo Rangel (Mozambique), all of them shown in Okwui Enwezor's first major exhibition *In/Sight—African Photographers 1940 to the Present*.[11]

In/Sight—African Photographers 1940 to the Present opened at the Guggenheim in May 1996 as a counterpart to *Africa: The Art of a Continent*, a massive, historical show on "classical" African sculpture, which the Guggenheim had taken over from the Royal Academy in London. Originally, the historical show was planned to be complemented by *Seven Stories about Modern Art in Africa*, which was running at London's Whitechapel Gallery as part of africa95, a nationwide UK season of arts that lasted

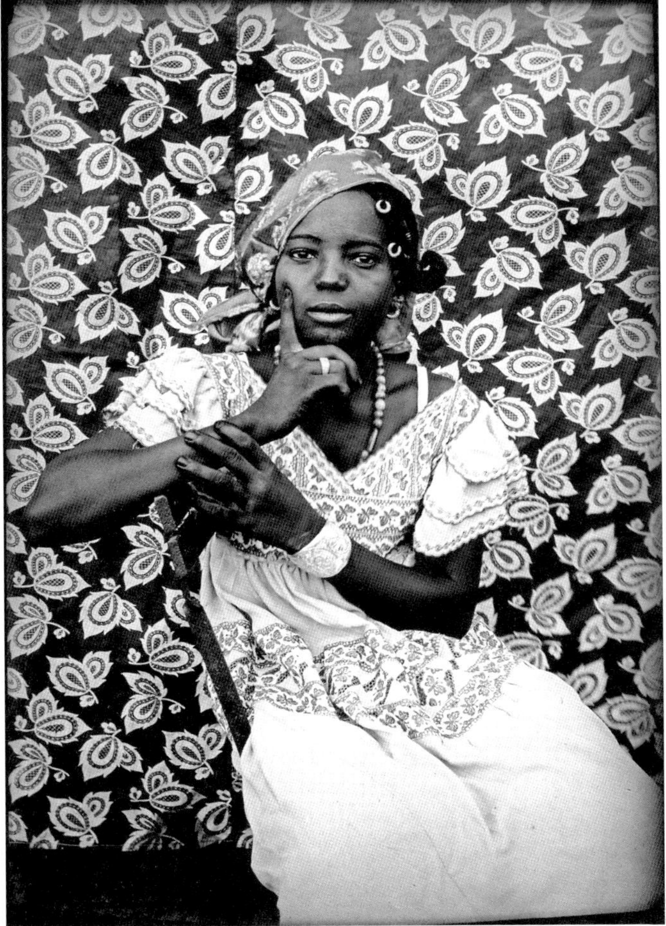

8.3 Seydou Keïta, *Untitled*, 1956–1959. Modern gelatin silver print. © Seydou Keïta / SKPEAC, courtesy of The Pigozzi Collection.

from September to December 1995. Thematically and conceptually, *Seven Stories* understood itself as a counterpart to the main *Africa* exhibition at the Royal Academy.[12] In accordance with the postcolonial demand for inclusion and visibility, the artistic director, Clémentine Deliss, commissioned five African artists and art historians to select works representing the development of modern art in their home country. The result was seven different "stories" of the development of modern art in Senegal (El Hadji Sy), Sudan and Ethiopia (Salah Hassan), Nigeria (Chika Okeke-Agulu), South Africa (David Koloane), and Kenya and Uganda (Wanjiku Nyachae). As it turned out, however, budget cuts as well as organizational and representational issues made the takeover of *Seven Stories* unfeasible;

the Guggenheim was forced to come up with a fast and financially affordable alternative.[13] The result was *In/sight*, cocurated by the Spanish critic Octavio Zaya, editor of the journal *Atlántica*; Guggenheim's Clare Bell; and Okwui Enwezor, whose new journal, *Nka*, had already earned plaudits in the art world. Weighing the options, the three decided to use the archives of *Revue Noire* and curate a show on African photography.

Framed by an African film series, lectures, panel discussions, and a host of other citywide activities, *In/Sight—African Photographers 1940 to the Present* presented 139 works from thirty photographers. Covering all the main regions of the continent as well as the diaspora, the work included categories such as photojournalism, documentary photography, and studio photography. About a quarter of the works on display were from the 1980s and 1990s. In the accompanying catalog, Clare Bell provided a general background to the exhibition project, while Zaya and Enwezor explained the agenda, that is, seeing Africa through African eyes. The only commissioned contributor to the catalog was Olu Oguibe, who reflected on the history and cultural practice of photography in Nigeria.

The show turned out to be a success. Alluding to the assemblage of anonymous works on display in the parallel exhibition, *Africa: The Art of the Continent*, Max Kozloff in *Artforum* wrote, "*In/Sight* was striking, above all, as a gallery of faces."[14] His colleague at the *New York Times*, Holland Cotter, similarly compared the two, declaring that *Africa: The Art of the Continent* represented an outdated model of curating, simply "obsolete," in contrast to *In/Sight*, a visit to which he deemed "mandatory."[15] The widely positive reception of *In/Sight* boosted not only Enwezor's career as an influential critic and curator but also the reputation of the journal *Nka*, whose editors were now regarded collectively as an important new voice in the debate over contemporary art. Three years after *In/Sight*, Oguibe and Enwezor leveraged their status by publishing the anthology *Reading the Contemporary: African Art from Theory to the Marketplace*.[16] Consisting of contributions by the editors themselves plus a host of other authors, the anthology provided an informative and authoritative panorama of the critical theory that had emerged since the exhibition *Magiciens de la terre* a decade earlier. Although the volume offered no unifying critical perspective, it did carry a clear message, as the cover picture signaled unambiguously: a photograph from Yinka Shonibare's *Diary of a Victorian Dandy*, showing Shonibare as a commanding black dandy figure standing among white male friends and female servants in the library of a late nineteenth-century Victorian mansion, thus challenging the racial roots of authority of white Westerners over the meaning of black (African) art (fig. 8.4).

The postcolonial posture was less resistant to the presence of white

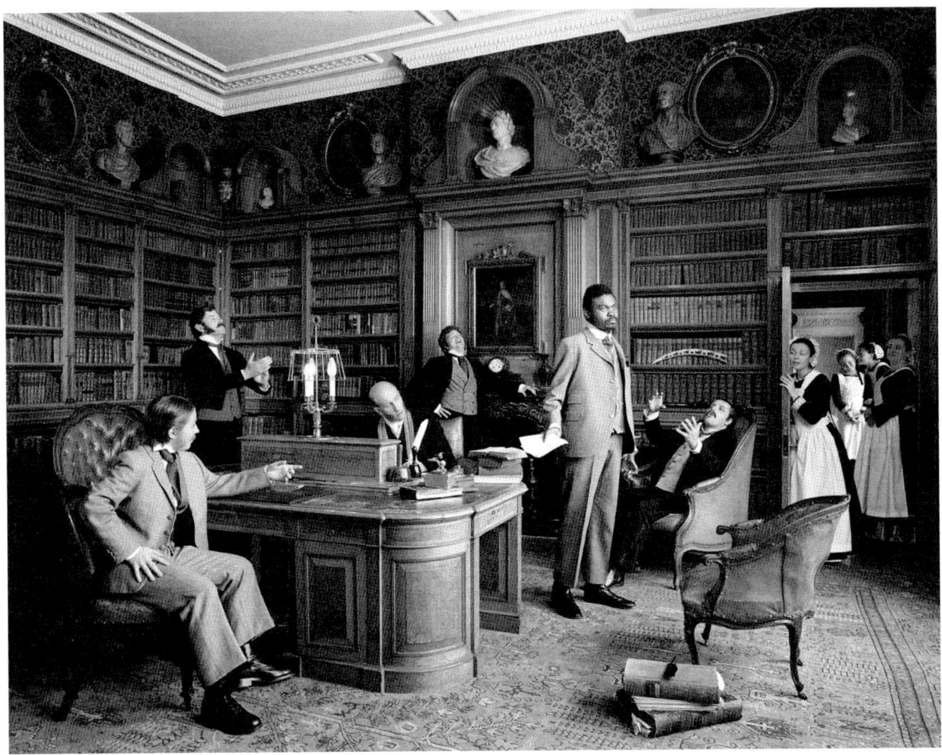

8.4 Yinka Shonibare, CBE. *Diary of a Victorian Dandy: 14.00 Hours*, 1998. © Yinka Shonibare CBE. All rights reserved, DACS / ARS, NY 2021.

scholars than to the predominance of white colonial forms of knowledge
production, especially anthropology and ethnographic fieldwork. Up
until the 1990s, this production of knowledge constituted an important
method for art historians working on African art. While some felt the
"the wind of change" (Oguibe) refreshing, others were alarmed. In an
intervention in the journal *African Arts*, the curator of the Baltimore Museum of Art, Fred Lamp, warned that the rise of postcolonial theory had
led to a withering of student interest in ethnographic fieldwork and a decline of research on so-called classical African art.[17] Lamp's observation
prompted the journal to start a dialogue on the matter. The invitation
to respond yielded a series of heated comments rejecting Lamp's claims
and defending the value and necessity of theory. Lamp himself called the
passionate rebuttals to his contentious claim an academic "Jerry Springer
Show," thus comparing the heated exchanges with a popular American
talk show well known for its often loud and shrill dramatization of banal
issues. In fact, with seminal works showing new paths in the study of so-

called power objects and masked performances,[18] Lamp's warning related to the withering of "classical" African art proved unfounded. It did mark a decisive rift, however, between different camps within the field.

Photography, Authorship, and the Market

If the message of Oguibe's and Enwezor's anthology *Reading the Contemporary* was clear, the subtitle of the anthology—*African Art from Theory to the Marketplace*—remained nebulous. Did it refer to the shift from the (white) monopoly of theory to the open market-like competition over the best ideas? Or did it mean a shift of value and importance from the bourgeois, modernist notion of the autonomy of art to the sober recognition of art as another element of the profit-driven logic undergirding global, neoliberal capitalism? Or—yet another reading—did it point to the discrepancy between the official assurances of inclusion and the real-life experience of exclusion in the art world/market?

While Oguibe's and Enwezor's *Reading the Contemporary* left the market question unanswered, Sidney Kasfir's *Contemporary African Art*—also published in 1999—addressed it openly and vigorously.[19] Conceived as a comprehensive review of the then newly (re)established field of contemporary art in Africa, Kasfir focused on the period between the 1950s and early 1990s. The seven chapters address different attitudes toward the creation of art. They range from popular and urban art to the role of patrons, the process of decolonization, and the question of migration, displacement, and diaspora. A key feature of these differences, tellingly discussed at the very center of the book, is the relationship between art and commodity. As Kasfir argued, local practices of art production did (and do) not follow the strict conceptual divide between art and commodity (or between art and craft for that matter), which colonialism introduced as a part of its civilizational/modernist package (see also chap. 5).[20] In practice, the lines were (and still often are) blurred, leaving questions of authorship, authenticity, and singularity to dealers and critics mediating between local and Western art worlds. As Kasfir put it,

> In Africa, emulation of one artist by another was an integral part of the workshop system and an important part of apprenticeship. Also, precolonial workshops (as well as individual artists outside the workshop system) turned out an established repertory of forms which their patrons required. The upshot is that African artists who have not been exposed to Western high-art categories do not make the same judgements about either utilitarian and non-utilitarian forms or the continued replication of a known prototype which are crucial to West-

ern assumptions about either art versus craft or artworks versus commodities. . . . The greatest difference between African and non-African assumptions about art and commodity can be seen where they are produced—in the workshop, the cooperative or the individual workplace. By contrast, it is where they are sold, be it at a gallery, kiosk, or street corner or illustrated catalogue, that an accommodation is attempted between producer and consumer, African artist and foreign collector. The dealer or trader is charged with bridging this divide and, once again, cultural mediation comes into play.[21]

A widely discussed example of this "cultural mediation" is the reception of the work of the Malian studio photographer Seydou Keïta. In 1999, parallel with the publication of Kasfir's *Contemporary African Art* and Oguibe's and Enwezor's *Reading the Contemporary*, Elizabeth Bigham discussed Keïta's authorship as a mix of different forces only partially controlled by Keïta himself.[22] According to Bigham, the story started in the 1970s. By then, Keïta had closed his studio but kept his negatives. When Susan Vogel was passing through Bamako, she purchased a number of negatives from Keïta. Vogel was interested in his work as an example of urban art that captured the presence and subjectivity of his sitters. In 1991, the photographs themselves, now enlarged, became part of her exhibition *Africa Explores* in New York (see chap. 7). In the meantime, however, the provenance of the pictures had gone missing, to the effect that Keïta's photographs in the exhibit were labeled "unknown photographer." As it happened, in New York, the photographs attracted the attention of André Magnin, curator of the private collection of Jean Pigozzi, an Italian French investor, art lover, and photographer. Pigozzi had begun collecting contemporary African art after having seen *Magiciens de la terre* in Paris. In 1992, Magnin traveled to Mali to meet with Keïta and review his oeuvre. Apparently with Keïta's permission, Magnin returned to Paris with over nine hundred negatives from which he made prints. Two years later, in 1994, Magnin began to show and publish Keïta's portraits, first in Paris at the Fondation Cartier and subsequently at other exhibitions in Europe and the US.[23] Equally, in 1994, the French photojournalist Françoise Huguier organized the first African Photo Biennale in Bamako, where she included Keïta's work as part of the newly developed interest in African photography. The visibility had an immediate and tangible effect. Thus, Keïta's growing artistic reputation and the price of his works went hand in hand with the changing size of his prints. The process culminated in 1997 with a big solo show in Zurich, and later that year at Gagosian Gallery in New York. By then, the price of Keïta's photographs had increased from around $700 to $16,000, correlating with the

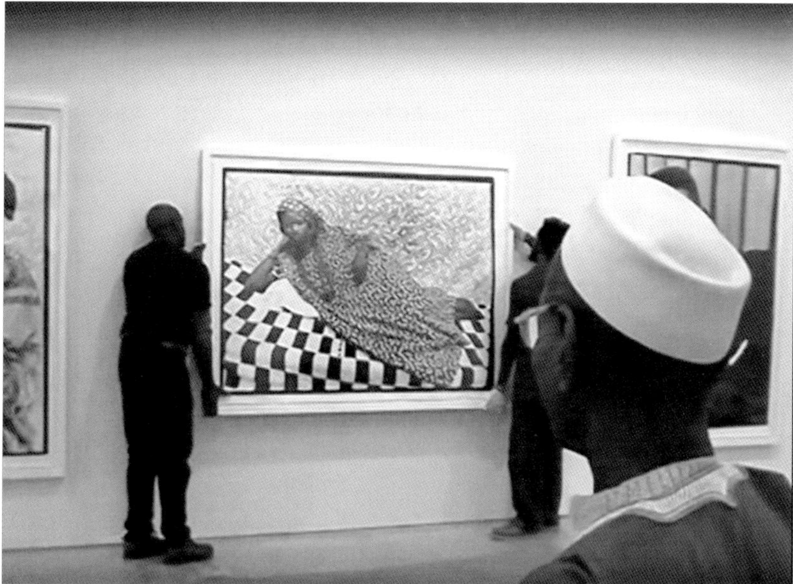

8.5 Film still, Seydou Keïta watching the mounting of his work at Gagosian Gallery, New York, 1997. © André Magnin, courtesy of Galerie Magnin-A, Paris.

increase of the size of the prints, from 5 by 7 inches, to 48 by 60 inches (fig. 8.5).[24] What appears to be a success story was actually the beginning of a bitter argument over authorship and ownership. It was not until 2001, however, shortly before his death, that Keïta finally formally severed ties with Magnin and Pigozzi and hired the Parisian gallerist Jean Marc Patras and his New York gallery partner Sean Kelly as his new agents.

The description of the clash between Keïta and his European middlemen echoed an awareness of the market dynamics. With venues, dealers, and gallerists initially residing almost exclusively outside the continent, the clash meant to illustrate not only the conflicts resulting from the distance between artist and client but also the asymmetry between "theory" and "marketplace," to cite again the subtitle of Oguibe's and Enwezor' seminal reader.

Biennales and Curators

Reading the Contemporary captured both the excitement and the tensions that dominated the decade between the mid-1990s and mid-2000s, when contemporary art from Africa began to attract attention, sales rose, and theory production boomed. A prime instrument in the expansion of the market and the production of "modernity at large"[25] was the biennale model. Initially conceived in the late nineteenth century as a way to showcase national artistic productions, the proliferation of the model increased the visibility of previously marginalized or silenced subjects and allowed for the creation of new transnational artscapes. However, it also generated new conflicts over the role of the curator.

A case in point was the short-lived (1995 and 1997) Johannesburg Biennale in South Africa. It illustrates the specific tensions and dynamics that characterized the globalization of the art world after the 1989 fall of the Berlin Wall and the corresponding globalization of neoliberalism. In South Africa, the geopolitical transformations meant the end of the apartheid regime and the gradual removal of the country's exclusion and isolation within the international art world.[26] In 1994, four years after Nelson Mandela's release from prison, South Africa held its first free elections. To demonstrate the country's ambition to become an open, democratic, and multicultural society, the South African Ministry of Culture and the Johannesburg city council approved the funds for the organization of the first Johannesburg Biennale.

Initially scheduled to coincide with the elections, the (first) Johannesburg Biennale started in late February 1995. With sixty-three national pavilions and twenty South African exhibitions, *Africus* aimed to introduce local artists to the world following South Africa's decades of cultural boycott and international isolation. Politically, the event was intended to represent the aspiration toward multiethnic unity and reconciliation in what the charismatic Archbishop Desmond Tutu termed the "Rainbow Nation"—that is, post-apartheid South Africa.[27] In line with this vision, *Africus* focused on inclusivity, outreach programs, and curatorial and civic education. Newspapers carried ads informing the public about the process for submitting works and becoming engaged. As a result, the spectrum of events, genres, and participants ranged widely from exhibition venues in townships to white cube galleries in downtown Johannesburg and Cape Town. The title of Thomas McEvilley's contribution to the exhibition catalog, "Here Comes Everybody," aptly captured the spirit of the biennale.[28]

But not "Everybody" was universally welcome. In a widely noted intervention, South African artist Sue Williamson and writer Ashraf Jamal criticized the vaunted inclusivity of the exhibition and argued that the demands for equal representation negatively affected the selection processes and thus the quality of the works on display.[29] They maintained that, far from boosting the country's international reputation, lowering standards would perpetuate clichés of African art as being steeped in craft and "community art." For David Koloane, the artist and curator of the South African part of the London *Seven Stories* exhibition (see above), the problem was less the quality of the art than the context in which it was seen. To him, the whole idea of the biennale was an alien "transplant" imported into and failing to reflect the complexities of South African society or to "encompass the African essence."[30] Last but not least, there was the debate over the alleged neoracial asymmetry of the event: white artists predominately contributed challenging conceptual art, which dominated over black township artists, who engaged in respected, community work.[31]

Despite these critiques, *Africus* was a powerful statement for the end of South Africa's exclusion from the art world. Steps were, therefore, taken to move forward with organizing a sequel. An organizing committee was formed to review and address the issues of the first edition and find an artistic director for the next biennale. The choice fell on one of the committee members, Okwui Enwezor, whose work for *In/Sight* had brought him into contact with key figures in the South African art world such as the photographer David Goldblatt and the filmmaker William Kentridge. Enwezor adopted a different approach from that of his predecessors; in contrast to *Africus*, which was rather inward looking, Enwezor conceived of the biennale as a way to embed South Africa in the wider (art) world. The result was 1997's *Trade Routes: History and Geography*, which explored South Africa's present and past in the context of global flows of capital, goods, and people. Conceptually and organizationally, *Trade Routes* was informed by the debate about new "global visions" in curating exhibitions.[32] In accordance with postcolonial discourse, Enwezor discarded the national pavilion model that had historically been foundational to the biennale concept, instead inviting six international curators to work with him on curating a series of exhibitions and selecting artists.[33] With 160 artists from sixty-three countries (instead of 250 artists from eighty countries), *Trade Routes* was smaller and more conceptual than *Africus*. Like Enwezor and the majority of his cocurators, more than half of the artists resided in countries other than those of their origin. In contrast to *Africus*'s wide reach—with events held in townships and in the countryside—*Trade Routes* had an exclusively urban and transnational focus. The various artists and speakers explored themes emanating from colonization, migration, and displacement, all of them intentionally transcending the South African art scene. The only event solely showing South African artists was Colin Richards's *Graft* show in Cape Town (fig. 8.6).

The public response to the program was unenthusiastic.[34] Enwezor's ambition to widen the internal discussion about the new "rainbow nation" by exploring its global history and geography turned out to be polarizing. Critics and audiences alike charged *Trade Routes* with pandering to an international audience, and in doing so, not only neglecting the

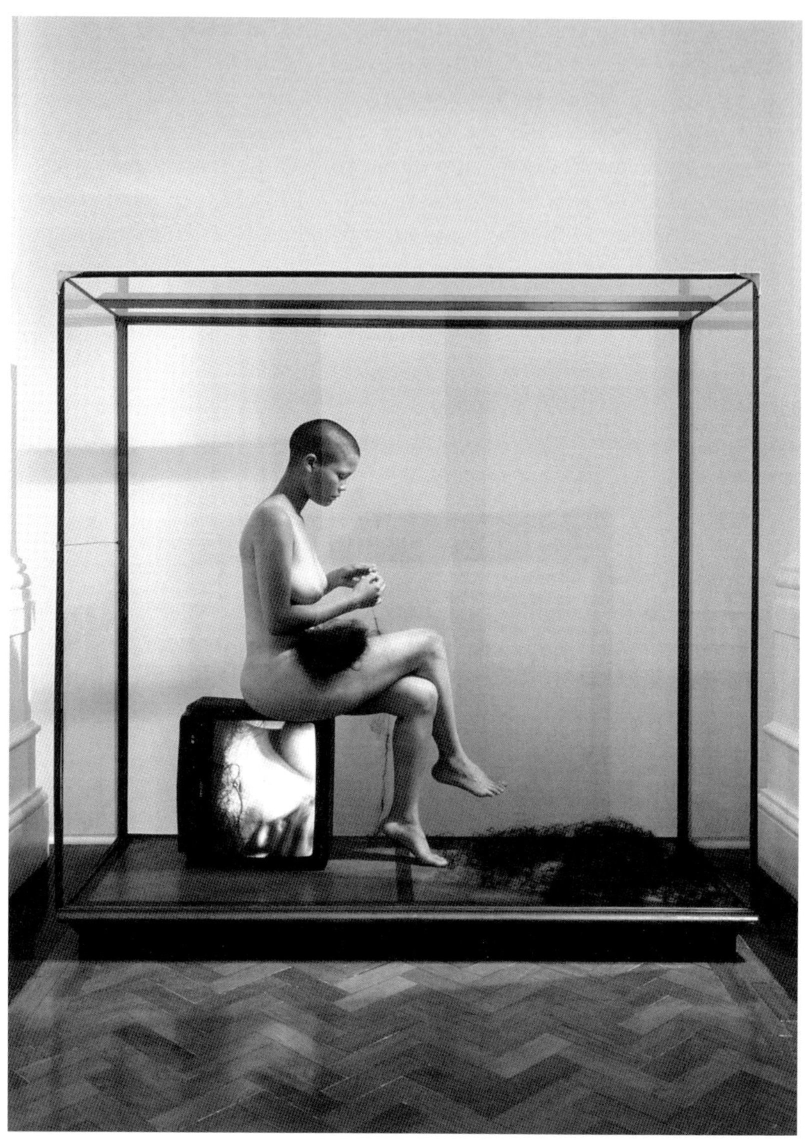

8.6 Tracey Rose, *Span II*, 1997. Performance at the South African National Gallery in the *Graft* show curated by Colin Richards during *Trade Routes*. Visitors saw the artist naked and clean shaven in a glass cabinet sitting on a television and knotting her hair. The performance was read as an act of resistance to the colonial male gaze represented by the close-up of a reclining nude displayed in the television as a prominent theme in modern European art. © Tracey Rose, courtesy of Dan Gunn Gallery, London.

immediate challenge—coming to terms with the legacy of apartheid—but actually creating a new "artistic apartheid." As the Spanish critic and curator Gabriel Perez-Barreiro put it,

> The most recent boom in cultural studies and postcolonialism is in danger of creating an artistic apartheid in which only particular types of art which conform to a specific vocabulary (still "made in the 'West'" incidentally) can enter. Thus, the center continues to pre-select and predetermine which of the peripheral arts can be exposed to the public according to its own agenda.[35]

In view of the dwindling numbers of visitors, the question Who was actually benefiting from the event? became more and more pressing. Eventually, the Johannesburg city council cut funding, and *Trade Routes* closed a month ahead of schedule.

The local fate of *Trade Routes* exemplified what anthropologists at the time called the "dialectics of flow and closure," which characterizes periods of accelerated change.[36] Thus, while South Africa's rapid transition to a post-apartheid society allowed for openness and access to new social and economic resources, it created an equal and opposite reaction of reluctance and resistance. As much as change was welcomed in some quarters, it was met with unease in others. Still, for all its flaws and shortcomings, *Trade Routes* succeeded in putting South Africa on the map in the international art world. Within the following years, shows on contemporary South African art were mounted in New York, Washington, London, and other places. *Trade Routes* also catalyzed the emergence of a new postcolonial type of both curator and curating, as Okwui Enwezor, embodying both, explained in 2002:

> The role of the curator can be many things. Based on my own experience, I want to make a distinction between curating within the canon and curating within culture. Curating within the canon means to curate facing the formidable examples that have been produced in the West. These are very valuable and we can never set that aside. There is something very particular about curating within art history itself—simply nibbling or making minor changes within that. The curator who endeavors to leave the institutional arena of history and the canon has to risk a little bit. That is, to curate within culture is to see art in a totality that is not simply bounded by art history. It is there that we begin to make room for new forms of knowledge, new possibilities of articulating different types of intelligence that are unruly and cannot be disciplined by the academic world.[37]

Enwezor's distinction between curating "within the canon" and curating "within culture" captured the postcolonial ambition to both critique and transcend established structures. In doing so, Enwezor's picture of the role of the curator was not unlike that of European patrons a generation earlier. In their presentation of African artists, art impresario figures such as Ulli Beier equally broke with the canon to make room for new forms of knowledge. In contrast to critics like Clement Greenberg and the high-modernist focus on artistic autonomy and medium specificity, they focused on cultural issues such as identity and tradition. However, the parallels end there; a generation later—with colonial "modern" having morphed into postcolonial "contemporary"—the political situation had changed. The former colonial subject had entered the stage and put the question of representation on the agenda again, this time, not just acquiring presence and demanding representation—as in the 1950s and 1960s—but curating it.

Given the global proliferation of the biennale model, it was not surprising that the focus of attention shifted to the mother of the biennale itself. Africa's representation at the Venice Biennale echoes the shifting understanding of the continent's art. Thus, the first time the Venice Biennale showed African art was in 1922, when African sculptures were shown in conjunction with works by the Italian artist Amedeo Modigliani. The exhibition still breathed the primitivist obsession with *art nègre*. The split between black sub-Saharan Africa and the Islamic North became apparent in 1952 when Egypt was assigned a permanent pavilion. Sub-Saharan Africa remained absent until the early 1990s. South Africa was given permission to have its own pavilion in 1993, thereby acknowledging the country's end of apartheid. However, South Africa's presence in Venice was overshadowed by Susan Vogel's *Fusion* exhibition, which showed artists from a region (West Africa) rather than a nation (see chap. 7).

Nearly a decade later, in 2001, the biennale presented still another idea of Africa when Salah Hassan and Olu Oguibe, Enwezor's coeditors from *Nka*, curated *Authentic/Ex-centric* at the Venice Biennale. Housed at Palazzo Fondazione Levi as part of the biennale's off-site program, Hassan and Oguibe presented seven artists as representatives of a new postmodern and postcolonial "African conceptualism" that resulted from living and working "between worlds."[38] Ranging from Yinka Shonibare's playful *Vacation*, in which he dressed a family of astronauts in his trademark "African fabrics," to Magdalena Campos-Pons's biographical multimedia exploration of Afro-Cuban family history, the works on display both commented on and explored experiences of displacement, diaspora, memory, and the (re)negotiation of identities.

By the time *Authentic/Ex-centric* was running in Venice (May to November 2001), Enwezor had just finished organizing *The Short Century*, a massive show on Africa's struggle for independence, and was in the final stages of working on *Documenta 11*, which opened on June 11, 2002.[39] Established in 1955 as a means to bring postwar Germany back into the international art world and since then running every five years, Documenta developed into the world's most important forum for current trends in contemporary art. Given this context, the appointment of Enwezor as the artistic director of the *Documenta 11* was a clear statement both enacting and acknowledging the shift toward a more inclusive, global, and postcolonial art world (fig. 8.7). Fittingly, Enwezor and his cocurators started the Documenta program with a series of five preexhibition "platforms"

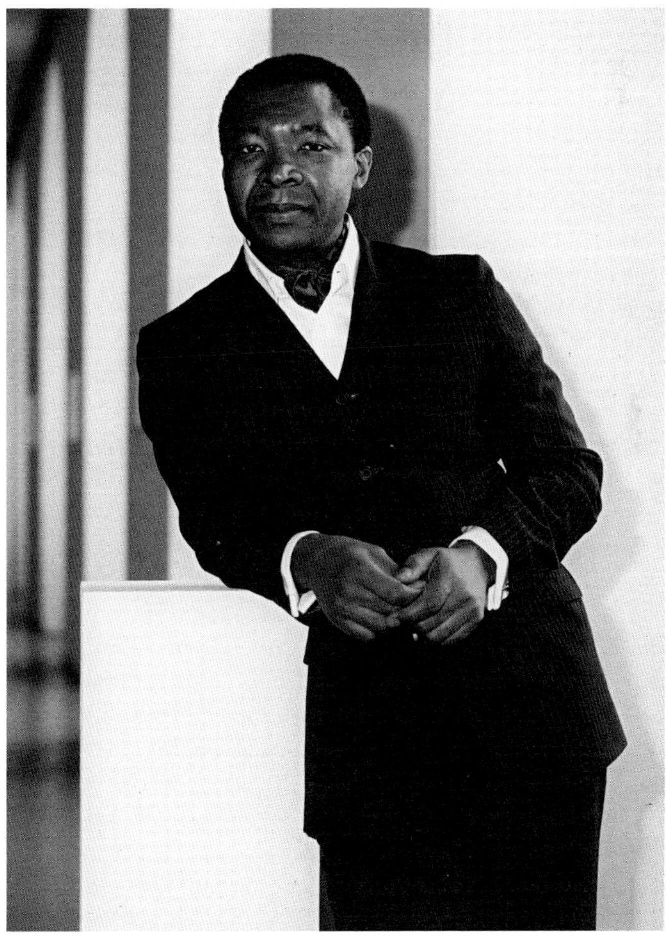

8.7 Okwui Enwezor at *Documenta 11*, Kassel, 2002. Photo: Rysard Kasiewicz. © Documenta Archive.

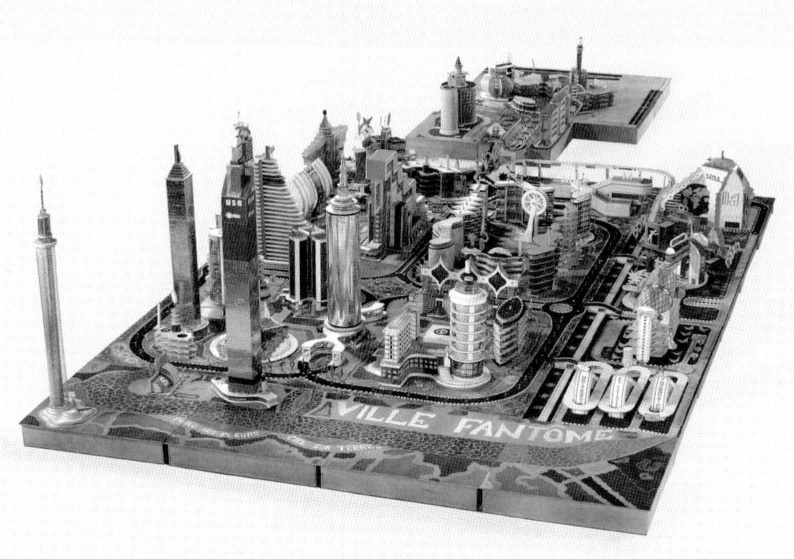

8.8 Bodys Kingelez, *Ville fantòme*, 1996, shown at *Documenta 11*. Paper, cardboard, plastic, 120 × 240 × 580 cm. © Bodys Isek Kingelez, courtesy of The Pigozzi Collection.

scattered around the world in Vienna, New Delhi, St. Lucia, Lagos, and Kassel, each addressing a particular topic relevant to both the region and the wider global concerns of the Documenta. Themes ranged from civil wars, transitional justice, and the unfulfilled dreams of democracy to urban dystopias and the dynamics of cultural creolization (fig. 8.8).

Of the 117 artists Enwezor and his cocurators selected, more than half came from countries other than the Euro-American zone. Yet only 10 percent hailed from Africa or the "African Diaspora," as non-African, black artists were now called. Thirteen years after *Magiciens de la terre*, *Documenta 11* returned to the issue of globalization—but not with the invitation to see all artists as "magicians." Instead, it presented art as a medium through which one can acknowledge political contemporaneity and think about the resulting ethics of relationships. In the words of Enwezor,

> The exhibition as a diagnostic toolbox actively seeks to stage the relationships. Conjunctions, and disjunctions between different realities: between artists, institutions, disciplines, genres, generations, processes, forms, media, activities; between identity and subjectification. Linked together the exhibition counterposes the supposed purity and

autonomy of the art object against a rethinking of modernity based on ideas of transculturality and extraterritoriality.[40]

Expectedly, the "rethinking" triggered a debate over the distinctly political agenda of the show. Critics argued that imposing ethics on aesthetics would reduce the value and quality of art. Others welcomed Enwezor's decision to open up contemporary art to diverse social and material conditions. At the end, "culture" trumped canon; in terms of attendance, *Documenta 11* was a success: 651,000 people visited the show during its duration of four months.

Outside the confines of the art world, however, the agenda of inclusion contrasted with the experience of exclusion. As art historian Sylvester Okwunodu Ogbechie noted in his review of *Documenta 11*,

> At the German consulate in Los Angeles, it took this author three days to explain to German consular officials why an art historian and professor in a major department of art history at a major American university should be interested in attending the most important contemporary art exhibition on the planet. One imagined other black attendees confronting the same problem of access at German embassies everywhere, worrying about securing a valid presence in an increasingly xenophobic Europe, clutching tightly to the transit visas that are now required of many black and brown peoples for passage through most European airports.[41]

Ogbechie's experience points to the discrepancy between the artistic and curatorial success of postcolonialism, in its attempts to effectively expand the art world, on the one hand and its detachment from actual contemporary politics (i.e., racism) on the other. While big traveling exhibitions like *Africa Remix*[42] and the presence of African artists at prominent venues like the Venice Biennale increased the visibility of global contemporary art, the concrete, political effects of the postcolonial discourse remained limited.

Gradually, the conceptual authority of postcolonialism began to fade. At the next Documenta in 2007 (*Documenta 12*), the Benin-based artist Romuald Hazoumè showed a large makeshift boat constructed from gasoline canisters in front of a large wall-size photograph depicting a dried-up oasis (fig. 8.9). Called *Dream*, the installation poignantly commented on the disjuncture between the curatorial success of postcolonialism in the art world and the continued drowning of African migrants trying to cross the Mediterranean Sea. In fact, with the institutionalization of postcolonial arguments in academia, and their arrival in the mainstream,

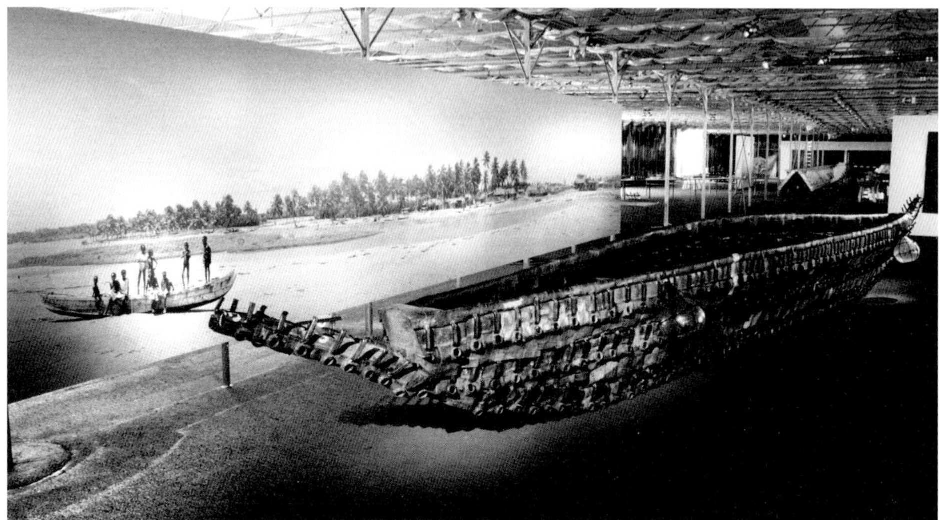

8.9 Romuald Hazoumè, *Dream*, 2007. Installation view, *Documenta 12*, 2007. Plastic canisters, glass bottles, corks, cords, letters, photographs. Photo: Rysard Kasiewicz. © 2021 Artists Rights Society (ARS), New York, ADADP, Paris.

the "postcolonial aura" waned until the waning itself became the subject of reflection.[43] Thus in 2008, the curators of the Guangzhou Triennial titled their event *Farewell to Post-Colonialism*. As the Chinese critic and cocurator Gao Shiming put it,

> Post-colonialism has earned a place in the endorsed and dominant worldview history of nation-states. It has been integrated with various social movements in the past 40 years. Its merits are obvious in literature, the arts, and politics. However, these merits have quickly degenerated to routines within the last 20 years. For instance, we often see and hear symbolic forms of cultural critique in various international exhibitions and seminars labeled with key terms like "identity," "the other," "translation," "immigrant," "migration," "indigenous," "difference," "diversity," "hegemony," "marginalization," "minority," "oppression," "visible-invisible," "class," "sex," and so forth. Today, given the existing postcolonial toolkit, these concepts and ideas that once possessed revolutionary critical force have become another form of dominant power discourse. . . . What this politics of discourse has created is a society formally free but unable to realise, a society that praises difference but that cannot create difference itself.[44]

Surely, Shiming was aware that postcolonial discourse is not monolithic. Rather, multiple voices and positions address different conditions in different postcolonial spaces. Thus, what mattered in Guangzou was primarily the situation in East Asia. Accordingly, the cast of characters prominent in debates about contemporary African art was largely missing. Still, the critique had an echo within the field and did not go unheard.

*   *   *

In hindsight, it is still remarkable how quickly the field of African art studies changed in the 1990s. Given the historical coupling of modernism and colonialism it was clear that the erosion of the former had to mean also the erosion of the latter. Postmodernism and postcolonialism transformed the field thoroughly and long-lastingly. Surely, the issues at stake were not new. Questions of race, knowledge, and representation had been discussed a generation before (chap. 5). But the dwindling of old certainties enabled a new generation of artists and scholars to reframe and rethink long-standing issues in a new postcolonial language and methodology. The "postcolonial turn," as the 1990s came to be seen later, had not only decentered the art world. It also shifted the public attention from traditional to contemporary African art. As we have seen, the "winds of change" (Oguibe) the new discourse unleashed were strong and prompted vehement reactions. Some ten years later, however, the excitement was over. The winds had died down. In 2008, the journal *Nka*, itself a postcolonial creation, convened three roundtables made up of curators and university professors to discuss the altered art world within the realms of museums, curation, and scholarship.[45] "How do we as individual scholars imagine the field of contemporary African art history and our place in it?" one of the journal editors, Chika Okeke-Agulu, asked. Given the diversity of the continent, how helpful and representative are big exhibitions? What does it mean that the great majority of scholarship still resides outside the continent? How can the continuing relocation of African scholars and artists to Europe and the US be stopped? The debate went in different directions, and consensus was hard to find. Positions differed. Yet, an odd mixture of staidness and anxiety was noticeable. No one declared a "Farewell to Postcolonialism," as the organizers of the Guangzhou Triennial had done. It was clear, however, that the vigor and momentum of the newness had passed. A change of direction was in the air.

CHAPTER 9

Undoing the Empire

DURESS, DEFIANCE, AND DECOLONIAL FUTURES

Today, the decolonizing project is back on the agenda worldwide.
ACHILLE MBEMBE, *Decolonization and the Question of the Archive,* 2016

Introduction

When in March 2015, a group of students started to demand the removal of the bronze statue of the British mining magnate and colonizer Cecil Rhodes from the entrance to the University of Cape Town, they could hardly have imagined their successful action would become one of defining events of the decade (fig. 9.1). In fact, if there was one topic that dominated the Africanist art world during the second decade of the twenty-first century, it was the ubiquity of the decolonization agenda. From decolonizing the archive to decolonizing the canon, the curriculum, the museum, the gallery system, the university, and the art establishment, the last decade has seen the emergence of numerous initiatives and campaigns aimed at undoing the empire in both the Global South and North.[1]

But what has fueled this "decolonial turn," as some observers have called it, and how does it differ from other forms of critique, namely postcolonial discourse?[2] Given the heterogeneity of the movement, the answers are necessarily numerous. Demands to decolonize the art collection of the University of Cape Town have a different background than demands to decolonize the Brooklyn Museum of Art in New York or the Humboldt Forum in Berlin. Certainly, the legacies of slavery and colonialism have gained public recognition. "Black lives matter." The anger at the existing conditions is manifest and widespread. So is the quest

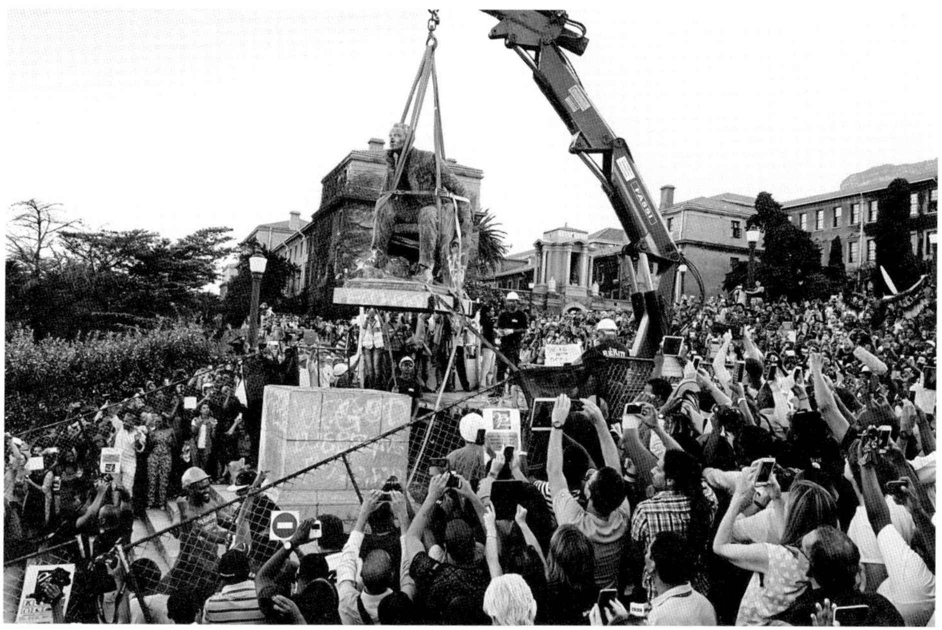

9.1 Cheering students surround the bronze statue of British colonialist Cecil John Rhodes as it was removed from the campus at the University of Cape Town, Cape Town, South Africa, April 9, 2015. © Associated Press. Photo: Schalk van Zuydam.

for action. While postcolonialism opened up discursive spaces and provided visibility and recognition for artistic expressions coming out of Global Africa, it did little to change the social and political situations for people on the ground. The need for more radical, action-oriented forms of critique has generated and (re)fueled a vibrant decolonial agenda that combines previous decolonizing projects with new epistomological and practical forms of critique.[3]

In the following, I will discuss the peculiar features of this constellation in three different contexts. I will start with a closer look at what observers have called the "shifting gravity" in the international art world.[4] The concept signifies the rise of new urban art festivals that challenge the vertical North-South relations of dominance by forging new horizontal South-South connections and invoking new decolonial futures. To illustrate the variations in these programs, the discussion looks at the biennale in Lubumbashi in the Democratic Republic of the Congo and DAK'ART in Senegal. Following the interest in alternative futures, I will discuss the corresponding interest in the function of archives and the emergence of the study of African modernism as a "new discipline" of Africanist research.[5] Over the last two decades the field has seen a surge in studies investigating the dynamics and historical specificities of modern African art in different parts of the continent. What drives this research is partly the ambition to recognize the work of modern African artists who had been excluded from the (art-)historical archive. Partly, it is effort to understand and come to terms with the disjuncture between the hopes and promises of the past and the failures and frustrations of the present. Given this constellation, I will come finally back to Cape Town, home and origin of the "Rhodes Must Fall" movement but also home of Zeitz MOCAA, the first large museum of contemporary art from Africa and its diaspora, which opened in Cape Town in September 2017. The movement and the museum seem to be sending different messages: while the former speaks to bitter frustrations over the lack of progress on the level of everyday life, the latter is a celebration of success and achievements in the realm of art. As I maintain, what drives the current decolonial/decolonization agenda within the art world is in many ways rooted in the gap between the two spheres. But let me start by visiting an art event in the southeast of the Democratic Republic of the Congo, near the border with Zambia.

Visions and Validations

From October 9 to November 8, 2017, the Picha Art Center in Lubumbashi, Democratic Republic of the Congo (DRC), organized the Fifth Lubumbashi Biennale. Picha, Swahili for "image," is an independent art initiative that supports and promotes artistic creation in the DRC. Unlike the organizers of the continent's most prominent biennales in Dakar, Bamako, or Cairo, Picha does not receive government support. Founded in the early twentieth century by the Belgian government as the administrative capital of the mineral-rich province of Katanga, the city's complex social, economic, and political history has crippled the urban infrastructure and left many of Lubumbashi's inhabitants impoverished. Picha is meant to be a creative counterpoint.

The theme of the 2017 biennale, *Éblouissements* (endazzlements) reflected on this condition. The term stems from the Congolese Gabonese sociologist Joseph Tonda in his critique of the global contemporary as both glittering and blinding, fascinating and hallucinatory, enchanting and utterly violent.[6] For the Congolese artist and biennale director Toma Muteba Luntumbue, Tonda's focus on the imaginary provided a fitting conceptual framework for the four-week-long event. Spread across several sites within the city, the biennale comprised exhibitions, performances, lectures, professional encounters, workshops, film cycles, and a variety of learning and outreach activities. Right from the start,

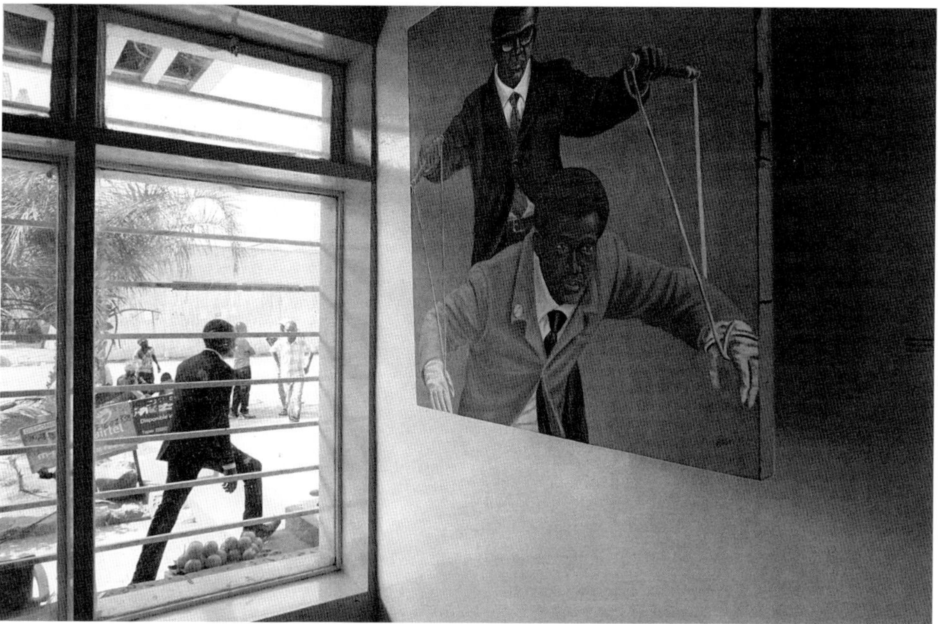

9.2 Zemba Luzamba, *Manipulation*, installation view. Lubumbashi Biennale, 2017. Photo: Elisabeth Weydt.

Luntumbue was eager to root the biennale in the city. Thus, all of the participants were asked to engage with Lubumbashi's public spaces and its colonial and postcolonial history (figs. 9.2, 9.3). In line with this idea, the opening began with a public performance by the Congolese performance artist Sarah Mukadi. Their bodies and clothes colored in earth tones, the dancers of Mukadi's troupe recalled a demonstration of Lubumbashi women who took to the streets nude to protest against oppression and sexual violence under Belgian colonial rule. The performance captured Luntumbue's ambition. As he explained in an interview,

> It is not a Biennale made for the art world: it is rather a Biennale made for the people. This is not demagogy: there is really something different which can rise from the local conditions and from the translation of the exhibition dispositive which we are setting up in a context where there is no institutional or independent art system.[7]

Lubumbashi exemplifies the efforts to counter the hierarchical Euro-American dominance in the global art world by creating new alternative platforms and fostering horizontal South-South relations. In fact, since the early 1990s, as a result of the end of the Cold War, the number of

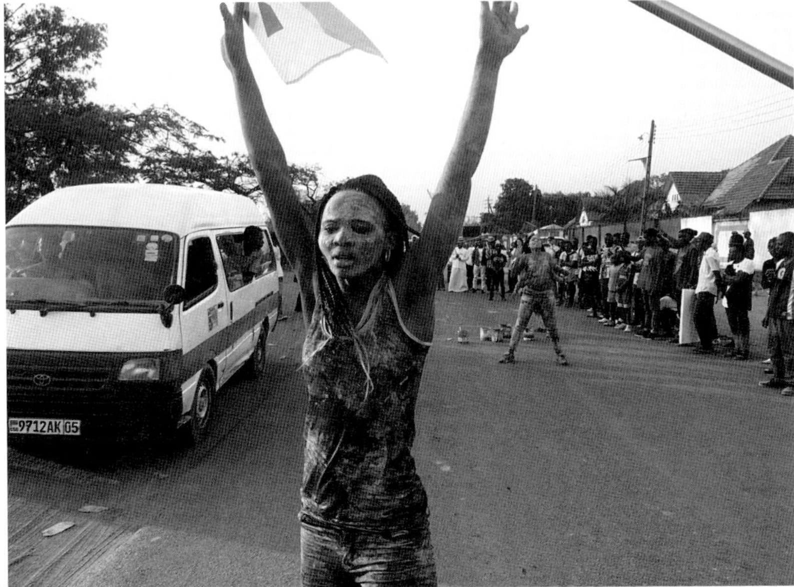

9.3 Sarah Mukadi, performance at the opening of the Lubumbashi Biennale, October 5, 2017. Photo: Elisabeth Weydt.

new art festivals, biennials, and triennials on the African continent has steadily increased. Just as the expansion of neoliberal economic regimes helped to generate a market boom for contemporary art, it also prompted a push back in the form of independent art spaces. In contrast to the established and well-known biennales like Dakar or Bamako, these new spaces are often independent initiatives led by artists and nonprofit organizations.[8] Defined by their distance from commercial and government-sponsored projects, they have provided not only platforms for the exploration and circulation of alternative visions, practices, and concepts but also have created spaces for the emergence of woman curators like the late Bisi Silva, who led the Contemporary Art Centre in Lagos, or Koyo Kouoh, who founded the Raw Material Company in Dakar and was later appointed executive director and chief curator at the Zeitz Museum of Contemporary African Art in Cape Town, South Africa.

Of course, distance and autonomy are relative. After all, Western cultural institutions and foundations like the Goethe Institut or the Alliance française often provide financial and organizational assistance. For them the existence of a lively art scene is essential for the functioning of modern civil societies in which art functions as a system to balance and negotiate competing social interests and positions.[9] But does the investment in art work? Far from being a field of experimentation and a rehearsal stage for a different world, curators and artists like Luntumbue are acutely aware of the hegemonic regime and "totalizating singularity" of the contemporary.[10] They realize the need to pluralize the contemporary and allow for the recognition of multiple temporalities, multiple pasts and multiple presents, existing in the same space.

To understand these pluralities, it is helpful to compare Luntumbue's *Éblouissements,* with another project: *Suturing the City,* a collaboration between the anthropologist Filip De Boeck and Sammy Baloji, photographer and cofounder of the Lubumbashi Biennale.[11] The joint project focuses on the ways Congo's urban dwellers stitch together the disparate realities out of which artistic projects are made. They ask how urbanity is lived and experienced in the midst of shattered memories of a precolonial past, decrepit remnants of modernist, (post)colonial architecture, Chinese posters of imaginary early Chéri Samba–style luxury homes, and huge billboards depicting planned futuristic structures with titles like *Modern Paradise* or *Crown Tower.* The answer is as hazy as the sky in Baloji's photographs. According to Baloji and De Boeck, uncertainty, instability, and unpredictability determine the life of Congo's urban dwellers, artists included. Conceived in this way, the project is not concerned with Congo's art world per se. There is no mentioning of the Lubumbashi Biennale. The authors don't visit artist studios, galleries, and museums. Instead, they delve deep into the local subjectivities that inform the space that these institutions inhabit. It is a text and image project about the relationship between the built environment and political imagination, about the duress and durability of false promises and failed improvements, and about mapping out the possibilities and limits for envisioning a fulfilling future.

An important center where these promises and futures were once made and conceived is the biennale in Dakar. As we have seen in chapters 5 and 6, the capital of Senegal occupies a prominent place in Africa's history of decolonization. In 1966, the *Premier Festival Mondial des Arts Nègres* (FESMAN) celebrated a vision of justice, equality, and recognition not just for Senegal but for the whole of Africa and its diaspora. In fact, FESMAN was an early example of the attempts to counter Western dominance, a condition that has helped to lend FESMAN's successor DAK'ART its reputation as arguably the most prominent African event in the global art world. Since its inception in the early 1990s, DAK'ART underwent several revisions.[12] Taking place from early May to early June, it is now the African flagship of the international biennale circuit. It is here, during the DAK'ART, where the promises and futures of the pasts are continuously resurrected, reworked, and reenvisioned.

Participation in the official program is only for artists "from Africa and the diaspora." Artists from other parts of the globe can participate but are restricted to the OFF program, whose venues are usually private and informal.[13] (fig. 9.4). The restriction is key. As Ugochukwu-Smooth Nzewi and Thomas Fillitz have recently argued, what is at stake is not the market value of the works on display but rather their "cultural validation" within the different parameters that constitute, frame, and enact the imagined community of the black world.[14] Invoking and reimagining the ideas of the founding fathers of Négritude and Pan-Africanism are key in this regard. At the center stand the visionary futures Négritude thinkers and politicians like Aimé Césaire and Léopold Sédar Senghor once imagined in their effort to overcome the French imperial nation-state.[15]

Let's take a closer look. In 2016, DAK'ART changed its selection process and moved to a star curator model. After a decline in importance and a series of experimentations, the directorate decided to invite the renowned Swiss Cameroonian writer, curator, and art critic Simon Njami as artistic director. Njami had started his career with the Paris-based journal *Revue Noire* and subsequently made himself a name by curating a series of prominent contemporary art exhibitions, including *Africa Remix*, which traveled from Germany, England, France, and Sweden to Japan and South Africa. For the 2016 iteration of DAK'ART, Njami picked Senghor's poem "The City in the Blue Day" as a general theme. Pointing to Senghor's vision of black solidarity, he invited artists to "invent new strategies and aesthetics in order to re-enchant the world and the

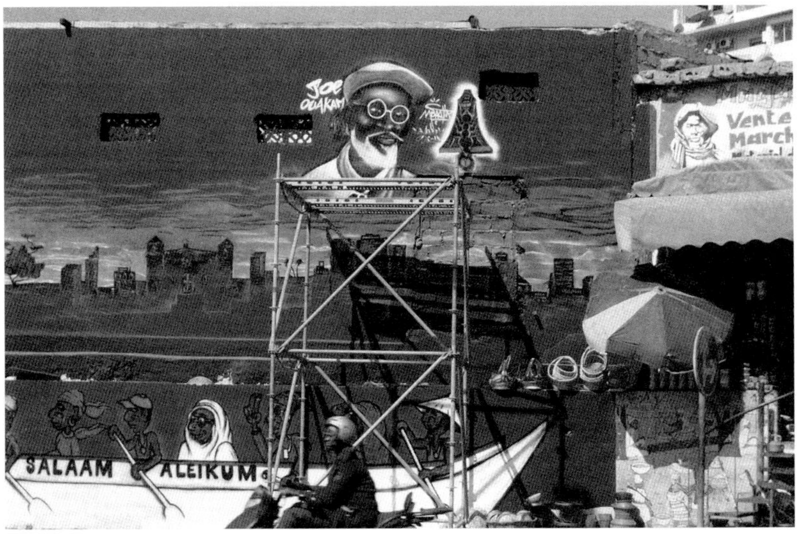

9.4 Docta Graffito with a depiction of Issa Samb alias Joe Ouakam, DAK'ART OFF 2018. Photo: Thomas Fillitz.

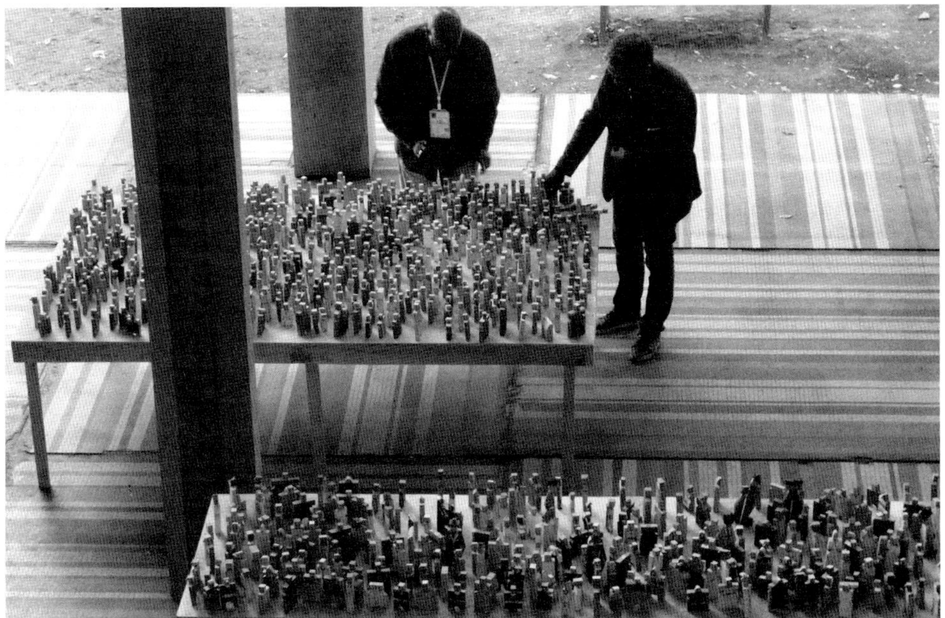

9.5 Installation view, main exhibition hall at the former Palais de Justice, DAK'ART 2016. Abdul Awofeso, *Fragments from the City*. On the right, artistic director Simon Njami. Photo: Thomas Fillitz.

continent."[16] To provide the appropriate architectural ambience for his program, Njami turned the abandoned former Palais de justice, which once housed FESMAN's modern/contemporary art show *Tendencies and Confrontations* (see chap. 5), into DAK'ART's main exhibition hall and transformed the early twentieth-century art deco railway station, the Gare ferroviaire, into the central meeting place for the event's international audience (fig. 9.5).

Njami's move did not remain unnoticed. In July of 2016, one month after the biennale had ended, the memory of FESMAN was invoked again. At the occasion of the inaugural conference of the new Musée des civilisations noires in Dakar, Ibrahima Thioub, one of Senegal's most prominent scholars and intellectuals, publicly noted,

> If the Premier Festival Mondial des Arts Nègres lived, its memory has wandered, as if suspended from an unfinished symphony. The Musée des Civilisations Noires, which must bear witness to the Black Eden to find new hopes, is the missing link in the symphony. It is imperative to achieve it in order to reconcile the black world with its history and offer a strong anchor to all memories in exile.[17]

It might be tempting to brush off the two events as poetically charged black nostalgia. Yet there is more to it. Njami's and Thioub's tapping into the utopian power of Négritude point to something bigger.

African Modernism and the Archival Impulse

A fitting entry point into the discussion is Elizabeth Harney's *In Senghor's Shadow: Art, Politics, and the Avant-Garde in Senegal, 1960–1995*.[18] Published in 2004, the book explores the artistic aftermath of Négritude in Senegal. It starts with a discussion of Senghor's and Césaire's writings on the poetics of blackness and ends with the emergence of DAK'ART and the negotiation of its place in the international art world. What unfolds in between is a captivating analysis of the contested formations and transformations of modern and contemporary Senegalese art. The spectrum ranges from the modernist Pan-African aesthetics of Papa Ibra Tall's tapestries and Senghor's nationalist patronage of the École des Dakar to the art collective Laboratoire Agit'Art with the performances of El Hadji Sy and the installations of Issa Samb alias Joe Ouakam (fig. 9.6).

Harney's anchoring of artistic practices in the shifting entanglements of different political and aesthetic milieus has been rightfully praised as a pioneering achievement. However, the acclaims call for an explanation. A decade before, Salah Hassan, one of the founders of *Nka*, had called for the need to study the "modernist experience." As he noted: "Of all the categories of African art, modern art, especially that of western trained artists, has received the least attention from art historians and other scholars of African art."[19] By then, Hassan's plea remained unheard. A decade later, the situation had changed. Following Harney's study, a surge of books began to address the dynamics of modernism in different parts of the continent. A real "archive fever" set in.[20] Why? What happened?

Hal Foster's essay "An Archival Impulse," published in the same year as Harney's Senegalese study, offers a clue.[21] What triggered Foster's attention was a shift in the interest in archives. As he argued, artists had worked with lost and found objects before. However, in the 1990s, artistic practices began to turn archives from "excavation sites" into "construction sites."[22] For Foster, the move was fueled by "a desire to turn belatedness into becomingness, to recoup failed visions in art, literature, philosophy, and everyday life into possible scenarios of alternative kinds of social relations."[23] While Foster conceived the surge of archival art as an effect of postmodernism, the proximity of his observation to post- and decolonial figures of thought is obvious. What one can see is an oscillation between different understandings and interests in archives

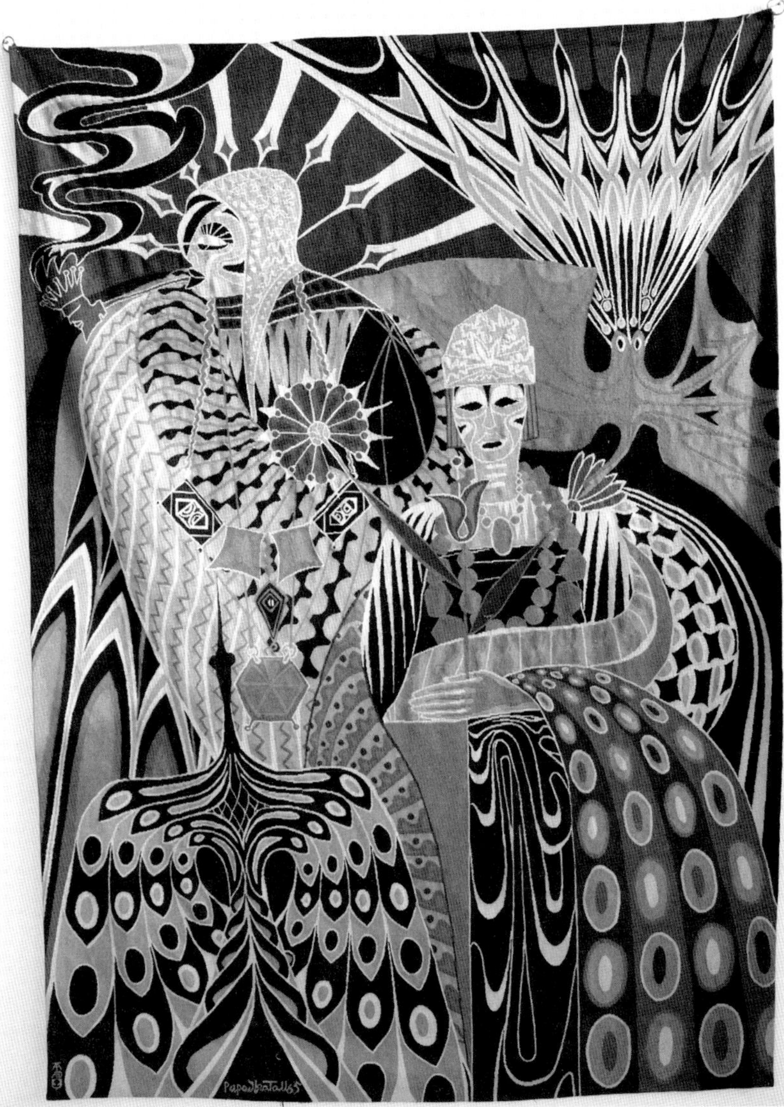

9.6 Papa Ibra Tall, *Royal Couple*, 1965. Tapestry, 222 × 155 cm. Photo courtesy of Ugochukwu-Smooth Nzewi, all rights reserved.

as sites of exclusion and dispossession on the one hand and reclamation and envisioning alternative futures on the other.[24]

Exemplary in this respect is Okwui Enwezor's exhibition *Archive Fever: Uses of the Document in Contemporary Art*.[25] Shown in 2008 at the International Center of Photography in New York, Enwezor's focus was on the way artists use photography to counter and interrogate the authority of the archive. As such, *Archive Fever* resonated with Enwezor's previous projects, specifically his photography exhibitions *In/Sight* and *Snap Judgments* and first and foremost the monumental historical show *The Short Century: Independence and Liberation Movements in Africa 1945–1994* from 2001. With its wealth of documents—on display were not just paintings, sculptures, and installations but also album covers, posters, theater, photojournalism, television programs, architectural plans, and commemorative textiles—*Short Century* had plunged deeply into the historical archive. But it did not explore the concept itself. *Archive Fever* did. A quote from Michel Foucault in Enwezor's long introductory essay set the tone:

> The archive is first the law of what can be said, the system that governs the appearance of statements as unique events. But the archive is also that which determines that all these things said do not accumulate endlessly in an amorphous mass, nor are they inscribed in an unbroken linearity, nor do they disappear at the mercy of chance external accidents; but they are grouped together in distinct figures, composed together in accordance with multiple relations, maintained or blurred in accordance with specific regularities; that which determines that they do not withdraw at the same pace in time, but shine, as it were, like stars, some that seem close to us shining brightly from far off, while others that are in fact close to us are already growing pale.[26]

Foucault's poetic language aimed to capture the blurred and fleeting nature of the subject. What he tried to identify, and what Enwezor enthralled, was the idea of the archive as an opaque, encapsulated system that is both within and outside ourselves, a kind of matrix that governs and limits both what we can say and how we can say it, the sedimented result of historical discourses of institutionalized power and systems of legitimation that had become naturalized and taken for granted. While *Archive Fever* did not have a specific racial focus, Enwezor realized that Foucault's understanding of the archive was compatible with decolonization discourse, especially the work of Frantz Fanon. In the 1950s, while working as a physician and psychiatrist in Algeria, Fanon analyzed the subtle psychological effects of colonialism to the effect that the subject incorporates the logic of power and begins to perpetuate its practice.[27] Seen from a black perspective, Enwezor understood the inherent dialogue of Fanon and Foucault. What mattered to him though was both: the archival process of erasure and exclusion as well as the archival practice of rescue, resistance, and reclamation.

Given this conceptual configuration, the growing research on Négritude and African modernism can be seen as aiming not just to correct and widen the art-historical archive but to come up with alternative, post- and decolonial readings of modernism, readings that counter the Western logic of artistic innovation that had consigned early twentieth-century primitivism the status of avant-garde while it relegated the work of modern African artists to the realm of belatedness and irrelevance.

Two studies on Nigerian modernism convey what's at stake. Chika Okeke-Agulu's *Postcolonial Modernism* and Sylvester Ogbechie's *Ben Enwonwu* focus on very much the same time span but paint a rather different picture of Nigerian modernism.[28] At the center of Okeke-Agulu's study stands a group of young artists who graduated in the late 1950s from the newly founded art college in Zaria in Northern Nigeria. Much of the book deals with notions of nationhood, modernity, and progress.[29] As Okeke-Agulu stresses, for the Zaria artists around the renowned Nigerian artist Uche Okeke, progress was tied to a temporal and aesthetic regime that had surged past the ideas of Négritude and Pan-Africanism favored by Ben Enwonwu, the subject of Ogbechie's book. Both Okeke and Enwonwu focus on how Nigerian artists wrestled with the question of the meaning of *modern*. How was the term to be aesthetically realized? Okeke's *Oja* and Enwonwu's *Africa Dances* series exemplify different programs (figs. 9.7, 9.8). Both are embedded in indigenous Igbo cultural practices—Igbo masquerades in the case of Enwonwu and *uli* mural and body paintings in the case of Okeke. Both aim to synthesize different life and art worlds, yet whereas Enwonwu's masked figures of the former maintain a strictly figurative stance, Okeke's spiral, curvilinear patterns follow and explore an abstract language. The stylistic difference correlates with different auctorial approaches. While Okeke-Agulu's *Postcolonial Modernism* effectively adopts an avant-garde position that situates the Zarian artists firmly within the political context of the transition to independence, Ogbechie's *Ben Enwonwu* aims to understand the artist's abiding attempts to both handle and grapple with modernism's multiple artistic temporalities. As different as the two perspectives are, both authors end their study by invoking an Igbo stance: While Ogbechie likens Enwonwu to an Igbo masquerade that requires multiple perspectives for its understanding, Okeke-Agulu compares the Zaria art school to *mbari*, the Igbo spirit house, that once brought the different factions of society together (see chap. 5). In both cases, the reference to Igbo heritage and identity aims to circumvent the catch-22 many African artists saw and at times still see themselves confronted with: because they came late into art history (as defined by the West) they were not among the main (Western) players, and because they did not belong to the main actors they were pushed to the sidelines and assigned the role of negligible latecomers. Invoking an Igbo stance challenges this logic. It's a position of

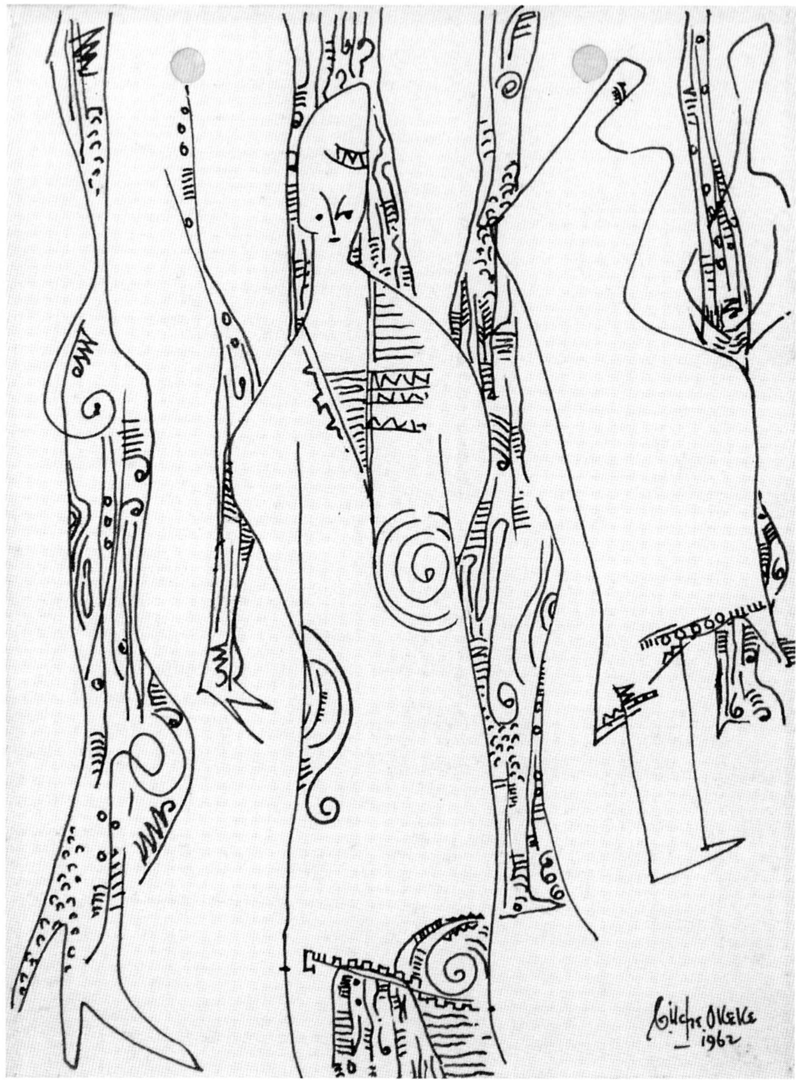

9.7 Uche Okeke, *Punishment* (*Oja Suite*), 1962. Pen and ink. The Simon Ottenberg Collection. Newark Museum. © The Professor Uche Okeke Limited (PUOLL).

difference that not only resonates with the calls for "delinking" and "epistemic disobedience" featured in the recent decolonial/decolonization discourse but also echoes the role of race and exclusion in this very discourse.[30] Let me come back then to South Africa, where the toppling of the Rhodes monument at the entrance to the University of Cape Town provided the fitting imagery for the volition of defiance that shapes the decolonial stance.

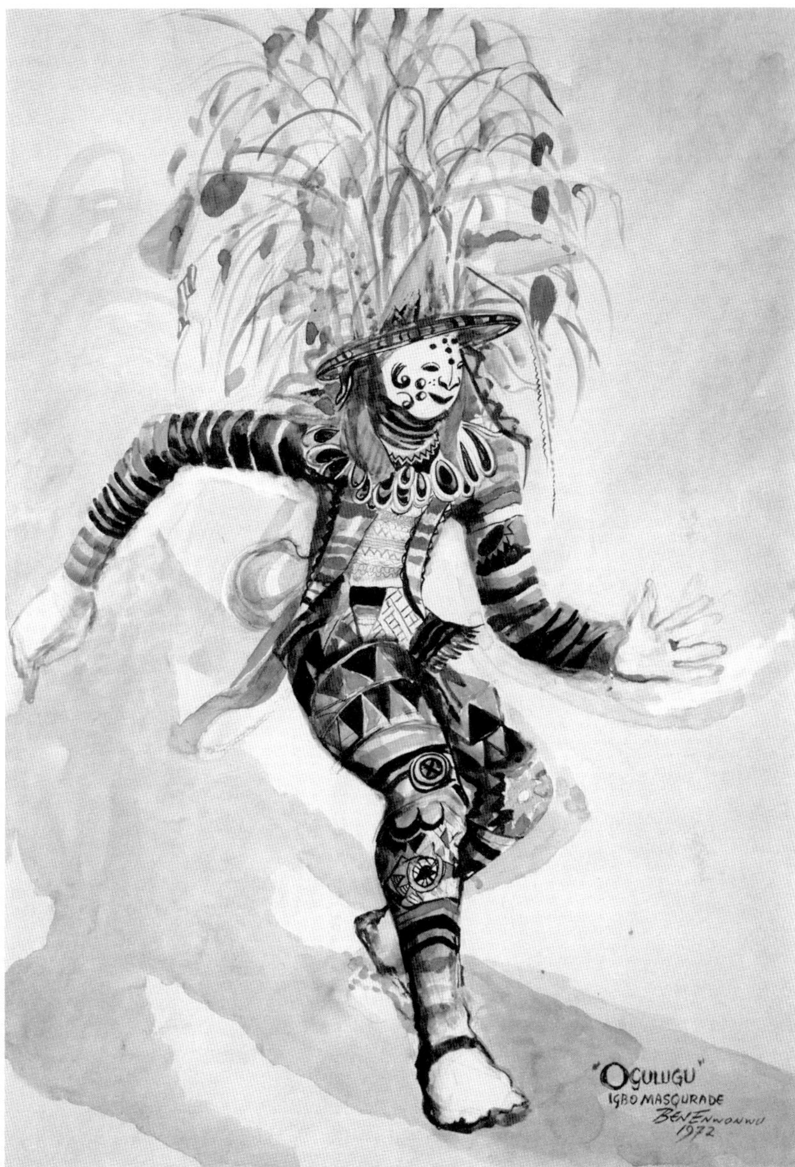

9.8 Ben Enwonwu, *Ogulugu*, 1972. Courtesy of The Ben Enwonwu Foundation.

The Rock and the Silo

In 1990 South African artist William Kentridge made an animated film called *Monument* as part of his *Drawing for Projection* series. At three minutes and twelve seconds long and made of eleven charcoal drawings, the film starts with the drawing of a barren landscape over a dark sky with rapidly moving clouds suggesting the imminent arrival of a thunderstorm. The next shot begins with a close-up of a man's face. Bowed and heavily breathing, we see him carrying a heavy load on his shoulder. Gradually, the man disappears, slowly walking with his load across into the distant landscape. The film then cuts and letters introduce "Soho Eckstein Civic Benefactor." Soho Eckstein emerges as a wealthy, white businessman standing behind microphones and reading a written speech. Megaphones and loudspeakers generate a stream of small black stripes that morph into a veiled statue inside an open, cage-like metal frame. Among billboards, lampposts, and an ever-denser mass of people Soho Eckstein waves his hands, gesturing praise and recognition for what the statue represents. Eventually, the statue is revealed, and we recognize the same load-wearing figure we encountered at the beginning of the film, but now its feet are chained to the plinth. With the figure raising its head, looking at the beholder who hears it breathing heavily, the film ends (fig. 9.9).

Kentridge's film represents an early intervention in South Africa's debate on how to come to terms with the legacy of apartheid. Earlier in 1990, South Africa's president F. W. de Klerk had announced he would

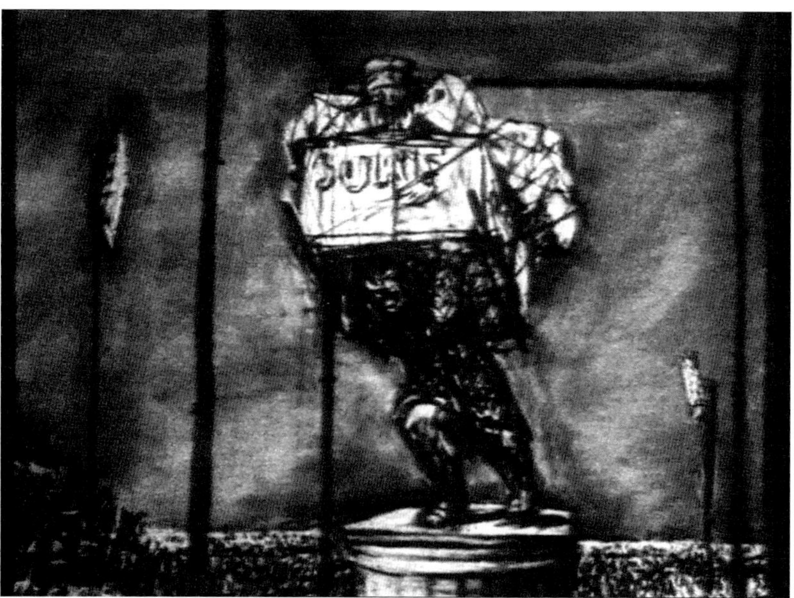

9.9 Still from William Kentridge's film *Monument*, 1990. © National Museum of African Art, Smithsonian Institution, courtesy of William Kentridge.

lift the ban on political parties and release political prisoners from prison. The decisions opened the door for free elections and gave rise to the public debate over questions of guilt and commemoration. Kentridge's focus on the public benefactor Soho Eckstein, whose wealth is derived from the exploitation of the black labor force his monument seeks to honor, brought to light the moral consequences members of the white cultural and critical elite saw themselves facing. That is, how would they come to terms with the past their race and status entailed? How would they expose the crimes of the past while at the same time feeling complicit? As curator and critic Dan Cameron put it in 1999,

> The film seeks to give voice to some of Kentridge' most profound misgivings concerning both his chosen vocation and the passivity of his position as spectator in relation to South Africa's ongoing political crisis. . . . We are invited to understand to experience Soho as an extension of the artist himself onto the morally complex playing field of South African public life. In such a context, as questions of identity become reduced to simplistic sketches of the group to which one belongs and whose interest one is expected to defend, personal imperfections become a kind of psychic armour. . . . Even if the decision to monumentalize the overburdened worker seems more like an expression of Soho's unconscious guilt than a deliberate attempt to atone for his exploitative behavior, *Monument* holds out the glimmer of hope that mutual sympathy, even across the widest of cultural boundaries, is possible.[31]

The hope Cameron's reading evokes has been difficult to sustain, though. Despite instituting a truth and reconciliation commission, passing a national heritage act, and establishing numerous new monuments, memorials, and museums aiming to address the injustices of the past, the latter are still felt to inform the injustices of the present.[32]

The recent uprising at the University of Cape Town with which I began this chapter exemplifies the ongoing volatility of the situation. The statue of Cecil Rhodes, a British-born mining magnate, empire proselytizer, and benefactor of the land on which the university is situated, had been the focus of sporadic protests in the past, but ten years after the end of apartheid and the first free elections, the critique acquired new meaning: the massive bronze work had become a symbol of the lack of change and the city's enduring racial and economic inequalities. The anger exploded on March 9, 2015, when Chumani Maxwele, a student at the University of Cape Town, picked up a bucket of human feces on the curbside in the township of Khayelitsha, brought it to the university, and threw it into the face of the Rhodes statue, shouting "Where are our heroes and ancestors?" [33] Protests continued for days and spread to the destruction of artworks from the university gallery to occupations of university offices and public art performances. On April 9, 2015, the university leadership finally gave in, agreeing to decolonize the university and its academic programs. But first, the symbolic act of removing the statue from the university premises by crane, before a crowd of spectators, had to take place. Performance and installation artist Sethembile Msezane highlighted the historical and colonial context.[34] In a nearly four-hour-long performance, Msezane stood on a mobile plinth with arms outstretched wearing a beaded headdress and hair adornments (fig. 9.10). The title of her performance, *Chapungu: The Day Rhodes Fell*, referenced the soapstone bird sculptures that once crowned monoliths in the ancient, precolonial settlement widely known as Great Zimbabwe that Rhodes annexed as part of his empire-building ambitions.

While iconoclasm is about destruction, its moral drive is geared toward renewal; it's about building and creating a better place.[35] Given the charged political climate, it is therefore no coincidence that this iconoclastic impulse also informed the opening of new Zeitz Museum of Contemporary Art in Africa in September 2017. Housed in an old repurposed

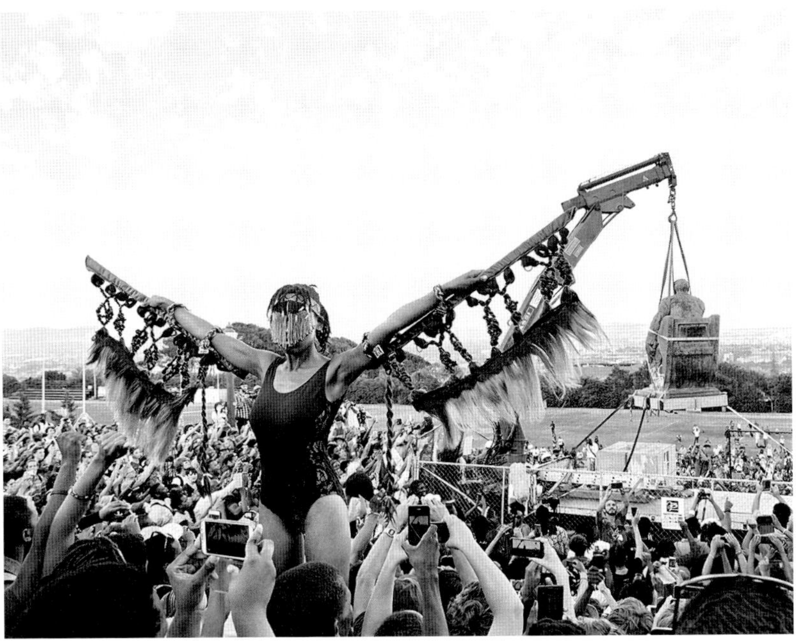

9.10 Sethembile Msezane, *Chapungu: The Day Rhodes Fell*, 2015. Print in Hahnemuhle photo rag paper, 84.1 × 118.9 cm. Photo courtesy of the artist. © Sethembile Msezane.

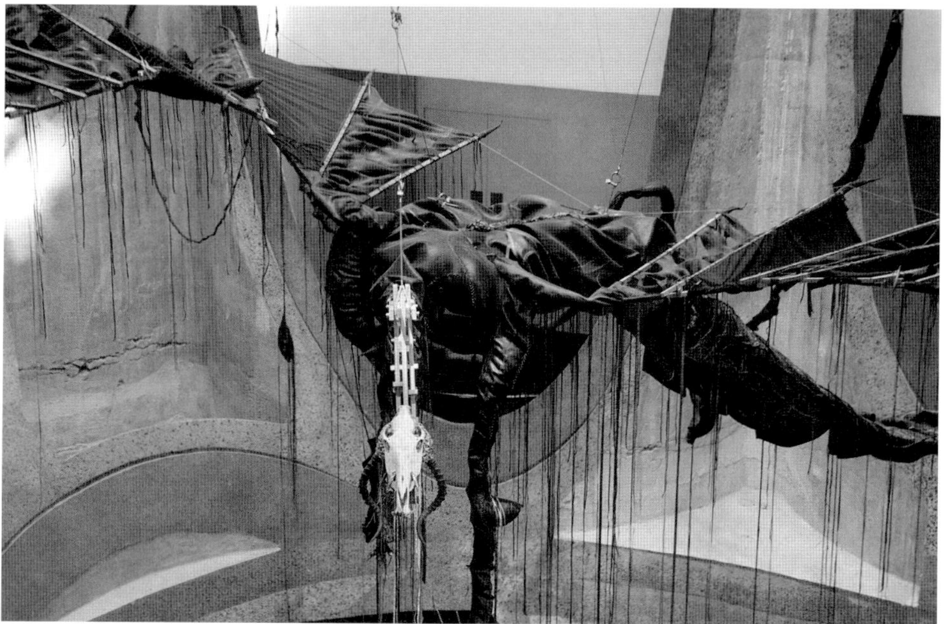

9.11 Nicholas Hlobo, *Iimpundulu Zonke Ziyandilandela*, 2017. Rubber, ribbon, mixed media, sound, 250 × 460 × 1,000 cm. Installation view. Courtesy Zeitz Museum of Contemporary Art Africa (Zeitz MOCAA).

grain silo on Cape Town's waterfront, the museum's inaugural exhibition, *All Things Being Equal*, showed over forty artists from Africa and its diaspora ranging from Kehinde Wiley, Wangechi Mutu, Chris Ofili, and El Anatsui to William Kentridge, Kendell Geers, Nandipha Mntambo, and Zanele Muholi as well as young local artists like Sethembile Msezane. The works on display in Cape Town came from the German businessman Jochen Zeitz, formerly CEO of the sports company Puma and owner of an extensive collection of contemporary African art.

The reception was widely positive. All major media outlets covered the opening with fanfare, celebrating both the stunning architectural design by the London Heatherwick studio and Nicholas Hlobo's massive flying rubber dragon dramatically hovering in the open museum's atrium (fig. 9.11). The artist Sue Williamson, a prominent South African voice in the art world, captured the hope and excitement that accompanied the opening:

> The opening of the museum marks an extraordinary milestone in the reception and presentation of contemporary art on the African continent, an opportunity—finally—for Africa to consistently play host

to the world, rather than to be always sending artists and their work to foreign art institutions through lack of funding and space to show the work here. . . . There is little doubt that the new Zeitz MOCAA has the potential to shine the light on the artists of Africa, to re-imagine the position which contemporary African art holds in the world right now, and to make Cape Town a fixed destination for curators wishing to see that art framed by local discourse.[36]

Still, the question of racism, poverty, and coloniality and that prompted the Rhodes Must Fall movement also informed the debate about the new Zeitz museum in Cape Town.[37] Thus, in addition to recognition and praise, the "local discourse" also expressed concern and critique. Questions stemmed from the critical dictionary of heritage and circled around ownership, representation, and control: Who is the museum's intended audience? Who speaks? On whose behalf?[38] All four of the initial public faces of the museum project—the executive director and chief curator, the owner of the collection, the architect of the museum, and the CEO of the waterfront redevelopment company—were white men, with the architect and the collection owner being nonnationals.[39] In view of the country's violent history of segregation and exclusion, this fact was quickly noted and linked to the institution's structure and location. Though the museum's leadership has emphasized its ambition to be a museum for all people in South Africa, the economics say otherwise. With

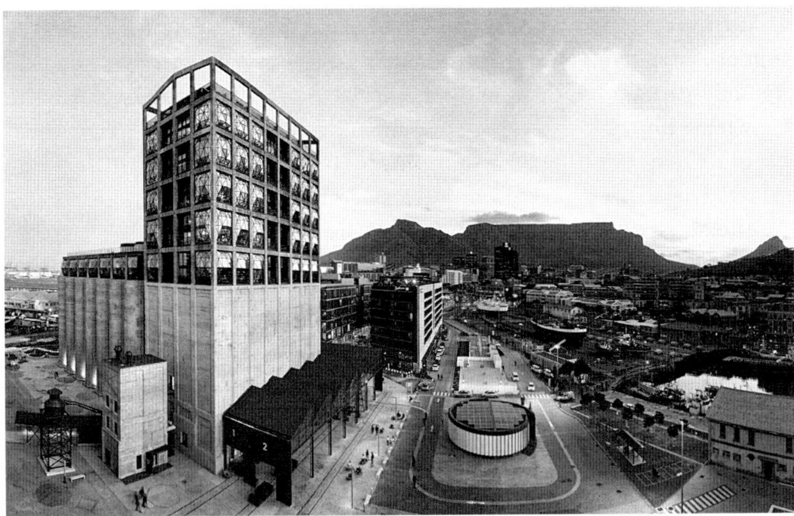

9.12 Zeitz Museum of Contemporary Art Africa (Zeitz MOCAA) in Cape Town. © hufton + crow.

its eighty galleries and a sculpture garden, the museum is part of a water-front redevelopment plan that aims to connect the far-flung mall, which attracts more than twenty million visitors annually, to a rapidly gentrifying lower city (fig. 9.12). In other words, the museum's target audience—those visitors who make the museum financially viable—is clearly not the economically precarious local population but foreign tourists and the South African upper middle class that can afford the hefty entrance fee of 210 Rand (US$13.52 in April 2022).[40] Tellingly, above the new museum sits a luxury hotel, ironically called The Silo, where room rates start at US$900 per night.

*   *   *

Perhaps it would have been naive to expect the first large African museum of contemporary art showing transnational works by artists from Africa and the African diaspora to be an exception to the old story of class, power, and privilege. In fact, some might see the arrival of global African contemporary art into the world of wealth as a sign of the field's maturity. However, from a decolonial perspective, the opening of the Zeitz MOCAA can't be disconnected from the toppling of the Rhodes monument. In 1990, the year he made his film *Monument,* William Kentridge referred to apartheid as the "rock" that weighs on the moral conscience of South Africa's citizens.[41] As he explained, the "rock" is everywhere. One can't get away from it. It is "possessive, and inimical to good work." It is for that very reason, Kentridge argued, that "the job of the artist is to escape from the rock."[42] After all, artists cannot let the rock impede their work. But how far can one escape? Might escape mean ending up in spaces of detachment, like the exclusive luxury hotel above the Zeitz museum, removed from the pain and suffering of the world below? Cape Town is not the only place where "the rock" and "the silo" go together. The tensions the union creates are palpable everywhere. So are the efforts to imagine a different world where "the rock" has given way to a decolonial future.

Epilogue

What do we talk about when we talk about African art? Let me end my interrogation of this question by following up on the notion of a decolonial future that concluded the final chapter. Is there a way "out of the dark night" the colonial legacies have bequeathed us, as Achille Mbembe recently put it?[1]

As we have seen, a defining feature of the decolonial agenda is its heterogeneity, or rather its multivalences as being a demand, a vision, an epistemological critique, and a stance of resistance and defiance all at once. The range of meanings reflects the long and varied semantic shadow that starts looming when one begins to talk about "African art." Location matters. Voices from the North dominate this talk. If voices of the South speak up, they need to publish in the North (and preferably in English) to get heard. The decolonial turn and agenda are not in the least a reaction to this condition. It aims to ward off the glaring light of the North casting its discursive shadow on the South. Let's recall that *Éblouissements*, the title of the 2017 Lubumbashi Biennale, was inspired by Joseph Tonda's critique of imperial modernity as a society of techno-capitalist spectacle that dazzles its subjects. Protective local glasses are necessary to see one's options moving forward—but in what direction? Which vantage point is used to envision the future?

Of course, there is no single position, only multiple, competing ones, a fact that makes talking about African art burdened with an excess of meaning. Again, location matters. It makes a difference whether one addresses the question at the Basel Miami art fair or in Lubumbashi. One option would be to get rid of the signifier all together; there is no African art, only art in Africa and its diasporas. The option has prominent proponents. As Shonibare and Enwezor once famously argued, the definition of *Africa* and *the West* go together. The two are intertwined. One cannot define *Africa* without *Europe*, just as it is impossible to define *Europe* without *Africa*. Both definitions are entangled; they work both ways.[2] Hence, practices of cultural translation—exemplified by the history of Dutch wax cloth, Shonibare's favorite medium—might be more fitting than the insistence on authenticity and difference. But there is a third diasporic option, an option of yearning and mourning, as it were, that keeps pushing the long history of domination and violence, erasure, and extraction into the fore. The manifold legacies of the transatlantic slave trade have made Africa also about remembrance and longing, a "project of desire," as the philosopher Souleymane Bachir Diagne recently put it.[3] Hence, whatever the position that one adopts, the "rock" remains. It breathes like the figure in Kentridge's film *Monument*.

In 1990, the rock was about the legacy of apartheid hovering over the hopes of the newly emerging "rainbow nation." Today, the image of the figure chained to the plinth alludes to the artefacts chained in the museums of the North and the attempts to free and repatriate them—to bring them home—one of the key demands of the decolonial agenda. Certainly, the agenda is not new.[4] Demands to return cultural property illegally amassed during imperial and colonial times have long been made. In recent years, however, the debate on restitution got new momentum (see the introduction). Hamady Bocoum, the director of the new Musée des civilisations noires in Dakar, and Malick Ndiaye, the artistic director of the 2022 DAK'ART, are clear on this point. They subscribe to a position of "insubordination" that rejects both the critical postcolonial stance for its neglect of the ancient riches of African history as well as the West's assumed connoisseurial authority in valuing and validating cultural artifacts. It is worth citing their reminder:

> Let us address history: When the modern museum took shape in eighteenth century Europe, its preoccupation with the systematic classification of knowledge by means of objects was derived from the great catalogues of the sixteenth century and from cabinets of curiosities, which aimed to be reflections of the world in miniature. The museum secularized the religious objects it contained, stripping them of their sacred dimension. Divorced from their ritual contexts, they became art objects seen as manifestations of a nation's creative spirit. It is important to recall this history that classifies objects as art as it has had profound consequences. It allowed for the appeal to a universal category that enabled museums to argue that objects that had been stripped of their original character no longer represented African

heritage. Exhibited in the museum, objects came to acquire a universal dimension that shifted questions of origin and ownership to notions of stewardship. But how valid are these reifications of art?[5]

One could extend the question by linking it to the question of repair and repatriation. Restitution, for a long time an anathema in the Global North, has become a reality and with it the debate over the prospects and possibilities of "resocializing" restituted objects in their original location.[6] How will the new meanings, translations, energies, and networks the objects formed abroad reconcile with the expectations, hopes, and anxieties awaiting them in their old homeland upon their return from exile?

It is too early to know the answer. What matters is the question. After all, it is only consequent that real practical steps toward the shaping the decolonial future of African art need to begin with the return of objects from the field's colonial past. The "new relational ethics" Sarr and Savoy have demanded in their restitution report echo a new sense of openness that results from an unraveling, decentering, and breaking down of distinct patterns of power and dependencies.[7] Surely, differences exist. Various options are on the table. But given the excess of meaning, what else would one expect? "African art," let alone "Africa," has turned into, or perhaps has always been, an inexhaustible quotation.[8] Its multiple translations have made it subject to many forms of (re)imaginations, and (re)configurations. As such, the talk about "African art" is likely to stay. What its future will look like—where, how, and what we will be talking about when we talk about "African art"—will depend on the emancipatory power of the talk, how much it can challenge, counter, and eventually overcome the structural asymmetry among those doing the talking.

ACKNOWLEDGMENTS

I am most grateful for the willingness of many friends, colleagues, and students who shared their thoughts with me over the years this book has been in the making.

Especially, I would like to thank Rowland Abiodun, George Abungu, Cynthia Becker, Suzanne Blier, Christa Clark, Skip Cole, Madi Cook-Comey, Till Förster, Mark Haxthausen, Paola Ivanov, Ferdinand de Jong, the late Sidney Kasfir, Prita Meier, John Monroe, Steven Nelson, Malick Ndiaye, Smooth Nzewi, Sylvester Ogbechie, Chika Okeke-Agulu, Kelsey Petersen, Kerstin Pinther, Allen Roberts, Ray Silverman, Zoë Strother, Susan Vogel, Tobias Wendl, and Megan Zembower.

Writing started in 2017 during a fellowship at the Getty Research Center in Los Angeles. I want to thank Thomas Gaehtgens and Alexa Sekyra for the invitation and my fellow fellows with whom I had the pleasure and privilege to exchange ideas. Thanks also to Susan Bielstein, senior editor at University of Chicago Press, for her trust, guidance, and unwavering confidence in the project during the challenging times of the pandemic. I am glad that the book found a home with UCP.

Finally, I want to thank Brigitte for her critique and companionship during this project. It is to her this book is dedicated.

NOTES

Introduction

1. Johannes Fabian, *Time and the Other: How Anthropology Makes Its Objects* (New York: Columbia University Press, 1983).

2. Valentin-Yves Mudimbe, *The Idea of Africa*, African Systems of Thought (Bloomington: Indiana University Press, 1994).

3. A prominent example is Meschac Gaba's installation *Museum of Contemporary African Art, 1997–2002*. In 2013, in an interview with Chris Dercon—then director of the Tate Modern in London, which had bought Gaba's museum installation—Gaba commented on the responses to his work: "I hate people telling me what I do is European art. It's mainly Africans who tell me that, not Europeans. What I do is to react to an African situation, which is linked to a Eurocentric problem." Cited from the Tate website, https://www.tate.org.uk/whats-on/tate-modern/exhibition/meschac-gaba-museum-contemporary-african-art/my-museum-doesnt-exist.

4. Felwine Sarr and Bénédicte Savoy, *Restituer le patrimoine africain* (Paris: Philippe Rey/Seuil, 2018). For the English translation, see http://restitutionreport2018.com/sarr_savoy_en.pdf.

5. Ibid., 4.

6. AFP, "Black Heritage Museum, 'Crucible of Creativity,' Opens in Dakar," France 24, December 6, 2018, https://www.france24.com/en/20181206-black-heritage-museum-crucible-creativity-opens-dakar. On the role of the new museum in the context of Senegal's history of cultural heritage policy, see also Ferdinand de Jong, "The Museum of Black Civilizations: Race, Repair, Restitution," in *Decolonizing Heritage: Time to Repair in Senegal* (Cambridge: Cambridge University Press, 2022).

7. Daniel Boffey, "Belgium's Revamped Africa Museum Triggers Request by DRC," *Guardian*, December 8, 2018, https://www.theguardian.com/world/2018/dec/08/belgium-revamped-africa-museum-demands-congo-kabila. For a discussion of the museum, see Elaine Ericksen Sullivan, "'Petit à Petit': Contemporary Art and Decolonial Horizons in Belgium's AfricaMuseum" (PhD diss., University of California, Los Angeles, 2020), https://escholarship.org/content/qt4d49z3xc/qt4d49z3xc.pdf.

8. Statement on the handling of the Benin Bronzes in German museums and institutions, April 29, 2021, https://www.bundesregierung.de/resource/blob/973862/1902356/bb1f9db17191f24d00ab3dccb2e70a08/2021-04-30-bkm-statement-benin-data.pdf?download=1.

9. Dipesh Chakrabarty, *Provincializing Europe: Postcolonial Thought and Historical Difference* (Princeton, NJ: Princeton University Press, 2000); Okwui Enwezor, ed., *Documenta 11: The Catalogue* (Osfildern: Hatje Cantz, 2002); Olu Oguibe, *The Culture Game* (Minneapolis: University of Minnesota Press, 2004).

10. Moni Adams, "African Visual Arts from an Art Historical Perspective," *African Studies Review* 32, no. 2 (September 1989): 55–103; Paula Ben Amos, "African Visual Arts from a Social Perspective," *African Studies Review* 32, no. 2 (September 1989): 1–53; Oguibe, *The Culture Game*.

11. Sidney Kasfir, "African Visual Cultures," in *Modern African History*, ed. John Parker and Richard Reid (Oxford: Oxford University Press, 2013), 438–49.

12. Achille Mbembe and Steven Rendall, "African Modes of Self-Writing." *Public Culture* 14, no. 1 (2002): 239–73.

13. At this point I should clarify what I mean by "field" and how the concept differs from that of the "art world." My use and understanding of the term *field* is informed by sociological theory. That is, a field is always a "social field" populated by a multitude of players (objects, humans, institutions) who compete over influence and authority within a given field-specific subject like "art." Understanding the "art world" as an "art field" not only stresses the relational and agonistic characteristics of the field/world, it also acknowledges the fact that players within the field/world do not have to share the same cultural background, as Danto has maintained in his classic definition of the art world: "The art world is the discourse of reasons institutionalized, and to be a member of the art world is, accordingly, to have learned what it means to participate in the discourse of reasons for one's culture." Artur Danto, "The Art World Revisited," in *Beyond the Brillo Box: The Visual Arts in Post-Historical Perspective* (Berkeley: University of California Press, 1992), 46. In fact it is the presence of multiple and competing cultures that characterizes the dynamics of an Africanist art world. On the relation of worlds and fields, see Hans van Maanen, *How to Study Art Worlds: On the Societal Functioning of Aesthetic Values* (Amsterdam: Amsterdam University Press, 2007).

14. See Prita Meier, *Swahili Port Cities: The Architecture of Elsewhere* (Bloomington: Indiana University Press, 2016).

15. Michael Baxandall, *Patterns of Intention: On the Historical Explanation of Pictures* (Oxford: Oxford University Press, 1985), 1.

16. Chinua Achebe, "The Art of Fiction No. 139: Interview with Jerome Brooks," *Paris Review*, no. 133 (Winter, 1994): 1–5.

17. Surely, Achebe is not the only literary voice on this question. Kenyan writer Ngũgĩ wa Thiong'o has famously opted for a different position by deciding to write in his native tongue Gikuyu; see his influential study *Decolonizing the Mind: The Politics of Language in African Literature* (London: Heinemann, 1986). In African art history the question remains unresolved. For three different positions, see Suzanne Blier, "Words about Words about Icons: Iconologology and the Study of African Art," *Art Journal* 46, no. 2 (Summer 1988): 75–87; Rowland Abiodun, *Yoruba Art and Language: Seeking the African in African Art* (Cambridge: Cambridge University Press, 2014); and Moyo Okediji's translational and dialogical reading of Abiodun's critique, "African Art and Language as Semioptic Text," *Art Bulletin* 97, no. 2 (2015): 123–39.

18. For a recent example stemming from an ethnography of art school education, see Gary Allen Fine, *Talking Art: The Culture of Practice and the Practice of Culture in MFA Education* (Chicago: University of Chicago Press, 2018).

19. The same goes for the signifier "African." Instead of asking what actually is "African" in African art, I argue it makes more sense to ask, How, when, and under what circumstances

does an object—and an artist—become, or cease to be, "African"? Needless to say, this applies also for other totalizing designations like "American," "Asian," or "Western."

20. See Edward Said, *Beginnings: Intentions and Methods* (New York: Columbia University Press, 1975).

21. Bogumil Jewsiewicki and David Newbury, eds., *African Historiography: What History for Which Africa?* (Beverly Hills: Sage, 1986).

22. For a recent example, see Allen Roberts, *Dance of the Assassin: Performing Early Colonial Hegemony in the Congo* (Bloomington: Indiana University Press, 2013).

23. Obviously, generational shifts and changes don't translate into a simple linear chronology. For an insightful discussion of the problems of a generational approach in art history, see Frederic J. Schwartz, "Ernst Bloch and Wilhelm Pinder: Out of Sync," *Grey Room*, no 3 (Spring 2001): 54–89.

24. Michael Baxandall, *Painting and Experience in Fifteenth-Century Italy: A Primer in the Social History of Pictorial Style* (Oxford: Oxford University Press, 1972).

25. See Fredric Jameson, "Modernism and Imperialism," in *Nationalism, Colonialism, and Literature*, ed. Terry Eagleton, Fredric Jameson, and Edward Said (Minneapolis: University of Minnesota Press, 1990), 42–66. See also, Oguibe, *The Culture Game*.

26. Ernst Bloch, *Heritage of Our Times*, trans. Neville and Stephen Plaice (Cambridge: Polity Press, 1991), originally published as *Erbschaft dieser Zeit* (Zurich: Oprecht & Helbling, 1935). See also Schwartz, "Ernst Bloch and Wilhelm Pinder."

27. See Suzanne Blier, *Art and Risk in Ancient Yoruba: Ife History, Power, and Identity, c. 1300* (Cambridge: Cambridge University Press, 2015); Alisa LaGamma, ed., *Sahel: Art and Empires on the Shores of the Sahara* (New Haven, CT: Yale University Press, 2020); Kathryn Gunsch, *The Benin Plaques: A 16th Century Imperial Monument* (London: Routledge, 2017); Kathleen Bickford Berzock, ed., *Caravans of Gold, Fragments in Time: Art, Culture, and Exchange across Medieval Saharan Africa* (Princeton, NJ: Princeton University Press, 2019).

28. On a general, comparative level, see Zoë Strother, *The Uncanny Guest: Masks in Theory and Practice, from Europe to Africa* (Los Angeles: Getty Publications, forthcoming).

29. Lowery Stokes Sims and Leslie King-Hammond, eds., *The Global Africa Project* (Munich: Prestel, 2010); Christa Clark, ed., *The Arts of Global Africa. The Newark Museum Collection* (Newark: Newark Museum, 2018); Cynthia Becker, *Blackness in Morocco: Gnawa Identity through Music and Visual Culture* (Minneapolis: University of Minnesota Press, 2020).

30. Dan Hicks, *The Brutish Museums: The Benin Bronzes, Colonial Violence and Cultural Restitution* (London: Pluto Press, 2020); Bénédicte Savoy, *Africa's Struggle for Its Art: History of a Postcolonial Defeat*, trans. Susanne Meyer-Abich (Princeton, NJ: Princeton University Press, 2022), originally published as *Afrikas Kampf um seine Kunst: Geschichte einer Postkolonialen Niederlage* (Munich: C. H. Beck, 2021).

31. See Silvia Forni and Christopher Steiner, eds., *Africa in the Market: 20th Century Art from the Amrad African Art Collection* (Toronto: Royal Ontario Museum, 2016); Yaëlle Biro, *Fabriquer le regard: Marchands, réseaux et objets d'art africains à l'aube du XXe siècle* (Dijon: Les presses du réel, 2018); John Warne Monroe, *Metropolitan Fetish: African Sculpture and the Imperial French Invention of Primitive Art* (Ithaca, NY: Cornell University Press, 2019); Maureen Murphy, *De l'imaginaire au musée: Les arts d'Afrique à Paris et à New York, 1931 à nos jours* (Dijon: Les presses du réel, 2020).

32. The main reason for this omission is my conviction that the subject demands and merits more attention than this book could accommodate. While the status of architecture was recognized as an integral part of the field early on, it has taken on a life of its own, with its own journals, professional organizations, and exhibitions.

33. Ikem Stanley Okoye, "Identity/Knowledge," *Critical Interventions: Journal of African Art History and Visual Culture* 1, no. 1 (2007): 5–13.

Chapter One

1. Alfred Ellis Burton, *The Land of Fetish* (London: Chapman and Hall, 1883), 73.

2. Kristin Mann, *Marrying Well: Marriage, Status and Social Change in Colonial Lagos* (Cambridge: Cambridge University Press, 1985).

3. Leo Frobenius, *The Voice of Africa: Being an Account of the Travels of the German Inner African Exploration Expedition in the Years 1910–1912*, trans. Rudolf Blind (London: Hutchinson, 1913), 1:39–40, originally published as *Und Afrika Sprach: Bericht über den Verlauf der dritten Reise Periode der D.I.A.F.E. in den Jahren 1910 bis 1912* (Berlin: Vita Deutsches Verlagshaus, 1912).

4. In 1904, by then thirty-five years old, Frobenius had established the "Inner African Research Expeditions" as both a business and a scholarly venture.

5. Leo Frobenius, *Der Ursprung Afrikanischer Kulturen* (Berlin: Borntraeger, 1898), iv. For a recent take on the framing of (African) art, see Bennetta Jules-Rosette and J. R. Osborn, *African Art Reframed: Reflections and Dialogues on Museum Culture* (Champaign: University of Illinois Press, 2020).

6. The museum grew out of the Royal Prussian Ethnographic collection, which in turn grew out of Brandenburg-Prussian royal *Kunstkammer*, or cabinet of art. The latter had its roots in the seventeenth century, when Brandenburg-Prussia established a small colony in what is now Ghana with close commercial ties to companies like the Dutch East India Company.

7. Kurt Krieger, "Abteilung Afrika," *Baessler Archiv: Beiträge zur Völkerkunde* 21 (1973): 106.

8. See François-Xavier Fauvelle, *The Golden Rhinoceros: Histories of the African Middle Ages*, trans. Troy Tice (Princeton, NJ: Princeton University Press, 2018), originally published as *Le rhinocéros d'or: Histoires du Moyen Âge africain* (Paris: Alma, 2013).

9. Glenn Penny, "Bastian's Museum," in *Worldly Provincialism: German Anthropology in the Age of Empire*, ed. Glenn Penny and Matti Bunzl (Ann Arbor: University of Michigan Press), 86–126.

10. Michel Leiris, *L'Afrique fantôme* (1934; Paris: Gallimard, 1984), 102–3 and 120–24.

11. See Enid Schildkrout and Curtis Keim, *The Scramble for Art in Central Africa* (Cambridge: Cambridge University Press, 1998).

12. Günther Tessmann. *Die Pangwe: Völkerkundliche Monographie eines Negerstammes* (Berlin: Ernst Wasmuth, 1913), 2:117.

13. It needs to be noted that up to the 1930s, the terms *Anthropology, Ethnologie,* or the German *Völkerkunde* echoed different and often rivaling traditions and attitudes toward the colonial, non-Western other. In the German context, for instance, *Völkerkunde* meant the comparative study of peoples (*Völker*) and included a romantic distinction between advanced and civilized peoples of culture (*Kulturvölker*) and primitive peoples of nature (*Naturvölker*). Others favored anthropology that initially focused mostly on the anatomical/physical study of man with the aim of defining and developing general laws that situated humans in the realm of nature. In a similar way, art historians differed between those who were interested in distinct regions or periods, *Kunstgeschichte* (literally, art history), and those who were interested in developing general principals of art, *Kunstwissenschaft* (literally, art science). See Peter Probst, introduction to *Ambivalent Allure: Encounters of Art History and Anthropology from 1870 to 1970*, eds. Joseph Imorde and Peter Probst (Los Angeles: Getty Publications, forthcoming).

14. John Garson and Charles Read, *Notes and Queries on Anthropology* (London: Anthropological Institute, 1884).

15. Gottfried Semper, *Style in the Technical and Tectonic Arts; or, Practical Aesthetics*, trans. Harry Francis Mallgrave and Michael Robinson (Los Angeles: Getty Publications, 2004), originally published as *Der Stil in den technischen und tektonischen Künsten oder praktische Ästhetik* (Munich: Bruckmann, 1860). Semper very much exemplified the modern (industrial) interest in ornaments. In 1851 he was commissioned to display the achievements of Turkey, Egypt, and other nations within the new Crystal Palace, which had been built completely out of glass for the first World's Fair in London. The encounter with other non-European artistic styles and traditions left a lasting impression that informed his theory about "practical aesthetics."

16. Gottfried Semper, "Über Baustile," in *Wissenschaft, Industrie, Kunst und andere Schriften über Architektur, Kunsthandwerk und Kunstunterricht* (Mainz: Florian Kupferberg, 1966), 107, first published 1869 by Friedrich Schultess (Zurich).

17. See Augustus Pitt Rivers, "Typological Museums," *Journal of the Society of Arts* 40 (1891): 115–22.

18. See William Chapman, "Rearranging Ethnology: W.H.L.F. Pitt Rivers and the typological Tradition," in *Objects and Others*, ed. George Stocking (Madison: University of Wisconsin Press, 1985), 15–48.

19. Henry Balfour, *The Evolution of Decorative Art* (London: Rivingstone, 1893).

20. See Priyanka Basu, "Art Historical 'Borderlands': Elisabeth Wilson, Martin Heydrich, and August Schmarsow on 'Primitive' Ornament," *Journal of Art Historiography* 12 (2015): 1–18.

21. Alois Riegl, *Problems of Style: Foundations for History of Ornaments*, trans. Evelyn Kain (Princeton, NJ: Princeton University Press, 1992), originally published as *Stilfragen: Grundlegungen zu einer Geschichte der Ornamentik* (Berlin: Seimans, 1893); on the concept of *Kunstwollen*, originally conceived in the 1850s by the classical archaeologist Heinrich Brunn, see Riegl's *Late Roman Art Industry*, trans. Rolf Winkes (Rome: Brettschneider, 1985), originally published as *Die spätrömische Kunstindustrie* (Vienna: n.p., 1901).

22. Ernst Grosse, *The Beginnings of Art* (London: Appleton, 1914), originally published as *Die Anfänge der Kunst* (Freiburg: Seibeck, 1894).

23. Georg Schweinfurth, *Artes Africanae* (Leipzig: F. A. Brockhaus; London: Sampson Low, 1875) (published simultaneously in German and English editions). The book served as a lavishly illustrated appendix to Schweinfurth's travelogue, *Im Herzen von Afrika: Reisen und Entdeckungen im Centralen Aequatorial Afrika während der Jahre 1868–1871* (Leipzig: F. A. Brockhaus, 1874).

24. Leo Frobenius, "Die Bildende Kunst der Afrikaner," *Mitteilungen der Anthropologischen Gesellschaft Wien* 27 (1896): 332.

25. See Jonathan Haynes, *Noah's Curse* (Oxford: Oxford University Press, 2007), in conjunction with Anne Lamont, *L'art et la race: L'Africain (tout) contre l'œil des Lumières* (Dijon: Les presses du réel, 2019).

26. On the history of fetishism, see William Pietz's seminal trilogy of articles in *RES*, especially "The Problem of the Fetish, III: Bosman's Guinea and the Enlightenment Theory of Fetishism," *RES: Anthropology and Aesthetics*, no. 16 (1988): 105–24.

27. G. W. F. Hegel, *Philosophy of History*, trans. J. Sibree (New York: Dover, 1956), 93, originally published as *Vorlesungen über die Philosophie der Geschichte* (Berlin: Duncker und Humblot, 1837).

28. Ibid., 95.

29. Ibid., 91.

30. Ludwig Wolf, *Im Innern Afrikas: Die Erforschung des Kassai während der Jahre 1833–1885* (Leipzig: F. A. Brockhaus, 1888).

31. On the Kuba experience of this development, see Jan Vansina, *Being Colonized: The Kuba Experience in Rural Congo 1880–1960* (Madison: University of Wisconsin Press, 2010).

32. Cited after Maarten Couttenier, "One Speaks Softly, Like in a Sacred Place: Collecting, Studying and Exhibiting Congolese Artefacts as African Art in Belgium," *Journal of Art Historiography*, no. 12 (2015): 27.

33. Barbara Plankensteiner, ed., *Benin Kings and Rituals: Court Arts from Nigeria* (Gent: Snoeck 2007).

34. Augustus Pitt Rivers, *Antique Works from Benin: Collected by Lieutenant-General Pitt Rivers* (London: privately printed, 1900), iv.

35. Economic reasons drove the raid. Benin's monopoly of trade blocked British ambitions to generate revenue in the region. In 1896 the British military attempted to get access to Benin's rich resources in palm oil, rubber, and ivory. However, the attempt failed, resulting in the killing of the British troops by the Benin army, which in turn prompted a "punitive expedition" a year later. The raid has generated a long and intensive debate on museums, violence, and the legacies of colonialism with the term *Benin Bronzes* becoming a collective signifier for the most precious parts of the loot that included, next to metal plaques and sculptures, also ivory objects. For the most recent discussion, see Dan Hicks, *The Brutish Museums: The Benin Bronzes, Colonial Violence and Cultural Restitution* (London: Pluto Press, 2020) and Barnaby Phillips, *Loot: Britain and the Benin Bronzes* (London: Oneworld, 2020).

36. Charles Read and Ormond Dalton, *Antiquities of the City of Benin and Other Parts of West Africa in the British Museum* (London: British Museum, Department of British and Medieval Antiquities, 1899). On Benin art in British imperial culture, see Annie Coombs, *Reinventing Africa: Museums, Material Culture, and Popular Imagination in late Victorian and Edwardian England* (New Haven, CT: Yale University Press, 1994).

37. Cited after Elazar Barkan, "Aesthetics and Evolution: Benin Art in Europe," *African Arts* 30, no. 30 (Summer 1997): 37.

38. Read and Dalton, *Antiquities*.

39. Pitt Rivers, *Antique Works*.

40. For a list of Benin brass plaques acquired by European museums, see Kathryn Wysocki Gunsch, *The Benin Plaques. A 16th Century Imperial Monument* (Abingdon: Routledge, 2017). On the market for Benin court art, see Felicity Bodenstein, "Notes for a Long-Term Approach to the Price History of Brass and Ivory Objects Taken from the Kingdom of Benin in 1897," in *Acquiring Cultures: Histories of World Art on Western Markets*, ed. Bénédicte Savoy, Charlotte Guichard, and Christine Howald (Berlin: De Gruyter, 2018), 267–88.

41. Felix Von Luschan, "Die Altertümer von Benin," *Zeitschrift für Ethnologie* 30 (1898): 150.

42. Felix von Luschan, *Die Karl Knorrsche Sammlung von Benin-Altertümern im Museum für Länder- und Völkerkunde in Stuttgart / im Auftrag des Vorstandes beschrieben von Felix v. Luschan* (Stuttgart: Kohlhammer, 1901), 15.

43. Felix von Luschan *Die Altertümer vom Benin* (Berlin: Walter de Gruyter, 1919), 2:244.

44. Cited in Glenn Penny, *Objects of Culture: Ethnology and Ethnographic Museums in Imperial Germany* (Chapel Hill: University of North Carolina Press, 2002), 75.

45. Von Luschan, *Die Altertümer von Benin*, 2:3.

46. The war was first and foremost political and resulted from the long-standing conflict between first comers and late comers as the two basic segments of the city. See Suzanne Blier, *Art and Risk in Ancient Yoruba: Ife History, Power, and Identity, c. 1300* (Cambridge: Cambridge University Press, 2015).

47. Frobenius, *The Voice of Africa*, 1:310.

48. On the conflict, see Editha Platte, *Bronze Head from Ife* (London: British Museum, 2010).

49. "German Discovers Atlantis in Africa," *New York Times*, January 11, 1911.

50. Charles Read, "Plato's 'Atlantis Re-discovered," *Burlington Magazine for Connoisseurs* 18, no. 26 (1911): 330, 331–35.

51. Two other Olokun heads found with terra cotta in Ife ended up in the British Museum; another is now in the Ife Museum in Nigeria. See, Platte *Bronze Head from Ife.*

52. Frobenius, *The Voice of Africa*, 1:348.

53. See Suzanne Marchand, "Leo Frobenius and the Revolt against the West," *Journal of Contemporary History* 32, no. 2 (1997): 153–70.

54. Leo Frobenius, "Ancient and Recent African Art," *Art in Translation* 1, no. 2 (2009): 196, originally published as "Alte und junge Africanische Kunst," *Die Kunstwelt* 2, no. 2 (1912): 97–114.

Chapter Two

1. https://www.moma.org/calendar/exhibitions/2748.

2. Paul Guillaume, cited in an interview with Aimé Césaire conducted by René Depestre, in Aimé Césaire, *A Discourse on Colonialism* (1972; New York: Monthly Review Press, 2000), 93.

3. From June 1935 to April 1936, a scaled-down version had traveled across the country, reaching seven museums and galleries in seven different states. In addition, Barr secured a grant from the education department of the Rockefeller Foundation to document the exhibition with photographs that were sent to every black college in the US where, up until the 1950s, education was still segregated.

4. James Johnson Sweeney, *African Negro Art* (New York: Museum of Modern Art, 1935), 21.

5. Robert Goldwater, *Primitivism and Modern Painting* (New York: Harper, 1938).

6. Thus, objects that showed signs of use, such as blood stains, were washed, waxed, and polished; any attached "extraneous" elements, such as strings, cloth, or feathers, were removed. But the purification process also worked with a focus on nonsculptural elements, especially the surface. The great majority of the artifacts on display in museums in Europe and the US had been made during colonial times. Yet with the growing commodification of African artifacts, patina became a desired feature. Dealers highlighted the existence of a patina as proof of a precontact, precolonial origin, thereby purifying the object from any contact with a secular, colonial modernity.

7. The respective claims and comments have been recounted numerous times. See Jean-Louis Paudrat, "From Africa," in *"Primitivism" in 20th Century Art: Affinity of the Tribal and the Modern*, ed. William Stanley Rubin (New York: Museum of Modern Art, 1984), 1:125–75.

8. Pablo Picasso, "Discovery of African Art," in *Primitivism and Twentieth-Century Art*, ed. Jack Flam and Miriam Deutch (Berkeley: University of California Press, 2003), 33; excerpt, originally published in André Malraux, *La Tête Obsidian* (Paris: Gallimard, 1974).

9. Andre Derain, "Early Encounter with African Art," in Flam and Deutch, *Primitivism and Twentieth-Century Art*, 29.

10. Gelett Burgess, "The Wild Men of Paris," *Architectural Record* 27, no. 5 (1910): 401–14.

11. Ibid., 401.

12. In 1912, the Société d'art et d'archéologie nègre (Society for Negro Art and Archaeology) was created, with Guillaume presenting himself as its representative, followed in 1913 by the Société des Mélanophiles (Society of Melanophiles).

13. Coady opened his gallery in 1914. His supplier of African sculptures was the Paris-based French Hungarian dealer Joseph Brummer who, like Guillaume, equally expanded his business to the US. See Yaëlle Biro, "African Art, New York, and the Avant-Garde," *African Arts* 46, no. 2 (2013): 88–97, as well as Biro's more extensive study, *Fabriquer le regard: Marchands, réseaux et objets d'art africains à l'aube du XXe siècle* (Dijon: Les presses du réel, 2018).

14. For a description of the exhibition, see Helen Shannon, "African Art, 1914: The Root of Modern Art," in *Modern Art and America: Alfred Stieglitz and His New York Galleries*, ed. Sarah Greenough (Boston: Bulfinch Press, 2001), 169–70.

15. Cited in Pamela Genova, "The Poetics of Visual Cubism: Guillaume Apollinaire on Pablo Picasso," *Studies in 20th Century Literature* 27, no. 1 (2003): 58.

16. See Patricia Leighton, "The White Peril and L'Art Nègre: Picasso, Primitivism, and Anticolonialism," *Art Bulletin* 72, no. 4 (1990): 609–30.

17. Gelett Burgess, "The Wild Men of Paris," *Architectural Record* 27, no. 5 (1910): 401–14.

18. Kahnweiler coined the phrase "conceptual painting" in his book on Juan Gris, which he published under the pseudonym Daniel Henry. See Daniel Henry, *Juan Gris* (Leipzig: Klinkhard und Biermann, 1929).

19. "Der Negerkünstler zeigt uns immer, was er *weiß*, nicht was er *sieht*." Daniel-Henry Kahnweiler, "Negerkunst und Kubismus," *Merkur, Zeitschrift für Europäisches Denken* 13 (1959): 723, https://volltext.merkur-zeitschrift.de/journal/mr_1959_08.

20. Carl Einstein, *Bebuquin oder die Dilettanten des Wunders* (Berlin: Wochenschrift, 1912).

21. Carl Einstein, *Negerplastik* (Leipzig: Verlag der Weissen Bücher, 1915). In the following I cite from the English translation of *Negerplastik* as "Negro Sculpture" in Carl Einstein, *A Mythology of Forms: Selected Writings on Art*, ed. Charles Haxthausen (Chicago: University of Chicago Press, 2019), 32–59.

22. On Brummer, see John Warne Monroe, *Metropolitan Fetish: African Sculpture and the Imperial French Invention of African Art* (Ithaca, NY: Cornell University Press, 2019), 45.

23. See Charles Haxthausen, introduction to *A Mythology of Forms*, by Carl Einstein, 1–15.

24. The argument is informed by Wilhelm Worringer's influential study *Abstraction and Empathy: A Contribution to the Psychology of Style* (New York: International Universities Press, 1953), originally published as *Abstraktion und Einfühlung* (Munich: R. Piper, 1908). As Worringer argued, "abstraction" and "empathy" mark two contrasting poles of feeling. While abstraction emerges in an environment that is perceived as disturbing, fearful, and confusing, empathy reflects a confidence in the material world, a sense of control over nature that allows for a realistic style.

25. Einstein, "Negro Sculpture," 49.

26. Carl Einstein, "African Sculpture," in *A Mythology of Forms*, 64–164.

27. Ibid.

28. Ibid., 64.

29. Leo Frobenius, *The Voice of Africa: Being an Account of the Travels of the German Inner African Exploration Expedition in the Years 1910–1912*, trans. Rudolf Blind (London: Hutchinson, 1913), 1:349, originally published as *Und Afrika Sprach: Bericht über den Verlauf der dritten Reise Periode der D.I.A.F.E. in den Jahren 1910 bis 1912* (Berlin: Vita Deutsches Verlagshaus, 1912).

30. Paudrat has suggested that there were 147 private collections of African sculpture in the city by 1930. Jean-Louis Paudrat, "Primitive Arts in Paris on the Threshold of the Thir-

ties," *Art Tribal: Bulletin de l'Association des amis du Musée Barbier-Mueller* (1996), 46. See also Monroe, *Metropolitan Fetish*.

31. See Petrine Archer-Straw, *Negrophilia: Avant-Garde Paris and Black Culture in the 1920s* (London: Thames & Hudson, 2000).

32. Carl Einstein, *Die Kunst des 20. Jahrhunderts* (Berlin: Propylaen, 1926), 161. On Einstein's "fatal attraction" of African art, see also the perceptive study of Charles Haxthausen, "Fatal Attraction. Carl Einstein's Anthropological Turn," in *Ambivalent Allure: Modern Encounters of Art History and Anthropology from 1870 to the 1970s*, ed. Peter Probst and Joseph Imorde (Los Angeles: Getty Publications, forthcoming).

33. See Monroe, *Metropolitan Fetish*, chaps. 3 and 4.

34. Léopold Senghor, *Liberté I: Négritude et Humanisme* (Paris: Stock, 1964), 313.

35. Gary Wilder, *The French Imperial Nation-State: Negritude and Colonial Humanism between the Two World Wars* (Chicago: University Press of Chicago, 2005), 142.

36. Cited in Christoph Miller, "The (Revised) Birth of Negritude: Communist Revolution and 'the Immanent Negro' in 1935," *PMLA* 125, no. 3 (2010), 745, 747.

37. Wilder, *The French Imperial Nation-State*.

38. When Marius de Zayas published *African Negro Art: Its influence on Modern Art* at his Modern Gallery in 1916, he did not think of New York's African American population as his target audience. The short text is outspokenly racist. While de Zayas acknowledged the artistic quality of the works he sold in his gallery, he made it clear that the mental capacity of their creators was not high.

39. A prominent exception was the collection of Kuba art amassed in 1892 by the African American Presbyterian missionary William Henry Sheppard (see chap. 1). Sheppard was a human rights activist who was instrumental in documenting and exposing the atrocities committed in Leopold II's Congo Free State. Upon his return to the US in 1910, he donated his collection to his alma mater, Hampton College, where it is now part of the collection of the Hampton University Museum.

40. W. E. B. Du Bois, "Criteria of Negro Art," in *The Norton Anthology of African American Literature*, ed. Henry L. Gates and Nellie McLay (New York: W. W. Norton. 2004), 777, originally published in *The Crisis* 32 (October 1926): 290–97.

41. Ibid.

42. Barnes was an ardent believer in the idea that aesthetic experience and social progress go hand in hand. See Christa Clark, *African Art in the Barnes Foundation: The Triumph of l'Art Nègre and the Harlem Renaissance* (New York: Skira Rizzoli, 2015).

43. Sonia Delgado-Tall, "The New Negro Movement and the African Heritage in a Pan-Africanist Perspective," *Journal of Black Studies* 31, no. 3 (January 2001): 289.

44. Kobena Mercer, *Alain Locke and the Visual Arts* (New Haven, CT: Yale University Press, forthcoming).

45. On the relationship of Locke and Barnes, see Mark Helbling, "Albert C. Barnes and Alain Locke," *Phylon* 43, no. 1 (1982): 57–67, as well as Clark, *African Art in the Barnes Foundation*.

46. Cited in Clark, *African Art in the Barnes Foundation*, 56.

47. Cited in Helbling, "Albert C. Barnes," 59.

48. Alain Locke, "A Note on African Art", *Opportunity*, May 1924, 135.

49. Alain Locke, "The Legacy of Ancestral Past," in *The New Negro: An Interpretation* (New York: Albert and Charles Boni, 1925), 254–70.

50. See Kobena Mercer, "Aubrey Williams: Abstraction in Diaspora," *British Art Studies*, no. 8, https://doi.org/10.17658/issn.2058-5462/issue-08/kmercer.

51. On Winold Reiss's relationship with Locke and Douglas, see Christian Kravagna, *Transmoderne: Eine Kunstgeschichte des Kontakts* (Berlin: B_Books, 2017).

52. Countee Cullen, "Heritage," in *The New Negro*. See also Elisabeth Mudimbe-Boyi, "Harlem Renaissance and Africa: An Ambiguous Affair," in *The Surreptitious Speech: Présence Africaine and the Politics of Otherness, 1947–1987*, ed. Valentin-Yves Mudimbe (Chicago: University of Chicago Press, 1992), 174–84.

53. Albert Barnes, "Negro Art in America," in *The New Negro*, 22.

54. W. E. B. Du Bois, *The Gift of Black Folk* (Boston: Stratford, 1924).

55. Part of this reduction was the distinction between the precolonial and the colonial black: "The black ruled by European masters is a different being from his ancestors. The slave of the rubber plantation, lazy or rebellious, the petty thief along the water-front, the chief with eyes of solemn dignity above a parody of European clothing, the mission school-boy puzzled with Christian doctrine—these are not the makers of African art." Paul Guillaume and Thomas Munro, *Primitive Negro Sculpture* (Philadelphia: Barnes Foundation, 1926), 2, 9–10, 13.

56. Cited in Clarke, *African Art in the Barnes Foundation*, 63.

57. Barnes had commissioned *Primitive Negro Sculpture* from Paul Guillaume, his African art dealer in Paris. Guillaume was supposed to provide the text. However, Guillaume only sent a few notes. In the end, Barnes commissioned Thomas Munro, who was in charge of the Barnes foundation's education department, to write the catalog essay. See Clark, *African Art in the Barnes Foundation*.

Chapter Three

1. Karl Scheffler, *Der Berliner Museumskrieg* (Berlin: Bruno Cassirer, 1921), 22.

2. Cited in Sigrid Westphal-Hellbusch, "Die Geschichte des Berliner Völkerkundemuseums," *Baessler Archiv*, n.s., 21 (1973): 27.

3. Alois Riegl, *Problems of Style: Foundation for History of Ornaments* (Princeton, NJ: Princeton University Press, 1992), originally published as *Stilfragen Grundlegungen zu einer Geschichte der Ornamentik* (Berlin: Georg Siemens, 1893); Heinrich Wölfflin, *Principles of Art History: The Problem of the Development of Style in Later Art* (New York: Dover, 1950), originally published as *Kunstgeschichtliche Grundbegriffe: Das Problem der Stilentwicklung in der neueren Kunst* (Munich: Bruckmann, 1915).

4. As Bernhard Berenson, the American Renaissance scholar and icon of connoisseurship, remarked in the early 1930s, "Photographs! Photographs! In our work one can never have enough." Bernhard Berenson. *Italian Pictures of the Renaissance: A List of the Principal Artists and Their Works with an Index of Place* (Oxford: Clarendon Press, 1932), x. On the visual process of art historical canon formation in Europe, see Friederike Kitschen, "Making the Canon Visible: Art Historical Book Series in the Late Nineteenth and Early Twentieth Century," in *Canons and Values. Ancient to Modern*, ed. Larry Silver and Kevin Terraciano (Los Angeles: Getty Publications, 2017), 216–44.

5. On the role of photography as a key medium in the production of artistic and commercial value, see also Sylvester Okwunodu Ogbechie, "Transcultural Interpretation and the Production of Alterity: Photography, Materiality, and Mediation in the Making of 'African Art,'" in *Art History and Fetishism Abroad: Global Shiftings in Media and Methods*, ed. Gabriele Genge and Angela Stercken (Bielefeld: Transcript, 2014), 113–28.

6. See, for example, Terence Ranger, "Colonialism, Consciousness and the Camera," *Past and Present*, no. 171 (May 2001): 203–15; Paul Landau, "Empires of the Visual: Photogra-

phy and Colonial Administration in Africa," in *Images and Empires: Visuality in Colonial and Postcolonial Africa*, ed. Paul Stuart Landau and Deborah Kaspin (Los Angeles: University of California Press, 2002), 141–62.

7. In fact, von Luschan refused to guide visitors through the collections, fearing the cramped showrooms would leave a negative impression. See Andrew Zimmermann, *Anthropology and Antihumanism in Imperial Germany* (Chicago: Chicago University Press: 2001), 191.

8. Felix von Luschan, *Die Altertümer von Benin*, 3 vols. (Berlin: Walter de Gruyter, 1919).

9. Giorgio Vasari, *Lives of the Most Excellent Painters, Sculptors and Architects*, trans. Jonathan Foster and Jean Paul Richter (London: H. G. Bohn, 1859–1864), originally published as *Le vite de più excellenti pittori, scultori e architettori* (Florence: Giunti, 1568).

10. Johann Joachim Winckelmann, *The History of Art in Antiquity*, trans. Henry Lodge (Boston: James Munroe, 1848), originally published as *Geschichte der Kunst des Alterthums* (Dresden: Walther, 1764).

11. Von Luschan, *Die Altertümer von Benin*, 1:15.

12. In his study on Ife, Frobenius mentioned that the palace of the ancient kingdom of Oyo was once adorned with bronze plaques similar to the ones in Benin. Leo Frobenius, *The Voice of Africa: Being an Account of the Travels of the German Inner African Exploration Expedition in the Years 1910–1912*, trans. Rudolf Blind (1912; London: Hutchinson, 1913), 1:178, originally published as *Und Afrika Sprach: Bericht über den Verlauf der dritten Reise Periode der D.I.A.F.E. in den Jahren 1910 bis 1912* (Berlin: Vita Deutsches Verlagshaus, 1912).

13. Henri Clouzot and André Level, *L'art nègre et l'art océanien* (Paris: Devambez, 1919). On Clouzot and Level as well as Georges Hardy discussed below, see the discussion by John Warne Monroe, *Metropolitan Fetish: African Sculpture and the Imperial French Invention of Primitive Art* (Ithaca, NY: Cornell University Press, 2019).

14. Georges Hardy, *L'art nègre: L'art animiste des noirs d'Afrique* (Paris: Henri Laurens, 1927).

15. Ibid., 117–18.

16. Eckart von Sydow, *Die deutsche expressionistische Kultur und Malerei* (Berlin: Furche, 1920).

17. Eckart von Sydow, "African Sculpture," *Africa: Journal of the International African Institute* 1, no. 2 (1928): 219.

18. Ibid., 224–25.

19. See Bernhard Ankermann, "Kulturkreise und Kulturschichten in Afrika," *Zeitschrift für Ethnologie* (1905), 57:5–84; Heinrich Baumann, "Die Afrikanischen Kulturkreise," *Africa: Journal of the International African Institute* 7, no. 2 (1934): 129–39. In his later writings, Frobenius distanced himself from the focus on formal style and resisted the art-historical tendency to favor figurative objects. He insisted that it was not enough to look merely at the outer form of culture. What mattered for Frobenius was not the object as such but the relationships among objects, from which the essential style or *Gestalt* of a culture would reveal itself. For an overview of Frobenius's scholarship, see Suzanne Marchand, "Leo Frobenius and the Revolt against the West," *Journal of Contemporary History* 32, no. 2 (1997): 153–70.

20. See Anne Baldassari, *Picasso and Photography: The Dark Mirror* (Paris: Flammarion and Museum of Fine Arts, Houston, 1997). On Picasso's use of ethnographic and anthropological illustrations, see also Suzanne Blier, *Picasso's Demoiselles: The Untold Origins of a Modern Masterpiece* (Durham, NC: Duke University Press 2019).

21. Vladimir Markov, "Negro Art," in *Vladimir Markov and Russian Primitivism: A Charter for the Avant-Garde*, ed. Jeremy Howard, Irena Bužinska, and Zoe S. Strother (Burlington, VT: Ashgate 2015), 217–52, originally published as *Iskusstvo negrov* (Peterburg, 1919). See also

Zoe Strother, "The Politics of Face in the African Art Photography of Vladimir Markov," in Howard, Bužinska, and Strother, *Vladimir Markov and Russian Primitivism*, 85–128.

22. Markov, "Negro Art," 242.

23. Charles Sheeler, *African Negro Sculpture Photographed by Charles Sheeler* (New York: Modern Gallery, 1918).

24. Wendy Grossman, *Man Ray, African Art, and the Modernist Lens* (Minnesota: University of Missouri Press, 2010).

25. Christa Clarke, *Defining Taste: Albert Barnes and the Promotion of African Art in the United States during the 1920s* (PhD diss., University of Maryland, 1998), 139. Sheeler declined, however, and the job eventually went to Barbara and Willard Morgan, who set out to capture the "aesthetic essences" of the works in question.

26. *Noire at blanche* is actually a title coined only later. See Wendy Grossman and Steven Manford, "Unmasking Man Ray's *Noire et Blanche*," *American Art* 20, no. 2 (2006): 134–47.

27. See Hans Himmelheber's discussion of Ivorian "export art" that was produced in the interwar period: "Fälschungen und andere Abweichungen von der traditionellen Kunst in Negerafrika," *Tribus* 16 (1967): 15–34.

28. Press Release MoMA 4-24-1935 / For release Saturday Afternoon/Sunday Morning, May 11 and 12, 1935. In New York, philanthropic organizations organized tours for young African American artists like Jacob Lawrence and Romare Bearden to see the show. See Patricia Hills, "Cultural Legacies and the Transformation of the Cubist Collage Aesthetic by Romare Bearden, Jacob Lawrence, and Other African-American Artists," in *Romare Bearden, American Modernist*, Studies in the History of Art, vol. 71, ed. Ruth Fine and Jacqueline Francis (New Haven, CT: Yale University Press, 2011), 221–47.

29. See Virginia Lee-Webb, "Art as Information: The African Portfolios of Charles Sheeler and Walker Evans," *African Arts* 24, no. 1 (January 1991): 60.

30. On the history of the figure, see Kerstin Schankweiler, "Double Trophy: *Gou* by Akati Ekplékendo," in *Reading Objects in the Contact Zone*, eds. Eva-Maria Troelenberg, Kerstin Schankweiler, and Anna Sophia Messner (Heidelberg: Heidelberg University Publishing, 2021), 140–47.

31. Carl Kjersmeier, *Centres de style de la sculpture nègre africaine*, 4 vols. (Paris: Morance, 1935–1938).

32. At least two photographs can be unquestionably attributed to him: one showing a Senufo figure, the other a Luba stool. Both feature harsh light and defining shadows.

33. For an elaboration of this argument, see Wendy Grossman, "Photography at the Crossroads: African Art in the Age of Mechanical Reproduction." In *Die Schau des Fremden: Ausstellungskonzepte zwischen Kunst, Kommerz und Wissenschaft*, ed. Cordula Grewe (Stuttgart: Steiner, 2006), 317–40.

34. Margaret Iversen, "Alois Riegl and the Aesthetics of Disintegration," in *Kunst und Kunsttheorie, 1400–1900*, ed. Peter Ganz (Wiesbaden: Harrasowitz, 1991), 439–51; Sidney Kasfir, "One Tribe, One Style? Paradigms in the Historiography of African Art," *History in Africa* 11 (1984): 163–93.

35. Riegl, *Problems of Style*.

36. Wölfflin, *Principles of Art History*.

37. For a discussion of the work of the institute, see Hellen Tilley, *Africa as a Living Laboratory: Empire, Development, and the Problem of Scientific Knowledge, 1870–1950* (Chicago: University of Chicago Press, 2011).

38. International African Institute, "Five-Year Plan of Research," *Africa*, no. 6 (1932): 1.

39. Von Sydow, "African Sculpture," 225–26.

40. Eckart von Sydow, "Ancient and Modern Art in Benin City," *Africa* 11, no. 1 (1938): 55–62. The title is obviously a reference to an article Frobenius had published some fifteen years earlier on "Ancient and Recent African Art." Eckart von Sydow, *Im Reiche Gottähnlicher Herrscher: Streifzüge durch Westafrika* (Braunschweig: Gustav Wenzel und Sohn, 1943).

41. Von Sydow, "Ancient and Modern Art," 57.

42. Hans Himmelheber, *Negerkünstler: Ethnographische Studien über den Schnitzkünstler bei den Stämmen der Atutu und Guro im Innern der Elfenbeinküste* (Stuttgart: Strecker und Schroeder, 1935); *Negerkunst und Negerkünstler* (Stuttgart: Strecker und Schroeder, 1960).

43. Rather than embarking on an academic career as a university professor or museum curator, Himmelheber preferred to work freelance, a status that allowed him to combine his various roles of collector, connoisseur, and scholar.

Chapter Four

1. Marla Berns, Mary Nooter Roberts, and Doran Ross, "African Art in the Fowler Museum at UCLA," in *Representing Africa in American Art Museums*, ed. Kathleen Bickford Berzock and Christa Clarke (Seattle: University of Washington Press 2011), 184–204.

2. Clifford Geertz, ed., *Old Societies and New States: The Quest for Modernity in Asia and Africa* (London: Free Press of Glencoe, 1963).

3. Daniel Biebuyck, introduction to *Tradition and Creativity in Tribal Art*, ed. Daniel Biebuyck (Berkeley: University of California Press, 1969), 7.

4. Melville Herskovits, a key figure in the development of African studies in the US, explicitly offered scholarly expertise to the CIA. In 1958, after having been elected president of the African Studies Association, Herskovits wrote to the CIA director Allen Dulles, "the Association, which represented the combined strength of those concerned with Africa in this country . . . would be happy to aid you in any way it can." Cited in William G. Martin and Michael O. West, "The Ascent, Triumph and Disintegration of the Africanist Enterprise in the US," in *Out of One, Many Africas: Reconstructing the Study and Meaning*, ed. William G. Martin and Michael O. West (Urbana: University of Illinois Press, 1999), 91–92.

5. Daniel Biebuyck, ed., *Tradition and Creativity in Tribal Art* (Berkeley: University of California Press, 1969); Warren d'Azevedo, ed., *The Traditional Artist in African Society* (Bloomington: Indiana University Press, 1973).

6. Biebuyck, introduction, 22.

7. On the role and importance of funding for the establishment of African art history, see Robyn Poyner, "Ancestors and Elders: Personal Reflections of an Africanist Art Historian," *African Arts* 50, no. 3 (July 2017): 8–21.

8. Franz Boas, *Primitive Art* (Oslo: H. Aschehoug,1927).

9. Melville Herskovits, "The Aesthetic Drive: Graphic and Plastic Arts," in *Man and His Works* (New York: A. Knopf, 1948), 413.

10. Meyer Shapiro, "Style," in *Anthropology Today: An Encyclopedic Inventory*, ed. Alfred Kroeber (Chicago: University Press of Chicago, 1953), 287–312; cf. Doran Ross, "Interview with Roy Sieber," *African Arts* 25, no. 4 (October 1992): 36–51.

11. See William Bascom, "Brass Portraits Heads from Ile Ife," *Man* 38 (1938): 176. "The Legacy of an Unknown Nigerian Donatello," *Illustrated London News*, April 8, 1939, 592–94.

12. James Fernandez, "Principles of Fang Opposition and Vitality in Fang Aesthetics," *Journal of Aesthetics and Art Criticism* 25, no. 1 (1966): 53–64; "The Exposition and Imposition of Order: Artistic Expression in Fang Culture," in *The Traditional Artist in African Societies*, ed. Warren d'Azevedo (Bloomington: Indiana University Press, 1973), 194–220; James Fer-

nandez and Renate L. Fernandez, "Fang Reliquary Art: Its Quantities and Qualities," *Cahiers d'études africaines* 15, no. 60 (1975): 723–46.

13. Fernandez, "Exposition and Imposition of Order," 204.

14. Ibid., 205.

15. A notable exception in the realm of anthropology was Simon Ottenberg, whose fieldwork on Igbo masquerades in South East Nigeria had put him in contact with artists teaching at the University of Nigeria, Nsukka. See Simon Ottenberg, *New Traditions from Nigeria: Seven Artists from the Nsukka Group* (Washington, DC: Smithsonian, 1997). See also chapters 5 and 9.

16. Yaëlle Biro, "The Museum of Primitive Art in Africa at the Time of Independence," *Metropolitan Museum of Art Bulletin* 72, no. 1 (Summer 2014): 38–46.

17. Kate Ezra, "Collecting African Art at New York's Museum of Primitive Art," in *Representing Africa in American Art Museums,* ed. Kathleen Bickford Berzock and Christa Clarke (Seattle: University of Washington Press, 2011), 123.

18. Alisa LaGamma, Joanne Pillsbury, Eric Kjellgren, and Yaëlle Biro, "The Nelson A. Rockefeller Vision," *Metropolitan Museum of Art Bulletin* 72, no. 1 (Summer 2014): 7.

19. In 1959, Rockefeller had been elected governor of New York.

20. Cited in 7.

21. Doran Ross, interview with Roy Sieber; Roy Sieber, *Sculpture of Northern Nigeria* (New York: Museum of Primitive Art, 1961).

22. Frans Olbrechts, "Contributions to the Study of the Chronology of African Plastic Arts," *Africa* 14, no. 4 (1943): 183–93; *Plastiek van Kongo* (Antwerp: Standaard, 1946). See also Constantin Petridis, "Olbrechts and the Morphological Approach to African Sculptural Art," in *Frans M. Olbrechts 1899–1958: In Search of Art in Africa,* ed. Constantin Petridis (Antwerp: Antwerp Ethnographic Museum), 119–42.

23. William Fagg, *Tribes and Forms in African Art* (London: Methuen. 1965), 11, 12.

24. The original title of the exhibition 1964 in Berlin was *Hundert Stämme, Hundert Meisterwerke* (Hundred Tribes, Hundred Masterpieces).

25. Fagg himself was skeptical of the allures of socialism: "In the perspective of history, when today's propaganda pamphlets have been blown away by further winds of change, it will doubtless be seen that the most important and significant contribution made in Africa by the colonial system was the political movements, at present usually called 'nationalism', which helped to bring about its dissolution, and which are largely traceable to the patterns established by the European Socialist revolutions of 1848. Somewhat similar, the philosophy of Négritude, which took its rise in Paris, should be judged on whether it can put down roots in Africa and draw sustenance from the native soil; so far has neither succeeded or failed." William Fagg and Margaret Plass, *African Sculpture* (London: Studio Vista, 1964), 7.

26. On the CIA activities, see Frances Saunders, *The Cultural Cold War: The CIA and the World of Arts and Letters* (New York: New Press, 1999).

27. Designed by Hugh Stubbins, formerly one of Walter Gropius's assistants at Harvard, the Congress Hall was initially the American contribution to an international architectural exhibition *Interbau,* which took place in Berlin in 1957.

28. Fagg, *Tribes and Forms,* 18.

29. Fagg and Plass, *African Sculpture,* 45. See also William Fagg, "The African Artist," in *Tradition and Creativity in Tribal Art* ed. Daniel Biebuyck (Berkeley: University of California Press, 1969), 203–13.

30. Fagg and Plass, *African Sculpture,* 45–46.

31. An early critical though largely ignored voice was the Caribbean artist and art his-

torian Denis Williams. In the 1960s, while working at the University of Ibadan, he studied the history of Nigerian metal sculpture, primarily in Ife and Benin. Employing a strictly art-historical approach, he rejected the category of "tribe" because of its lack of precision, arguing instead for the existence of different schools of art similar to European art history. See Denis Williams, *Icon and Image: A Study of Sacred and Secular Forms in African Classical Art* (New York: New York University Press, 1974). For a general summary of the critique of the one tribe/one style model, see Sidney Kasfir, "One Tribe, One Style? Paradigms in the Historiography of African Art," *History in Africa* 11 (January 1984), 163–93.

32. Roy Sieber, *African Textiles and Decorative Arts* (New York: Museum of Modern Art, 1972); John Picton and John Mack, *African Textiles* (London: British Museum, 1979).

33. Labelle Prussin, *Architecture in Northern Ghana: A Study of Forms and Functions* (Berkeley: University of California Press, 1969); *Hatumere: Islamic Design in West Africa* (Berkeley: University of California Press, 1986); Suzanne Blier, *The Anatomy of Architecture: Ontology and Metaphor in Batammaliba Architectural Expression* (Chicago: University Press of Chicago, 1987).

34. Herbert Cole, "Art as a Verb in Iboland," *African Arts* 3, no. 1 (1969): 34–41, 88.

35. Among Sieber's Nigerian PhD students were Babatunde Lawal and Chike Aniakor.

36. As Roslyn Walker, one of Sieber's students, recalled, it was the idea of the "sacredness of the object" that he planted in the mind of his students. Roslyn Adele Walker, "Remembering Roy Sieber (1923–2001)," *African Arts* 50, no. 3 (Autumn, 2017): 23.

37. Rubin came to be a prominent figure in the Californian art and counterculture scene. Well known is the influence of his article "Accumulation: Power and Display in African Culture," *Artforum* 13, no. 9 (1975): 35–47, on LA-based African American artists like Betye Saar and David Hammons.

38. Cole, "Art as a Verb." Cole was a student of Herbert Fraser at Columbia University in New York, where Fraser directed Columbia's program on "primitive art." While the program echoed and made use of the nearby Museum of Primitive Art, Fraser was acutely aware of the limitations of a formalist and comparative approach. He therefore encouraged his students to leave the museum and do fieldwork. See Cole's recollections of Fraser in Herbert Cole, "A Mighty Tree Has Fallen," *African Arts* 50, no. 3 (Autumn 2017): 31–37.

39. In his poem entitled "Hunting Is Not Those Heads on the Wall," Jones had written: "Art-ing is what makes art, and is thereby more valuable. But we speak of the muse, to make even a verb a thing." LeRoi Jones, *Home: Social Essays* (New York: Morrow, 1966), 199. On Jones, a.k.a. Amiri Baraka, see also chapter 6.

40. Thurston Shaw, "Excavations at Igbo-Ukwu, Eastern Nigeria: An Interim Report," *Man* 60 (1960): 161–64.

41. Chinua Achebe, *Things Fall Apart* (London: Heineman, 1958).

42. Cole, "Art as a Verb," 38, 41. For the extensive elaboration of this argument, see Herbert Cole, *Mbari: Art and Life among the Owerri Igbo* (Bloomington: Indiana University Press 1982), and Herbert Cole and Chike Aniakor, *Igbo Arts: Community and Cosmos* (Bloomington: Indiana University Press, 1984).

43. Herbert Cole, *African Arts of Transformation* (Santa Barbara: University of California Santa Barbara Arts Gallery, 1970). See also the glowing exhibition review by John Povey in *African Arts* 4, no. 2 (Spring 1971): 56–57.

44. Robert Farris Thompson, *African Art in Motion* (Berkeley: University of California Press, 1974).

45. Robert Farris Thompson, "Yoruba Dance Sculpture: Its Contexts and Critics" (PhD diss., Yale University, 1965).

46. J. Carter Brown and Gerald Nordland, foreword to Thompson, *African Art in Motion*, vii.

47. White was a relative latecomer among African art collectors. She had started to collect only in 1960, thus after the end of colonialism.

48. Thompson, *African Art in Motion*, xii. See also the work of some of Thompson's students: Anita Glaze, *Art and Death in a Senufo Village* (Bloomington: Indiana University Press, 1981); Henry Drewal and Margret Thompson Drewal, *Gelede: Art and Female Power among the Yoruba* (Bloomington: Indiana University Press. 1983); Sylvia Boone, *Radiance from the Waters: Ideals of Feminine Beauty in Mende Art* (New Haven, CT: Yale University Press, 1986).

49. Over the course of his career Thompson elaborated this theme in a series of articles; see Robert Farris Thompson, *An Aesthetic of the Cool: Afro-Atlantic Art and Music* (Pittsburgh, PA: Periscope, 2011).

50. Thompson, *African Art in Motion*, xiv.

51. As ambitious as the exhibition design was, from the point of view of the exhibition audience the success remained limited. Visitors complained about the difficulty of really appreciating the objects. When the exhibition was shown at the National Gallery in Washington, DC, a few months later, the curators not only separated the objects and the visual information, they also changed the title. Thus, instead of "African Art *in* Motion" the title was now "African art *and* Motion." See also Barbara Newsom and Adele Silver, eds., *The Museum as Educator* (Berkeley: University of California Press, 1978), 99–101.

52. In an extended review for the *African Studies Review*, the dance anthropologist Judith Lynne Hanna, for instance, concluded, "There is no question that Thompson is innovative within the field of art history in emphasizing the reality of art forms' meaning in a context which is frequently motional. However, his expressed aim to develop an existential definition of dance as art in motion would have been better fulfilled had he let his collection of existential experts and films speak for themselves or had he developed a better fit between what he views as the aesthetic and what his informants say is their aesthetic; and if there is a discrepancy an explanation is called for." Judith Lynne Hanna, "Review of African Art in Motion: Icon and Act by Robert Farris Thompson." *ASA Review of Books* 1 (1975): 9. The reception in the field's flagship journal *African Arts* was equally reserved. See William Bascom, "Review of Robert Farris Thompson's African Art in Motion," *African Arts* 7, no. 4 (1974): 85–86; Robert Ellis, "Review of Robert Farris Thompson's African Art in Motion" *African Arts* 7, no. 2 (1974): 30–33.

53. Michael West and William Martin, "A Future with a Past: Resurrecting the Study of Africa in the Post-Africanist Era," *Africa Today* 43, no. 3 (1997): 309–26.

Chapter Five

1. The conference was meant to be an art-related follow-up to the first Asian-Afro Conference a year before in Bandung, Indonesia. The original French title of the conference was Premier Congrès International des Ècrivains et Artistes Noirs.

2. Ben Enwonwu, "Problems of the African Artist Today," *Présence Africaine*, no. 8/10 (1956): 177.

3. The concept has been used in different ways. Rather than the artistic and aesthetic meaning of autonomy in terms of claiming an independent, "autonomous" representation of reality and space, I am interested in the political meaning of the concept.

4. Olu Oguibe cites the governor of the Gold Coast, Sir Hugh Clifford, who posited in

1918, "The West African Negro has often been reproached with his failure to develop any high form of civilization. It has been pointed out *ad nauseam* that he has never sculptured a statue, painted a picture, produced a literature, or even invented a mechanical contrivance worthy of the name, all of which are perfectly true." Olu Oguibe, *The Culture Game* (Minneapolis: University of Minnesota Press, 2004), 48.

5. Ola Oloidi, "Defender of African Creativity: Aina Onabolu, Pioneer of Western Art in West Africa," *Africana Research Bulletin* 17, no. 2 (1991): 21–49.

6. On the biography of Onabolu's life, see Simon Ikpakronyi, "Aina Onabolu: His Life, His Works, and His Contribution to the Development of Contemporary Nigerian Art," in *Aina Onabolu: Symbol of the National Studios of Art*, ed. Paul Chike Dike and Patricia Oyelola (Lagos: National Gallery of Art, 1999), 8–50.

7. Aina Onabolu, "A Short Discourse on Art" (unpublished manuscript, 1920), 6–7.

8. Ola Oloidi, "Art and Nationalism in Colonial Nigeria," *Nsukka Journal of History* 1, no. 1 (1989): 97.

9. Ikpakronyi, "Aina Onabolu," 20.

10. Based on these efforts, in 1943 Murray was appointed Nigeria's first Surveyor of Antiquities.

11. Murray's attitude resembled that of G. A. Stevens, who was sent to teach art at Achimota College in what was then Gold Coast (later Ghana). See Rhoda Woets, "The Recreation of Modern and African Art at Achimota School in the Gold Coast (1927–52)," *Journal of African History* 55, no. 3 (2014): 445–65.

12. Ben Enwonwu, "Into the Abstract Jungle. A Criticism of a New Trend in Nigerian Art," *Drum*, June 1963, 25–29.

13. Léopold Senghor, "L'esprit de la civilization ou les lois de la culture, négro-africaine," *Présence Africaine*, no. 8 (1956): 60. Senghor first conceived the ideas of Négritude in 1939 in an essay titled "What the Black Man Contributes." See Léopold Senghor, *Liberté I, Négritude et humanism* (Paris: Seuil, 1964).

14. Frantz Fanon, *Black Skin, White Masks*, trans. Charles Markman (New York: Grove Press 1967), originally published as *Peau noire, masque blancs* (Paris: Éditions du Seuil, 1952); *The Wretched of the Earth*, trans. Constance Farrington (New York: Grove, 1963), originally published as *Les damnés de la terre* (Paris: Francois Maspero, 1961).

15. Frantz Fanon, "Racisme and culture," *Présence Africaine*, nos. 8–10 (1956): 129.

16. Richard Wright, "Tradition and Industrialization: The Plight of the Tragic Elite in Africa," *Présence Africaine*, nos. 8–10 (1956): 357. Wright's skepticism vis-á-vis Négritude recalls Countee Cullen's 1925 poem "Heritage" in which Cullen asks, "What is Africa to me?" "What's your nakedness to me?" "Not yet has my heart or head / In the least way realized / They and I are civilized." See chapter 2.

17. Wright, "Tradition and Industrialization," 362.

18. Ibid., 368–69.

19. Aimé Césaire, "Culture and Colonization." *Présence Africaine*, nos. 8–10 (1956): 207. For an insightful eyewitness account of the conference, see James Baldwin, "Princes and Powers," in *The Price of the Ticket* (New York: St. Martin Press, 1985), 41–64.

20. See Helena Cantone, "Italy—Africa: A Contradictory Inventory of Modernity," *Critical Interventions* 10, no. 1 (2016): 5–27.

21. For a recent discussion of the Dakar festival, see David Murphy, ed., *The First World Festival of Negro Arts, Dakar 1966: Contexts and Legacies* (Liverpool: Liverpool University Press, 2016).

22. The term *classical African art* was formally introduced by the Caribbean artist and art historian Denis Williams, *Icon and Image: A Study of Sacred and Secular Forms of African Classical Art* (New York: New York University Press, 1974).

23. Senghor's interest in Leo Frobenius goes back to 1936, when Frobenius's magnum opus, *Kulturgeschichte Afrikas* (Zurich: Phaidon, 1933), first appeared in French as *Histoire de la civilisation africaine*. On the complex relationship between Senghor and Frobenius, see Jean Ita, "Frobenius, Senghor, and the Image of Africa," in *Modes of Thought: Essays of Thinking in Western and Non-Western Societies*, ed. Robin Horton and Ruth Finnegan (New York: Humanities Press, 1974), 306–36.

24. For Gabus, the concept of the "dynamic museum" meant primarily the possibility of flexible exhibition spaces. See Lucia Allais, *Designs of Destruction* (Chicago: University Press of Chicago, 2018), 191.

25. Works from Nigeria, which Senghor regarded as "the ancient Greece of Africa," were absent from this exhibition, having been accorded their own dedicated exhibition space in the city hall where William Fagg was in charge of the curation.

26. On the difficulties and challenges the exhibition had to cope with, see Cédric Vincent, "Tendencies and Confrontations: Dakar 1966," *Afterall: A Journal of Art, Context and Enquiry*, no. 43 (Spring/Summer 2017): 88–101. Joseph L. Underwood, "Tendances et Confrontations: An Experimental Space for Defining Art from Africa," *World Art* 9, no.1 (2019): 43–65.

27. Iba N'Diaye, *La jeune peinture en Afrique Noire: Quelques réflexions d'un artiste africain', oeuvres africaines nouvelles* (Paris: Musée de l'homme, 1970).

28. Engelbert Mveng, "The Function and Significance of Negro Art in the Lives of Black People," *Colloquium: Function and Significance of African Negro Art in the Life of the People and for the People, March 30–April 8, 1966*, ed. Société Africaine de Culture (Paris: *Présence Africaine*, 1968), 26.

29. William Fagg, "Tribality," in *Colloquium: Function and Significance of African Negro Art in the Life of the People and for the People, March 30–April 8, 1966*, ed. Société Africaine de Culture (Paris: *Présence Africaine*, 1968), 107–20.

30. See Iba N'Diaye, *La jeunesse africaine face a l'impérialisme* (Paris: Maspero, 1971), 49, and Elisabeth Harney, *Senghor's Shadow: Art, Politics, and the Avant-Garde in Senegal, 1960–1995* (Durham, NC: Duke University Press, 2006).

31. Ben Enwonwu, "The African View of Art and Some Problems Facing the African Artist Today," in Société Africaine de Culture, *Colloquium*, 417–18.

32. John Povey, "The First World Festival of Negro Arts at Dakar," *Journal of the New African Literature and the Arts* (Autumn 1966): 64–75.

33. Ibid., 75.

34. John Povey and Paul Proehl, "First Word," *African Arts* 1, no. 1 (1967): 1, 58, 59. For a discussion of the early years of *African Arts*, see also Steven Nelson, "Daringly Experimental and Versatile: African Arts and the Contemporary," *African Arts* 50, no. 1 (2017): 16–21.

35. Exemplified by the ruins of Great Zimbabwe, the capital of the old precolonial state of Mapungubwe, sculpting stone had a long tradition in Zimbabwe. From the 1920s onward, Christian missionaries had begun to incorporate it into their practical education. McEwen followed this tradition of patronage but gave it a new market-oriented and contemporary twist. See Jonathan Zilberg, "Zimbabwean stone sculpture: The invention of a Shona tradition" (PhD diss., University of Illinois, 1996).

36. On the congress and the exhibition see Barbara Murray, "The 1962 First International Congress of African Culture: A Brief Report." *Nka*, no. 42/43 (2018): 74.

37. Ulli Beier, *Contemporary Art in Africa* (London: Praeger, 1968).

38. For a filmic reflection of the debate on African art, see the film by Alain Resnais and Chris Marker, *Les statues meurent aussi* (Statues also die), commissioned by *Présence Africaine*. On the voice-over for the film, see Chris Marker, "Statues Also Die," *Art in Translation* 5, no. 4 (2013): 429–38.

39. On Osogbo, see my *Osogbo and the Art of Heritage: Monuments, Deities, and Money* (Bloomington: Indiana University Press, 2011), as well Chika Okeke-Agulu, "Rethinking Mbari Mbayo: Osogbo Workshops in the 1960s," in *African Art and Agency*, eds. Till Förster and Sidney Kasfir (Bloomington, Indiana University Press, 2013), 154–79.

40. Frank McEwen, "'Return to Origins': New Directions for African Art," *African Arts* 1, no. 2 (1968): 18–88.

41. Beier, *Contemporary Art in Africa*; Susanne Wenger, *The Timeless Mind of the Sacred: Its Manifestation in the Osun Grove* (Ibadan: Institute of African Studies, 1977).

42. Frank Speed and Ulli Beier, *New Images for a Changing Society*, documentary film (Liverpool, 1964).

43. Rolf Italiaander, *Neue Kunst in Afrika* (Mannheim: Bibliographisches Institut, 1957); Janheinz Jahn, *Muntu. Umrisse der neoafrikanischen Kultur* (Düsseldorf: Diederichs, 1958). In the US, the English translation, *Muntu: An Outline of Neo-African Culture* (London: Faber and Faber, 1961), became a best seller and was widely received.

44. Evelyn Brown, *Africa's Contemporary Art and Artists* (New York: Harmon Foundation, 1966).

45. Beier, *Contemporary Art in Africa*, 14.

46. Accordingly, Beier dedicated the book to three young intellectuals representing this new environment in Nigeria: Chinua Achebe as a writer, Onuora Nzekwu as a civil servant, and Lazarus Ukeje as a lawyer.

47. Jahn, *Muntu.*

48. Beier, *Contemporary Art in Africa*, 169.

49. Marshall Mount, *African Art: The Years Since 1920* (Bloomington: Indiana University Press, 1973), 193.

Chapter Six

1. For recollections of the participants, see the Panafest web documentary developed by Dominique Malaquais and Cédric Vincent, http://webdocs-sciences-sociales.science/panafest/#1-Les_festivals_-_The_festivals.

2. William Greaves, dir., *The First World Festival of Negro Arts* (1966), 40 min.

3. Irina Venzher and Leonid Makhnatch, dir., *Ритмы Африки* (African Rhythms) (1966), 52 min., http://webdocs-sciences-sociales.science/panafest/#USSR_movie_dakar_66. On Soviet scholarship on African art, see Kate Cowcher, "Soviet Supersystems and American Frontiers: African Art Histories amid the Cold War," *Art Bulletin* 101, no. 3 (2019): 146–66.

4. Ousmane Sembène, "Novelist-Critic of Africa," *West Africa*, September 1962, 1041.The critique echoed that of Wole Soyinka, for whom Négritude was an expression of insecurity and weakness. As he famously argued, "A tiger does not proclaim his tigritude, he pounces. In other words, a tiger does not stand in the forest and say: 'I am a tiger.' When you pass where the tiger has walked before, you see the skeleton of the duiker, you know that some tigritude has been emanated there." Cited in Janheinz Jahn, ed., *A History of Neo-African Literature* (London: Faber, 1968), 265–66, originally published as *Geschichte der neoafrikanischen Literatur: Eine Einführung* (Düsseldorf: Dietrichs, 1966).

5. James Baldwin, "Letter from a Region of My Mind," *New Yorker*, November 17, 1962, 11–17.

6. Es'kia Mphahlele, "On Négritude in Literature," *Rand Daily Mail*, June 7, 1963, retrieved from https://www.blackpast.org/global-african-history/speeches-global-african-history/1963-eskia-ezekiel-mphahlele-negritude-literature/.

7. Critical reports about the political engineering that enabled the reconnection did not go unheard. In March 1967, months after the Dakar festival, the American magazine *Ramparts* caused a national sensation by publishing an exposé of the CIA's secret funding of education groups and cultural events, including the secret funding of the Dakar festival and AMSAC. See Frances Stonor Saunders, *The Cultural Cold War: The CIA and the World of Arts and Letters* (New York: New Press, 1999), and the recollections of Harold Weaver, a participant of FESMAN, http://webdocs-sciences-sociales.science/panafest/#FESMAN_66-Harold_Weaver. For a personal reflection on (American) African art studies during the period of the Cold War, see Robin Poynor, "Ancestors and Elders: Personal Reflections of an Africanist Art Historian," *African Arts* 50, no. 3 (Autumn 2017): 8–21.

8. See the documentary on Herskovits by Llewellyn Smith, Vincent Brown, and Christine Herbes-Sommers, *Herskovits at the Heart of Blackness* (San Francisco: Vital Pictures Production, 2009).

9. Melville Herskovits, "The Negro's Americanism," in *The New Negro*, ed. Alain Locke (New York: Albert & Charles Boni, 1925), 353–60.

10. Melville Herskovits and Frances S. Herskovits, *Rebel Destiny: Among the Bush Negroes of Dutch Guiana* (New York: Whittlesey House, 1934).

11. Melville Herskovits, "The Negro in the World: The Statement of a Problem," *American Anthropologist* 32, no. 1 (1930): 145–55.

12. Melville Herskovits, "African Gods and Catholic Saints in New World Negro Belief." *American Anthropologist* 39, no. 4 (1937): 635–43; *Life in a Haitian Valley* (New York, Alfred A. Knopf, 1937).

13. Suzanne Blier, "Field Days: Melville J. Herskovits in Dahomey," *History in Africa: A Journal of Method* 16 (1989): 12.

14. Melville Herskovits, *The Myth of the Negro Past* (Boston: Beacon Press, 1941).

15. *The Myth of the Negro Past* had been funded by the Carnegie Foundation, which also financed the research of the Swedish economist, Gunnar Myrdal. Myrdal published his findings in 1944 under the title *The American Dilemma: The Negro Problem and Modern Democracy*. The title pointed to the conflict between the willingness of African Americans to assimilate and accept the ideology of the melting pot and the unwillingness of mainstream society to accept African Americans as part of American society.

16. Melville Herskovits, "Afro-American Art," in *Encyclopedia of World Art*, ed. Bernard Myers (New York: McGraw Hill, 1959), 1:150–58, Herskovits's argument for the existence of "Africanisms" was far from being shared by African American intellectuals. Well known is his dispute with the African American sociologist Franklin Frazier, who strongly rejected Herskovits's work. Frazier maintained that African Americans had left behind Africa and adapted to their new environment. Where Frazier saw a rupture with African culture, Herskovits argued for an "acculturative continuum" in the sense of a permanent change. Its specific achievements were adaption, integration, and recombination best understood as syncretism. Ironically, what was praised in the US as innovation was perceived as dangerous in Africa.

17. Partly to blame for this apparent lack of interest in the visual arts was Herskovits's devotion to the performing arts, especially dance. Dance worked best for his (largely implicit) theory of motor or habitual body memory, and it is, therefore, no coincidence that

he showed an active interest in those researchers who focused on the body, like the dancer, choreographer, and dance anthropologist Katherine Dunham. See Joyce Aschenbrenner, *Dancing a Life: Katherine Dunham* (Urbana: University of Illinois Press, 2002).

18. The congress came on the heels of the First International Congress of African Culture, which took place in August 1962 in Harare, Zimbabwe, then Salisbury, Southern Rhodesia. See chapter 5.

19. Kwame Nkrumah, "Address Delivered to Mark the First International Congress of Africanists," in *Proceedings of the First International Congress of Africanists, Accra, 11–19 December 1962*, ed. Lalage Bown and Michael Crowder (Accra: Longmans, 1964), 11.

20. Alioune Diop, "The Spirit of Présence Africaine," in Brown and Crowder, *Proceedings*, 49. The statement was a hardly concealed reference to Hans Himmelheber, whose presentation at the congress focused on the cultural dimensions of Dan sculpture.

21. The passage is cited from Charles Patterson's report to the chairman of the Institute of Current World Events, an American fellowship program to advance American understanding of foreign affairs, http://www.icwa.org/wp-content/uploads/2015/09/CJP-10.pdf.

22. As shown in chapter 4, Jones/Baraka also informed Cole's plea for a performative turn in the study of African art.

23. Amiri Baraka, "The Black Arts Movement: Its Meaning and Potential," *Nka*, no. 29 (2011): 30.

24. See Kay Brown, "The Weusi Artists," *Nka*, no. 30 (2012): 60–67.

25. The popularization of Shango and its emergence in black culture is often associated with W. E. B. Du Bois. Du Bois made Shango into one of the lead characters of his pageant *The Star of Ethiopia*, which he wrote in 1913 to commemorate the fiftieth anniversary of the Proclamation Act (1863). See Babatunde Lawal, "Reclaiming the Past: Yoruba Elements in African American Arts," in *The Yoruba Diaspora in the Atlantic World*, ed. Toyin Falola and Matt D. Childs (Bloomington: Indiana University Press, 2004), 291–324, and Moyo Okediji, *The Shattered Gourd: Yoruba Forms in Twentieth Century Art* (Seattle: University of Washington Press, 2003), 63–87.

26. Ademola Olugebefola was one of the founding members of WEUSI. Born in St. Thomas, Virgin Islands, as Bedwick Lyola Thomas, Olugebefola had migrated with his parents to the US in 1945 at the age of five. In the mid-1960s, he moved to Harlem, where he joined the Yoruba temple and WEUSI and adopted a Yoruba name.

27. Okediji, *The Shattered Gourd*, 92.

28. It needs to be mentioned that *bad* in black American dialect means "good" or "intense." According to the *Oxford English Dictionary*, its use in this sense can be traced back to the nineteenth century.

29. Jeff Donaldson, "Ten in Search of the Nation," *Black World*, October 1970, 80–89. For a personal account of the events, see Wadsworth Jarell, *Africobra* (Durham, NC: Duke University Press, 2020).

30. Sylvester Ogbechie, *Ben Enwonwu: The Making of an African Modernist* (Rochester, NY: University of Rochester Press, 2008), 181.

31. Barbara Jones-Hogu, "The History, Philosophy and Aesthetics of AFRICOBRA," *Nka*, no.94 (Spring 2012): 90–97.

32. "Cool ade" played with the Yoruba term *ade*, meaning "crown" and "royalty." As such it was a pun on "Kool-Aid," a popular brand of an artificial pulverized drink mix that was and still is marketed with strong colors representing the different fruit flavors. Jarell, *Africobra*, 98–99.

33. Jones-Hogu, "History, Philosophy and Aesthetics of AFRICOBRA," 94.

34. Ibid.

35. A prominent venue was CONFABA, the Conference on the Functional Aspects of Black Art, held in 1970 at Northwestern University in Evanston, Illinois.

36. Robert Farris Thompson, "Yoruba Artistic Criticism," in *The Traditional Artist in African Societies*, ed. Warren d'Azevedo (Bloomington: Indiana University Press, 1973), 62–78.

37. Donald Cosentino and Robert Farris Thompson, "Interview with Robert Farris Thompson," *African Arts* 25, no. 4 (1992): 59.

38. Ibid.

39. George Kubler, *The Shape of Time: Remarks on the History of Things* (New Haven, CT: Yale University Press, 1962).

40. Armstead Robinson, preface to *Black Studies in the University*, ed. Armstead L. Robinson, Craig C. Foster, and Donald H. Ogilvie (New Haven, CT: Yale University Press, 1969), vii.

41. David Davis, "Reflections," in Robinson, Foster, and Ogilvie, *Black Studies in the University*, 222.

42. Robert Farris Thompson, "African Influence on the Art of the United States," in Robinson, Foster, and Ogilvie, *Black Studies in the University*, 122–70.

43. Robert Farris Thompson, "An Aesthetic of the Cool: West African Dance," *African Forum* 2, no. 2 (Fall, 1966): 85–102; "An Aesthetic of the Cool," *African Arts* 7, no. 1 (1973): 40–43, 64–67, 89–91.

44. Eckart von Sydow, "African Sculpture," *Africa: Journal of the International African Institute* 1, no. 2 (April 1928): 214.

45. Hans Himmelheber, *Negerkünstler: Ethnographische Studien über den Schnitzkünstler bei den Stämmen der Atutu und Guro im Innern der Elfenbeinküste* (Stuttgart: Strecker und Schroeder, 1935).

46. Claude Lévi-Strauss, *The Savage Mind* (Chicago: University Press of Chicago, 1966), originally published as *La pensée sauvage* (Paris: Plon, 1962); Donald Cosentino, and Robert Farris Thompson, "Interview with Robert Farris Thompson," *African Arts* 25, no.4 (1992): 53–58.

47. Ibid., 56.

48. Robert Farris Thompson, "An Introduction to Transatlantic Black Art History: Remarks in Anticipation of a Coming Golden Age of Afro-Americana," in *Rediscovering Afro-America*, ed. Roger Abrahams (Leiden: Brill, 1975), 192–201.

49. A less-well-known but far-reaching event was the exhibition *African Accumulative Sculpture: Power and Display* at the Pace Gallery in New York organized by Arnold Rubin in 1974.

50. Robert Farris Thompson, *Flash of the Spirit: African and Afro-American Art and Philosophy* (New York: Vintage, 1983).

51. Ibid., xiv.

52. For a collection of articles covering his wide-ranging work, see Robert Farris Thompson, *Aesthetic of the Cool: Afro-Atlantic Art and Music* (Pittsburg, PA: Periscope, 2011).

53. Paul Gilroy, *The Black Atlantic: Modernity and Double Consciousness* (London: Verso, 1993).

54. Paul Gilroy, "Paul Gilroy," in *Conversations in Postcolonial Thought*, ed. Katy P. Sian (New York: Springer, 2014), 181.

55. Gilroy, *The Black Atlantic*, 19.

56. Robert Farris Thompson, "Afro-Modernism," *Art in America International*, September 1991, 91.

57. It thus anticipated the heated discussion sparked by the curatorial notion of "post-black" first conceived in 2001 by Thelma Golden in her contribution to the exhibition catalog *Freestyle* at the Studio Museum New York. See Thelma Golden, "Post . . . ," in *Freestyle*, ed. Christine Y. Kim and Franklin Sirmans (New York: Studio Museum in Harlem, 2001), 14–15.

Chapter Seven

1. "African Art at 50: National Museum of African Art Marks Its 50th Anniversary in 2014 with Year of Exhibitions and Programs," Smithsonian National Museum of African Art, https://africa.si.edu/50years/.

2. Henry Drewal and Margret Drewal, *Gelede: Art and Female Power among the Yoruba* (Bloomington: Indiana University Press, 1983).

3. Henry Drewal, "African Art Studies Today," in *African Art Studies: The State of the Discipline*, ed. E. Lifschitz (Washington, DC: Smithsonian Institution, 1990), 50.

4. A telling example of this challenge is the reaction to Jan Vansina, *Art History in Africa* (London: Longman, 1984). A historian by training, Vansina provided a solid and much-welcomed methodological basis for the historical study of traditional African art. Only two years later, in a symposium on African art, Valentin-Yves Mudimbe commented, "The conceptual framework of African studies is both a mirror and a consequence of a hegemonic experience." Valentin-Yves Mudimbe, "African Art as a Question Mark," *African Studies Review* 29, no. 1 (1986): 4.

5. I borrow the term *exhaustion* from Andreas Huyssen, "Modernity and Postmodernity," *New German Critique*, no. 33 (Autumn 1984): 11.

6. Leslie Fiedler, "Cross the Border, Close the Gap," *Playboy*, December 1969, 230, 252–54, 256–58.

7. Jean-François Lyotard, *The Postmodern Condition: A Report on Knowledge*, trans. Geoff Bennington and Brian Massumi (Minneapolis: University of Minnesota Press, 1984), originally published as *La condition postmoderne: Rapport sur le savoir* (Paris: Minuit, 1979).

8. Hans Belting, *The End of the History of Art?* (Chicago: University of Chicago Press, 1987), originally published as *Das Ende der Kunstgeschichte?* (Munich: Berlin Deutscher Kunstverlag, 1983).

9. Michel Foucault, *Power/Knowledge: Selected Interviews and Other Writings 1972–1977* (New York: Pantheon, 1980); Valentin-Yves Mudimbe, *The Invention of Africa: Gnosis, Philosophy and the Order of Knowledge* (Bloomington: Indiana University Press, 1988).

10. Edward Said, *Orientalism* (New York: Vintage, 1978).

11. Stuart Hall, "Cultural Studies: Two Paradigms," *Media, Culture and Society* 2, no. 1 (1980): 57–72.

12. Johannes Fabian, *Time and the Other: How Anthropology Makes Its Object* (New York: Columbia University Press, 1983); James Clifford, *The Predicament of Culture: Twentieth-Century Ethnography, Literature, and Art* (Cambridge, MA: Harvard University Press, 1988); Ivan Karp and Steven D. Lavine, eds., *Exhibiting Cultures: The Poetics and Politics of Museum Display* (Washington, DC: Smithsonian Institution Press, 1991).

13. Drewal, "African Art Studies Today," 50.

14. Kirk Varnedoe, "Contemporary Explorations," in *"Primitivism" in Twentieth Century Art: Affinities between the Tribal and the Modern* (New York: Museum of Modern Art, 1984), 679.

15. Ibid., 682.

16. For a prominent example of the critique, see James Clifford, "Histories of the Tribal and the Modern," *Art in America*, April 1985, 164–77.

17. See Raymond Moulin, *Le marché de l'art: Mondialisation et nouvelles technologies* (Paris: Flammarion, 2003).

18. Cited in Françoise Gilot and Charles Lake, *Life with Picasso* (New York: McGraw-Hill, 1964), 266. For a list of artists participating in the show, see "Exhibition Histories: Magiciens de la terre," C&, August 12, 2016, https://www.contemporaryand.com/magazines/magiciens-de-la-terre/.

19. Rasheed Araeen, *The Other Story* (London: Hayward Gallery, 1989).

20. Rasheed Araeen, "Our Bauhaus, Others' Mudhouse," *Third Text* 3, no. 6 (1989): 11.

21. Benjamin Buchloh, "The Whole Earth Show: An Interview with Jean Hubert Martin," *Art in America* 77 (May 1989): 150–59, 211, 213.

22. Jean Fisher, "Other Cartographies," *Third Text* 3, no. 6 (1989): 79–82.

23. Sally Price, "Art autre: Art nôtre," *Cahiers du Musée national d'art moderne*, no. 28 (1989): 61–68; Sally Price, *Primitive Art in Civilized Places* (Chicago: University of Chicago Press, 1989).

24. Thomas McEvilley, "Marginalia: Thomas McEvilley on the Global Issue," *Artforum* 28, no. 7 (March 1990): 21.

25. Ulli Beier, *Art in Nigeria* (Cambridge: Cambridge University Press, 1960).

26. Ilona Szombati-Fabian and Johannes Fabian, "Art, History, and Society: Popular Painting in Shaba, Zaire," *Studies in the Anthropology of Visual Communication* 3 (1976): 1–21; Johannes Fabian, "Popular Culture in Africa: Findings and Conjectures," *Africa* 48, no. 4 (1978): 15–34.

27. Johannes Fabian, *Remembering the Present: Painting and Popular History in Zaire* (Berkeley: University of California Press, 1996).

28. Karin Barber, "African Popular Culture," *African Studies Review* 30, no. 3 (1987): 1–78.

29. Joseph Cornet, "African Art and Authenticity," *African Arts* 9, no. 1 (January 1975): 52–55.

30. Cornet, "African Art and Authenticity," 54.

31. For an insightful discussion of this period, see Sarah Van Beurden, *Authentically African: Arts and the Transnational Politics of Congolese Culture* (Athens: Ohio University Press, 2015).

32. Ibid., 55.

33. Marilyn Houlberg, "Ibeji Images of the Yoruba," *African Arts*, 7, no. 1 (January 1973): 91–92.

34. Daniel Biebuyck, introduction to *Tradition and Creativity in Tribal Art*, ed. Daniel Biebuyck (Los Angeles: University of California Press, 1969), 12.

35. Marilyn Houlberg, "Collecting the Anthropology of African Art," *African Arts* 9, no. 3 (April 1976): 15–19, 91.

36. Sydney Kasfir, "African Art and Authenticity: A Text with a Shadow," *African Arts* 25, no. 2 (April 1992): 40–53, 96–97.

37. Sydney Kasfir, "One Tribe, One Style? Paradigms in the Historiography of African Art," *History in Africa* 11 (1984): 163–93.

38. Roland Barthes, *The Pleasure of the Text* (New York: Hill & Wang, 1975), 32, originally published as *Le plaisir du texte* (Paris: Seuil, 1973).

39. For an extended, book-length version of this argument, see Sidney Kasfir, *African Art and the Colonial Encounter: Inventing a Global Commodity* (Bloomington: Indiana University Press 2007).

40. Henry Drewal, "Contested Realities: Inventions of Art and Authenticity," *African Arts* 25, no. 4 (October 1992): 4.

41. Philip Ravenhill, "On the Cross-Cultural Appreciation of Art," *African Arts* 25, no. 4 (October 1992): 18.

42. Thomas Beidelman, "Authenticity and Appropriation," *African Arts* 25, no. 3 (July 1992): 25.

43. Pierre Bourdieu, *Distinction: A Social Critique of the Judgement of Taste* (Cambridge, MA: Harvard University Press, 1984), originally published as *La distinction: Critique sociale du jugement* (Paris: Minuit, 1979).

44. Arjun Appadurai, ed., *The Social Life of Things* (Cambridge: Cambridge University Press, 1986).

45. Ibid.

46. Igor Kopytoff, "The Cultural Biography of Things: Commoditization as Process," in Appadurai, *The Social Life of Things*, 64–91. The impact of Appadurai's volume was immediate and triggered similar models. Perhaps the best-known example is James Clifford's "On Collecting Art and Culture," in Clifford, *The Predicament of Culture*, 215–51.

47. Christopher Steiner, "Fake Masks and Faux Modernity: The Crisis of Misrepresentation," *African Arts* 25, no. 3 (July 1992): 18.

48. Christopher Steiner, *African Art in Transit* (Cambridge: Cambridge University Press, 1994).

49. For example, Daniel Crowley, "The West African Art Market Revisited," *African Arts* 7, no.4 (1974): 54–59.

50. Ilisa Barbash and Lucien Taylor, dir., *In and Out of Africa* (Berkeley: Media, 1993).

51. For an extension of this argument with regard to the distinction between art and commodity in Euro-American art, see Christopher Steiner, "Rights of Passage: On the Liminal Identity of Art in the Border Zone," in *The Empire of Things: Regimes of Value and Material Culture*, ed. Fred Myers (Santa Fe, NM: School of American Research, 2001), 207–32.

52. Johannes Fabian, "Quibbles and Questions," *African Arts* 25, no. 3 (July 1992): 27.

53. Grace Stanislaus, *Contemporary African Artists: Changing Traditions* (New York: Studio Museum of Harlem, 1990). On display were works from El Anatsui (Ghana/Nigeria), Youssouf Bath (Côte d'Ivoire), Ablade Glover (Ghana), Tapfuma Gutsa (Zimbabwe), Rosemary Karuga (Kenya), Souleymane Keita (Senegal), Nicholas Mukomberanwa (Zimbabwe), Henry Munyaradzi (Zimbabwe), and Bruce Onobrakpeya (Nigeria).

54. John Povey, "First Word," *African Arts* 23, no. 4 (October 1990): 1.

55. Ibid.

56. James Baldwin et al., *Perspectives: Angles on African Art* (New York: Prestel, 1987). In 1992–1993 the center renamed itself the Museum for African Art and moved to a more spacious location in SoHo, Lower Manhattan. In 2002, the museum relocated again to Long Island City in Queens, where it exhibited until 2006.

57. Susan Vogel, ed., *ART/Artifact: African Art in Anthropology Collections* (New York: Prestel, 1988).

58. Susan Vogel, foreword to *Africa Explores: 20th Century African Art*, ed. Susan Vogel (New York: Prestel, 1991), 9.

59. Ibid., 11–12.

60. "Africa Explores: 20th Century African Art," New Museum, http://archive.newmuseum.org/index.php/Detail/Occurrence/Show/occurrence_id/206.

61. Susan Vogel, *Exhibition-Ism* (New York: Prestel, 1994), 102–3.

62. See the various reviews in *African Arts* in 1992 and 1993.

63. Vogel, foreword, 10.

64. Olu Oguibe, "Africa Explores: 20th Century African Art," *African Arts* 26, no 1 (January 1993): 16–22.

65. Ibid.

66. Ibid., 22.

67. Susan Vogel, "West African Artists at the Venice Biennale," in *Fusion: West African Artists at the Venice Biennale*, ed. Thomas McEvilley (New York: Prestel, 1993), 6.

68. The selection of the artists was done by Vogel, Santoni, and Ousmane Sow from Senegal.

69. Thomas McEvilley, "Doctor, Lawyer, Indian Chief: 'Primitivism' in Twentieth Century Art at the Museum of Modern Art," *Artforum* 23, no. 3 (1984): 60.

70. McEvilley, *Fusion*, 13.

71. Ibid., 20.

72. Ibid., 7.

73. Oguibe, "Africa Explores," 16.

Chapter Eight

1. See Ruth Nielsen, "The history and development of wax-printed textiles intended for West Africa and Zaire," in *The Fabrics of Culture: The Anthropology of Clothing and Adornment*, ed. Justine Cordwell and Ronald Schwarz (New York: Mouton, 1979), 467–98. For an early insightful take on Shonibare's textile strategy, see John Picton, "Yinka Shonibare: Undressing Ethnicity," *African Arts* 34, no. 3 (2001): 66–73.

2. Jonathan Rutherford, "The Third Space: Interview with Homi Bhabha," in *Identity: Community, Culture, Difference* (London: Lawrence and Wishart, 1990), 207–21; Homi Bhabha, *The Location of Culture* (London: Routledge, 1994); Olu Oguibe, "Art, Identity, Boundaries: The Rome Lecture," *Nka*, no. 3 (1995): 26–33.

3. Stuart Hall, "New Ethnicities," in *Black Film British Cinema*, ICA Documents 7, ed. Kobena Mercer (London: ICA Publications, 1988), 27–31.

4. Olu Oguibe, "Forward to the Future," *African Arts* 31, no. 4 (1998): 1.

5. Ben Enwonwu, "The African View of Art and Some Problems Facing the African Artist Today," in *Colloquium: Function and Significance of African Negro Art in the Life of the People and for the People, March 30–April 8, 1966*, ed. Société Africaine de Culture (Paris: *Présence Africaine*, 1968), 420–21.

6. Okwui Enwezor, "Redrawing the Boundaries: Towards a New African Art Discourse," *Nka*, no. 1 (Fall/Winter 1994): 4.

7. Ibid., 7.

8. *Revue Noire* stopped printing the journal in 2001 and shifted its activities to publishing, curating, and posting content online in a blog. For a history of the project, see Jean Loup Pivin, "*Revue Noire*, une histoire," *Continents Manuscrits*, no. 3 (2014), http://journals.openedition.org/coma/433.

9. Jean-François Bayart, *Les études postcoloniales: Un carnaval académique* (Paris: Karthala, 2010). Mamadou Diouf, "Les postcolonial studies et leur réception dans le champ académique en France," in *Ruptures postcoloniales: Les nouveaux visages de la société française*, ed. Nicolas Bancel et al. (Paris: La Découverte, 2010), 149–58.

10. One prominent exception was a study on the aesthetic practices of photography among Yoruba in Nigeria by Stephen Sprague, "Yoruba Photography: How the Yoruba See Themselves," *African Arts* 12, no. 1 (November 1978): 52–59. Consonant with the new interest

in questions of power and representation, studies had looked primarily at the colonial use of photography in postcards. See Christraud Geary, "Photographs as Materials for African History: Some Methodological Considerations," *History in Africa* 13 (1986): 89–116, and anthropological depictions of racial types, for example, *Anthropology and Photography*, ed. Elizabeth Edwards (New Haven, CT: Yale University Press, 1992).

11. Okwui Enwezor, Olu Oguibe, and Octavio Zaya, eds., *In/Sight: African Photographers 1940 to the Present* (New York: Guggenheim Museum, 1996).

12. Clémentine Deliss, ed., *Seven Stories about Modern Art in Africa* (London: Whitechapel Gallery and Flammarion, 1995). John Picton, "africa95 and the Royal Academy," *African Arts* 29, no. 3 (1996): 22–23.

13. For a discussion of the show's reception, see Maureen Murphy, "L'art de la polémique: Africa95 et *Seven Stories about Modern Art in Africa*," *Cahiers d'études africaines* 56, no. 223 (2016), 663–78.

14. Max Kozloff, "In/Sight: African Photographers, from the 1940s to the Present," *Artforum* 35, no. 2 (October 1996): 114–15.

15. Holland Cotter, "An African Anthology of Rewarding Objects," *New York Times*, June 7, 1996.

16. Olu Oguibe and Okwui Enwezor, eds., *Reading the Contemporary: African Art from Theory to the Marketplace* (London: Institute of International Visual Art, 1999).

17. Frederick Lamp, "Africa Centered," *African Arts* 32, no.1 (Spring, 1999): 1–10. Lamp boosted his warning with numbers from the triennial conferences of the Arts Council of the African Studies Association, the biggest institutional assembly of people involved in African arts. While in 1989 papers on so-called classical art still made up 60 percent of the conference presentations, in 1998 the number was down to 30 percent.

18. For example, Suzanne Blier, *African Vodun: Art, Psychology, and Power* (Chicago: University of Chicago Press, 1994); Sarah Brett-Smith, *The Making of Bamana Sculpture: Creativity and Gender* (Cambridge: Cambridge University Press, 1995); Zoe Strother, *Inventing Masks: Agency and History in the Art of the Central Pende* (Chicago: University of Chicago Press, 1998).

19. Sidney Kasfir, *Contemporary African Art* (London: Thames and Hudson, 1999).

20. For a recent study of these blurred lines between art and commodity, see Atta Kwami, *Kumasi Realism. 1951–2007: An African Modernism* (London: Hurst, 2011).

21. Kasfir, *Contemporary African Art*, 104–5.

22. Elizabeth Bigham, "Issues of Authorship in the Portrait Photographs of Seydou Keïta," *African Arts* 32, no. 1 (Spring 1999): 56–67.

23. André Magnin, *Seydou Keïta* (Paris: Fondation Cartier, 1994); *Seydou Keïta* (Zurich: Scala, 1997).

24. See Michael Rips, "Who Owns Seydou Keïta?" *New York Times*, January 22, 2006.

25. Arjun Appadurai, *Modernity at Large: The Cultural Dimensions of Globalization* (Minneapolis: University of Minnesota Press, 1996).

26. In 1987, the Weltkulturen Museum (formerly Museum für Völkerkunde) in Frankfurt, Germany, had shown *Botschaften aus Südafrika: Kunst und künstlerische Produktion schwarzer Künstler*, which aimed to present an overview of black contemporary South African art. The push into the art world proper began shortly after. In 1990, the same year Mandela was released from prison, the Museum of Modern Art in Oxford showed *Art from South Africa*. In 1993, after decades of isolation and boycott, South Africa was allowed to participate in the Venice Biennale.

27. Marylin Martin, "The Rainbow Nation. Identity and Transformation," *Oxford Art Journal* 19, no. 1 (March 1996): 3–15.

28. Thomas McEvilley, "Here Comes Everybody," in *Africus: Johannesburg Biennale. Johannesburg*, ed., Okwui Enwezor et al. (Johannesburg: Transitional Metropolitan Council, 1995), 53–57.

29. Sue Williamson and A. Jamal, *Art in South Africa: The Future Present* (Cape Town: David Phillip, 1996).

30. David Koloane, "Africus: The Johannesburg Biennale. A Perspective," *African Arts* 21, no. 1 (Spring 1996): 56.

31. On this part of the discussion, see John Peffer, *Art and the End of Apartheid* (Minneapolis: University of Minnesota Press, 2009), 123.

32. See Jean Fisher, ed., *Global Visions: Towards a New Internationalism in the Visual Arts* (London: Institute of International Visual Art, 1994), and the discussion in chapter 7.

33. With Octavio Zaya, Olu Oguibe, Hou Hanru, and Gerardo Mosquera, more than half of the curators Enwezor selected for *Trade Routes* had participated in Jean Fisher's 1994 conference at the Tate Gallery in London on "Global Visions."

34. On the reception of *Trade Routes*, see the compilation of articles and recollections *Trade Routes Revisited: A Project Marking the 15th Anniversary of the Johannesburg Biennale*, ed. Joost Bosland (Cape Town: Stevenson, 2012), https://issuu.com/stevensonctandjhb/docs/trade_routes_book_issuu?e=9663888/5488475.

35. Gabriel Pérez-Barriero, "Earth and Everything: Recent Art from South Africa," *Third Text*, no. 37 (1999): 92.

36. Birgit Meyer and Peter Geschiere, eds., *Globalization and Identity: Dialectics of Flow and Closure* (Oxford: Blackwell, 1999).

37. Okwui Enwezor, *The Black Box: Introduction to Documenta 11, Platform 5* (Ostfildern-Ruit: Hatje Cantz, 2002), 26.

38. Salah Hassan and Olu Oguibe, "Authentic/Ex-centric at the Venice Biennale: African Conceptualism in Global Contexts," *African Arts* 34, no. 4 (Winter 2001): 64–75, 96; Okwui Enwezor, "Between Worlds: Postmodernism and African Artists in the Western Metropolis," *Atlántica*, no. 12 (1995–1996): 119–33.

39. Okwui Enwezor, *The Short Century: Independence and Liberation Movements in Africa 1945–1994* (Munich: Prestel, 2001).

40. Enwezor, *The Black Box*, 55.

41. Sylvester Ogbechie, "Ordering the Universe: Documenta 11 and the Apotheosis of the Occidental Gaze," *Art Journal* 64, no. 1 (Spring 2005): 80–89.

42. Simon Njami, ed., *Africa Remix: Zeitgenössische Kunst eines Kontinents* (Stuttgart: Hatje Cantz, 2004).

43. Arif Dirlik, "The Postcolonial Aura: Third World Criticism in the Age of Global Capitalism," *Critical Inquiry* 20, no. 2 (Winter 1994): 328–56.

44. Gao Shiming, "Observations and Presentiments after Postcolonialism," in *Farewell to Post-Colonialism*, ed. Sarat Maharaj, Chang Tsong-Zung, and Gao Shiming (Guangzhou: Guangdong Museum of Art, 2011): 34–35. See also Patricia Yaeger, "Editor's Column: The End of Postcolonial Theory? A Roundtable with Sunil Agnani, Fernando Coronil, Gaurav Desai, Mamadou Diouf, Simon Gikandi, Susie Tharu, and Jennifer Wenzel," *PMLA* 122, no. 3 (Autumn 2007), 633–50.

45. Salah Hassan, ed., "The Twenty-First Century and the Mega Shows: A Curators' Roundtable," *Nka*, no. 22/23 (Spring/Summer 2008): 152–88; Chika Okeke-Agulu, ed., "Roundtable II: Contemporary African Art History and the Scholarship," *Nka*, no. 26 (Spring 2010): 80–151. Chika Okeke-Agulu, ed., "Roundtable III: Contemporary African Art and the Museum," *Nka*, no. 31 (2012): 46–111.

Chapter Nine

1. For a recent example, see Catherine Grant and Dorothy Price, eds., "Decolonizing Art History," *Art History* 43, no. 1 (February 2020): 8–66.

2. Nelson Maldonado-Torres, "Thinking through the Decolonial Turn: Post-Continental Interventions in Theory, Philosophy, and Critique," *Transmodernity: Journal of Peripheral Cultural Production of the Luso-Hispanic World* 1, no. 2 (Fall 2011), retrieved from https://escholarship.org/uc/item/59w8j02x.

3. Respective decolonial attempts to rethink history against the grain can be traced back to the 1950s and 1960s. Yet the emergence of a popular, far-reaching decolonial stance in terms of untangling or "delinking" modes of the production of knowledge from a primarily Eurocentric episteme only happened in the 2000s by way of a fusion of African decolonization theory, French poststructuralism, South Asian postcolonial thought, and Latin American liberation philosophy. See Anibal Quijano, "Coloniality and Modernity/Rationality," in *Globalization and the Decolonial Option*, ed. Walter D. Mignolo and Arturo Escobar (New York Routledge, 2010): 23-32; Walter Mignolo, "Delinking," *Cultural Studies* 21, no. 2/3 (2007): 449–514, and his influential "Epistemic Disobedience, Independent Thought and Decolonial Freedom." *Theory, Culture and Society* 26, no. 7/8 (2009): 159–81.

4. *Shifting Gravity* was the title of first World Biennale Forum at Gwanju, South Korea in 2012.

5. Prita Meier, "Modernism in Africanist Art History: The Making of a New Discipline," in *The Modernist World*, ed. Allana Lindgren and Stephen Ross (New York: Routledge, 2017), 214–24.

6. Joseph Tonda, *L'impérialisme postcolonial: Critique de la société des éblouissements* (Paris: Karthala, 2015).

7. Lucrezia Cipitelli, "Toma Muteba Luntumbue and the 5th Lubumbashi Biennale," *Dopopiozero*, November 18, 2007, http://www.doppiozero.com/materiali/toma-muteba-luntumbue-and-5th-lubumbashi-biennale.

8. For a history and discussion of these new spaces, see Kerstin Pinther, Ugochukwu-Smooth Nzewi, and Berit Fischer, eds., *New Spaces for Negotiating Art and Histories in Africa* (Berlin: Lit, 2015).

9. A prominent blueprint for these kinds of cultural development aids is Niklas Luhmann, *Art as a Social System* (Stanford, CA: Stanford University Press, 2000), originally published as *Die Kunst der Gesellschaft* (Frankfurt am Main: Suhrkamp, 1995).

10. See the interview with the sociologist Rolando Vázquez, "The End of the Contemporary," *C&*, June 5, 2017, https://www.contemporaryand.com/magazines/the-end-of-the-contemporary/, and Walter Escobar, *Designs for the Pluriverse* (Durham, NC: Duke University Press, 2018).

11. Filip De Boeck and Sammy Baloji, *Suturing the City: Living Together in Congo's Urban Worlds* (London: Autograph, 2016). The joint project builds on the authors' previous work and intimate knowledge of the area. Since the mid-2000s, Baloji has been invested in the visual exploration of Congo's urban and industrial landscapes, especially in the Katanga area. His photographs, films, and photomontages address questions of memory, abandonment, and violence, themes that intersect closely with De Boeck's work. In 2002, De Boeck participated in the Lagos platform, one of five Enwezor organized for *Documenta 11*. Two years later, his exhibition *Kinshasa, The Imaginary City* won the Golden Lion of the Venice Architectural Biennale. Filip De Boeck and Marie-Françoise Plissart, *Kinshasa: Tales of the Invisible City* (Leuven: Leuven University Press, 2004).

12. For a recent overview of the history and specifics of the biennale, see Ugochukwu-Smooth Nzewi and Thomas Fillitz, eds., *Dak'Art: The Biennial of Dakar and the Making of Contemporary African Art* (London: Bloomsbury, 2020).

13. Joanna Grabski, "All the City Is an Exhibition: The DAK'ART-OFF in the Biennale and in Dakar's Art World City," in Nzewi and Fillitz, *Dak'Art*, 151–64.

14. Nzewi and Fillitz, introduction to *Dak'Art*, 10.

15. Gary Wilder, *Freedom Time: Negritude, Decolonization, and the Future of the World* (Durham, NC: Duke University Press, 2015); Ferdinand de Jong, *Decolonizing Heritage: Time to Repair in Senegal* (Cambridge: Cambridge University Press, 2022).

16. Simon Njami, ed., *Réenchantements: La cité dans le jour bleu/Reenchantments: The City in the Blue Daylight* (Bielefeld: Kerber, 2016).

17. Cited in Hamady Bocoum and Malick Ndiaye, "Le Musée des civilisations noires: A Continuous Creation of Humanity," in *National Museums in Africa: Identity, History and Politics*, eds. Raymond Silverman, George Abungu, and Peter Probst (London: Routledge, 2021), 128.

18. Elizabeth Harney, *In Senghor's Shadow: Art, Politics, and the Avant-Garde in Senegal, 1960–1995* (Durham, NC: Duke University Press, 2004).

19. Salah Hassan, "The Modernist Experience in African Art: Visual Expressions of the Self and Cross-Cultural Comparisons." *Nka*, no. 2 (Spring/Summer 1995), 31.

20. For examples of this surge, see Sylvester Okwunodu Ogbechie, *Ben Enwonwu: The Making of an African Modernist* (Rochester, NY: Rochester University Press, 2008); John Peffer, *Art and the End of Apartheid* (Minneapolis: University of Minnesota Press, 2009); Gitti Salami and Monica Visonà, eds., *A Companion to Modern African Art* (Walden, MA: Wiley, 2013); Atta Kwami, *Kumasi Realism 1951–2007: An African Modernism* (London: C. Hurst, 2013); Chika Okeke-Agulu, *Postcolonial Modernism: Art and Decolonization in Twentieth-Century Nigeria* (Durham, NC: Duke University Press, 2015); Elizabeth Harney and Ruth Phillips, eds., *Mapping Modernisms: Art, Indigeneity, Colonialism* (Durham, NC: Duke University Press, 2018); Elizabeth Giorgis, *Modernism in Ethiopia* (Athens: Ohio University Press, 2019); Joshua Cohen, *The Black Art Renaissance: African Sculpture and Modernism across Continents* (Oakland: University of California Press, 2020).

21. Hal Foster, "An Archival Impulse," *October* 110 (Autumn 2004): 3–22.

22. Ibid., 22.

23. Ibid.

24. For an informative overview, see Ferdinand De Jong, "At Work in the Archive," *World Art* 6, no. 1 (2016): 3–17.

25. Okwui Enwezor, *Archive Fever: Uses of the Document in Contemporary Art* (Göttingen: Steidl, 2008). The title stemmed from Jacques Derrida's essay *Archive Fever: A Freudian Impression* (Chicago: University of Chicago Press, 1996), originally published as *Mal d'archive: Une impression freudienne* (Paris: Gallée, 1995). Contrary to the Foucauldian understanding of archives as sites of erasure and exclusion, Derrida pointed to the openness and messianic character of the archive in terms of the feverish promise and hope to extend the accumulation of data endlessly into the future.

26. Enwezor, *Archive Fever*, 1. Michel Foucault, *The Archaeology of Knowledge and the Discourse on Language*, trans. A. M. Sheridan Smith (New York: Pantheon Books, 1972), 129, originally published as *L'archéologie du savoir* (Paris: Gallimard, 1969).

27. Frantz Fanon, *Black Skin, White Masks*, trans. Charles Markman (New York: Grove Press 1967), originally published as *Peau noire, masque blancs* (Paris: Éditions du Seuil, 1952).

28. Chika Okeke-Agulu, *Postcolonial Modernism*; Sylvester Ogbechie, *Ben Enwonwu*.

29. The famous first sentence in Uche Okeke's *Natural Synthesis* manifesto of 1960 reads, "Young artists in a new nation, that is what we are!" It ended with the verdict, "Today's social problems are different from yesterday's, and we shall be doing grave disservice to Africa and mankind by living on our father's achievements. For this is like living in an entirely alien cultural background." Uche Okeke, "Natural Synthesis," in *Seven Stories about Modern Art in Africa*, ed. Clémentine Deliss (London: Whitechapel Gallery and Flammarion, 1995), 208–9.

30. Mignolo, "Epistemic Disobedience."

31. Dan Cameron, "Survey," in *William Kentridge*, ed. Dan Cameron, Carolyn Christov-Bakargiev, and John Maxwell Coetzee (London: Phaidon 1999), 57.

32. Sabine Marschall, *Landscape of Memory: Commemorative Monuments, Memorials and Public Statuary in Post-Apartheid South Africa* (Leiden: Brill, 2010); Kim Miller and Brenda Schmahmann, eds., *Public Art in South Africa: Bronze Warriors and Plastic Presidents* (Bloomington: Indiana University Press, 2017).

33. For a description of the events, see Francis Nyamnjoh, *#RhodesMustFall: Nibbling at Resilient Colonialism in South Africa* (Bamenda: Langaa, 2016).

34. See Tamar Garb, "Falling and Rising: In the Wake of Cecil John Rhodes," *Nka*, no. 44 (May 2019): 24–37.

35. Zoe Strother, "Iconoclasms as Site for the Production of Knowledge," *HAU: Journal of Ethnographic Theory* 10, no. 3 (2020): 985–88.

36. Sue Williams, "Zeitz MOCAA Is Here," ArtThrob, September 13, 2017, https://artthrob.co.za/2017/09/13/zeitz-mocaa-is-here/.

37. See the various articles on the museum at ArtThrob, https://artthrob.co.za/, and Gemma Sieff, "From Maize to Museum: The Long-Awaited Zeitz Museum of Contemporary Art Africa Aims to Let the Continent Tell Its Own Story," ARTnews, September 7, 2017, http://www.artnews.com/2017/09/07/from-maize-to-museum-the-long-awaited-zeitz -museum-of-contemporary-art-africa-aims-to-let-the-continent-tell-its-own-story/.

38. The questions recall a prominent dispute over an exhibition in 1996, thus two years after the end of apartheid, at National Gallery in Cape Town. Under the title *Miscast: Negotiating the Presence of Bushmen*, the white South African artist Pippa Skotnes addressed the organized killing, exploitation, abuse, and museal representation of indigenous Khoisan people in South Africa. Though Skotnes took pains to consult and involve Khoisan communities in the exhibition, it was strongly condemned by Khoisan groups and black critics who questioned Skotnes's right as a white South African to "reframe" the black subject. See Sandra Klopper, "Whose Heritage? The Politics of Cultural Ownership in Contemporary South Africa," *Nka*, no. 5 (Fall/Winter 1996): 34–37.

39. Things changed in early summer 2018 when Mark Coetzee, MOCAA's executive director and chief curator, stepped down after allegations of misconduct. In March 2019, MOCAA named Koyo Kouoh as the museum's new director and chief curator.

40. Exceptions have been made to provide greater accessibility. For visitors under eighteen, the museum is free of charge. There is also free entry for African citizens every Wednesday between 10:00 a.m. and 1 p.m. (last checked, April 2022).

41. "These two elements—our history and the moral imperative arising from that—are the factors for making that personal beacon rise into the immovable rock of apartheid. To escape this rock is the job of the artist. These two constitute the tyranny of our history. And escape is necessary, for as I stated, the rock is possessive, and inimical to good work. I am not saying that apartheid, or indeed, redemption, are not worthy of representation, description or exploration, I am saying that the scale and weight with which this rock presents itself is

inimical to that task." Carolyn Christov-Bakargiev, *William Kentridge* (Brussels: Société des Expositions du Palais des Beaux-Arts des Bruxelles, 1998), 75.

42. Ibid.

Epilogue

1. Achille Mbembe, *Out of the Dark Night: Essays on Decolonization* (New York: Columbia University Press, 2021), originally published as *Sortir de la grand nuit* (Paris: Éditions La Découverte, 2010).

2. Yinka Shonibare, "Hedonism, Masquerade, Carnivalesque and Power: A Conversation with Okwui Enwezor," In *Looking Both Ways: Art of the Contemporary African Diaspora*, ed. Laurie Ann Farrell (Gent: Snoeck, 2004), 162–77.

3. Souleymane Bachir Diagne and Jean-Loup Amselle, *In Search of Africa(s): Universalism and Decolonial Thought*, trans. Andrew Brown (Cambridge: Polity Press, 2020), originally published as *En quète d'Afrique(s): Universalisme et pensée decoloniale* (Paris: Albin Michel 2018).

4. Raymond Silverman, George Abungu, and Peter Probst, eds., *National Museums in Africa: Identity, History, Politics* (New York: Routledge, 2021); Bénédicte Savoy, *Africa's Struggle for Its Art: History of a Postcolonial Defeat*, trans. Susanne Meyer-Abich (Princeton, NJ: Princeton University Press, 2022), originally published as *Afrikas Kampf um seine Kunst: Geschichte einer Postkolonialen Niederlage* (Munich: C. H. Beck, 2021).

5. Hamady Bocoum and Malick Ndiaye, "Le Musée des civilisations noires: A Continuous Creation of Humanity," in *National Museums in Africa: Identity, History and Politics*, ed. Raymond Silverman, George Abungu, and Peter Probst (London: Routledge, 2021), 131.

6. Felwine Sarr and Bénédicte Savoy, *Restituer le patrimoine africain* (Paris: Philippe Rey/Seuil, 2018), http://restitutionreport2018.com/sarr_savoy_en.pdf. See also Ferdinand de Jong, *Decolonizing Heritage: Time to Repair in Senegal* (Cambridge: Cambridge University Press, 2022). On the question of restitution, resocialization, and translation, see also Souleymane Bachir Diagne, *De langue à langue: L'hospitalité de la traduction* (Paris: Albin Michel, 2022).

7. Sarr and Savoy, *Restituer le patrimoine africain*.

8. Valentin-Yves Mudimbe, *The Idea of Africa* (Bloomington: University of Indiana Press, 1994).

INDEX

Page numbers in italics refer to illustrations.